Ius Gentium: Comparative Perspectives on Law and Justice

Volume 107

Ius Gentium is a book series which discusses the central questions of law and justice from a comparative perspective. The books in this series collect the contrasting and overlapping perspectives of lawyers, judges, philosophers and scholars of law from the world's many different jurisdictions for the purposes of comparison, harmonisation, and the progressive development of law and legal institutions. Each volume makes a new comparative study of an important area of law. This book series continues the work of the well-known journal of the same name and provides the basis for a better understanding of all areas of legal science.

The *Ius Gentium* series provides a valuable resource for lawyers, judges, legislators, scholars, and both graduate students and researchers in globalisation, comparative law, legal theory and legal practice. The series has a special focus on the development of international legal standards and transnational legal cooperation.

Pınar Kara

Tort Liability in Multinational Corporate Groups

A Comparative Analysis with Particular Focus on Turkey

Springer

Pınar Kara
Minerva Business and Human Rights
Association
Istanbul, Turkey

ISSN 1534-6781 ISSN 2214-9902 (electronic)
Ius Gentium: Comparative Perspectives on Law and Justice
ISBN 978-3-031-29335-1 ISBN 978-3-031-29336-8 (eBook)
https://doi.org/10.1007/978-3-031-29336-8

This Springer imprint is published by the registered company Springer Nature Switzerland AG
The registered company address is: Gewerbestrasse 11, 6330 Cham, Switzerland

Nihal ile Ahmet'e
For the eternal olive trees of my country

Preface

This publication is a further revised and updated version of the author's PhD thesis completed at Istanbul Bilgi University Law Faculty in Private Law, which was accepted by the decision of the Doctorate Board on 27 January 2021. The publication was lastly revised in February 2022 to reflect the recent developments on this subject matter.

Paris, France

Pınar Kara

Acknowledgments

So much time and so many places: this thesis sprouted its first shoots in London, discovered its authentic voice in Paris, and finally came to fruition in Normandy. So much support and so much gratitude: my work has been guided and inspired by different people at different times, with each person contributing something unique and valuable.

My PhD journey—which has, in total, spanned around nine years of my life—has been both enlightening and transformative for me personally. First of all, a big thank you to my dear family and friends, who have been so generous with their compassion, support, and understanding. This extended period of research and writing has been challenging and introspective, and my life would have been cold without them.

All else aside, this PhD thesis would not have been born if my path had not crossed with my two esteemed professors:

Firstly, I would like to express my gratitude to my dear professor and esteemed thesis advisor, Prof. Yeşim M. Atamer, who never hesitated in diving into the depths of this subject with me, especially when I reached out to her with only a vague initial idea in my head. Again and again, she offered me her time, effort, and feedback and broadened my horizons.

I would also like to express my gratitude to my dear professor, Prof. Gül Okutan Nilsson, who has given so much of her invaluable time and effort on my thesis, and even more, who has supported me with great enthusiasm throughout the whole PhD process. I am so grateful for all the motivation and all the advice that she has given me always with that sparkle in her eyes.

I would also like to thank my valued professors Prof. Başak Baysal, Assoc. Prof. İpek Sağlam, and Dr. Candan Yasan Tepetaş. They comforted me with their kindness, helping to dissolve the distance inevitably inserted between us by the screen, on what must be the most exciting day of my life to date—the day of my PhD thesis defense—and enabled me to deepen my study with their invaluable comments and contributions.

I would like to express my deep gratitude to a cherished lawyer, my dearest Av. Şeyma İnal, whom I have been fortunate to have a close connection with—

someone who has always believed in me, always known that I was capable of achieving more, and who has been so generous with her support, her warmth, and her inspiring ideas.

I would like to thank Prof. Janet Dine, who read the very first draft of this thesis and offered me her insightful comments, as well as the enthusiasm I needed to carry on.

I would also like to thank a valued academic, dear Prof. Sanem Aksoy, who was kind and patient enough to read the roughest earliest draft of this thesis and then to discuss it with me, line by line.

I would like to thank Dr. Çiğdem Çımrın for her solidarity, for sharing our interest on business & human rights, for those long moments of brainstorming and, last but not least, for Minerva's owl. I feel hopeful and enthusiastic for all that awaits us in near future.

I would like to thank Tracy Starreveld, my patient editor, who helped me more clearly express what I really wanted to say by diligently and virtuously working through every single sentence of this thesis.

I would like to thank Melda Otara, who provided me with all the support I needed throughout my long PhD period, always with a smile on her face, and the teams from Istanbul Bilgi University Law Faculty, of the Institute of Graduate Programs and of Bilgi University Library.

I would like to express my gratitude to my dear uncle Mehmet Ali Kara, who has taught me many invaluable things by his silent wisdom and his infinite curiosity for knowing more in life.

My deepest gratitude to my loving father Ahmet Ali Kara, the stable presence in my life and my constant support, who has showed me the true meaning of conscience and kindness, and who has luckily passed onto me a love of animals and nature.

My deepest gratitude to my loving mother Prof. H. Nihal İncioğlu, the most compassionate person I have ever met, who has been a best friend for as long as I can remember, with whom I love sharing everything in life. My parents are such an essential and cherished part of this person I have become.

Finally, a heartfelt thank you to my dear Kerem Balcıoğlu, the love of my life—*et le tourbillon de ma vie*—who has relentlessly put his analytical perspective into every scenario presented in this thesis, who has patiently supported me and who has never stopped expressing how he is proud of me. I love living this life with you.

I am so grateful to you all. Thanks to each and every one of you, a book has been born.

February 2023

Paris, France Pınar Kara

Contents

Abbreviations

ATS	Alien Tort Statute
Austl. Int'l L.J.	Australian International Law Journal
AÜHFD	Ankara Üniversitesi Hukuk Fakültesi Dergisi
BATİDER	Banka ve Ticaret Hukuku Dergisi
BHRJ	Business and Human Rights Journal
Brit. J. Am. Legal Stud.	British Journal of American Legal Studies
Brussels I	Council Regulation (EC) No 44/2001 of 22 December 2000 on jurisdiction and the recognition and enforcement of judgments in civil and commercial matters
Brussels I Recast	Regulation (EU) No 1215/2012 of the European Parliament and of the Council of 12 December 2012 on jurisdiction and the recognition and enforcement of judgments in civil and commercial matters
CC	Turkish Civil Code No. 4721
CPC	Turkish Civil Procedure Code No. 6100
CSR	Corporate social responsibility
EBLR	European Business Law Review
EBOR	Economics Business Organization Law Review
ECCJ	European Coalition for Corporate Justice
ECFR	European Company and Financial Law Review
ECHR	European Convention on Human Rights
ECJ	European Court of Justice
ERÜHFD	Erciyes Üniversitesi Hukuk Fakültesi Dergisi
EU	European Union

EÜHFD	Erzincan Üniversitesi Hukuk Fakültesi Dergisi
EWCA	England and Wales Court of Appeal
EWHC	England and Wales High Court of Justice
FDL	Foreign direct liability
Geo. J. Int'l L.	Georgetown Journal of International Law
HRDD	Human rights due diligence
ILO	International Labour Organization
İÜHFM	İstanbul Üniversitesi Hukuk Fakültesi Mecmuası
J. Bus. Ethics	Journal of Business Ethics
J. Fac. L. Inonu U.	Journal of Faculty of Law of Inonu University
McGill Int'l J. Sust. Dev. L. & Pol'y	McGill International Journal of Sustainable Development Law and Policy
MHB	Milletlerarası Hukuk ve Milletlerarası Özel Hukuk Bülteni
mHRDD	Mandatory human rights due diligence
MNC	Multinational corporate groups
MÜHFD-HAD	Marmara Üniversitesi Hukuk Fakültesi Hukuk Araştırmaları Dergisi
NGO	Non-governmental organisation
OECD	Organisation for Economic Co-operation and Development
OEIGWG	Open-ended intergovernmental working group
OHCHR	United Nations Office of the Human Rights Office of the High Commissioner
OJ	Official Journal
PIPC	Turkish Code on Private International and Procedural Law No. 5718
QB	Queen's Bench Division
Queen's L.J.	Queen's Law Journal
Queensland L.J.	The University of Queensland Law Journal
RabelsZ	Rabels Zeitschrift für ausländisches und internationals Privatrecht
Rome II	Regulation (EC) No 864/2007 on the law applicable to non-contractual obligations
SCCJ	Swiss Coalition for Corporate Justice
SDGs	Sustainable Development Goals
SMEs	Small and medium-sized enterprises
Suffolk U. L. Rev.	Suffolk University Law Review
SÜHFD	Selçuk Üniversitesi Hukuk Fakültesi Dergisi

SZW/RSDA	Schweizerische Zeitschrift für Wirtschafts- und Finanzmarktrecht
TCC	Turkish Commercial Code No. 6102
TCO	Turkish Code of Obligations No. 6098
TFM	Ticaret ve Fikri Mülkiyet Hukuku Dergisi
UKHL	United Kingdom House of Lords
UKSC	United Kingdom Supreme Court
UN	United Nations
UNCITRAL	United Nations Commission on International Trade Law
UNCTC	United Nations Centre on Transnational Corporations
UNDHR	Universal Declaration of Human Rights
UNGPs	United Nations Guiding Principles on Business and Human Rights
ZGR	Zeitschrift für Unternehmens- und Gesellschaftsrecht

Chapter 1
Introduction

Globalisation has had a significant impact on all aspects of life, including business transactions. As transactions became globalised, so did companies. There have been innovations in corporate structure that have led to an expansion of the limits on the global operations of businesses.[1] Companies that started operating in the global arena have now transcended the realm of nation states.[2] However, globalisation also cast doubts on the ability and willingness of national governments to fulfil their human rights responsibilities.[3] On the other side of the spectrum, international law remained insufficient to regulate multinational corporations (MNCs),[4] as the general position of companies in international law is questionable.

Due to several reasons, ranging from convenience in accessing resources, easy production and lower costs, it has become a trend for companies established in developed Western (or Northern) countries to operate in developing or the least developed countries through their subsidiaries, where the law is usually not developed enough to sufficiently address corporate liability. In other words, as *Muchlinski* powerfully stated, "*(. . .) liberal Western powers (. . .) had to live with the paradox of the observance of human rights at home and their denial in overseas colonial possessions*".[5] In turn, developing countries, who are in need of foreign investment, have often opted to regulate the issues of liability in a limited manner in their laws, while local institutions have failed to act impartially against foreign investors for the

[1] UN Special Representative of the Secretary-General, Protect, Respect and Remedy: a Framework for Business and Human Rights, UN Doc. A/HRC/8/5 (7 April 2008), para. 104.

[2] Woodroffe (1999), p. 133.

[3] Cragg et al. (2012), p. 2.

[4] The terms of 'multinational corporate group', 'multinational corporations', 'multinationals' and 'transnational corporations' are all tantamount to each other and expressed by the acronym of MNC (s) in this study.

[5] Muchlinski (2001), p. 34.

P. Kara, *Tort Liability in Multinational Corporate Groups*, Ius Gentium: Comparative Perspectives on Law and Justice 107,
https://doi.org/10.1007/978-3-031-29336-8_1

same reason.[6] The aforementioned trend of MNCs, established in developed countries, engaging in business in developing or the least developed countries in order to benefit from legal loopholes and advantages—against third world countries that wish to attract foreign investment—creates a so-called 'downward spiral'[7] or race-to-the-bottom.

The mismatch between the concept of the nation state and the globalised nature of MNCs created a way to eliminate liability by leaning towards state boundaries, separate legal personality and corporate veil. The existence of a corporate veil, caused by the separation of legal entities, supplemented by a jurisdictional veil, caused by the multinational nature of corporate groups, has become a feasible mechanism for disregarding liability in foreign direct liability (FDL) cases, where the parent company's liability is sought for damage arising from the activities of transnational subsidiaries.[8] Hence, the discussions on the parent company's liability in corporate groups has gained momentum in the last few years, as it has become a primary need—in terms of socio-legal policy—to address the liabilities of parent companies of MNCs for the acts committed by their transnational subsidiaries.

These theoretical concerns have also been embodied in specific cases in practice, where irreparable damage was caused for many people without any imposition of liability. One of these cases is the Bhopal incident of 1984, which concerned the leakage of forty tons of the poisonous gas methyl isocyanate from a Union Carbide pesticide plant in Bhopal, India, which affected the surrounding areas and caused numerous deaths and permanent injuries.[9] While the US courts rejected jurisdiction, the Indian Supreme Court decided on a settlement amount to be paid to the victims, which was insufficient to cover the damage. The finalisation of FDL cases by way of settlement also constitutes a particular problem, as it seriously hinders the future of FDL claims by enabling multinational corporations to avoid any admission of liability. Another striking example is the Rana Plaza incident of 1983, which concerned the collapse of an eight-storey commercial building in Bangladesh that included five garment factories, causing many casualties. Following this disaster, the Accord on Fire and Building Safety in Bangladesh[10] was signed between many clothing companies. This accord is a legally independent and binding agreement between brands and trade unions, aiming to ensure a safe and healthy work environment for the textile and garment industry in Bangladesh. Even though measures like these, taken intentionally by companies, have a positive impact in practice, they are insufficient to ensure a fully effective and harmonised approach with respect to multinational tort cases. The magnitude of these disasters and the wideness of the

[6]Nygh (2002), p. 56.

[7]Woodroffe (1999), p. 132.

[8]Muchlinski (2010), s. 920.

[9]Business & Human Rights Resource Centre, Union Carbide/Dow lawsuit (re Bhopal), https://www.business-humanrights.org/en/latest-news/union-carbidedow-lawsuit-re-bhopal/.

[10]Accord on Fire and Building Safety in Bangladesh (2013). https://admin.bangladeshaccord.org/wp-content/uploads/2018/08/2013-Accord.pdf.

area affected thereby highlight the necessity of regulating FDL in statutory law. As a matter of fact, past experience shows that, compared to previous times where damage was mostly limited to personal injuries and individual deaths, the risks in today's world often involve a general peril for the public, such as radioactive and chemical disasters,[11] which need to be addressed in law.

The liability of a parent company for human rights violations and environmental damage caused by the operations of its transnational subsidiaries has found life in so-called 'foreign direct liability claims'. These claims are initiated by 'involuntary creditors', such as tort victims, who have no voluntary engagement with the parent companies of MNCs.[12] These are actions that target the parent company's direct responsibility, based on their alleged duty of care towards third parties, thus under the tort of negligence. This is not a straightforward conclusion, as it has many complicated legal layers that should be handled very carefully. In fact, FDL cases touch upon many fields of law: (i) company law, which challenges these claims by its very basic principles of separate legal entity and limited liability, (ii) tort law, which seems to provide the only viable basis for the reasons to be dealt hereunder, (iii) private international law, which serves to determine the applicable law and jurisdiction in these cases, and finally (iv) international human rights law and environmental law, which both regulate the violations considered within these claims. This study focuses on the private international law, tort law of negligence and company law aspects of the matter, without dealing with the nature of violations under human rights law or the state responsibility under public international law.

It is not easy to effectively regulate MNCs. First of all, it is difficult to position them in international law, given their nature as private actors that are not subject to international law in the traditional context. For this reason, it becomes important to regulate these actors in domestic laws, which is a growing trend nowadays, as countries including France, Switzerland, Germany and the Netherlands have taken solid steps to adopt liability provisions in their statutory laws by way of mandatory

---

[11] Slapper (2011), p. 83.

[12] 'Voluntary creditors' are those who have voluntarily entered into a commercial relationship with an entity; e.g. business creditors, contractual counterparties, commercial partners, employees. Employees of a subsidiary, however, are seen as third parties for a parent company, thus they might be deemed to be involuntary creditors against a parent company. The same rationale applies to the sub-contractors and suppliers of a subsidiary. Although these would be deemed to be voluntary creditors in respect of their relationship with the subsidiary, they will be involuntary creditors in their claims brought against the parent company. It could be argued that consumers are also voluntary creditors, in the sense that they enter into the relevant relationship voluntarily. And yet, their position can be argued in the case of patronage statements made by parent companies in a group, which are not the subject matter of this study. 'Involuntary creditors' are those who have been engaged in a relationship with a party without their voluntary involvement, thus they are unable to contract around liability or to negotiate in advance for risk-shifting. In this case, there is no contract or any other voluntary engagement between the parties, but rather an act by one of them which inflicts damages upon the other. Tort victims are typical examples of involuntary creditors, as they suffer damages due to a third party's unlawful act; e.g. people living in the vicinities of the place where the subsidiary operates, employees of a transnational subsidiary (who are third parties to the parent company).

human rights due diligence (mHRDD). Hence, it appears that mHRDD will be important in the future of FDL claims. In fact, regulating this issue in domestic laws might serve as effective and clear grounds for accommodating FDL claims and triggering liability for the breach of the duty of care under tort law.

This study focuses—in the second chapter—on the concerns surrounding the operation of MNCs that lead to a necessity to regulate responsible business conduct, then explains the nature of FDL, followed by a presentation and delimitation of the scope of this study.

The third chapter focuses on the definitions of companies, corporate groups and MNCs, mostly within the scope of Turkish law in comparison with other jurisdictions, as well as on certain relevant international legal instruments. Within this framework, special focus is put on the basic company law principles of separate legal personality and limited liability, which challenge FDL claims. The terms 'corporate groups' and 'groups of companies' are hereby used with the meaning prescribed thereto under Turkish law (i.e. the relevant provisions of Turkish Commercial Code[13] (TCC) and Trade Registry Regulation[14]). As it is analysed in detail in the second chapter, the concept of corporate groups is defined quite broadly under Turkish law, which might even cover business partners such as suppliers or sub-contractors, depending on the level of control exercised in the relevant relationship. Accordingly, it is considered that Turkish law might be useful for FDL claims, although not well equipped enough to accommodate them. On this point, the analysis of liability is presented differently for 'pure holdings' and 'mixed holdings', which have different levels of intervention by parent companies in the business operations of their subsidiaries. With regard to MNCs, their positions in international law and specific concerns which are triggering the need for regulation are discussed. Within this context, various sources of international law, including corporate social responsibility instrument such as the UN Global Compact,[15] Organisation for Economic Co-operation and Development (OECD) Guidelines for Multinational Enterprises[16] ('OECD Guidelines for MNEs') and the ILO Tripartite Declaration of Principles concerning Multinational Enterprises and Social Policy[17] ('ILO Tripartite Declaration') are analysed, and suggestions are given regarding a potential

[13]Turkish Commercial Code numbered 6102, OJ 14.02.2011/27846, in force as of 01.07.2012.

[14]Trade Registry Regulation numbered 2012/4093, OJ 27.01.2013/28541, in force as of 27.01.2013.

[15]The Ten Principles of the United Nations Global Compact, https://www.unglobalcompact.org/what-is-gc/mission/principles.

[16]2011 edition of OECD Guidelines for Multinational Enterprises ("OECD Guidelines for MNEs"), http://www.oecd.org/daf/inv/mne/48004323.pdf.

[17]ILO Tripartite Declaration of Principles concerning Multinational Enterprises and Social Policy, adopted by the Governing Body of the International Labour Office at its 204th Session (Geneva, November 1977) and amended at its 279th (November 2000), 295th (March 2006) and 329th (March 2017) Sessions. The fifth edition (March 2017) is available at http://www.ilo.org/wcmsp5/groups/public/%2D%2D-ed_emp/%2D%2D-emp_ent/%2D%2D-multi/documents/publication/wcms_094386.pdf ("ILO Tripartite Declaration").

reform to national laws to effectively regulate MNCs within the scope of FDL claims.

The fourth chapter of the study examines the substantive legal aspects of FDL claims. In this regard, claims by 'involuntary creditors',[18] who have no opportunity to negotiate with the corporation over the allocation of risks,[19] and more specifically tort victims, stand at the focal point of the analysis.

As the legal framework of this study is predominantly Turkish law, the substantive analysis of FDL claims are made under the relevant Turkish law, in comparison with English case law (and to some extent Dutch case law) where these claims have been discussed in detail.[20] Within this context, the potential legal grounds of FDL claims are analysed, based on two main categories; (i) tort liability, with specific focus on the breach of duty of care, and (ii) strict liability.

Within the scope of tort liability, the mandatory elements constructing this liability under Turkish law—namely fault, unlawfulness, causation and damage—are analysed in terms of FDL claims, in the context of the provisions of the Turkish Code of Obligations[21] (TCO) on general fault liability (Art. 49 et seq). In relation to fault, it is considered that the parent company's acts would, in most FDL cases, consist of an omission, which would constitute an act of negligence. Parent company liability for a breach of the duty of care is evaluated within the scope of the element of unlawfulness, whereby attention is drawn to the need for a specific provision in statutory law regulating the aforesaid duty of care in order to establish unlawfulness—although in FDL cases the violated right is an absolute right (e.g. physical integrity), for which unlawfulness in result is considered sufficient. The element of causation, in particular, is evaluated within the scope of the theory of adequate causation, which is dominant in Turkish law, whereby it is assessed in which cases causation could be deemed to exist in FDL claims and whether the parent company could avoid liability by proving that the causation was broken (in cases of *force majeure*, victim's fault or third party's fault). Finally, the damage in terms of FDL cases is analysed, with a particular focus on violation of physical integrity which includes cases of death, injury and deterioration of health, as the most common types of damage occurring in these cases. To this end, pecuniary

[18] Muchlinski (2012), p. 151.

[19] Muchlinski (2010), p. 918; Muchlinski (2011), p. 679.

[20] Although there is a comparative legal study whereby the parent company's liability of its subsidiary's tortious acts has been analysed including Turkish law aspects (Eroğlu 2008), the mentioned study did not encompass the new texts of TCO and TCC, both of which came into force in July 2012 and introduced significant novelties for the subject of this study. One of the mentioned novelties is the regulation of corporate groups for the first time under Turkish law (Art. 195-210 TCC), which have mostly been adopted from German *Konzernrecht*. Another significant novelty is the strict liability for dangerous activities regulated in Article 71 of the TCO as a cover-all liability type, which might be useful in calling the parent company's liability in FDL claims. Moreover, the mandatory rules on human rights due diligence are also part of recent improvements, not to mention the continuous developments in global field, including the works on an international treaty to regulate this issue.

[21] Turkish Code of Obligations numbered 6098, OJ 04.02.2011/27836, in force as of 01.07.2012.

damages and non-pecuniary (moral) damages are also explained as a means of legal remedy for the victims of FDL claims. It is important to note that there are currently no provisions in Turkish statutory law to establish a parent company's duty of care. For this reason, after exploring English case law on a parent company's duty of care in terms of FDL cases, a statutory provision is suggested to regulate this liability in Turkish law.

As for the strict liability grounds under Turkish law, mild causal liability of the employer (Art. 66 TCO), strict liability for dangerous activities (Art. 71 TCO) and strict liability for polluting the environment (Art. 28 Environmental Law[22]) are all explored. Amongst these grounds, employer's liability appears to be a challenge in terms of establishing parent company liability in FDL claims, as it is difficult to prove the required relationship of subordination and dependence between two separate legal entities, i.e. the parent company and its subsidiary. Strict liability for dangerous activities might also be unlikely to serve as adequate legal grounds for FDL claims, as in this case it would be necessary to prove that the parent company had acted as the owner or operator of the enterprise that caused the relevant damage—which is, in fact, owned and operated by the subsidiary. Strict liability for polluting the environment would also require an assessment of whether the parent company could be deemed to be economically and organisationally in control of the subsidiaries' operations that led to the relevant environmental damage, in which case it might be possible to establish the parent company's liability as the 'polluter'.

As additional legal grounds that might serve as complementary to tort liability, the recent trend of mHRDD is examined. In this respect, first of all, international legal instruments (that are mainly soft law instruments) that regulate non-financial reporting obligations for companies are assessed. Thereafter, the current French law, the proposal and counter-proposal in Switzerland, the draft law in Germany and the draft law in the Netherlands are also explored. Based on all these legal instruments, a suggestion is put forward to regulate mHRDD under Turkish law, as part of the already existing provisions concerning corporate groups in the TCC.

The fifth chapter of the study focuses on the private international legal aspects of FDL claims. Within this context, the questions of jurisdiction and applicable law are analysed under the relevant Turkish law, along with the relevant legislation in the UK, the EU and the US, which may also be applicable depending on the corporate structure of MNCs. The analysis also comprises the relevant case law on the questions of jurisdiction and applicable law, especially in common law jurisdictions where they have flourished. To this end, regarding the question of jurisdiction, discussions are mostly focused on the point of whether the place where the tortious act was committed may be deemed as the home country, where the parent company has made the decisions (concerning its subsidiaries) that led to the relevant damage in the host country, or where it has failed to take such decisions or measures to prevent the damage. Regarding the question of applicable law, the heart of the

[22] Environmental Law numbered 2872, OJ 11.08.1983/18132, in force as of 11.08.1983.

discussion centres on the point of whether the home country, as the place where the alleged omission of the parent company happened, might be deemed as the most closely connected law to the relevant claim. The analysis focusing on the aforementioned points explore the relevant grounds under Brussels I Recast[23] and ATS[24] regarding jurisdiction, and Rome II[25] regarding applicable law.

References

Online Sources

Accord on Fire and Building Safety in Bangladesh, (2013). https://admin.bangladeshaccord.org/wp-content/uploads/2018/08/2013-Accord.pdf

Business & Human Rights Resource Centre, Union Carbide/Dow lawsuit (re Bhopal), https://www.business-humanrights.org/en/latest-news/union-carbidedow-lawsuit-re-bhopal/

Legislation, Reports, Resolutions and Opinions

Alien Tort Statute or Alien Tort Claims Act, 28 U.S.C. § 1350

ILO Tripartite Declaration of Principles concerning Multinational Enterprises and Social Policy, adopted by the Governing Body of the International Labour Office at its 204th Session (Geneva, November 1977) and amended at its 279th (November 2000), 295th (March 2006) and 329th (March 2017) Sessions

Regulation (EU) No 1215/2012 of the European Parliament and of the Council of 12 December 2012 on jurisdiction and the recognition and enforcement of judgments in civil and commercial matters: OJ L 351/21 (20.12.2012)

Regulation (EC) No 864/2007 of the European Parliament and of the Council of 11 July 2007 on the law applicable to non-contractual obligations (Rome II): OJ L 199/40 (31.07.2007)

2011 edition of OECD Guidelines for Multinational Enterprises, http://www.oecd.org/daf/inv/mne/48004323.pdf

The Ten Principles of the United Nations Global Compact, https://www.unglobalcompact.org/what-is-gc/mission/principles

---

[23] Regulation (EU) No 1215/2012 of the European Parliament and of the Council of 12 December 2012 on jurisdiction and the recognition and enforcement of judgments in civil and commercial matters: OJ L 351/21 (20.12.2012).

[24] Alien Tort Statute or Alien Tort Claims Act, 28 U.S.C. § 1350; it was embedded in a statute that was enacted in 1789.

[25] Regulation (EC) No 864/2007 of the European Parliament and of the Council of 11 July 2007 on the law applicable to non-contractual obligations (Rome II): OJ L 199/40 (31.07.2007).

UN Special Representative of the Secretary-General, Protect, Respect and Remedy: a Framework for Business and Human Rights, UN Doc. A/HRC/8/5 (7 April 2008)

Literature

Cragg W, Arnold DG, Muchlinski P (2012) Guest Editors' introduction human rights and business. Bus Ethics Q 22(1):1–7

Eroğlu M (2008) Multinational enterprises and tort liabilities, an interdisciplinary and comparative examination. Edward Elgar Publishing

Muchlinski P (2001) Human rights and multinationals: is there a problem?. Int Aff 77 (I):31–47

Muchlinski P (2010) Limited liability and multinational enterprises: a case for reform?. Cambridge J Econ 34:915–928

Muchlinski P (2011) The changing face of transnational business governance: private corporate law liability and accountability of transnational groups in a post-financial crisis world. Indiana J Glob Legal Stud 18 (2):665–705

Muchlinski P (2012) Implementing the New UN corporate human rights framework: implications for corporate law, governance, and regulation. Bus Ethics Q 22(1):145–177, ISSN 1052-150X

Nygh P (2002) The liability of multi-national corporations for the torts of their subsidiaries. Eur Bus Org Law Rev 3:51–81

Slapper G (2011) Violent corporate crime, corporate social responsibility and human rights. In: Voiculescu A, Yanacopulos H (eds) The business of human rights – an evolving Agenda for corporate responsibility. Zed Books, pp 79–100

Woodroffe J (1999) Regulating multinational corporations in a World of Nation states. In: Addo MK (ed) Human rights standards and the responsibility of transnational corporations. Kluwer Law International

Chapter 2
Introduction to FDL and the Nature of FDL Claims

2.1 Concerns Regarding MNCs: "Is There a Problem?"[1]

MNCs comprise different local entities, yet internationally they act as a single entity.[2] The complex structure of MNCs has created concerns in the international business and legal arena. While host countries were concerned that MNCs, which are usually large corporate groups, could act as agents to home countries by safeguarding the interests of home countries, the home countries were concerned about the migration of jobs leading to MNCs engaging in a signficant amount of manufacturing and production outside the borders of home countries, thus reducing job opportunities at home.[3] The UN's working group (called the 'Group of Eminent Persons to Study the Impact of Multinational Corporations on Development and International Relations') had also mentioned these concerns in their report of 1974 as, in short, (i) home country concerns about domestic employment, balance of payments and competition, (ii) host country concerns about ownership and control of key economic sectors by foreign companies, their potential effects on political sovereignty and on socio-cultural values, (iii) labour's concerns about the effect of MNCs on the bargaining strength of trade unions, (iv) consumers' concerns about the potential effects on the quality and price of goods, and finally (v) the MNCs' concerns about a potential expropriation of their assets along with restrictive, unclear and unsteady government policies.[4] It is considered as no surprise then that MNCs

[1] The phrase "is there a problem?" is quoted from Muchlinski (2001), p. 1.

[2] Palombo (2019), p. 267.

[3] Zerk (2006), p. 10.

[4] Economic and Social Council Resolution 1721 (LIII), quoted in UN, 'The Impact of Multinational Corporations on Development and on International Relations', UN DOC. E/5500/Rev. 1., ST/ESA/ 6 (New York: UN, 1974), 13 ILM 800, p. 19; Zerk (2006), p. 11.

P. Kara, *Tort Liability in Multinational Corporate Groups*, Ius Gentium: Comparative Perspectives on Law and Justice 107,
https://doi.org/10.1007/978-3-031-29336-8_2

often engage in lobbying with host country governments for a business-friendly legislation, whereby they influence political decision-making in the host countries.[5]

This structure which comprises different legal entities presents a significant challenge for effective regulation, especially due to the main principles company law of separate legal entityship and limited liability. Not surprisingly, when a corporate group is multinational, and therefore disseminated to a number of different countries via subsidiaries, the issue of effective regulation becomes even more challenging, as it involves a jurisdictional barrier in addition to the corporate one. In other words, these complicated group structures allow parent companies to lower their risks of liability in general, and for the purposes of this study, in tort.[6] Another challenge is, conversely, being able to control these different companies and have them all complying with the parent company's policies and ethical guidelines. In fact, especially in cases where the corporate group has foreign subsidiaries or where there is a joint venture between two or more companies established in different countries, the cultural differences may make it difficult to ensure a centralised control.[7]

It might still be difficult to identify or understand problems in the structure and operations of MNCs all over the world, especially given the principles of the free market and free economy. However, MNCs have a destablising effect on the market against the governments and the people of the host countries. In fact, MNCs are able to act flexibly in their operations, as they have the opportunity to choose the host country where they operate through local subsidiaries. These host countries are usually developing or least developed countries, which need foreign investment to create more jobs, cash flow and thus contribute to their economies. Frequently, host country governments have shareholdings in these subsidiary companies, which enables MNCs to mask their group structures and secure their social licence to operate in a foreign country.[8] Therefore, the reliance of the host countries on foreign investment against the freedom, flexibility, bargaining power, wealth and knowledge of MNCs creates an imbalance between these actors to the benefit of MNCs.[9] The dependence of the developing or least developed host countries on foreign investment also results in a favourable approach to these issues in their legislation, specifically concerning liability. This situation, in turn, renders them more attractive to foreign investment from developed home countries, where the legislation is developed and the liability terms are stricter. The end result often harms the people of host countries, and MNCs are able to wash their hands clean of any damages incurred due to their operations.[10]

---

[5]Enneking (2012), p. 365.

[6]Rühmkorf (2015), p. 172.

[7]Loomis (1999), pp. 150–151.

[8]Dowling (2020), p. 223. For instance, Indian government held shares in UCC's Indian subsidiary, which operated the Bhopal plant, in turn of the land on which the factory was built.

[9]Enneking (2012), p. 366.

[10]Enneking (2012), p. 367.

On a different note, it would be false to believe that MNCs have bargaining power only against host countries. Their power against the home countries where their parent companies are located is also significant as these countries understand the importance of providing a favourable climate for establishment in order to pave the way for local and international competition between international companies located there.[11] In a manner of speaking, MNCs may become economically stronger than nation states.[12] All of these concerns and risks have, in time, led to a need for regulations on MNCs that would be adequate for their supra-national and flexible character, either in international law or in home country or host country domestic laws.

2.2 Nature of FDL Claims

The main purpose of FDL claims does not lie in holding the parent company liable for the damage caused by the operations of its subsidiaries. Rather, the goal is to hold the parent company liable for its own actions (or omissions) concerning the damage caused by the operations of its subsidiaries. More specifically, in these claims, parent company liability is invoked for the parent company's own actions (or omissions) in relation to the operations of its subsidiaries that resulted in damage on third parties (e.g. local people in the host country). It is thereby claimed that the parent company owes a duty of care directly against the relevant third parties, which is allegedly breached. FDL cases are seen as important tools in ensuring corporate social responsibility and accountability, as they incentivise MNCs to behave responsibly at home and abroad, to provide transparency in their transnational activities and to allow the host country citizens to receive remedies for the harm suffered due to the activities of MNCs. [13]

This form of liability addressed against parent companies of MNCs under FDL claims is a primary and direct liability arising from the actions of the parent company itself. Therefore, these claims are direct in nature against the parent company, unlike the cases of piercing of the corporate veil, where the parent company's liability is claimed indirectly through the subsidiary. Under any circumstances, piercing of the corporate veil doctrine, which suggests that the distinction between the legal entity

[11] Enneking (2012), p. 369.

[12] Antunes (1994), p. 38. As a supporting point to the economic power of MNCs, data pertaining to the financial year 2017 compiled by Global Justice Now shows that amongst 200 biggest economies in the world, 157 are corporations and not countries. As an example, the annual revenue generated by Royal Dutch Shell in 2017 exceeds the GDPs of Mexico and of Sweden, while BP's and ExxonMobil's exceed that of India and Switzerland. See Global Justice Now, 69 of the richest 100 entities on the planet are corporations, not governments, figures show, 17.10.2018, https://www.globaljustice.org.uk/news/2018/oct/17/69-richest-100-entities-planet-are-corporations-not-governments-figures-show.

[13] Enneking (2013), p. 137.

and its real person creators (so called the 'veil') should be disregarded in certain cases by deeming them a single legal entity,[14] proves to be more challenging in practice than FDL claims. This is a complex doctrine, applied in very exceptional cases where it is proven that there is a fraudulent use of the separate legal entity structure by the parent company, and where the subsidiary is acting as some kind of façade – or 'alter ego' – for the parent company.[15] It is mostly the case that the creditors of an insolvent subsidiary address their claims against the parent company, arguing that the the parent company and the subsidiary disregarded the separate legal entity principle by acting as a single entity. This is usually applied as a last resort in cases where there has been a misuse of separate legal personality or the assets of the two companies are mixed. The main difference between FDL claims and piercing the corporate veil is that in cases of FDL the veil is left intact.[16] Another important difference between these two methods lies in the scope of the claim. FDL that is based on parent company tort liability concerns the parent company's responsibility for its own wrongful acts, while piercing of the corporate veil creates a much wider liability on the parent company's side as this covers the whole claim against the subsidiary, regardless whether the parent company had any fault in the occurrence of the respective harm.[17]

FDL cases consist of claims initiated against parent companies of MNCs before the courts of the developed home countries where the parent companies are based, in relation to the harms occurred due to the activities of their subsidiaries in developing or least developed host countries.[18] Typically, in these cases, the MNC has operations that are harmful to the environment or to the local people of the host country, where the law and the judicial system remain insufficient to cover these claims. Even if the law of the developing or least developed host country may be adequate to accomodate FDL claims, the local environment may not be favourable. For instance, the lack of legal aid or the insufficiency of legal expertise in a specific matter might seriously affect the benefits of the tort victims expected from filing these claims.[19] Another possibility is the unavailability of fair trial that in times occurs because of corruption or political instability.[20] For these reasons, the plaintiffs of FDL claims try their chances before the courts of the home country, which is usually a developed country with adequate law and legal environment in place to address the relevant claims.

Another crucial aspect of FDL claims is that these claims do not aim to recover the financial inability or insufficiency of the transnational subsidiary, by seeking compensation from the supposedly wealthier parent company. In fact, any such

[14] Sağlam (2020), p. 1122.

[15] Sağlam (2020), p. 1122.

[16] Enneking (2012), p. 249.

[17] Enneking (2012), p. 250.

[18] Enneking (2008), p. 285; Enneking (2009), pp. 903–904.

[19] Nygh (2002), p. 56.

[20] Weller and Thomale (2017), p. 514.

claim would have been considered a type of secondary and indirect liability for parent companies. Instead, the main goal is to accommodate these claims under a more effective and fair justice system, which might be achieved before the courts of the developed home country.[21] Hence, FDL claims aim to introduce a potential gateway for tort victims in countries where the rule of law is barely established and where access to a fair trial and effective remedy is difficult, especially when tried against MNCs, who act as powerful foreign investors.

There is a structurally unequal distribution of power which significantly reduces tort victims' ability to invoke the responsibility of MNCs, as these corporations use complex corporate structures that enable them to hide from liability.[22] It is acknowledged that the corporate structure of a group makes its creditors more vulnerable compared to the creditors of independent companies, due to the corporate group's ability to reduce transparency and create the impression that the whole group stands for each single company's debts.[23] This inequality also includes technical issues such as difficulty accessing information and evidence, financial insufficiency or inability to cover legal costs, which significantly hinder the tort victims' access to an effective remedy. In fact, involuntary creditors could be considered to be weaker and less likely to receive compensation for their damages compared to voluntary creditors who are protected by their contracts in addition to the law. Involuntary creditors have no means to bargain for compensation in advance or to avoid the risks they face, and the losses they incur are ineffectively externalised by the relevant wrongdoer.[24] For this reason, this study takes involuntary creditors as its focus, as it seeks to shed light upon the tort liability of an MNC's parent company for human rights abuses committed by its transnational subsidiaries.

2.3 Aim and Focus of the Study: Presentation and Delimitation of the Scope

The focal point of this study is FDL claims, which are aimed at invoking parent companies' liability in tort of negligence[25] due to the actions of its transnational subsidiaries in host countries. These are actions giving rise to specific human rights abuses in violation of physical integrity—such as death, injury and deprivation of

[21] Jones (2019), p. 2.

[22] Africa is a country - The Zambian farmers who are suing a mining company in a British court (15.02.2019), https://africasacountry.com/2019/02/the-zambian-farmers-who-are-suing-a-mining-company-in-a-british-court.

[23] Kraakman et al. (2009), p. 127.

[24] Eroğlu (2008a, b), p. 89.

[25] Tort liability and its sub-category tort of negligence are Common Law concepts, which correspond roughly to delicts or extra-contractual liability in Continental European legal systems, to which Turkish law also belongs. Nevertheless, the term of 'tort liability' is used within this study, as this term has already become common parlance in legal doctrine (van Dam (2007), p. 4).

health—which at the same time constitute tortious acts. The plaintiffs in these cases are the involuntary creditors, who are tort victims harmed by the activities of an MNC's subsidiary.[26] Although the violations that are subject to FDL claims mostly constitute human rights abuses, the human rights aspects of the matter—concerning state duty—are not dealt with in this study, as it is hereby focused on the tort liability of non-state actors, and more specifically, corporations.[27]

Nevertheless, it is useful to briefly mention the specific human rights that might be relevant in the context of FDL claims. In fact, the UN Global Compact,[28] which is considered to be the leading instrument in business and human rights, is mainly focused on three pillars: (1) respect for human rights defined under the Universal Declaration of Human Rights (UNDHR),[29] (2) compliance with the standards and rules concerning labour and employment under ILO's Declaration on Fundamental Principles and Rights at Work, and (3) compliance with standards and rules concerning the protection of the environment under the Rio Declaration of the UN Conference on Environment and Development.[30] Human rights, within the context of FDL claims, mainly refer to the right to life,[31] protected under Article 3 of the UNDHR[32] and under Articles 6 (right to life) and 9 (right to liberty and security) of the International Covenant on Civil Political Rights.[33] The right to life is acknowledged as having crucial importance in FDL claims since in most cases the victims

[26]Consequently, no specific analysis is hereby made on liability for confidence (fiduciary duty) of parent companies (including Article 209 of TCC), as this liability would require a voluntary contact between the relevant company and the victim, which would then lead to a liability that is neither in tort nor in contract.

[27]In fact, the human rights violations committed by non-state actors, more specifically by MNCs and global supply chains, has led to the emergence of a new field of law: Business and human rights. This field focuses both on state obligation to ensure the protection of human rights in business and corporate duty to respect and protect human rights in business operations. With the continuous effect of globalization and proliferation of MNCs, it has become necessary to regulate business and human rights not only in non-binding international instruments, but also mandatory domestic laws. For some introductory remarks on business and human rights, see Smith (2018), pp. 406–407.

[28]The Ten Principles of the United Nations Global Compact, https://www.unglobalcompact.org/what-is-gc/mission/principles.

[29]The Universal Bill of Human Rights, Universal Declaration of Human Rights, adopted and proclaimed by General Assembly resolution 217 A (III) of 10 December 1948.

[30]Muchlinski (2017), p. 35. The basic values on which the UN Global Compact was based are human rights, labour and environment; anti-corruption was added in the UN Global Compact in 2004 (de Schutter (2010), p. 397).

[31]Right to life is described as the most fundamental of all rights, which is non-derogable, and it covers the positive obligation of States to protect life, including ensuring legal protection of life, investigation of deaths and provision of adequate healthcare (Smith (2018), pp. 219–221; Zielonka (2014), pp. 248–249).

[32]Article 3 of the UNDHR: "Everyone has the right to life, liberty and the security of person."

[33]International Covenant on Civil and Political Rights, adopted and opened for signature, ratification and accession by General Assembly resolution 2200A (XXI) of 16 December 1966, entry into force 23 March 1976, in accordance with Article 49.

suffer death or injuries, which all touch upon the right to life.[34] Furthermore, loss of livelihood due to disability caused by a damaging act that is made subject to FDL claim can also be deemed a violation of Article 25 of UNDHR.[35] The right to privacy and home and the right to protection by law against interference or attacks to one's home, covered by Article 12 of UNDHR, might also be relevant to FDL claims and especially those claims involving environmental damage.[36] Although there are other types of violations of basic human rights that frequently become subject to FDL claims, such as forced labour or child labour, these are also excluded here, as the following analysis is based on solutions available under tort law and company law, leaving aside any labour law-related assessments. Environmental claims are not, *per se*, included in the scope of this study, especially those claims concerning administrative or criminal law aspects, while claims concerning damage caused by environmental pollution (e.g. physical injuries and illnesses) are included. The delimitation of the subject of this study in no way suggests that there are no other types of implications of corporate behaviour on human rights. It has, however, been necessary to determine a limited scope for this study in order to capture several different aspects of the relevant human rights violations, including tort law, company law and private international law.

In general, tort claims in FDL cases arise either from issues concerning environmental damages and related health damages, or from poor labour standards, ranging from child labour to health and safety issues. This study's scope is limited to the tort law aspects of these claims and does not include any labour law analysis. FDL cases concern the allegation of the parent company's direct liability against third parties. The employees of subsidiaries are third parties to the parent company and therefore—if the prerequisites are established—they can, in fact, address FDL claims against the parent company. Having said that, any employment matter that may arise between these employees and the subsidiaries are not within the scope of this study.

The debate surrounding business and human rights has emerged because of the pressing need to address human rights concerns and violations arising from corporate behaviour. In fact, the worlds of human rights and of business have been completely separate from each other, especially because human rights obligations have traditionally been imposed on states by international legal instruments and domestic laws. Hence, for a long time, corporations have been staying clear of any obligations arising from human rights violations, although their operations and behaviour could have caused such violations. Turkey is one of those countries where even the debate around business and human rights has only recently begun. Therefore, Turkish law does not currently accommodate any specific regulations nor are there any court decisions on this subject. Having said that, Turkey's Action Plan on Human Rights of 2021 sets the subject of business and human rights as a goal

[34] *Slapper* states that the right to life should be respected by corporations as a part of corporate social responsibility and a way of carrying out ethical business; see Slapper (2011), p. 80.

[35] Muchlinski (2017), p. 43.

[36] Öztekin Gelgel (2006), p. 171.

under 9.3(b), reading as follows: "*Taking into consideration the UN Guiding Principles on Business and Human Rights, a national set of guiding principles with regard to business and work life will be prepared and awareness-raising activities will be conducted*".[37] Inclusion of this goal in the Action Plan on Human Rights constitutes a valuable improvement on the long way to achieve corporate responsibility for human rights abuses. In fact, even the achievement of this goal would result solely in implementation of soft law instruments, such as guidelines, and certain supporting activities, which would lack any binding character and the stringency offered by hard law instruments.

The main purpose of this study is to explore the legal grounds available in Turkish law that could serve for business and human rights claims in FDL actions. As there are currently no FDL claims made under Turkish law, the relevant legal grounds available under current laws are analysed in view of the relevant comparative law. Hence, the point of departure is *de lege lata*. To this end, both soft law instruments and hard law instruments are analysed. Consequently, suggestions are set forth *de lege ferenda* in light of the relevant comparative law, which would require new regulations in Turkish law. Accordingly, the study adopts a *de lege lata-de lege ferenda* approach, based on all available legal instruments.

Although the point of focus is Turkish law, a comparative legal approach is adopted throughout the study as the statutory laws and case laws (where relevant) of several different countries are analysed. Case law in the UK and court judgments in the Netherlands have developed significantly due to the popularity of these jurisdictions in FDL cases, particularly because there are many English and Dutch companies with subsidiaries operating in the less developed parts of the world. The US also has considerable case law on the matter mostly due to the Alien Tort Statute (ATS), which allows (or has so far allowed) for exceptional cases of extraterritorial application in human rights violation claims. France, Switzerland and Germany have also recently been contributing significantly to the field of business and human rights and FDL, by integrating or discussing the integration of mHRDD regulations in domestic laws.

This study aims to outline the reasons why Turkey could potentially play a significant role in the field of business and human rights, particularly in terms of FDL claims. The first reason is more socio-political than legal. Turkey is an important country for many industries (e.g. garment, mining, energy) that are accepted as posing high-risk in terms of human rights. Currently, there are numerous Western companies operating subsidiaries in Turkey, and others that even have close-linked suppliers or sub-contractors. This brings us to the second reason, which is based on law. The popularity of Turkey as a location for several important industries makes it essential to either ensure that home country laws are applicable and home country courts have jurisdiction in FDL claims arising from these activities, or alternatively, if Turkish courts would have jurisdiction and Turkish law

[37] Ministry of Justice of the Republic of Turkey, Action Plan on Human Rights, March 2021, https://insanhaklarieylemplani.adalet.gov.tr/resimler/eylemplani-eng.pdf.

would be applicable, then Turkish law should address these claims on the parent company's civil liability in tort. Hence, this study aims to examine those aspects of Turkish law that could be helpful in addressing parent company liability in FDL claims, and to recommend new ones in light of the relevant comparative law.

Several case studies concerning FDL claims are presented in Chap. 4 on substantive analysis. Having said that, an example case scenario would be useful in explaining both the substantive and private international law aspects. The scenario presented concerns a gold mine operating in a rural region of Turkey, by company S (a Turkish company), which is a wholly owned subsidiary of company P (a UK company). The mine's search for gold is conducted using cyanide which, when leaked, is proven to be detrimental to soil, water and human health. As a result of a few years of operation in the gold mine, certain damage is detected in the soil, which is harvested for several agricultural products by farmers. In addition to the loss of fertility in the soil, water sources are also polluted significantly due to the cyanide that leaked in the water through the soil. This has caused severe illnesses in the community living in the near surroundings of the mine. Workers of S are also affected by close contact with cyanide; vocational illnesses have occurred, some of which resulting in death.

There are three main pillars to the substantive legal aspects of this study. The first one is tort law, which is mainly based on the breach of the duty of care, the second is strict liability, which is most likely to be applicable in exceptional circumstances in FDL cases, and the third one concerns mHRDD, which might serve to complement tort liability.

As FDL is a very dynamic field, it has proven to be a challenge to successfully cover all legal aspects of the matter. Therefore, this study specifically focuses on environmental damages and related human rights abuses, arising from the operations of the foreign subsidiaries of an MNC. The study covers civil liability, but leaves aside criminal,[38] administrative and tax liability. Issues of labour law are also not covered hereunder, given that tort liability is related to third party claims, which naturally leave employee claims out of the scope; employees of subsidiaries, of course, are third parties for a parent company and their claims would therefore count as made in tort.

With the background concerning FDL is now provided by this chapter, the next chapter focuses on the subject of this liability: 'Multinational corporate groups'.

[38] Criminal liability, although mandatory and assuring, prioritizes public penalty over private individuals' compensation claims. It also does not provide the victims with the ability to determine the extent of damage they incur; see Thomale and Hübner (2017), p. 389.

References

Online Sources

Accord on Fire and Building Safety in Bangladesh (13 May 2013). https://admin.bangladeshaccord.org/wp-content/uploads/2018/08/2013-Accord.pdf
Africa is a country - The Zambian farmers who are suing a mining company in a British court (15.02.2019). https://africasacountry.com/2019/02/the-zambian-farmers-who-are-suing-a-mining-company-in-a-british-court
CORE - Ahead of Supreme Court ruling in human rights case against mining company, UK NGOs and unions call for new law to curb multinationals' global abuses (10.04.2019). https://corporate-responsibility.org/news/press-releases/
Global Justice Now, 69 of the richest 100 entities on the planet are corporations, not governments, figures show (17.10.2018). https://www.globaljustice.org.uk/news/2018/oct/17/69-richest-100-entities-planet-are-corporations-not-governments-figures-show
The Ten Principles of the United Nations Global Compact. https://www.unglobalcompact.org/what-is-gc/mission/principles

Legislation, Reports, Resolutions and Opinions

Economic and Social Council Resolution 1721 (LIII), quoted in UN, 'The Impact of Multinational Corporations on Development and on International Relations', UN DOC. E/5500/Rev. 1., ST/ESA/6 (New York: UN, 1974), 13 ILM 800
International Covenant on Civil and Political Rights, adopted and opened for signature, ratification and accession by General Assembly resolution 2200A (XXI) of 16 December 1966, entry into force 23 March 1976, in accordance with Article 49.
UN "Protect, Respect and Remedy" Framework for Business and Human Rights (7 April 2008) A/HRC/8/5

Literature

Antunes JE (1994) Liability of corporate groups. Kluwer Law
de Schutter O (2010) International human rights law. Cambridge University Press
Dowling P (2020) Limited liability and separate corporate personality in multinational corporate groups: conceptual flaws, accountability gaps, and the case for profit-risk liability. In: Enneking L, Giesen I, Schaap AJ, Ryngaert C, Kristen F, Roorda L (eds) Accountability, international business operations, and the law: providing justice for corporate human rights violations in global value chains. Routledge, pp 219–239
Enneking L (2008) the common denominatory of the Trafigura Case, Foreign direct liability cases and the Rome II Regulation, an essay on the consequences of private international law for the

feasibility of regulating multinational corporations through tort law. Eur Rev Priv Law 2:283–311
Enneking L (2009) Crossing the Atlantic? The political and legal feasibility of European foreign direct liability cases. George Wash Int Law Rev 40:903–938
Enneking L (2012) Foreign direct liability and beyond. Eleven International Publishing
Enneking L (2013) Multinationals and transparency in foreign direct liability cases. Dovenschmidt Quarterly 3:134–147
Eroğlu M (2008a) Multinational enterprises and tort liabilities, an interdisciplinary and comparative examination. Edward Elgar Publishing
Eroğlu M (2008b) Limited liability in Turkish law. Eur Bus Org Law Rev 9:237–265
Jones G (2019) It's not easy being a parent: AAA v. Unilever and the control conundrum – when a controlling shareholder may owe a duty of care in respect of the acts or omissions of a subsidiary. Bus Law Rev 40(1):2–6
Kraakman R et al (2009) The anatomy of corporate law, a comparative and functional approach, 2nd edn. Oxford University Press
Loomis W (1999) The responsibility of parent corporations for the human rights violations of their subsidiaries. In: Addo MK (ed) Human rights standards and the responsibility of transnational corporations. Kluwer Law International
Muchlinski P (2001) Human rights and multinationals: is there a problem? Int Aff 77(I):31–47
Muchlinski P (2017) The development of human rights responsibilities for multinational enterprises. In: Sullivan R (ed) Business and human rights. Dilemmas & Solutions, New York, pp 33–51
Nygh P (2002) The liability of multi-national corporations for the torts of their subsidiaries. Eur Bus Org Law Rev 3:51–81
Öztekin Gelgel G (2006) Akit Dışı Borç İlişkilerine Uygulanacak Hukuk Hakkındaki Avrupa Birliği Düzenlemesi (EU Regulation on Applicable Law in Non-Contractual Obligations). Istanbul
Palombo D (2019) The duty of care of the parent company: a comparison between French law, UK precedents and the Swiss proposals. BHRJ 4:265–286
Rühmkorf A (2015) Corporate social responsibility, private law and global supply chains. Edward Elgar Publishing
Sağlam İ (2020) Opinion on Legal Entity – Sustainability Nexus. Marmara University Law Faculty. J Legal Res MÜFHD-HAD 26(2):1111–1125
Slapper G (2011) Violent corporate crime, corporate social responsibility and human rights. In: Voiculescu A, Yanacopulos H (eds) The business of human rights – an evolving Agenda for corporate responsibility, pp 79–100
Smith RKM (2018) International human rights law, 8th edn. Oxford University Press, Oxford
Thomale C, Hübner L (2017) Zivilgerichtliche Durchsetzung völkerrechtlicher Unternehmensverantwortung (Civil Judicial Enforcement of International Corporate Responsibility). Juristenzeitung 8:385–397
van Dam C (2007) European tort law. Oxford University Press
Weller MP, Thomale C (2017) Menschenrechtsklagen gegen deutsche Unternehmen (Human rights lawsuits against German companies). ZGR 4:509–526
Zerk JA (2006) Multinationals and corporate social responsibility, limitations and opportunities in international law. Cambridge University Press
Zielonka SM (2014) The universality of the right to life: Article 2 and the margin of appreciation in the Jurisprudence of the European Court of Human Rights. N Y Univ J Int Law Polit 47(1): 245–278

Chapter 3
Multinational Corporate Groups, Their Position in International Law and Regulating Multinational Corporate Groups

3.1 Multinational Corporate Groups

In order to be able to provide an accurate definition of MNCs, it is first of all necessary to look at companies in general. Hence, this section firstly explains the concept of 'company' and the main features of companies in general, then focuses on the concept of 'corporate groups', taking Turkish law as the basis for the discussion, and finally turns to MNCs, which stand in the centre of this study.

3.1.1 Companies in General: Theories and Main Features

3.1.1.1 Defining 'Company'

Companies might be generally defined as legally and economically independent partnerships that are formed by shareholders in order to fulfil a common economic objective.[1] In the general theory of company law, the main elements of a company are identified as the elements of person, agreement, capital, common purpose and making an equal effort to reach the common purpose (also known as 'active cooperation' or *affectio societatis*).[2] Hence, it is possible to describe a company as an association of persons,[3] which come together by expressing their intentions to establish a company to achieve a common purpose, to allocate a certain amount of

[1] Dündar (2013), p. 81.

[2] Kırca and Şehirali (2013), p. 45. Sağlam emphasizes the importance of the perpetuality of the mentioned common objective, i.e. that the activity that is carried out to reach the objective should be of a constant feature; see Sağlam (2020), p. 1113.

[3] Although the company is described as an association of persons, companies with a single shareholder are allowed under Turkish law (TCC Art. 338/1 for joint stock companies).

P. Kara, *Tort Liability in Multinational Corporate Groups*, Ius Gentium: Comparative Perspectives on Law and Justice 107,
https://doi.org/10.1007/978-3-031-29336-8_3

capital and to show equal effort and diligence for achieving the relevant common purpose. Commercial company (*ticaret şirketi*),[4] is defined in Turkish legal doctrine as an association of one or more persons based on articles of association, under a common trade name and for an economic purpose, whereby they gather their effort, property or rights within the framework stipulated by law.[5]

In the classical theory of company law, the main characteristics of a company are set as (i) legal personality, (ii) limited liability, (iii) transferable shares, (iv) centralised management, and (v) shared ownership, which are deemed to be complementary to each other.[6] Having said that, for the purposes of the FDL debate and the scope of this study, the important characteristics of a company are determined as separate legal personality and limited liability. Therefore, this section discusses the effects of these two characteristics on the FDL debate.

3.1.1.2 Separate Legal Personality

A main principle of corporate law and an important main feature of a company is separate legal personality, which means that the company has a distinct and separate legal personality to all corporate actors surrounding it (i.e. shareholders, directors, creditors, employees etc.).[7] Separate legal personality may be deemed to consist of two separate capacities: legal capacity and the capacity to act. Legal capacity refers to a company's capacity to bear its own rights and duties, while the capacity to act refers to its ability to exercise its own rights and duties.[8]

In Common Law legal doctrine, under the 'theory of fiction', companies are seen as legal fictions invented by national law,[9] based on the logic that only real persons could be the holder of rights and be liable for debts.[10] This view results in the conclusion that companies lack the capacity to act and consequently have no capacity to be held responsible for torts.[11] It is in fact true that companies are created to facilitate and expedite commercial life by serving as a buffer zone for real-person

[4]As per Article 124/1 of TCC, commercial companies (*ticaret şirketleri*) are general partnerships (*kollektif şirket*), limited partnerships (*komandit şirket*), joint stock companies (*anonim şirket*), limited liability companies (*limited şirket*) and cooperative companies (*kooperatif*). Amongst these types of commercial companies, general partnerships (*kollektif şirket*) and limited partnerships (*komandit şirket*) are identified as partnerships (*şahıs şirketleri*), while joint stock companies (*anonim şirket*), limited liability companies (*limited şirket*) and limited partnerships with capital divided into shares (*sermayesi paylara bölünmüş komandit şirket*) are capital stock companies (*sermaye şirketleri*) (Art. 124/2 TCC).

[5]Pulaşlı (2013), pp. 45–46.

[6]Cahn and Donald (2018), p. 5.

[7]Antunes (1994), p. 58.

[8]Antunes (1994), p. 57.

[9]Dine and Koutsias (2014), p. 30; Sağlam (1995), p. 12.

[10]Sağlam (2020), p. 1118.

[11]Kırca and Şehirali (2013), p. 65; Sağlam (1995), pp. 13–14; Sağlam (2020), p. 1118.

investors by way of a separate legal personality and limited liability, which serve to separate them from their founders. In this manner, it can be assumed that the risks of operating a business are diminished, and in some instances even eliminated. On the other hand, in Continental European legal doctrine, which mainly adopts the 'reality theory', companies are deemed to be persons that are separate and independent from their founders, hence they are not created but merely acknowledged by laws.[12] This view results in an acceptance that companies have a free will separate from the real persons who have created it, hence the capacity to act and therefore can be held liable for the torts of their bodies.[13] Articles 125 and 126 of TCC, with reference to Article 48 of CC, regulate that commercial companies (*ticaret şirketleri*) are legal entities, subject to the terms and consequences attached thereto, which is a resonation with the Continental European legal doctrine.[14]

Companies become vested with legal personality upon incorporation, which results in two important consequences: (i) the company becomes a legal entity that is separate from its owners and (ii) the company's assets are separated from its owners' assets. It follows that the company itself is a person at law and can enter into contract, own assets and sue and be sued by others. Having a separate legal personality for a company contributes to the company's corporate character, as it distinguishes the company from its shareholders, keeping it separate from them and hence giving it a certain independence to continue as a separate entity.[15] The consequences of having a separate existence from its shareholders and having separate assets are actually intertwined with each other; in other words, the separate legal personality of an incorporated company brings about the result that its assets are also identified and separated. The separation of assets principle is valid throughout the term of activity of a company, including through its liquidation process.[16] Therefore, the capital of the company is identified and separated from its shareholders. [17] In other words, the assets of the company are owned by the company itself and are not subject to any ownership by the founders or the shareholders of the company, i.e. a separate patrimony accompanied by 'entity shielding', which serves to protect the company's assets from the creditors of the shareholders.[18] Hence, the shareholders do not have the right or authority to dispose of the assets of the company.[19]

---

[12] Sağlam (2020), p. 1119; Sağlam (1995), p. 15.

[13] Sağlam (2020), p. 1119; Sağlam (1995), p. 16. A company's legal capacity is considered to result in autonomous patrimonial structure, while its capacity of action results in autonomous organizational structure (Antunes (1994), pp. 58–61). Also see Kırca and Şehirali (2013), p. 65.

[14] In corporate legal theory, it is accepted that legal persons (including companies) are constructed and regulated upon the model of natural persons, as legal personality applies equally to both natural and legal persons (Antunes (1994), pp. 57–58).

[15] Kırca and Şehirali (2013), p. 70.

[16] Tekinalp (2013), p. 46.

[17] Watson (2015), p. 131.

[18] Kraakman et al. (2009), pp. 6, 9–10; Kırca and Şehirali (2013), p. 82.

[19] Kırca and Şehirali (2013), p. 82.

As a separate legal person, having separate assets from its shareholders, a subsidiary company in principle would also be separate from its parent company. This is normally followed by the logic that a parent company in a corporate group should not be held liable for the debts of its subsidiary. As held by the House of Lords in the famous *Salomon v Salomon* [20] decision, "*The company is at law a different person altogether from [those forming the company]*", thus the company is a separate entity from the people who are involved in it. [21] The *Salomon* case concerned a limited liability company, Aron Salomon Ltd., founded by Aron Salomon, who was in the leather business. Mr. Salomon sold the business to his company upon incorporation, against which he received a promissory note and a certain amount of shares. The payment, however, was postponed as the company did not have sufficient capital to cover it at the time of incorporation. Therefore, when the company went bankrupt, Mr. Salomon appeared as the primary creditor as his debt was secured by the promissory note. The case was initiated by the liquidator who was asking whether Mr. Salomon had the right to be the primary creditor of his own company, which was under his control. Hence the case scrutinised the ability of the company to enter into transactions that would bind the company. In its well-known decision, the House of Lords did not agree with the interpretations of the lower courts that the company was an agent or a trustee of the shareholders. Instead it confirmed that a company is a separate legal entity from its incorporators and shareholders and that this legal fiction could be eliminated in the event of an illegitimate purpose pursued by that company.[22]

The feature of separate legal personality is often used in FDL actions as a point of defence to rebut claims of legal responsibility addressed to a parent company for the harms occurred due to the activities of its transnational subsidiaries. Defendants tend to argue that, despite the shareholding and control, the parent company is a separate legal entity, and therefore should not be held liable for any harms occurring due to its subsidiary's activities. This argument could be deemed relevant in terms of piercing the corporate veil, which is allowed only in very limited circumstances due to the very nature of corporations, and particularly due to separate legal personality. It is, however, difficult to accept this line of argument in terms of FDL. This form of liability is not secondary to the liability of the subsidiary, but it is rather primary, as it constitutes the parent company's liability for its own actions or omissions concerning the operations of its subsidiaries. As it will be further discussed in the following chapter, parent company liability could be based upon breach of the parent company's duty of care, its strict liability or breach of its obligations concerning mHRDD. None of these grounds form a secondary liability for the parent company; they are, instead, all based on the wrongsful acts committed by the parent company. Therefore, separate legal personality does not constitute a viable argument for rebutting FDL claims against parent companies.

[20] [1896] UKHL 1, [1897] AC 22, Salomon v A. Salomon & Co. Ltd.

[21] Dine and Koutsias (2014), p. 28.

[22] Watson (2015), p. 135.

3.1.1.3 Limited Liability

Another significant feature of modern companies is the limited liability principle, which states that the shareholders' liability is limited to the share capital they undertake to pay into the company and that, in principle, no other contribution is expected from them. The economic rationale of this principle is described as the allocation of business risks and costs, which results in economic efficiency.[23] The limited liability principle aims to protect company shareholders from certain types of liability and thus it facilitates entrepreneurial activity.[24] The policy for the acceptance of limited liability for corporations is widely recognised as facilitating investment in business enterprises.[25] Limited liability constitutes an effective incentive for making investments, as the personal assets of the investor will be protected. In fact, limited liability is seen as a form of 'owner shielding', which refers to the protection of the assets of the shareholders from the claims of their creditors.[26] In other words, a distinction is made between the debts of the company and the debts of the shareholders against third party creditors.

This principle is recognised under Turkish law by Article 329 of TCC, which stipulates that a joint stock company is a company having a certain amount of capital which is divided into shares, where the company is responsible for its debts only with its assets, and that the shareholders can only be responsible to the company and limited to the amount of share capital they undertook to pay. This responsibility of the shareholders is called the 'single-debt principle' under Turkish law. Hence, the shareholders in stock companies, in principle, do not have a secondary liability towards company creditors.[27] Limited liability principle incorporated in Article 329 of TCC implies that the company's legal entity is solely responsible for the company's debts. Therefore, the shareholders are not responsible towards the company's creditors, but only towards the company for the payment of capital they undertake to invest.[28]

The economic efficiency sought by the principle of limited liability seems to fade within the context of MNCs. This is specifically the case for involuntary creditors who lack the ability to negotiate on liability or risk-shifting in advance, as they cannot prevent the risk of damages and also cannot spread the resulting costs.[29]

---

[23] Antunes (1994), p. 127.

[24] Kershaw (2012), p. 21.

[25] Dowling (2020), p. 220.

[26] Kraakman et al. (2009), pp. 9–10.

[27] Eroğlu (2008b), p. 244.

[28] From Turkish legal aspect, it is worth noting that limited liability principle is only applicable to capital stock companies (joint stock companies, limited liability companies and partnerships limited by shares) and some cooperatives. Some other types of partnerships that have legal personality (e.g. general partnerships) are not subject to limited liability principle.

[29] Antunes (1994), p. 136.

Accordingly, it can be said that limited liability in corporate groups increases market efficiency, rather than economic efficiency, for parent companies.[30]

The principle of limited liability, along with separate legal personality, is often used as a line of defence for parent companies. However, as will also be discussed further in this study, there appears to be a need for reform in corporate law, especially when the specific case of MNC is envisaged. In fact, an asymmetry of risk may arise between shareholders and creditors of a company, particularly for involuntary creditors (including tort victims), who often face obstacles in seeking economic redress from the relevant corporations due to the principles of limited liability and separate legal personality.[31]

3.1.2 Corporate Groups: A Brief Analysis with a Particular Focus on Turkish Law

3.1.2.1 Concept of Corporate Group and Regulatory Goals

Corporate groups, which can be generally defined as independently incorporated companies connected mostly by a chain of participations to form one commercial unit,[32] are very common in the modern world. Yet, it has been a challenge to provide a clear and unified definition for corporate groups in general, as these are dynamic structures that tend to change shape over time.

The issue of ensuring a certain level of harmonisation in the laws of the EU member states concerning corporate groups was discussed by Forum Europaeum, based on the logic that a total lack of harmonisation would create competitive advantages for countries where the issue is not regulated, and thus some kind of EU legislation was necessary for certain subjects within corporate group law.[33] However, the EU finally chose not to impose on member states any obligations to regulate corporate groups in domestic laws. Almost to the contrary, it was enunciated throughout the works concerning the Ninth Directive[34] and the Winter Report[35] that a framework had been determined for the EU on the subject, but it was left to the discretion of member states to choose whether or not to adopt a more detailed regulation.

---

[30] Antunes (1994), p. 136.

[31] Dowling (2020), pp. 220–221.

[32] Forum Europaeum Corporate Group Law (2000), p. 167.

[33] Forum Europaeum Corporate Group Law (2000), pp. 179–180.

[34] A draft "Ninth Company Law Directive on the Conduct of Groups containing a Public Limited Company as a Subsidiary" was circulated by the European Commission in 1984, which was later not adopted as it did not receive sufficient support by the Member States.

[35] Final Report of the High Level Group of Company Law Experts on a Modern Regulatory Framework for Company Law in Europe (2002).

The Winter Report had determined three basic reasons for having the corporate groups regulated by law: (1) to ensure transparency, (2) to strike a balance between the interests of the corporate group and of the group members, and (3) to resolve the problems of pyramidal structures.[36] The main objective of regulating corporate groups in statutory law might be addressed as protecting the interests of subsidiaries and their creditors[37] against parent companies based on the principles of transparency, accountability and balance of interests.[38] In fact, given that the transparency of subsidiaries in a corporate group is less compared to independent companies, subsidiaries' creditors are usually in a disadvantaged position since they cannot properly assess the risks.[39] A more secondary objective for group regulation in statutory law is addressed as assisting business and the economy by recognising corporate groups and facilitating group management.[40]

Moreover, the limited liability principle applied to the parent companies of corporate groups might result in irreparable damages.[41] *Antunes* refers to these incidents as 'moral hazards' which are mainly caused by the incentive provided by the limited liability principle for parent companies to engage in risky activities, usually through their subsidiaries, resulting in damages to society—the costs of which cannot be compensated.[42] Because of these concerns, there have been discussions and attempts to regulate corporate groups in statutory law.

There are only a few jurisdictions where the concept of corporate groups is regulated in domestic law, and only a few more where the concept has been defined either by law, by jurisprudence or by scholars. Turkey is one of those countries where corporate groups are regulated by law and have been subject to legal doctrine, which are analysed below. It is emphasised also in Turkish legal doctrine that one of the main features of corporate groups lies in the balance of interests; as unlike a sole company, a member of a group may at times act against its own interests for the sake of fulfilling the group's or the parent company's interests, depending on how effective the centralised management of the group is.[43] It therefore follows that the independence and discretionary powers to affect the decisions of the subsidiaries in

[36]Embid and José (2005), p. 88.

[37]The concept of 'creditors' might be different from the concept of 'stakeholders'. *Hopt* points out that the concept of 'stakeholders' is usually interpreted more broadly, including for instance consumers, the state, the environment, fundamental rights; see Hopt (2015), p. 4.

[38]Okutan Nilsson (2009), p. 13, 15.

[39]Hopt (2015), p. 7.

[40]Hopt (2015), p. 3.

[41]The limited liability principle, which was considered as an incentive for investors, is now regarded as an incentive to create complex structured corporate groups, which enable shareholders to minimize the risks and liabilities of doing business (Cahn and Donald (2018), p. 829).

[42]Antunes (1994), p. 138.

[43]In groups where the centralised management has created a strong effect, the bodies of the subsidiary will tend to act in accordance with the interests of the parent company, rather than the subsidiary (See Harsa (2007), p. 7).

corporate groups are significantly restricted.[44] In other words, corporate groups, by their very nature, conflict with the principle of each company being separate and independent, as the management of a corporate group is in fact the domain of the parent company.[45]

For these reasons, it becomes important to regulate corporate groups in order to address such conflicts and provide protection to those that might be affected by this imbalance of interests.[46] Hence the aim for regulating corporate groups might be to address the imbalance of interests between the group and the subsidiary and to protect the subsidiary's interests against the whole group and the interests of the subsidiary's creditors, which is considered to be the approach adopted by the TCC.[47]

In general terms, corporate groups may be defined as entities that are comprised of different companies or business enterprises which are linked to each other through patrimonial, contractual or personal links that come under a common centre of control.[48]

Before engaging in this brief analysis on Turkish law provisions concerning corporate groups, it is worth noting that corporate groups are considered to be the actors of the FDL claims studied within the scope of this study, while Turkish law on corporate groups does not accommodate any legal grounds for effectively addressing this liability. In fact, as mentioned, the provisions concerning corporate groups mainly aim to regulate an 'inwards' liability, which concern the protection of the subsidiary's interests against the parent company's and group's interests. Although Turkish law provisions concerning corporate groups regulate the legal remedies for the creditors of the subsidiary, this issue again constitutes a form of protection against the parent company's misuse of the subsidiary's assets. Consequently, any FDL claims that concern a more 'outwards' responsibility (i.e. parent company liability towards tort victims) are not covered by the corporate group provisions in Turkish law.

3.1.2.2 Parent Company and Subsidiary

TCC, in Article 195/1, defines corporate groups or, as referred to under the TCC, the 'group of companies' based upon the concepts of 'parent company' and 'subsidiary'. As per this definition:

A 'parent company' is a commercial company which directly or indirectly:

[44] Eminoğlu (2017), p. 17.

[45] Uygun (2015), p. 6.

[46] Susuz (2012), p. 272.

[47] Okutan Nilsson (2011), pp. 90–91.

[48] Starc-Meclejan (2013), p. 238.

(i) owns the majority of the voting rights; or
(ii) based on the articles of association of the company, has the right to procure the appointment of the decision-making majority of the members of the management body; or
(iii) in addition to its own voting rights, forms the majority of the voting rights, either alone or together with other shareholders based on an agreement; or
(iv) controls, based on an agreement or in any other manner, another commercial company, while the other commercial company under this control is a 'subsidiary'.

As it is clear from the wording and as also stated in the reasoning of Article 195 of TCC, it is deemed sufficient if one of the above-mentioned criteria is met to address the formation of a group of companies. It is accepted in legal doctrine that the mere existence of one of the criteria given under Article 195/1(a) (i.e. majority of voting rights, right to procure the appointment of the decision-making majority of the members of the management body, majority of voting rights based on an agreement) would be sufficient to deem the existence of control, without any possibility to prove otherwise and regardless of whether these criteria are actually exercised or not.[49] The same assumption of control might be adopted also in cases where the control is based upon a dominance agreement (Art. 195/1(b)), which should be approved by the company's general assembly and registered with the trade registry in order to become valid (Art. 105/2 Trade Registry Regulation). In other types of control (i.e. "*dominance in any other manner*" as expressed under Article 195/1(b) of TCC) it will be necessary to check if the control is actually exercised in practice.

As per the TCC, in the event that at least one of the members of a group of companies has headquarters located in Turkey, the relevant provisions of the TCC shall become applicable (Art. 195/1 TCC). Thus, it would be sufficient for the application of TCC provisions to have the headquarters of either the parent company or one of its subsidiaries in Turkey. With this provision, Turkish legislators aimed to keep the scope of the application wide enough to cover the MNCs that have one of their members in Turkey.

The specific TCC provisions concerning corporate groups permit only commercial companies to be a parent or subsidiary, which is first of all in line with the concept of 'groups of companies'.[50] The first draft of TCC referred to the term 'capital stock companies' which covers only joint stock companies, limited liability companies and partnerships limited by shares. The Justice Sub-Commission, however has extended the scope of the provisions with the term 'commercial companies', to cover partnerships (i.e. companies with unlimited liability)[51] in addition to capital stock companies.[52]

[49] Okutan Nilsson (2009), p. 102. As a matter of fact, the control grounds mentioned under Article 195/1(a) of TCC are the ones that can be assessed and calculated mathematically.

[50] Pulaşlı (2013), p. 151.

[51] According to Article 124/2 of TCC, partnerships are general partnerships (*kollektif şirket*) and limited partnerships (*komandit şirket*).

[52] Okutan Nilsson (2009), p. 68.

Corporate groups have no legal personality, thus they are merely an association of persons and/or entities.[53] This is especially important in the sense that it is not possible to address a claim against a corporate group, as the group itself has no legal personality. Therefore, FDL claims are addressed against the parent company of a corporate group, which is a separate legal entity.

3.1.2.3 'Undertaking' as the Parent

Another subject of corporate groups under Turkish law is the 'undertaking'.[54] Article 195/5 of TCC stipulates that the provisions concerning TCC shall apply to corporate groups where the parent is an undertaking, with its head office or residence in Turkey or elsewhere. The Turkish system of corporate groups does not permit entities other than commercial companies to form a corporate group. In other words, corporate groups can only be comprised of commercial companies (i.e. joint stock companies, limited liability companies, cooperatives, general partnerships and limited partnerships). However, the law provides an exception to this rule by stipulating that an undertaking can be a parent of a corporate group. The main objective for bringing this exception of undertaking into this study is to allow a wider scope to the rule and prevent any potential circumvention of the law.[55] In light of the clear wording of this article, it is understood that while it is possible for an undertaking to be the parent of a corporate group, the subsidiaries should always be commercial companies.[56]

The term 'undertaking' is not defined in TCC. However, the reasoning of Article 195 of TCC states that any private or public entity, real person or commercial enterprise could be the parent of a corporate group, which would be subject to the relevant provisions.

The term 'undertaking' aims to cover any type of real person, union of persons or assets that have the ability to contribute to a stock company, regardless of whether they have legal personality or not.[57] The rationale for including 'undertakings' as parent companies within corporate groups is that these undertakings may have economic interests other than those of their subsidiaries if they are engaged in other economic activities. Hence, it is thought that an undertaking should be engaged

---

[53] Tekinalp (2013), p. 543.

[54] The Turkish term '*teşebbüs*' literally means 'attempt', but within this framework it is translated in English as 'undertaking' or 'enterprise' (see Glossary for the European Union, Basic Terms, Secretariat General for the European Union Affairs (2003), https://www.ab.gov.tr/files/Sozluk/Sozluk_Baski.pdf). For the sake of consistency, the term 'undertaking' is used throughout this study.

[55] Uygun (2015), p. 18.

[56] Çakır Çelebi (2018), p. 22.

[57] Tekinalp (2013), p. 545.

in an economic activity, in addition to its corporate group, even if it does not act exclusively for the purpose of making profits.[58]

The 'economic activity' is interpreted in a broader sense. Therefore, for instance, being a parent company of more than one subsidiary, operating a commercial enterprise or even engaging in artisan or craftwork activities might be deemed as having other economic interests.[59] In order to be considered an undertaking, it is not required that the relevant undertaking operates in the same field of business as its subsidiaries or that these entities are in competition with each other.[60]

According to one opinion within legal doctrine, an undertaking should be economically independent and its dominance over subsidiaries should be continuous, but it is not required that it carries an economic activity.[61] However, there are still grey areas concerning the concept of undertaking within the scope of corporate group provisions, because the law does not define the term 'undertaking' and also because the legislator's explanations given in Article 195 refer to private and public entities, real persons and commercial enterprises. Simple partnerships (*adi şirket*), which lack legal personality, may also be undertakings at the top of a corporate group.[62] On the other hand, simple partnerships formed by different persons or entities in the case of a joint or collective control cannot be deemed as undertakings, given that these partnerships are focused on the internal management of the company, without being engaged in any business activity or interaction with third parties.[63]

3.1.2.4 Control and Dominance in Corporate Groups

Those jurisdictions where the concept of corporate groups is regulated in law have adopted different systems concerning the exercise of management in these groups. While some of them have opted to take the concept of 'dominance' as its basis (e.g. Swiss law), others have chosen the concept of 'control' (e.g. EU, French law). It was the opinion of Forum Europaeum on regulating corporate group law in member states that the concepts of 'control' and 'dominance' were interchangeable, but in reality dominance extended beyond control, as it could also be present when a company is in a position to control another, despite not holding the majority of the shares.[64] Yet the Forum Europaeum chose to adopt the concept of control in regulation of corporate groups, for the sake of achieving legal certainty and harmony

---

[58] Gürel (2009), p. 27.

[59] Gürel (2009), p. 28.

[60] Göktürk (2015), p. 22.

[61] Okutan Nilsson (2009), p. 75; Çakır Çelebi (2018), p. 27.

[62] Susuz (2012), p. 272.

[63] Okutan Nilsson (2009), pp. 150–151.

[64] Forum Europaeum Corporate Group Law (2000), p. 188.

with the domestic laws of the majority of member states.[65] Accordingly, the proposed regulation of corporate groups within the EU was based on (i) holding the majority of the voting rights, (ii) dominance contracts, or (iii) the authority to appoint and remove the majority of the members of the management body, while regulating *de facto* control was left to the discretion of member states.[66]

Systems that adopted the concept of dominance require that decisive influence is actually exercised, thus the mere existence of an ability to exercise it is not deemed sufficient. On the other hand, for systems that adopted the concept of control, the potential ability to exercise decisive influence is sufficient, regardless of whether this is actually used in practice.[67]

The provisions concerning corporate groups under Turkish law are mainly based upon the element of 'control'. Accordingly, the parent company shall have control if it holds the legal means to make decisions regarding its subsidiary in line with its own policies and instructions.[68] The mere ability to exercise decisive influence on strategic decisions is found to be sufficient for the existence of control—thus it is not necessary for this power to be actually exercised over the subsidiary.[69] TCC identifies cases of parent company's control over its subsidiary, in which the parent has the ability and means to legally control the subsidiary (i.e. by a majority of voting rights, the power to have the majority of the members of the management body appointed) and has control based on a dominance agreement (i.e. contractual control) or control by other means. Therefore, the means of control mentioned under the TCC are not *numerus clausus* and thus require evaluation on a case-by-case basis.[70] The legislator's explanations presented in the section on corporate groups and on Article 195 clarify that the legislator has chosen the concept of 'control' rather than 'dominance', stating that while control bears a mathematical aspect, dominance is mostly based on presumptions and therefore is less straightforward. On the other hand, TCC's provisions on corporate groups do not completely exclude dominance, as control in any manner other than the criteria mentioned in Article 195 is cited as one of the grounds of control. This system adopted by the TCC is defined as 'enhanced control or dominance' in Turkish legal doctrine.[71]

3.1.2.4.1 Ownership of the Majority of Voting Rights

Owning the majority of the voting rights in a company is accepted as a state of control. As also stipulated in the legislator's explanations given in Article 195, the

---

[65] Forum Europaeum Corporate Group Law (2000), p. 189.
[66] Forum Europaeum Corporate Group Law (2000), p. 189.
[67] Harsa (2007), p. 56.
[68] Dündar (2013), p. 86.
[69] Doğan (2014), p. 11.
[70] Doğan (2014), p. 14.
[71] Okutan Nilsson (2009), p. 97; Eminoğlu (2017), p. 23.

ownership of the majority of voting rights proves the existence of dominance, without any possibility of rebuttal.[72] This situation may occur as a result of owning shares in a company that add up to more than 50% of the total share capital. It is also possible to own the majority of voting rights in the case of privileged votes or differences in the share values.[73] Another important point in determining the majority of voting rights is to consider that there may be different voting quorums set for different types of decisions, which will need to be taken into account. As the concept of dominance is based on having decisive influence over important decisions concerning the management of business affairs, the majority of voting rights should also be determined in respect of votes that can affect these types of decisions.[74] Therefore, in case there are specific quorums set for these types of decisions, the voting rights should be calculated accordingly.

3.1.2.4.2 Power to Appoint Management

The second criterion which concerns having the power to procure the appointment of the decision-making majority of the members of the management body based on the company's articles of association—refers to a privilege right granted to a group of shareholders, who usually do not form the majority in shares. As this situation leads to the exercise of a decisive influence on the company's strategic decisions, it is deemed to be the existence of control. In principle, those who have the majority of voting rights shall also have the power to appoint the majority of the members of the management body of the relevant company. However, it is possible to provide other rights and authorities in the articles of association on this issue, which might also lead to a type of control that cannot be rebutted.[75]

3.1.2.4.3 Voting Agreements

The third criterion involves holding the majority of voting rights either alone or along with other shareholders, based on an agreement. This type of agreement is a voting agreement, whereby one party undertakes to vote (or to abstain from voting) in line with another party's instructions and interests. This is seen as one of the methods for achieving control within the definition of corporate groups, which cannot be rebutted.

---

[72] Okutan Nilsson (2009), p. 103.

[73] Doğan (2014), p. 56.

[74] Okutan Nilsson (2009), pp. 104–105.

[75] Doğan (2014), p. 61.

3.1.2.4.4 Dominance Agreements

Control achieved by way of a dominance agreement is another ground for control, which might form a corporate group within the meaning given under TCC (Art. 195/1-b). The legislator's explanations presented on this article stipulate that this term refers to the one defined under German law.[76] The concept of 'management' within this context would have the same scope as the strategic decisions outlined under Article 195/1(a), e.g. decisions related to the financing, investment, senior management, budget etc. The term 'dominance agreement' is defined in Trade Registry Regulation (Art. 106/1) as "*an agreement between parties that are not engaged in a direct or indirect subsidiary relation (and even if they are, independently from that relationship), which entails the authority to give instructions to the management body of the other company, which is a stock company,*[77] *without being subject to any conditions*". Therefore, any agreement that would satisfy the aforementioned conditions and leave a company's strategic decisions to the discretion of another, will be deemed a 'dominance agreement'. Dominance agreements may lead to the formation of a corporate group regardless of whether the dominant company (i.e. parent company) has shareholding in the subsidiary.[78] It is possible to establish a corporate group by way of a dominance agreement regardless whether there is a *de facto* dependence amongst the parties to the agreement (thus, the parent company and its subsidiary).[79]

The vagueness of the TCC provision has raised questions in practice as to whether any agreement that might be deemed to confer the authority to effect the management of another would qualify as a dominance agreement. Accordingly, the Trade Registry Regulation, which came into force around 6 months after the TCC, aimed to clarify certain aspects of this new concept under Turkish law. Loan agreements that bear provisions requiring the prior consent of the bank or finance institution for certain transactions that might jeopardise the payment of the loan do not *per se* qualify as dominance agreements (Art. 106/4 Trade Registry Regulation).[80] Moreover, shareholders' agreements that are signed by the shareholders only, without the company being a party, whereby rights and obligations of the shareholders and their management of the company are regulated, also do not *per se* qualify as dominance agreements within the meaning given under the TCC.

[76] Okutan Nilsson (2009), p. 135.

[77] The term of 'stock company' is different than 'commercial company' under Turkish law and is addressed under Article 124/2 of TCC as joint stock companies, limited liability companies and limited partnerships divided into shares.

[78] Dündar (2013), p. 109.

[79] Göktürk (2015), p. 29.

[80] Before the enactment of the Trade Registry Regulation it was debated in legal doctrine whether certain loan agreements bearing provisions on restrictions of distribution of dividends, change of board members or the use of the loan could be deemed as a way of exercising dominance, especially in cases where the bank or credit institution was given the authority to veto some of the decisions of the borrower company (See Gürel (2009), pp. 72–74).

However, where the relevant agreements satisfy any of the criteria given under Article 195 of TCC, then control and dominance may arise, which might lead to the formation of a corporate group under Turkish law.

TCC brings a condition for validity for dominance agreements, which is to be registered and announced with the trade registry (Art. 198/3). According to Trade Registry Regulation (Art. 106/2), dominance agreements should also be approved at the general assembly of the subsidiary. Having said that, in order to eliminate any possible misuse of law, TCC clearly states that the lack of mandatory registration and announcement will not prevent the exercising of provisions concerning the obligations and liabilities of corporate groups. In fact, considering the objective of regulating corporate groups in statutory law, it is possible to consider that the failure to register dominance agreements should not give rise to any invalidating effect on third parties, but might only trigger invalidity amongst its parties.[81]

3.1.2.4.5 Dominance in Any Other Manner

Finally, the TCC recognises the 'dominance in any other manner' exercised on a certain company as a way of exercising control within the context of corporate groups (Art. 195/1-b). It is, therefore, necessary to define what is meant by dominance under this clause. *Okutan Nilsson* interprets dominance within this framework as "*having a decisive influence in the determination of business and finance policies of a company, in particular in the process of taking decisions concerning production, sale and marketing activities, investment costs, budget and financing planning and distribution of dividends, that procure the fulfilment of the scope of activity*".[82]

Article 195/1(b) of the TCC introduced a liberal approach to the definition of corporate groups by including the existence of dominance in any other manner[83] as one of the criteria to create control. It is possible to say that the legislator has purposefully set this type of control in the widest possible manner, which will be analysed case-by-case.[84]

This system is similar to the one under Albanian law, whereby a group is deemed to exist "*where one company regularly behaves and acts subject to the directions or*

[81] Dündar (2013), p. 109.

[82] Okutan Nilsson (2009), p. 98.

[83] Dominance in any other manner, as regulated under Article 195/1(b) of TCC, requires a state of *de facto* control, which should be exercised in practice. The term of *de facto* control within this context is different than the *de facto* control under German *Konzernrecht* (see Section 311 of German Stock Corporation Act of 6 September 1965), which refers to a control formed by unilateral declaration without any dominance agreement (Hopt (2015), p. 10), and which mainly corresponds to the criteria sought by the TCC under Article 195/1(a) to form *de jure* control.

[84] Unlike the other cases of control regulated in under Article 195 of TCC, here it is necessary that the control is exercised, thus the mere existence of a right to exercise control is not *per se* sufficient to have control (Okutan Nilsson (2009), p. 140). Therefore, this type of corporate group is exclusively based on a relationship of dependence between the parties (Göktürk (2015), p. 30).

instructions of another company".[85] Albanian law recognises the relationships of franchising or distribution as a form of dominance as long as they bear the characteristics of a group.[86] On the other hand, under Turkish law, it is not very certain which relationships are to be considered dominance in any other manner. The legislator's reasoning presented in this article stipulates that the term 'dominance in any other manner' is to be interpreted widely, so as to include mergers, acquisitions and share purchase agreements, while it is still not clear if other types of agreements such as loan agreements, franchising or distribution agreements could be considered within this context. In light of the interpretation of the other criteria of control under Article 195/1, it would be reasonable to propose that any type of agreement, whether that be of a corporate or commercial nature, could be deemed to establish a type of control, provided that it exerts decisive influence on the management decisions concerning the main policies of the company, such as sales, production, marketing and finance.[87] Accordingly, where a commercial agreement grants a company the right to affect strategic decisions for another company and if this right is actually used by that company, then this might be seen as an existence of control that could lead to the formation of a corporate group.

Accordingly, it is possible to conclude that there are three types of control concerning corporate groups within the scope of the TCC provisions: (1) through shareholding, which can be in the form of holding the majority of voting rights, holding sufficient shares to appoint directors or managers to make decisions, or holding the majority of share capital, (2) through an agreement of dominance, even where there is no shareholding, and (3) in any other manner, which entails a *de facto* control over the company by being able to effect crucial financial or investment decisions.[88] As can be seen, Turkish law brings a broad definition to the groups of companies by referring to several different types of control. Therefore, a corporate group might be deemed to exist even where there is no direct or indirect shareholding of the majority of a subsidiary's shares, as long as one of the aforementioned types of control is present.

3.1.2.4.6 Presumption of Control

Notwithstanding the above-mentioned criteria, Turkish law also includes a presumption of control in two specific cases, the mere existence of which can be deemed as presence of control, which can be rebutted by showing evidence to the contrary. As per Article 195/2 of TCC, in the event that a commercial company owns the majority of another company's shares or where the amount of shares is sufficient to effect decisions managing the relevant company, this is seen as a presumption of control.

[85] For a thorough analysis on Albanian law on groups of companies see Dine (2012), pp. 44–69.
[86] Dine (2012), p. 66.
[87] Okutan Nilsson (2009), p. 142.
[88] Okutan Nilsson (2011), pp. 92–94.

The first case of this so-called presumption of control is holding the majority of the shares in a company. In such a scenario, it is presumed that the majority shareholder has control over its subsidiary. However, if the majority shareholder can prove that it has no decisive influence on the decision-making mechanism of its subsidiary, by showing that it cannot—either alone or collectively, directly or indirectly—have the majority of the voting rights or the right to determine the sufficient number of members in the company's management, this can be deemed a rebuttal of the presumption.[89]

The second case, on the other hand, is considered quite different to the first one, as it relates to the ownership of the number of shares sufficient to effect decisions that would manage the subsidiary. Even though this specific case is regulated as a presumption, in *Okutan Nilsson*'s opinion, the state of holding sufficient shares to take decisions to manage the company is not merely a mathematical calculation that can be exercised *per se*, and thus it would be necessary to prove this in practice.[90] This makes it difficult to be exercised as a presumption, as the existence of this situation requires practical proof.

The regulation of the aforementioned presumption is interpreted as a sign that the Turkish legislator has actually adopted a mix of two theories, i.e. dominance and control. However, the legislator's explanations presented in the TCC section on corporate groups clearly stipulate that despite the existence of the presumption of control, the law has opted to base the concept of corporate groups on 'control'.

3.1.2.5 Composition of Corporate Groups Under TCC

The mere existence of a parent company and a subsidiary, as defined in the TCC, is not sufficient to form a corporate group within the meaning given under Turkish law. There is a specific number of companies or persons that can compose a corporate group. Furthermore, holding companies require special assessment within the scope of corporate groups, as these companies do not necessarily form corporate groups, and when they do, they might be subject to a different analysis in terms of FDL. Therefore, the issues concerning the required number of below.

3.1.2.5.1 The Number of Companies Required to Form a Corporate Group

The number of companies required to qualify as a corporate group is not regulated under the TCC. About 6 months after the enactment of the TCC, a threshold for this required number of companies was introduced by the Trade Registry Regulation.[91] According to Article 105 of this regulation, in order to qualify as a group of

[89] Okutan Nilsson (2009), p. 132.

[90] Okutan Nilsson (2009), p. 134.

[91] Published in the official journal dated 27.01.2013 and numbered 28541.

companies, there should be at least one commercial company (parent company) and two commercial companies (subsidiaries) directly or indirectly connected under one of the criteria set out in the TCC. In the event that an 'undertaking' that does not qualify as a commercial company is the parent of a group, then the number of subsidiaries should be more than two. This aspect of Turkish law on corporate groups is distinct from other jurisdictions, including German law, in the sense that the criteria of corporate groups under Turkish law are regulated in two separate folds, one based on the concept of control or dominance and the other based on the composition of a group.[92]

Although TCC does not bear any provisions regarding the minimum number of entities that would form a corporate group, Trade Registry Regulation stipulates that there should exist a connection between at least three companies (plus an entity, where the parent is an undertaking) in order to be deemed a corporate group. In other words, if the minimum number of entities is not present, even though the criteria for control sought under Article 195 are met, a connection between only two companies can never be considered a corporate group within the meaning given under Turkish law.[93]

Evidently, by adopting the above-mentioned additional regulation the Turkish legislator has opted to follow the German approach, which requires—for the formation of a corporate group—that the relevant enterprises[94] act with 'another economic interest'.[95] This concept relates to real persons or legal entities that are in control of another entity and that also have other economic interests that might conflict with the interests of the controlled entity. The concept of 'another economic interest' is to be interpreted broadly so as to cover not only commercial activities but also any kind of competing interests, such as being the parent of another enterprise.[96]

The delimitation of the scope of corporate group provisions might also be considered to suit the main objective of the legislator, as the liability regime envisaged for the parent company and its board members is particularly severe in

[92] Eminoğlu (2017), p. 36.

[93] The fact that the minimum number of entities required to form a corporate group is regulated in the secondary legislation (i.e. Trade Registry Regulation) instead of the law itself (i.e. TCC) is criticised as being against the law, as the TCC bears no provisions signalling that the number of entities to form a corporate group would be stipulated in a secondary legislation, and that the relevant provision of Trade Registry Regulation should not be applied (Çakır Çelebi (2018), p. 23). Although it might be reasonable to consider that a secondary legislation cannot regulate any issue that is not present in law, the aforementioned article of Trade Registry Regulation aims to clarify and bring further details to the provisions of TCC, rather than introducing a provision that falls against the stipulation of the TCC. Hence, it would not be legally correct nor would it be reasonable to claim that the aforesaid article is legally invalid.

[94] German *Konzernrecht* is based on 'enterprises' rather than stock companies as in Turkish law; see Okutan Nilsson (2009), p. 75.

[95] Opposing opinion, Çakır Çelebi (2018), p. 27.

[96] Okutan Nilsson (2009), p. 76.

order to protect the interests of subsidiaries and their creditors.[97] Hence, it follows that this severe liability regime will only apply to corporate groups that satisfy both the criteria of control and composition of a group stipulated in the relevant legislation. Accordingly, Article 195 of TCC and Article 105 of Trade Registry Regulation should be read as being complementary to each other when addressing the definition and composition of a corporate group under Turkish law.

Altogether, the provisions of TCC and Trade Registry Regulation bring a clear definition of the group of companies under Turkish law. According to these provisions, the following structures—that are relevant within the context of this study—will be recognised as corporate groups, provided that they are always comprised of at least one parent company and two subsidiaries or at least one parent undertaking (who may be a real person) and three subsidiaries:

- Where a company, on its own or collectively, owns the majority of the shares or voting rights in the other companies;
- Where a company is entitled to appoint a majority of the members of the management body of other companies;
- Where a company can exercise control over other companies via a dominance agreement, subject to the conditions set out in the legislation;
- Where a company has control over the others by any other possible means (e.g. distributorship agreement, franchising agreement, production agreement etc.), which is actually exercised in practice.

This definition allows for a broad range of structures in MNCs to fall within the scope of corporate groups. In fact, to the extent that the conditions required under the relevant legislation are met, not only corporate groups with shareholding links but also supply chains with certain features could be deemed to be corporate groups that would trigger the application of the TCC and secondary legislation. Needless to say, this would require a thorough case-by-case analysis, including the legal relationship between these entities as well as the exercise of 'control' in practice, and it is not a straightforward assumption.

3.1.2.5.2 The Issue of 'Holding Companies'

Another issue concerning the composition of corporate groups under Turkish law relates to holding companies. Holding companies can form part of a group of companies, provided that they comply with the criteria set out in law. On the other hand, holding companies do not necessarily correspond to the concept of the corporate group and it is not required that the parent of a corporate group be a

---

[97] *Eminoğlu* defines corporate groups that satisfy the criteria of control but fail to comply with the criterion of composition of a group as 'non-regulated corporate groups', which should be subject to liability rules other than the ones on corporate groups (e.g. duty of care); see Eminoğlu (2017), p. 38.

holding company.[98] In fact, the type of relationship between a parent company and its subsidiaries is different to the one between a holding company and its subsidiaries. While the first one requires the existence of dominance, a holding company might also contribute to another company without presence of any kind of dominance and it is not required for a holding company to have subsidiaries in the first place.[99]

Although there is no clear definition of holding companies under the TCC, it is inferred from the wording of Article 519 on general legal reserve funds in joint stock companies that these are companies whose main scope of activity is to contribute to and invest in other companies (or enterprises). For this reason, contribution to and investment in other companies should be a continuous activity in holding companies.[100] Contrastingly, groups of companies can be comprised of different types of companies with different scopes of activity, which is not always to invest in other companies.[101]

A sub-segmentation of holding companies is suggested to distinguish between their different ranges of activity. To this end, a pure holding company is considered to be one that merely invests in others and holds subsidiary shares without having its own business operations, while a mixed holding company is seen as one that provides a commercial or industrial service in addition to investing in and creating dominance over other companies.[102] It is, however, worth noting that the TCC only regulates 'pure' holdings, yet corporate groups can be formed with a pure holding parent company as well as a mixed holding parent company, since corporate group provisions in TCC deem it sufficient to have a link between capital companies without making any distinction for holding companies.[103]

This sub-segmentation of pure holding companies and mixed holding companies has a crucial place in addressing the parent company's duty of care in FDL claims. While pure holding companies might be more inclined to be able to avoid

---

[98] Okutan Nilsson (2009), p. 69.

[99] Uygun (2015), p. 24.

[100] Gürel (2009), p. 13.

[101] Bahtiyar (2014), p. 69.

[102] Demir (2008), p. 13; Gürel (2009), p. 6, fn. 2; Okutan Nilsson (2009), pp. 69–70; Petrin and Choudhury (2018), pp. 776–778; Yıldırım (2015), pp. 12–13. Mixed holding companies are also referred to as 'holding-operating companies' as they control other companies while they also engage in their own operations, which are mostly in the same business line with their subsidiaries; in fact, the holding-operating companies that operate in different business lines with their subsidiaries are referred to as 'conglomerates' (Holding Company – Definition, How it Works, Types, Corporate Finance Institute-CFI, https://corporatefinanceinstitute.com/resources/knowledge/strategy/holding-company/.

[103] Okutan Nilsson (2009), p. 70. According to Gürel's opinion, the concept of holding referred to under Article 519 of TCC reflects holding companies in broad terms, which is a company whose activity is to contribute to other companies or enterprises; while the concept of holding in a narrower sense is a company that contributes to others with an aim to achieve dominance, which reflects the concept of groups of companies (Gürel (2009), pp. 16–17).

liability,[104] mixed holding companies which operate in the same or a similar field with their subsidiaries are expected to have superior knowledge and experience and thus would most probably be subject to liability. Having made this point, the substantive legal analysis concerning the parent company's duty of care and the importance of the distinction between pure and mixed holding companies are discussed in Chap. 4 of this study.

3.1.2.6 A Specific Basis for Compensation Claims Under Turkish Law: Article 202/1 of TCC

TCC provisions concerning corporate groups regulate a specific claim protecting the interests of the subsidiary and the subsidiary's creditors against the parent company's potential mismanagement and misuse of the subsidiary's assets. This claim is regulated under Article 202, while Article 206 refers to the case of whole ownership (full dominance) which bears different characteristics to a partial dominance.

Article 202 of TCC, first of all, prevents the parent company to use its dominance resulting in a loss for the subsidiary. Accordingly, in the event that the parent company has brought losses on its subsidiary and it has not covered these losses within the same financial year, the subsidiary's creditors can initiate a lawsuit requesting that the relevant amount is paid back to the subsidiary. It is the explicit wording of the provision that the subsidiary's bankruptcy is not a pre-condition for the use of this right. The article provides examples of certain scenarios that might bring about losses for the subsidiary, which are (i) legal transactions such as the assignment of business, assets, funds, staff, receivables and debts; (ii) the reduction in or transfer of its profits; (iii) the restriction on its assets with rights *in rem* or rights *in personam*; (iv) liabilities such as surety or guarantee; (v) the making of payments; (vi) the failure to renew the subsidiary's facilities without any rightful cause; (vii) any decisions or measures that would hinder the subsidiary's productivity or its operations, such as a restriction on its investments, or refraining from creating measures that would lead to the subsidiary's development. If the parent company's instructions or directions on the subsidiary have caused a loss for the subsidiary, the parent company shall be held liable under this clause.[105]

There are different opinions in Turkish legal doctrine as to whether the parent company's fault will be sought in establishing its liability under Article 202 of TCC. According to one opinion within Turkish legal doctrine, the parent company's liability in this respect will be based on tort in *de facto* corporate groups and on

[104] Regarding the rebuttal of liability by pure holding parent companies, UK Court of Appeal decision in Thompson v Renwick case (detailed analysis made in Sect. 4.1.2.2.4 of this study) is important.

[105] Akın (2014), p. 181.

contractual liability in the case of contractual corporate groups.[106] In the relevant scholar's opinion, this liability might be deemed to be an exception to the limited liability principle in corporate law, as in this case the intervention of the parent company in its subsidiary's affairs and the subsidiary's losses lead to a specific and much stricter type of liability for the parent company.[107] However, by the explicit wording of Article 202/1(d) of TCC,[108] the parent company's liability under Article 202 of TCC is connected to the standard of care regulated for board members (Art. 369 TCC). This provision constitutes a potential for the parent company to escape liability. In the event that the parent company can prove that, in giving the instructions or directing the subsidiary, it has acted in line with the standard of care determined for board members, then it will not be held liable to recover the relevant loss incurred by the subsidiary.[109] In other words, the parent company's liability under this provision is a liability based on fault, rather than strict liability. Therefore, it is also not possible to agree with the opinion that the liability under Article 202 of TCC presents an exception to the limited liability principle. In fact, this liability, even if established, does not concern parent company liability as a shareholder of the subsidiary, but rather the parent company's own act (mismanagement or misuse of dominance) that results in a loss for the subsidiary. This is not relevant to the principle of limited liability.

In light of the foregoing explanations on the nature of the claim under Article 202/1 of TCC (and under Article 206 of TCC for full dominance cases), it is possible to say that this claim is different to the FDL claims in many aspects, and would not constitute an adequate legal ground to accommodate FDL claims. This provision regulates the internal relationship between the parent company and its subsidiary and its main aim is to prevent any misuse of the resources of the subsidiary by its parent company. As a matter of fact, the main purpose of the TCC provisions on corporate groups is to deal with the negative consequences of the conflict of interest that may arise between a parent company and its subsidiaries as a result of the parent company's exercise of control over the subsidiary in contradiction with the subsidiary's interests.[110] As a consequence, the claim is not a typical claim for compensation, whereby the claimants would be compensated for the losses they suffered. In fact, the creditors of the subsidiary claim that the losses allegedly suffered by the subsidiary (which were not recovered) be paid by the parent company to the subsidiary, and not directly to the creditors. In other words, the creditors would aim to recover their receivables from the subsidiary through the

[106] Akın (2014), p. 181.

[107] Akın (2014), p. 177.

[108] Article 202/1(d) of TCC: "No compensation shall be granted in case it is proven that the action resulting in loss would have been done or refrained from being done under the same or similar circumstances by the board members of an independent company, protecting company's interests in line with the principle of good faith and acting with a diligent manager's care".

[109] This rule applies both in whole ownership (full dominance) and partial dominance cases (Göktürk (2015), p. 224).

[110] Okutan Nilsson (2018), p. 36.

parent company's restitution of the subsidiary's losses. Hence, it is possible to say that the claim under Article 202/1 of TCC is not a standard compensation claim, as it does not result in creditors obtaining their receivables. This claim is rather a specific claim regulated for corporate groups, which aims at preventing the mismanagement or misuse of a subsidiary's assets by the parent company. Furthermore, the creditors requesting the recovery of the subsidiary's loss under the aforementioned provision are the creditors of the subsidiary, unlike the claimants in FDL cases who claim a direct liability of the parent company based on the breach of duty of care. Hence the nature of these claims are different to each other. Moreover, in FDL claims, it might be difficult to claim that the subsidiary has suffered a loss due to the breach of the duty of care by the parent company. First, no such loss may have occurred, and second, even if it had, this is not the subject matter of the FDL claim; FDL claimants are not concerned about the losses incurred by the subsidiary, as they are directing their claims to the parent company. Therefore, this provision cannot be used by tort victims to bring FDL claims against the parent companies of a corporate group.

Having said that, as per *Anker-Sørensen*'s opinion, this mechanism under Turkish law can become an additional barrier for tort victims, who may have to bring a claim against the subsidiary first, rather than trying to bring their claim directly against the parent.[111] For the reasons explained above, it is not possible to agree with this opinion. In fact, tort claims based on the subsidiary's actions are not covered by this provision, especially because it relates to preventing the parent company's misuse of the subsidiary. The action under Article 202/1 can at most be described as an indirect liability case, in which the creditors of the subsidiary can only request that the relevant loss is paid to the subsidiary.[112] In FDL claims, the claims of tort victims are based on the allegation that the parent company is directly liable as it has breached its duty of care towards third party victims. This has no relevance within the provision of Article 202/1.

3.1.3 Multinational Corporate Groups: A View Through International Legal Instruments and Legal Doctrine

MNCs are entities of private corporate law[113] with complex structures consisting of separate companies linked to each other in different ways,[114] from shareholding to contractual or *de facto* control, whose parents and subsidiaries are established in different countries, which are subject to different laws and jurisdictions. In light of the explanations offered above regarding corporate groups under Turkish law, it is possible to say that there are many potential different structures that could be defined

[111] Anker-Sorensen (2014), p. 11.

[112] Okutan Nilsson (2018), p. 38; Akın (2014), pp. 257–258.

[113] Antunes (1994), p. 38.

[114] Dine and Koutsias (2014), p. 30.

as MNCs, including simple groups with a single parent and wholly owned subsidiaries, conglomerates and even supply chains. Although there is no unified definition of MNC in international law, there have been attempts to define the term in certain international legal instruments and in legal doctrine. In fact, for the last two decades, there have been improvements with respect to defining and regulating MNCs in the international arena.

The UN was the first body to recognise and address that there was an issue concerning MNCs. In 1974, as per the recommendation of the UN Economic and Social Council (ECOSOC), the UN Secretary-General issued a report on the impact of MNCs on the development process and on international relations. The UN Programme on Transnational Corporations was then integrated within the UN Conference on Trade and Development (UNCTAD) and finally replaced by the Commission on International Investment and Transnational Corporations of UNCTAD.[115] During this period, the UN Commission on Transnational Corporations prepared the Draft UN Code of Conduct on Transnational Corporations, which was not accepted or enacted by the member states. The Norms on the Responsibilities of Transnational Corporations and Other Business Enterprises were approved by the UN Sub-Commission on the Promotion and Protection of Human Rights on 13 August 2003, which were then considered by the UN Commission on Human Rights but not approved—with the explanation that they had no legal standing.[116] The Norms were seen as a restatement of human rights obligations imposed on companies by international law, as they set out to address an obligation for transnational corporations and other business enterprises to respect the principles under the UN treaties and international instruments.[117] The Norms defined the 'transnational corporation' as;

> an economic entity operating in more than one country or a cluster of economic entities operating in two or more countries – whatever their legal form, whether in their home country or country of activity, and whether taken individually or collectively.[118]

In 2005, John G. Ruggie was appointed as the Special Representative of the UN Secretary-General on business and human rights. Ruggie drafted the UN Guiding Principles on Business and Human Rights (UNGPs), which were unanimously

[115] United Nations Commission on Transnational Corporations – UIA Yearbook Profile – Union of International Associations, https://uia.org/s/or/en/1100059616.

[116] United Nations Sub-Commission Norms on business & human rights: Explanatory materials, Business & Human Rights Resource Centre, https://www.business-humanrights.org/en/united-nations-sub-commission-norms-on-business-human-rights-explanatory-materials.

[117] De Schutter (2010), p. 398.

[118] "Norms on the Responsibilities of Transnational Corporations and Other Business Enterprises with Regard to Human Rights", approved August 13, 2003, by U.N. Sub-Commission on the Promotion and Protection of Human Rights resolution 2003/16, U.N. Doc. E/CN.4/Sub.2/2003/L.11 at 52 (2003).

adopted by the UN Human Rights Council on 16 June 2011. [119] The UNGPs do not provide a definition of MNCs but imply that these are companies or enterprises with a presence in more than one country, which are referred to as the home and host countries.

Another international instrument concerning MNCs is the Organisation for Economic Co-operation and Development (OECD) Guidelines for Multinational Enterprises[120] ('OECD Guidelines'), which was adopted in 1976 and updated for the fifth time in 2011, and which is a non-binding instrument. The OECD Guidelines stipulate that while "*a precise definition of multinational enterprises is not required for the purposes of the Guidelines*",[121] MNCs;

> (…) operate in all sectors of the economy. They usually comprise companies or other entities established in more than one country and so linked that they may coordinate their operations in various ways. While one or more of these entities may be able to exercise a significant influence over the activities of others, their degree of autonomy within the enterprise may vary widely from one multinational enterprise to another. Ownership may be private, State or mixed.[122]

ILO's approach to the issue of MNCs was expressed in the ILO Tripartite Declaration,[123] which is a non-binding instrument. The definition of the term 'multinational enterprise' offered in this declaration is similar to the one made in the OECD Guidelines, stating that any precise definition of the term was not necessary and referring to the term as:

> enterprises – whether fully or partially state owned or privately owned – which own or control production, distribution, services or other facilities outside the country in which they are based.[124]

In light of these definitions presented in several major international legal instruments, it is possible to draw a general framework for MNCs for the purpose of this study. As the first condition, it is required that the structure be comprised of several entities, which can either be companies or enterprises, each with their own legal personalities.[125] Referring to the provisions under the TCC and the relevant

[119] United Nations Guiding Principles on Business and Human Rights – Implementing the United Nations "Protect, Respect and Remedy" Framework, United Nations Human Rights Office of High Commissioner, New York and Geneva (2011).

[120] OECD Guidelines for Multinational Enterprises, 2011 edition ("OECD Guidelines"), http://www.oecd.org/daf/inv/mne/48004323.pdf.

[121] OECD Guidelines, p. 17, para. 4.

[122] OECD Guidelines, p. 17, para. 4.

[123] ILO Tripartite Declaration of Principles concerning Multinational Enterprises and Social Policy, adopted by the Governing Body of the International Labour Office at its 204th Session (Geneva, November 1977) and amended at its 279th (November 2000), 295th (March 2006) and 329th (March 2017) Sessions. The fifth edition (March 2017) is available at http://www.ilo.org/wcmsp5/groups/public/%2D%2D-ed_emp/%2D%2D-emp_ent/%2D%2D-multi/documents/publication/wcms_094386.pdf ("ILO Tripartite Declaration").

[124] ILO Tripartite Declaration (2017), p. 3.

[125] Eroğlu (2008a), p. 71.

secondary legislation, which broaden the concept of corporate group to cases where a real person is controlling a corporate structure of at least three commercial companies, it might also be reasonable to expect here that an MNC can also be comprised of several entities and real persons, who are undertakings.

The second condition for an MNC would naturally be to have a parent company and subsidiaries domiciled in different countries. The peculiarity of MNCs is that while the parent company is incorporated in a certain country, the subsidiaries are dispersed worldwide for several purposes.

Another criterion for MNC would be to determine a certain degree of liaison or control between the entities that constitute the corporate group. The definitions referred to above clearly draw on the approach of considering the whole supply chain and contractors to be within the scope of MNC, to the extent that there is a certain degree of control or influence.

3.2 Positioning Multinationals in the International Legal Arena and the Problem of Effective Regulation

3.2.1 Theories on the Position of Multinationals in International Law

The position of companies in international law is much debated in legal doctrine. According to one opinion, there are no actual impediments against imposing liabilities on corporations under international law, but instead the traditional approach is based on the opinions of international lawyers and corporate lobbying with political interests.[126] However, numerous obstacles appear to exist in relation to positioning MNCs in international law.

At the core of this debate lies the opinion that only states can be subject to international law and that corporate actors, as private entities, cannot acquire this role and only limited human rights obligations can be imposed directly on them.[127] In fact, international law is defined as rights and obligations regulating the relationships between states. It is mostly accepted that companies are not directly subject to international conventions, including those governing human rights, and thus cannot be held liable by international human rights courts. [128] It follows that corporate actors, by themselves, are not obliged to respect human rights, but they must obey the law put in place by nation states.[129] In other words, in a traditional context, the subjects of human rights law are nation states, who are responsible for ensuring that the individuals and legal entities within their jurisdiction also comply with these

[126] Buhmann (2016), p. 703.

[127] Muchlinski (2012), p. 151; Weller and Thomale (2017), p. 516.

[128] Weber and Baisch (2016), p. 674.

[129] Muchlinski (2017), p. 36.

laws. This approach may only allow the acceptance of indirect obligations on non-state actors, including corporations, whose compliance is ensured by a nation state's regulations and enforcement mechanisms, while no direct obligation on corporations is envisaged.

There are various arguments supporting this traditional view, such as: (i) the only social responsibility of companies is making profits, (ii) companies are private actors with no duty to observe human rights, (iii) multinational companies are not able to actively protect civil and political rights, and (iv) NGOs are already balancing the claimed unfairness.[130]

The point of departure for this issue is actually linked to the discussion regarding the very nature of companies. According to traditional opinion, companies are organisations of individuals, thus they have no autonomous existence separate from the individuals that create them (e.g. shareholders, directors). Legal entityship is merely a fiction to impose liabilities on companies. It follows that companies, by themselves, have no moral status and cannot bear any responsibilities or have any rights. They do, however, act through their human agents, and their actions are ascribable to the company.[131] Therefore, a kind of corporate moral agency and thus corporate liability should be accepted.

The second opinion, on the other hand, mainly stipulates that companies are not merely fictions but real entities. It follows that they should be accepted as moral persons, with a moral responsibility to respect human rights. Hence, companies should be considered moral agents that can have duties and assume moral responsibility for their actions, especially because their internal decision-making is made by human agents.[132] This approach is based on the reasoning that MNCs are also comprised of individuals on whom the relevant human rights standards are binding and therefore this should be considered as part of the cost of doing business for a company.[133] As for parent companies, specifically, this view supports the opinion that controlling shareholders should be morally culpable for corporate wrongdoings in line with corrective justice, in the sense that the wrongdoer should compensate the victim.[134] The moral culpability argument seems to fit better with controlling shareholders, rather than shareholders acting merely as ordinary investors, as the former are better positioned to foresee and prevent damages occurring from their subsidiary's actions.[135] Followers of the first theory find the second one on real entity too simple, as they insist that companies are actually not independent from their shareholders, so they should be held morally responsible secondarily, along with their human agents.[136]

[130] Muchlinski (2001), pp. 35–36.
[131] Werhane (2016), p. 14.
[132] Arnold (2016), p. 262.
[133] Arnold (2010), p. 384.
[134] Crowe (2012), p. 160.
[135] Crowe (2012), p. 162.
[136] Werhane (2016), p. 17.

The traditional view that corporations cannot be subject to international law appears to fail when it comes to MNCs. In fact, the nation-state approach adopted by law fails dramatically in a world of global economic transactions and corporations operating at an international level above nation-state realms.[137] There may be several theoretical and technically legal arguments that could support this claim.

First of all, the above-mentioned traditional approach might lead to an excessive dependency on the domestic legislation of nation states, which might in turn lead to a lack of consistency across the international arena. This might be as a consequence of the argument that international treaties, including the ones concerning human rights, are ratified by states and therefore not binding on non-state actors. Such an argument might lead to the emergence of mandatory rules to be binding on non-state actors in domestic laws.[138] In other words, the lack of any regulation in international law that would be binding on non-state actors could boost the importance of domestic laws. Therefore, the imposition of direct obligations on non-state actors may pose a viable solution for ensuring their compliance with human rights laws. In fact, MNCs [139] often carry out activities that directly or indirectly impact various stakeholders[140] who are subject to international law, especially in less developed countries.[141] Hence, MNCs should also be deemed to be participants in international law due to their power and influence on other stakeholders. MNCs mostly have the power to affect the economic welfare of the countries where they operate, and therefore must be deemed to have an impact on human rights, specifically on economic and social rights by using their leverage.[142] Consequently, those who have relationships with MNCs (e.g. employees, contractors, communities in the areas where MNCs operate) or who are being impacted by them (e.g. due to pollution) should be able to bring successful claims against MNCs.[143] Moreover, there are concerns that the indirect

[137] Woodroffe (1999), p. 133.

[138] In fact, in order to impose human rights obligations on non-state actors, it might be necessary that these obligations are regulated elsewhere than in international treaties (de Schutter (2010), p. 55).

[139] Some scholars are of the view that not only MNCs but also local or small corporations should have the obligation to respect human rights, as nowadays all corporations can potentially act transnationally. See Carrillo-Santarelli (2018), p. 53.

[140] The concept of 'stakeholders' is interpreted widely, so as to cover the so-called 'primary stakeholders' consisting of those who are directly involved in transactions with the company, such as employees, customers and shareholders, and the 'secondary stakeholders' consisting of those who affect or are affected by the operations of the company; see Amao (2011), p. 191. Involuntary creditors, including FDL plaintiffs, fall within the secondary group of stakeholders.

[141] Bantekas (2004), p. 315.

[142] Muchlinski (2017), p. 37. In fact, according to a research made based on 2017 data, 157 of top 200 economic entities by revenue are corporations, and some MNCs have higher annual revenues than the GDPs of some countries; e.g. Royal Dutch Shell's revenues were determined to be higher than the GDPs of Mexico and Sweden, while Apple's revenues exceeded the GDPs of Switzerland, Norway and Austria (Global Justice Now, 69 of the richest 100 entities on the planet are corporations, not governments, figures show, 17.10.2018, https://www.globaljustice.org.uk/news/2018/oct/17/69-richest-100-entities-planet-are-corporations-not-governments-figures-show).

[143] Arnold (2016), p. 264.

approach might be insufficient in that states may fail to comply with their duties meaning that victims would not receive adequate remedies.[144] A direct approach, on the other hand, would be more effective in determining violation under international law, regardless of where the MNCs might be located.[145]

Another argument supporting this idea of the failure of traditional theory is the abandonment of the belief that the main goal of a company is the maximization of profits, which is based on shareholder primacy.[146] Shareholder primacy is a theory favouring shareholders' benefits, based upon the assumption that the company is owned by shareholders and that they have control over the company's assets.[147] This theory rests on three sub-segments: (i) a company's objective is to maximise shareholder wealth, (ii) shareholders should control the company, and (iii) directors should manage the company in a way that maximises shareholder wealth.[148] In fact, shareholders' interest is often seen as a self-centred interest, focused on obtaining profits from their participation in the company.[149] However, it is a point of discussion in legal doctrine that the shareholder primacy theory may be flawed, in that shareholders do not actually have sole control over the company's assets and cannot be deemed the owners thereof.[150] In today's world, the maximisation of profit for shareholders should not be seen as the only objective of a company; social responsibility and commitment to the achievement of social wealth are also important, as they contribute to achieving sustainability. Corporations can no longer survive in the market if they do not respect human rights, as they risk facing negative public opinion which in turn would harm their reputation and ultimately their business. Therefore, it is possible to put forth that human rights are good for business and corporations that do business need to respect human rights.[151] Consequently, this would also benefit the shareholders, as they would eventually profit by considering the interests of other stakeholders.[152] In fact, as *Buhmann* points out, "*societal expectations become normative as they drive and motivate corporate practice*".[153] These societal expectations concern responsible business behaviour, including in terms of respecting human rights and ensuring sustainability. The social and environmental dimensions of sustainable development should also be incorporated in the process of decision-making of companies, which is defined by *Sjåfjell* as the "*internalisation of externalities*".[154] Human rights violations and environmental

---

[144]Carrillo-Santarelli (2018), pp. 41–42.
[145]Carrillo-Santarelli (2018), pp. 41–42.
[146]Choudhury (2009), p. 635.
[147]Keay (2010), p. 394.
[148]Keay (2010), p. 375.
[149]Houben and Straetmans (2016), p. 616.
[150]Choudhury (2009), p. 635.
[151]Muchlinski (2001), p. 38.
[152]Houben and Straetmans (2016), p. 617.
[153]Buhmann (2011), p. 152.
[154]Sjåfjell (2011a), p. 15; Sjåfjell (2011b), pp. 12–13.

harms occurring due to the activities of corporations should also be considered as externalities that ought to be internalised in this sense; hence, they should be undertaken by the companies as costs of the business. Compliance with international human rights, in fact, would create additional costs for MNCs. Hence, the extent of the company's compliance with human rights could constitute a trade-off between the company's obligations to its shareholders and its obligations to society in general, whereby some of each could be prioritised over others.[155]

The pressing need to abandon shareholder primacy was also expressed in the Davos Manifesto 2020, concerning "*the universal purpose of a company in the fourth industrial revolution*".[156] The manifesto highlights, amongst other issues, the requirement for a company to consider its suppliers as partners in value creation and to integrate respect for human rights into the entire supply chain.[157] The manifesto describes 'company' as more than an economic unit, which "*fulfils human and societal aspirations as part of the broader social system*" and that a company's performance should not only focus on return to shareholders, but also on achieving environmental, social and good governance objectives.[158] Finally, the manifesto specifically refers to multinational companies, stipulating that these should serve all stakeholders, as part of their corporate global citizenship.[159]

The argument surrounding the private status of MNCs is also no longer relevant to their compliance with human rights. In fact, MNCs may even have sufficient power to influence and benefit from international law in that they can be seen as "*the invisible power behind the negotiators*".[160] In other words, nation states are no longer the sole players in this arena.[161] As a result of privatisation policies, many of the tasks that were previously undertaken by nation states are now within the scope of MNC activity, which serves as another reason to bind these organisations by human rights obligations.[162] It may also be observed that powerful MNCs are often connected to lobbies, which assist them in exercising bargaining power before international institutions in accordance with their own interests. Therefore, in order to provide some protection to individuals against powerful MNCs, it is required to include them in the system. [163] MNCs are often allowed to bypass supranational institutions and directly impact individuals.[164] This leads to the view that MNCs are

[155]Zerk (2006), p. 79.

[156]Davos Manifesto (2020): The Universal Purpose of a Company in the Fourth Industrial Revolution, World Economic Forum, https://www.weforum.org/agenda/2019/12/davos-manifesto-2020-the-universal-purpose-of-a-company-in-the-fourth-industrial-revolution/.

[157]Davos Manifesto (2020), para. A.iii.

[158]Davos Manifesto (2020), para. B.

[159]Davos Manifesto (2020), para. C.

[160]Dine (2005), p. 168.

[161]Dine (2005), p. 175.

[162]Zerk (2006), pp. 77–78.

[163]Carrillo-Santarelli (2018), p. 52.

[164]Muchlinski (2001), p. 40.

"*at least centers of unchecked power with no democratic control over them*", as they are able to evade and supersede the regulations of nation states.[165] In fact, although corporations are deemed entities of national law, corporate groups with parents and subsidiaries in different countries are of a transnational nature, which hinders the possibility of being subject to national legislations.[166] According to *Sjåfjell*, this creates a situation where the parent company's control over the corporate group is perversely matched by the limited possibility of holding the parent company liable for its subsidiaries' actions. [167] This is particularly challenging in the case of MNCs, considering that they use a kind of regulatory or jurisdictional arbitrage[168] and mostly choose to operate in developing countries with fewer mandatory regulations on their activities. In the case of tort victims, who are involuntary creditors of corporations, receiving an effective remedy proves to be even more challenging, as they are not in a position to negotiate fairly with the relevant corporations.[169] Accordingly, even if the corporation itself is seen as a nexus of several contracts, with contracting parties having the power to bargain for adequate compensation, tort victims of multinationals are not seen to receive any potential benefit from this.[170]

Another argument in support of having MNCs as addressees in international human rights law is the balance between rights and responsibilities. It is already accepted that corporations have certain human rights, e.g. the right to property, free speech, a fair trial and privacy.[171] As they can have human rights, it is therefore logical that they also bear obligations within the context of human rights law. It is also possible to say that respecting human rights is becoming a requirement of the free market, as corporations who choose to comply with human rights have a competitive disadvantage against those who are less conscientious in this respect. This is because they would be choosing to spend both time and money on protecting human rights and might even be willing to lose some business opportunities in those countries with poor human rights records, thus leading to a 'free-rider problem'. [172]

Positioning MNCs in the international legal arena should not be seen as being mutually exclusive with the obligations of states within the same context. States are obliged to ensure effective remedy under their domestic legal systems for the victims of corporate wrongs and MNCs can also be held responsible for the wrongs that they

[165] Dine (2008), pp. 179–181; Dine and Koutsias (2014), p. 6.

[166] Sjåfjell (2018), pp. 39–40.

[167] Sjåfjell (2018), p. 40.

[168] Dine (2012), p. 49.

[169] It is also considered that while voluntary creditors are mostly able to foresee the risks and protect themselves by way of conducting a due diligence and negotiate accordingly with MNCs, involuntary creditors have no such opportunity and therefore are vulnerable parties (Petrin and Choudhury (2018), p. 780).

[170] Choudhury (2009), p. 640.

[171] Muchlinski (2001), p. 33.

[172] Muchlinski (2001), p. 35. Antunes explains the concept of free-riding within this context as "incentives to overinvest in hazardous industries through the use of a network of disproportionate capitalized subsidiaries and to under-invest in accident prevention", Antunes (1994), p. 136.

have committed. [173] States carry an obligation to provide protection against the violations of private actors within their jurisdiction by monitoring the actions of these private actors and providing adequate remedies.[174] Nevertheless, holding states accountable for their violations might not be sufficient to effectively remedy the damages suffered by the victims. Developing or least developed host countries might lack the financial and technical means required for an adequate monitoring and compliance mechanism. Hence, given the imbalance of powers, their exclusive liability would not provide sufficient protection for individual victims.[175] Furthermore, in the event that a state is held responsible for a violation, it would be difficult to propose that an apology and guarantee of non-repetition, without any reparation, would constitute an effective remedy for the victim.. [176] This could be seen as another concern justifying that corporations should be recognised as actors in the international legal arena and carry obligations and responsibilities under international human rights law.

It is worth noting that making MNCs subject to international law would also require the establishment of international courts in order to hear the claims concerning the violations of the aforesaid international laws by MNCs. In fact, if MNCs were directly bound by the terms of international law, it would also be necessary to have specialised international courts in place. Otherwise, the current trend would continue to be MNCs being held only indirectly bound by the terms of international law, through state duty to regulate (in domestic laws) the issues required by the relevant international law. This would constitute a secondary and indirect liability on MNCs. Also the latest suggestions regarding the draft UN treaty, which will be discussed further in the upcoming sections, impose obligations on states to regulate corporate liability for human rights violations and environmental harms in their domestic laws, rather than imposing direct obligations on corporations in this respect. This aspect might be interpreted as signalling a future trend in this field, indicating no crucial change in subjecting MNCs to international law, but rather leaving it to countries to regulate the relevant issue more specifically in their laws.

3.2.2 International Legal Instruments Related to Responsible Business Behaviour and Corporate Social Responsibility

There are various international legal instruments that have a crucial role in determining the legal landscape surrounding business responsibility for human rights,

[173] Carrillo-Santarelli (2018), p. 36.
[174] Zerk (2006), p. 84.
[175] Zerk (2006), p. 85.
[176] Carrillo-Santarelli (2018), p. 40.

which guided the way to mandatory legislations. Explanations of the main international legal instruments concerning issues of responsible business behaviour and corporate social responsibility are provided below.

3.2.2.1 UN Instruments

The social and economic gap between developing and developed countries has been addressed in the UN GA Declaration on the Establishment of a New International Economic Order (1974).[177] This declaration pointed to the ever-growing gap between countries and addressed the importance of achieving international cooperation for development, which it identified as "*a shared goal and common duty of all countries*". In its declaration, the UN has assumed a role in the establishment of a new international economic order, which is to protect the interests of all countries equally. Consequently, an autonomous body within the Secretariat of UN, United Nations Centre on Transnational Corporations (UNCTC) began operations in 1975. The UNCTC led the negotiations on the UN Code of Conduct on Transnational Corporations, which in the end, however, failed.

All of these steps have finally led to the UN Global Compact, which might serve as a good example of an engagement by private actors to provide undertakings on social responsibility. Evolving from a need to achieve corporate sustainability, the then UN Secretary General Kofi Annan introduced UN Global Compact in 2000, which now forms the largest corporate sustainability initiative in the world, with 161 countries and over 9500 companies pledging to comply with its principles.[178] The Global Compact provides ten principles within the framework of ensuring responsible business behaviour, focusing on the fundamental areas of human rights, labour, environment and anti-corruption. Despite efforts to form a universal platform for responsible business behaviour, the Global Compact has been criticised as being ineffective, based on several factors such as the vagueness of terms used and of duties imposed on private companies, as well as the lack of sanctions.[179]

Another important tool on the subject of business and human rights is the UN Guiding Principles on Business and Human Rights (UNGPs), which was unanimously adopted by the UN Human Rights Council on 16 June 2011, with its resolution 17/4. [180] UNGPs follow the 'Protect, Respect and Remedy' policy framework[181] developed by the UN Special Representative for Business and

[177] United Nations General Assembly – Sixth Special Session, Resolution No. 3201 (S-VI), Declaration on the Establishment of a New International Economic Order (1 May 1974).

[178] UN Global Compact, https://www.unglobalcompact.org/.

[179] Arnold (2010), p. 373.

[180] United Nations Guiding Principles on Business and Human Rights – Implementing the United Nations "Protect, Respect and Remedy" Framework, United Nations Human Rights Office of High Commissioner, New York and Geneva (2011).

[181] UN "Protect, Respect and Remedy" Framework for Business and Human Rights, A/HRC/8/5 (7 April 2008).

Human Rights, John Ruggie, and provide voluntary guidelines for companies and states to prevent human rights violations in business operations. The framework recognises states as the primary actors of international human rights law, while also imposing positive duties on non-state actors in addition to a 'do no harm' principle.[182] This is considered a big step towards structuring the discussion on the human rights responsibilities of MNCs, especially in relation to the developing host countries where they choose to operate via subsidiaries.[183] Ruggie's policy framework suggests a due diligence mechanism whereby companies would comply with the principles and manage the risks of violating human rights.[184] The recommendation entails that due diligence should cover three main aspects: the risks pertaining to the country where the company operates; the risks pertaining to the activities that the company is engaged in; and the risks to which they may contribute through the business relationships they have established, such as with their suppliers, or business partners, etc.[185] The principles do not provide any fixed scope for the suggested due diligence, with the reasoning that due diligence should depend "*on the potential and actual human rights impacts resulting from a company's business activities and the relationships connected to those activities*".[186]

Although for the time being, the UNGPs are of a non-binding nature—posing 'societal expectations' rather than legal requirements—it is observed that these principles have a significant impact on domestic regulations. [187] In fact, the UNGPs are described as connecting elements of the state-centred international law to national law, legal institutions and to market forces with the ultimate aim of creating the maximum possible impact on business conduct.[188] To this end, they are seen as different to the UN Global Compact by providing clearer business governance guidance, connecting state duties and business responsibilities, focusing on remedies and influencing other instruments that govern business conduct.[189]

UNGPs set three basic principles: (i) the state's duty to protect against human rights abuses committed by third parties, including companies, through effective policies, regulation, legislation and adjudication, (ii) corporate responsibility for respecting human rights in their business operations, and (iii) access to remedy for victims of business and human rights abuses.

As the state's duty to protect requires them to ensure that private actors are prevented from abusing human rights by way of effective regulation, this imposes an indirect responsibility on companies as well.[190] The references to a state's duty

[182]De Schutter (2010), pp. 398–399.

[183]Cragg et al. (2012), p. 3.

[184]UN "Protect, Respect and Remedy" (2008), para. 25.

[185]UN "Protect, Respect and Remedy" (2008), para. 57.

[186]UN "Protect, Respect and Remedy" (2008), para. 72.

[187]Zerk (2014), p. 12.

[188]Buhmann (2015), p. 401.

[189]Buhmann (2015), p. 402.

[190]Dine (2005), pp. 179–180.

and a corporation's responsibility are made on purpose. The state's duty refers to a moral or legal obligation, while the corporation's responsibility implies accountability for the negative or positive consequences of corporate actions, which may result in blame or praise.[191] Corporations are private actors who, traditionally, are not considered to be subject to international law. The term 'responsibility' is chosen to address this issue along with the deduction that the responsibility of corporations is regarded as a standard of expected conduct rather than an obligation. [192]

The second pillar, 'corporate responsibility to respect', is interpreted as a consensus on moving from "naming and shaming" to "knowing and showing" for corporate actors, whereby companies are expected to understand the impacts of their operations on human rights and to take measures to protect them. [193] This aspect of corporate responsibility mainly stems from the due diligence concept, which requires companies to internalise human rights by preparing a policy, making periodic assessments, and putting in place a control and reporting system including grievance procedures.[194] Unlike some mandatory provisions on HRDD recently introduced in some domestic laws, which will be further dealt with in Chap. 4 below, the UNGPs explicitly stipulate that the principles apply to all enterprises regardless of their size, sector, operational context, ownership or structure. Nevertheless, the principles also state that HRDD will vary depending upon the size of the enterprise, the risk of human rights violations, and the nature and context of its operations. As it is declared in the commentary of Principle 17, while potential risks need to be reported along with mitigation and prevention methods, any violations that have already occurred should be remediated. The commentary of the relevant principles suggests ways to prevent and mitigate the risks of human rights violations for various scenarios:

- If business operations are directly giving rise to human rights violations, then the business should take measures to prevent and mitigate these;
- If business operations are contributing to human rights violations, then it should cease its contribution and exercise its leverage to eliminate or mitigate risks;
- If human rights impacts are caused by the business relationship between two enterprises, then the situation should be considered in light of various factors, such as the enterprise's leverage over the other, the importance of the relationship, and the severity of the violation. The enterprise should use any leverage it has, or try terminating the relationship, when it is not crucial to its own business.

The assessment of all these factors would surely require a diligent approach in practice, as it is not easy to prove that a company has leverage over another or that the relevant relationship is of crucial importance to its existence. It is also worth noting that Principle 22 on remediation and its commentary do not refer to any clear

[191] Arnold (2010); Kara (2018), p. 120.

[192] Muchlinski (2012), pp. 147–148.

[193] Zerk (2014), p. 10.

[194] Muchlinski (2012), p. 149.

mechanisms or ways to remediate any human rights abuses which have already occurred, which might be deemed to leave the issue unresolved.

As a result of the UN Summit in September 2015, the UN also issued 17 Sustainable Development Goals (SDGs) of the 2030 Agenda for Sustainable Development,[195] which have been in force since 1 January 2016 and adopted by all member states.[196] The SDGs aim to universally address issues such as poverty, hunger, gender equality and climate change with action by local governments. One of the first sentences from the preamble of the UN's decision on SDGs is "*All countries and all stakeholders, acting in collaborative partnership, will implement this plan*". Therefore, it is not reasonable to put forward that MNCs would not be covered by the SDGs. However, based on the questions previously discussed on the positioning of MNCs in the international legal arena, the impact of SDGs on MNCs remains unclear. It was observed that MNCs actively supported the SDGs upon their enactment. However, this support mostly took the form of adopting internal mechanisms within the company, rather than imposing SDGs on their supply chains.[197] For the purpose of increasing the implementation of these SDGs by MNCs, it is suggested that governments adopt an active stance.[198] This signals the need for a mandatory approach adopted in domestic laws.

3.2.2.2 OECD Instruments

Another international instrument concerning responsible business conduct is the OECD Guidelines, which are recommendations by governments addressed to MNCs. Although they put forth voluntary principles for responsible business conduct, the signatory countries undertake to implement these in their domestic laws.[199] The Guidelines further stipulate that if there is a contradiction between domestic laws and the principles and standards of the Guidelines, enterprises should try to comply with the Guidelines to the fullest extent without violating domestic law.[200] These guidelines have introduced a due diligence obligation for companies on all the substantive issues covered by the Guidelines, except for science and technology, competition and taxation, which is broader than what is envisaged in the UN Framework and UNGPs.[201] Unlike the lack of monitoring mechanisms in

[195] Take Action for the Sustainable Development Goals – United Nations, https://www.unglobalcompact.org/sdgs.

[196] UN Global Compact – Making Global Goals Local Business, https://www.unglobalcompact.org/sdgs.

[197] van Tulder and van Zanten (2018), https://discovery.rsm.nl/articles/detail/351-multinationals-and-the-uns-sustainable-development-goals-what-do-first-steps-reveal/.

[198] van Tulder and van Zanten (2018).

[199] OECD Guidelines, Preface, para. 1.

[200] OECD Guidelines, I. Concepts and Principles, para. 2.

[201] OECD Guidelines, Commentary to General Principles, para. 14; Buhmann (2016), p. 708.

UNGPs, the OECD Guidelines introduced National Contact Points to assist local business communities to comply with the principles and promote effectiveness.[202] These are grievance mechanism schemes that draw on legal method for the investigation and handling of complaints. [203] Nevertheless, it is suggested in legal doctrine that OECD Guidelines should apply to operations outside the borders of the member states, as well as within their borders, in order to be effective. [204] In fact, although the OECD Guidelines provide for these grievance mechanisms, these would not ensure the same level of efficiency as mandatory laws. *Buhmann* suggests that the EU might be in a position to adopt mandatory laws with direct effect for companies, although in certain subjects—such as labour and human rights—its powers are usually limited, as these areas are left to the discretion of member states.[205] Given that the areas where the EU's law-making power is limited are significantly relevant to corporate accountability, it remains questionable whether the suggested approach would have a lasting effect in practice.

3.2.3 The Way Forward: Alternative Methods Complementary to FDL

Further to the discussions presented on the position of MNCs in international law and the challenges involved in effectively regulating them, it is also worth presenting some complementary and supplementary methods that would support the way forward in FDL cases.In light of the analysis offered on the traditional approaches to company law regarding the different features of companies, some suggestions can be made with a view to creating a more favourable atmosphere for stakeholders in general, rather than only shareholders. This discussion is significant for the future of FDL claims as it might change the general thinking about corporations and their liability schemes. One alternative method concerns the attempt to have an international treaty by the UN on business and human rights, which aims to impose duties on states and regulate MNCs, amongst other types of businesses. The final draft issued by the relevant UN working group is, therefore, analysed below, specifically on the new ideas it could bring to FDL. Finally, on the procedural side of the matter, private arbitration in business and human rights is evaluated as a potential legal mechanism to address FDL claims under the Hague Rules on Business and Human Rights Arbitration (December 2019) (Hague Rules).[206]

---

[202] Weber and Baisch (2016), p. 674.

[203] Buhmann (2011), p. 148.

[204] Woodroffe (1999), p. 137.

[205] Buhmann (2016), p. 703.

[206] Hague Rules for Business and Human Rights Arbitration (December 2019), available at Permanent Court of Arbitration (PCA), Other Conventions and Rules, https://pca-cpa.org/en/documents/other-conventions-and-rules/the-hague-rules-for-business-and-human-rights-arbitration/.

3.2.3.1 Suggestions of Reform in Company Law

The concepts of FDL and the duty of care of parent companies are linked with other legal doctrines, such as shareholder primacy and multi-stakeholder approach, and therefore, the development of these concepts might trigger improvements in other areas.

The European Commission has been actively engaged in corporate social responsibility and the adaptation of company law to the needs of the modern world. For this purpose, the Commission presented the Green Paper, 'Promoting a European Framework for Corporate Social Responsibility' (Commission's 2001 Green Paper).[207] This Green Paper makes reference to a preferred definition of CSR: *"(...) a concept whereby companies integrate social and environmental concerns in their business operations and in their interaction with their stakeholders on a voluntary basis".*[208]

The European Commission's Communication on Corporate Social Responsibility[209] set out to invite all stakeholders—including companies, shareholders, unions, associations, as well as the public, to join the initiative to promote corporate social responsibility. To this end, the Commission referred to the already existing approach of businesses to view corporate social responsibility as a requirement to ensure long-term sustainability and shareholder value, while still taking the view (expressed in the Commission's 2001 Green Paper) that it constitutes a voluntary practice.[210] On the other hand, it adopted an almost revolutionary approach at the time in terms of addressing stakeholders within the context of CSR, by including not only business partners and investors, but also customers, NGOs representing local communities and the environment, and also recognised that CSR should expand beyond Europe to include any global supply chains.

The Commission then renewed its strategy on CSR, as a result of calls from the European Council and the European Parliament, and issued the Communication on a renewed EU strategy for Corporate Social Responsibility.[211] In this Communication, the Commission described the benefits of CSR as not only being for society and the environment, but also for business, stating that it would provide advantages to enterprises regarding risk management, cost savings, access to capital, customer

[207] European Commission, Green Paper "Promoting a European Framework for Corporate Social Responsibility", DOC/01/9, Brussels, (18 July 2001).

[208] Commission's 2001 Green Paper, p. 8.

[209] Communication from the Commission concerning Corporate Social Responsibility: A business contribution to Sustainable Development ("Commission Communication on CSR"), Brussels, 2.7.2002, COM(2002) 347 final.

[210] Commission Communication on CSR, p. 5.

[211] Communication from the Commission to the European Parliament, the Council, the European Economic and Social Committee and the Committee of the Regions, "A renewed EU strategy 2011–14 for Corporate Social Responsibility" ("Renewed EU Strategy for CSR"), Brussels, 25.10.2011, COM(2011) 681 final.

relationships, human resource management and innovation capacity.[212] Accordingly, a new CSR definition has been adopted: "*the responsibility of enterprises for their impacts on society*".[213] By eliminating the reference to voluntary practice, the Commission has surely made a significant improvement in its approach towards CSR. It has also set the aim of CSR as not only maximising the creation of shared value for shareholders/owners, but also for other stakeholders and for society as a whole.[214] Amongst other agenda for action, the Commission invited large European enterprises to commit to at least one of the following: the UN Global Compact, the OECD Guidelines for Multinational Enterprises, or the ISO 26000 Guidance Standard on Social Responsibility, in forming their CSR policies by 2014, and all European-based MNCs to commit to respecting the ILO Tri-partite Declaration by 2014.[215]

The Commission's action plans on company law and corporate governance also include important observations and suggestions concerning company law theory and sustainability. In its 2003 Action Plan on Modernising Company Law and Enhancing Corporate Governance in the EU,[216] the Commission refers to its Communication on CSR, which resulted in the establishment of a European Multi-Stakeholder Forum, aimed at defining the environmental and social practices of businesses, even if only voluntary. The action plan speaks of the importance of establishing an effective and proportionate protection of both shareholders and third parties in company law policy.[217] It also stipulates that in order to achieve sufficient transparency in corporate groups, it is required to ensure that there is adequate legislation in place concerning the disclosure of both financial and non-financial information for listed as well as non-listed companies.[218] In December 2012, the Commission adopted a new action plan on company law and corporate governance.[219] In this new action plan, the Commission set the following initiatives that it intended to take with the ultimate purpose of modernising company law and corporate governance: Enhancing transparency in companies, engaging shareholders in corporate governance, and supporting growth and competitiveness in companies by simplifying

[212] Renewed EU Strategy for CSR, p. 3.

[213] Renewed EU Strategy for CSR, p. 6.

[214] Renewed EU Strategy for CSR, p. 6.

[215] Renewed EU Strategy for CSR, p. 13.

[216] Communication from the Commission to the Council and the European Parliament, Modernising Company Law and Enhancing Corporate Governance in the European Union - A Plan to Move Forward ("2003 Action Plan on Company Law"), Brussels, 21.5.2003, COM (2003) 284 final.

[217] 2003 Action Plan on Modernising Company Law, p. 8.

[218] 2003 Action Plan on Modernising Company Law, p. 19.

[219] Communication from the Commission to the European Parliament, the Council, the European Economic and Social Committee and the Committee of the Regions, Action Plan: European company law and corporate governance – a modern legal framework for more engaged shareholders and sustainable companies ("2012 Action Plan on Company Law"), Strasbourg, 12.12.2012, COM (2012) 740 final.

cross-border operations.[220] Within the initiative to enhance transparency, the Commission recommended reporting requirements on non-financial aspects, with the aim of providing a long-term and sustainable strategy for companies.[221]

In addition to the challenges faced in regulating MNCs in the international legal arena, it is overall difficult to regulate MNCs, even in domestic laws, because of legal obstacles such as the structure and logic of company law, as well as jurisdictional limits. [222] *Enneking* describes these difficulties as follows: "*the intangible nature of multinational corporations, the transboundary nature of the activities, the difference in regulatory standards between developed home countries and developing host countries, and the aversion towards extraterritorial regulation make this an exercise that is far from easy*". [223] Therefore, the most feasible approach would be to create a regulatory framework within the scope of domestic laws with support of the international system, thereby complementing each other. A similar approach is defined as 'transnational law' by *Buhmann*, referring to the UNGPs, which are based on international law while also regulating business conduct across territorial borders. [224]

The aforementioned approach is clearly destined to be rather ineffective without the support of domestic laws. Therefore, it is crucial that reforms are realised in certain fields of law, as the current legal system appears to be insufficient on the effective regulation of MNCs. Company law, especially—with principles of separate legal personality and limited liability—bears certain impediments to regulating MNCs. In fact, these two basic principles of company law significantly restrict the chances of success in FDL cases. The corporate liability shield is seen as resulting in a cost for society, especially in cases where it is extended to corporate shareholders and where it involves more hazardous activities with a greater potential to cause environmental damages or human rights abuses. [225] The Modern Corporation Statement on Company Law, prepared and signed by a group of company law academics as part of the Modern Corporation Project and the Purpose of the Corporation Project[226] emphasises the role of the limited liability principle in the avoidance of liability by corporations. The following statement sums up this concern:

> As a result of the 'limited liability' of shareholders the creditors of corporations can only enforce their claims against the corporation's assets, not against those of the shareholders. In reality, therefore, for shareholders, 'limited liability' means 'no liability.' Shareholders are

---

[220] 2012 Action Plan on Company Law, pp. 4–5.

[221] 2012 Action Plan on Company Law, p. 6.

[222] Muchlinski (2012), p. 151.

[223] Enneking (2008), p. 308.

[224] Buhmann (2015), p. 410.

[225] Anker-Sorensen (2014), pp. 5–6.

[226] The Modern Corporation – Corporate Governance for the twenty-first Century, https://themoderncorporation.wordpress.com/.

> affected by the corporation's failures only indirectly and their losses limited to any decline in the value of the shares they hold.[227]

In light of the above concerns, it is possible to suggest that a reform is indeed necessary in corporate law, a reform which is traditionally grounded on a narrow shareholder primacy principle that leads to a justification of every corporate action as generating profit for the shareholders. A wider stakeholder approach needs to be adopted in a way that would take into account the benefits of all persons affected by corporate action, [228] including society in general and tort victims who are external to the company. It is discussed in legal doctrine whether limited liability principle should in fact extend to cover tort acts resulting from the company's negligent behaviour and whether this ought to be a necessary feature of the corporate structure.[229] It is emphasised that from a historical perspective the doctrine of limited liability does not expand to cover the tort liability of a company, especially a parent company which controls its subsidiary through its involvement in its management.[230] *Muchlinski* refers to this proposition as "*reorientation of corporate law away from the neoliberal conception of the 'asocial corporation', (...) toward the older tradition of the 'socially embedded corporation'*". [231] This effectively proposes a reformed 'civil corporation' which considers business and society as not mutually exclusive and which embeds the relevant social discourses of our time.[232]

On the other hand, *Choudhury* considers that profit maximisation alone cannot represent all shareholder interests, but also that a total shift from shareholder primacy might not be realistic given the diversity of shareholders investing especially in public corporations, and therefore a balance could be found between profit maximisation and non-financial interests, by 'serving these two masters'.[233] This approach seems to be compatible with the concept of internalisation of externalities, as these two approaches both refrain from denying the maximisation of profits, but also intend to focus on non-financial interests.

---

[227] The Modern Corporation Statement on Company Law, coordinated together with another disciplinary statement by Dr. Jeroen Veldman, Modern Corporation Project, which is hosted by Cass Business School, City University, London, Purpose of the Corporation Project: purposeofcorporation.org - themoderncorporation.org. Having said that, it would be too far-fetched to consider that all shareholders should be liable for the debts of the company against company creditors indefinitely with their own assets. This would eliminate all the benefits expected by the limited liability principle, which is not vicious *per se*. An assessment should be made to distinguish between the positions of different shareholders to consider their liability in this respect. In fact, I believe that the Modern Corporation Project's approach is also to put more importance on multi-stakeholder theory to strike a reasonable balance.

[228] Muchlinski (2011), p. 699.

[229] Kraakman et al. (2009), p. 11.

[230] H C Lo (2014), p. 15.

[231] Muchlinski (2011), p. 704.

[232] Muchlinski (2011), p. 692.

[233] Choudhury (2009), p. 649.

To conclude this discussion on effective regulation for corporate sustainability, including the roles of MNCs, a regulatory framework may be described as follows, in *Sjåfjell*'s words:

> (...) as when businesses (or, more broadly, economic actors) in aggregate create value in a manner that is (a) environmentally sustainable in the sense that it ensures the long-term stability and resilience of the ecosystems that support human life, (b) socially sustainable in the sense that it facilitates the respect and promotion of human rights and other basic social rights as well as good governance, and (c) economically sustainable in the sense that it satisfies the economic needs necessary for stable and resilient societies. [234]

3.2.3.2 A UN Treaty on Business and Human Rights

The UN Human Rights Council passed resolution 26/9 on 14 July 2014, concerning the elaboration of an international instrument that is legally binding on transnational corporations and other business enterprises with respect to human rights.[235] This was a resolution taken for the purpose of establishing an open-ended intergovernmental working group (OEIGWG) to develop an internationally binding instrument concerning business and human rights. It is noteworthy that while almost all developed countries chose not to participate in this resolution, the developing countries voted in favour.[236] The reason for this opposition is proposed as: "*the very appropriateness of international law in imposing binding human rights obligations on all types of business enterprises*".[237] The current global situation no longer seems to justify this abstaining approach by developed countries towards an internationally binding instrument on this subject, given the flow of foreign direct investment is no longer one-directional from developed to developing countries; there is an emerging trend of MNCs operating also from developing countries.[238]

In line with resolution 26/9, the OEIGWG was formed to work on the human rights responsibilities of transnational corporations and other business enterprises.

---

[234] Sjåfjell (2018), p. 36.

[235] UN Human Rights Council resolution 26/9 on the elaboration of an international legally binding instrument on transnational corporations and other business enterprises with respect to human rights, (14 July 2014), A/HRC/RES/26/9, https://documents-dds-ny.un.org/doc/UNDOC/GEN/G14/082/52/PDF/G1408252.pdf?OpenElement.

[236] The resolution was adopted with 20 votes in favour against 14, and 13 abstentions. In favour: Algeria, Benin, Burkina Faso, China, Congo, Côte d'Ivoire, Cuba, Ethiopia, India, Indonesia, Kazakhstan, Kenya, Morocco, Namibia, Pakistan, Philippines, Russian Federation, South Africa, Venezuela (Bolivarian Republic of), Viet Nam; against: Austria, Czech Republic, Estonia, France, Germany, Ireland, Italy, Japan, Montenegro, Republic of Korea, Romania, the former Yugoslav Republic of Macedonia, United Kingdom of Great Britain and Northern Ireland, United States of America; abstaining: Argentina, Botswana, Brazil, Chile, Costa Rica, Gabon, Kuwait, Maldives, Mexico, Peru, Saudi Arabia, Sierra Leone, United Arab Emirates.

[237] Deva (2018), p. 21.

[238] Deva (2018), pp. 21–22; Macchi (2018), p. 80.

During the first session's panel discussions,[239] some states pointed to the need for a balance between protecting human rights and protecting foreign investments, which could be ensured by a form of smart regulation mixing hard and soft law mechanisms. It is stipulated that human rights should be recognised as universal, indivisible and interdependent. As for the scope of the treaty, it was suggested by some panellists that it should cover not only transnational corporations but all types of business enterprises. As for the subject matter of the treaty, it was discussed that human rights should be covered broadly, so as to include core rights and all those on which corporations could have an impact. It was further proposed that abolishing the doctrine of *forum non conveniens* could be helpful in ensuring the state's responsibility for human rights abuses and that the state's responsibility in this respect should extend to both home and host countries. The importance of adopting legislation to prevent negative human rights impacts and to establish due diligence mechanisms was also emphasised.

During the panel discussions held at the second session,[240] it was reiterated that the treaty must be built on UNGPs, without undermining these principles. Therefore, the UNGPs should be implemented in domestic laws; within this context, the example of French Law on Duty of Vigilance[241] was given. It was also stated that the treaty should operationalise the principles of separate legal identity and limited responsibility in a way that could be adapted to the specific structure of transnational corporations. It was again recognised that voluntary instruments remained insufficient to regulate MNCs. A suggestion was made to establish an international court to enforce the treaty. It was also referred to an International Court of Justice decision where it was held that the state's obligation to respect human rights did apply beyond its territory when there was a link between the relevant state and the activity that was carried out abroad. It was further discussed that imposing direct obligations on a non-state actor (i.e. corporations) would facilitate the search for a remedy for the victims. Finally, specific examples of challenges to access to remedy were evaluated.

At the third session,[242] there was a debate around what the scope of application of the treaty should be in terms of *rationae materiae* and *rationae personae*, concluding that it should cover all internationally recognised human rights and activities of

[239] See the "Report on the first session of the open-ended intergovernmental working group on transnational corporations and other business enterprises with respect to human rights, with the mandate of elaborating an international legally binding instrument" of the Human Rights Council, dated 5 February 2016, https://documents-dds-ny.un.org/doc/UNDOC/GEN/G16/018/22/PDF/G1601822.pdf?OpenElement.

[240] See the "Report on the second session of the open-ended intergovernmental working group on transnational corporations and other business enterprises with respect to human rights" of the Human Rights Council, dated 4 January 2017, https://documents-dds-ny.un.org/doc/UNDOC/GEN/G17/000/94/PDF/G1700094.pdf?OpenElement.

[241] Loi no. 2017-399 du 27 Mars 2017 relative au devoir de vigilance des sociétés mères et des entreprises donneuses d'ordre, https://www.legifrance.gouv.fr/affichTexte.do?cidTexte=JORFTEXT000034290626&categorieLien=i.

[242] See the "Report on the third session of the open-ended intergovernmental working group on transnational corporations and other business enterprises with respect to human rights" of the

transnational corporations, as well as those of other business enterprises. It was proposed that the treaty should cover not only the companies, but also any business activities of a transational nature, without focusing on whether the relevant company is transnational or local. This point, however, remained unresolved.[243] Finally, it was decided that a draft internationally binding instrument be prepared and submitted to the member states and other parties for their review before the fourth session.

Following several sessions, the OHCHR finally issued a Zero Draft of the legally binding instrument dated 16.7.2018.[244] The draft convention was aimed at achieving protection and fulfilment of human rights in transnational business operations, access to an effective remedy, as well as international cooperation. The Zero Draft was revised by OEIGWG Chairmanship on 16.07.2019 (the 'Revised Draft'),[245] then again on 06.08.2020 (the 'Second Revised Draft'),[246] and finally on 17.08.2021 (the 'Third Revised Draft').[247] It is worth noting that the Third Revised Draft introduced a new category to the concept of vulnerable groups, 'older persons', as an undeniable impact of the COVID-19 pandemic.[248] It has also made clear reference to climate change, in addition to environmental impacts and standards.[249]

The scope of the legally binding instrument was kept wide in the Revised Draft, the Second Revised Draft and the Third Revised Draft. Despite the debates taking place at the third session, the scope was finally regulated as "*This (Legally Binding Instrument) shall apply to all business activities, including business activities of a transnational character*",[250] therefore not only focusing on companies but on

---

Human Rights Council, dated 24 January 2018, https://documents-dds-ny.un.org/doc/UNDOC/GEN/G18/017/50/PDF/G1801750.pdf?OpenElement.

[243] Cassel (2018), p. 280.

[244] OHCHR, Legally Binding Instrument to Regulate, in International Human Rights Law, the Activities of Transnational Corporations and Other Business Enterprises, (16.07.2018), https://www.ohchr.org/documents/hrbodies/hrcouncil/wgtranscorp/session3/draftlbi.pdf.

[245] Open-Ended Intergovernmental Working Group on Transnational Corporations and Other Business Enterprises With Respect to Human Rights (IGWG) (2019), https://www.ohchr.org/Documents/HRBodies/HRCouncil/WGTransCorp/OEIGWG_RevisedDraft_LBI.pdf.

[246] Open-Ended Intergovernmental Working Group on Transnational Corporations and Other Business Enterprises With Respect to Human Rights (OEIGWG), Legally Binding Instrument to Regulate, in International Human Rights Law, the Activities of Transnational Corporations and Other Business Enterprises, OEIGWG Chairmanship Second Revised Draft (06.08.2020), https://www.ohchr.org/Documents/HRBodies/HRCouncil/WGTransCorp/Session6/OEIGWG_ChairRapporteur_second_revised_draft_LBI_on_TNCs_and_OBEs_with_respect_to_Human_Rights.pdf.

[247] Open-Ended Intergovernmental Working Group on Transnational Corporations and Other Business Enterprises With Respect to Human Rights (OEIGWG), Third Revised Draft Legally Binding Instrument to Regulate, in International Human Rights Law, the Activities of Transnational Corporations and Other Business Enterprises (17.08.2021), https://www.ohchr.org/EN/HRBodies/HRC/WGTransCorp/Session7/Pages/Session7.aspx.

[248] Third Revised Draft, Preamble PP13, Articles 6.4.c and 16.4.

[249] Third Revised Draft, Preamble PP10, Articles 6.4.a and 6.4.e.

[250] Third Revised Draft, Article 3/1 (Scope). The Second Revised Draft referred to business enterprises rather than business activities; however, considering that the terms of 'business

business activities in general, regardless of whether these are of a transnational character or not.[251] The transnational character of business activities is described as (a) being undertaken in one or more jurisdiction or state, or (b) with the most substantial part of its preparation, planning, direction, control, design, processing, manufacturing, storage or distribution taking place through any business relationship in another state or jurisdiction, or (c) creating significant effect in another state or jurisdiction.[252] The Third Revised Draft makes it clear that it covers all internationally recognised human rights and fundamental freedoms, including environmental rights.[253] The damage suffered by the victims of human rights violation or abuse was kept quite wide in the Second Revised Draft, as it covered not only physical and economic losses but also mental injuries, emotional suffering and substantial impairment of human rights,[254] which went far beyond the traditional definition of human rights. This was amended in the Third Revised Draft, which more simply refer to those who "*have suffered harm that constitute human rights abuse*".[255] Direct victims, and also their immediate family or dependents, are defined as victims of human rights abuses.[256] However, the persons who have suffered harm by intervening to assist victims in distress or to prevent victimisation, who were included in the definition of victims in the Second Revised Draft,[257] were removed from the Third Revised Draft.

The Third Revised Draft provides for specific remedies against human rights violations that fall within its scope, which are not *numerus clausus*, but including restitution, compensation, rehabilitation, satisfaction and guarantees of non-repetition, environmental remediation and ecological restoration.[258] HRDD is also regulated as a means of prevention, according to which state parties undertake to adopt the required measures to ensure that all persons carrying out business activities undertake HRDD in line with the requirements set forth in the treaty.[259]

The system of liability provided by the Third Revised Draft (which adopted the exact same wording of the Second Revised Draft) is quite revolutionary.

---

activities' and 'business activities of a transnational character' are defined in the legally binding instrument, the Third Revised Draft's approach appears to be more adequate.

[251] It was previously discussed during OEIGWG meetings that domestic companies need not be regulated within the international treaty, as these are already covered by domestic laws, while MNCs are the ones who manage to hide between different jurisdictions, which need to be regulated by an internationally binding instrument; see Lopez and Shea (2016), p. 114; Bilchitz (2016), p. 221.

[252] Third Revised Draft, Article 1/4 (Definitions).

[253] Third Revised Draft, Article 3/3 (Scope); Article 1/2 (Definitions). This was a point that was agreed upon by the parties during OEIGWG sessions; see Lopez and Shea (2016), p. 114.

[254] Second Revised Draft, Article 1/1 (Definitions).

[255] Third Revised Draft, Article 1/1 (Definitions).

[256] Third Revised Draft, Article 1/1 (Definitions).

[257] Second Revised Draft, Article 1/1 (Definitions).

[258] Third Revised Draft, Article 4/2 (Rights of Victims).

[259] Third Revised Draft, Article 6 (Prevention).

Accordingly, state parties undertake to ensure that their domestic laws provide for a liability for persons conducting business activities (including transnational ones) for their failure to prevent their contractual parties from causing damage to third parties, provided that they legally or factually control or supervise the relevant business enterprise or activity that caused the damage, or should foresee or should have foreseen risks of human rights violations arising from the relevant activities, but failed to adopt the required measures to prevent the relevant damage.[260] This means that any natural or legal person who conducts business activities (regardless of whether they are of a transnational nature) shall be responsible for any harm caused by the activities of their suppliers or sub-contractors (including transnational ones), as long as they have control or supervision over the relevant enterprises or their activities. Alternatively, even if they do not have control or supervision, they could still be held responsible if they are able to foresee the risks of human rights abuses pertaining to such activities. In any case, the liability within this context is linked to the failure to take the required measures to prevent the damage. As an additional remark on legal liability it is noted that HRDD, which is regulated as a method of preventing human rights abuses under Article 6, shall not automatically absolve liability and that the court shall consider the liability issue by considering the relevant business entity's compliance with applicable HRDD standards.[261] This provision serves as a positive condition to ensure that HRDD is not conducted as a tick-box exercise.

As can be noted, both the Second and the Third Revised Drafts have clearly opted for imposing duties on states rather than imposing direct obligations on corporations. In fact, the liability provisions stipulate that state parties are to ensure certain conditions that would result in the sought-after corporate compliance. This approach eliminates the risk of criticism that corporations, as private parties, cannot be subject to instruments of international law.[262]

The jurisdiction clause of the Third Revised Draft introduces a provision which favours transnational tort claim victims. It is stated in this clause that the jurisdiction shall vest upon the courts of the place (i) where the human rights abuse has occurred and/or produced effects, or (ii) where acts or omissions contributing to the relevant human rights abuse have occurred, or (iii) where the natural or legal persons who have allegedly committed the relevant human rights abuses or contributory acts or omissions are domiciled, or (iv) where the victim is a national of or is domiciled.[263] This provision almost word-by-word follows the Second Revised Draft, but it takes a step backwards in providing an advantage to tort victims in FDL claims by

[260] Third Revised Draft, Article 8/6 (Legal Liability).

[261] Third Revised Draft, Article 8/7 (Legal Liability).

[262] However, in the opinion of *Bilchitz*, this argument is flawed as the act of imposing duties on states to ensure that third parties (including corporations) comply with human rights is actually a recognition that the relevant third parties are bound by international law. See Bilchitz (2016), p. 208.

[263] Third Revised Draft, Article 9/1 (Adjudicative Jurisdiction).

reinserting the reference to the courts of the place where the victim is a national of or where the victim is domiciled. Rejection of jurisdiction based on *forum non conveniens* is prohibited if claimants bring their cases to one of the courts set out in the relevant clause of jurisdiction,[264] which is to the benefit of victims and in line with recent developments concerning *forum non conveniens*. It is possible to say that the Third Revised Draft adopts a strict approach by way of imposing obligations on states parties to remove legal obstacles, including *forum non conveniens*, in cases of human rights abuses concerning transnational business activities.[265]

The clause on applicable law of the Third Revised Draft, firstly refers to the law of the court having jurisdiction.[266] The provision further stipulates that, subject to domestic law, the claim may be governed by the law of the country where (i) the acts or omissions have occurred or produced effects, or (ii) the person who has allegedly committed the acts or omissions is domiciled.[267] The Revised Draft, differently from the Second and Third Revised Drafts, referred also to the use of the domicile of victims as an alternative method for determining applicable law, which might have led to undesirable results in terms of FDL claims, as the host country's law could have been the applicable law. This risk is eliminated by the explicit wordings of the Second and Third Revised Drafts. However, it would still be important to determine what the acts or omissions that gave rise to the relevant human rights violations actually were. Considering the nature of FDL claims, whereby victims allege that they have suffered damages due to the acts or omissions of the parent company, this provision seems likely to be effective in serving the interests of these victims as they would be allowed to bring their claims before the courts and under laws of the home country. The clear reference to the place where the acts or omissions produced effects favours this interpretation.

The possibility of achieving a consensus on a UN treaty is looking hopeful on so many levels, but most importantly, it shows that there is a shared understanding and motivation between different countries to effectively regulate business and human rights. As a way forward based on the establishment of an international treaty, *Choudhury* suggests establishing *ad hoc* or specialised courts for transnational corporate abuses, which would combine different aspects of these claims—such as criminal law, human rights law, corporate and commercial law.[268] It is clear that in order to reach such a goal, it would first be necessary to prepare a treaty to regulate the obligations of MNCs and the penalties for any breaches, as well as the procedural aspects—such as whether the rules would be based on common law or civil law—which would also require an international consensus.[269]

---

[264] Third Revised Draft, Article 9/3 (Adjudicative Jurisdiction).

[265] Third Revised Draft, Article 7.3.d (Access to Remedy).

[266] Third Revised Draft, Article 11/1 (Applicable Law).

[267] Third Revised Draft, Article 11/2 (Applicable Law).

[268] Choudhury (2005), p. 61.

[269] Choudhury (2005), pp. 62–63.

3.2.3.3 Private Arbitration in Business and Human Rights

Another important step forward might be related to the dispute resolution mechanism in FDL claims. Although, up until now, court litigation has been the main method for solving these disputes, there are also downsides to it, such as the problem of jurisdiction, costs of litigation, unfair judicial systems and also most cases resulting in out-of-court settlement without any admission of liability. Based on these concerns, there have been recent attempts to introduce private arbitration as an alternative to court litigation, which might be a useful method to provide an effective remedy to FDL victims.

The Hague Rules,[270] prepared as a result of a project supported by the City of the Hague and the Ministry of Foreign Affairs of the Netherlands, sets out rules concerning arbitration proceedings in business and human rights disputes.[271] Although they were drafted based on the Arbitration Rules of the United Nations Commission on International Trade Law (2013 UNCITRAL Rules),[272] the Hague Rules were modified to reflect the particular characteristics of business and human rights disputes, necessity for special measures, importance of transparency and special expertise of arbitrators, as well as special mechanisms for collecting evidence and hearing witnesses.[273] It is worth noting that the Hague Rules reflects all three pillars of the UNGPs: Pillar I on state responsibility to protect human rights by incentivising arbitration in FDL claims, Pillar II on corporate responsibility to respect human rights by choosing arbitration as a method of dispute resolution, and Pillar III on access to remedy by facilitating the FDL victims' access to remedy in cases of violation.[274]

As mentioned in the Preamble of the Hague Rules, arbitration as a dispute resolution mechanism poses only an alternative to the general state-based judicial mechanisms and is in no way a substitute thereof. Claimants are entitled to bring their claims before an arbitral tribunal without having to exhaust the available domestic legal remedies.[275] It is, however, necessary that the parties have agreed to refer to arbitration under the Hague Rules in case a dispute arises in their legal relationship, whether contractual or not.[276] Although the provision appears to cover

[270] Hague Rules for Business and Human Rights Arbitration (December 2019), available at Permanent Court of Arbitration (PCA), Other Conventions and Rules, https://pca-cpa.org/en/documents/other-conventions-and-rules/the-hague-rules-for-business-and-human-rights-arbitration/.

[271] Information on the project available at: The Hague Institute for Global Justice, Business and Human Rights Arbitration, https://www.thehagueinstituteforglobaljustice.org/portfolio/business-and-human-rights-arbitration/.

[272] Arbitration Rules of the United Nations Commission on International Trade Law, United Nations Commission on International Trade Law, (February 2014).

[273] Izzo (2019), http://arbitrationblog.kluwerarbitration.com/2019/09/13/a-further-step-towards-business-and-human-rights-arbitration-the-hague-rules/.

[274] Izzo (2019), p. 1546.

[275] Tarman (2020), p. 1547.

[276] Hague Rules, Art. 1/1.

non-contractual relationships too, it would be challenging if not impossible to consider the majority of FDL cases within this framework, as these mostly concern transnational tort claims between two parties who had no relationship prior to the relevant damage subject to the dispute. FDL claims that concern occupational health and safety violations that caused harms on the employees of transnational subsidiaries might be accommodated safely within scope of arbitration under the Hague Rules, as their contracts could make reference to arbitration in cases of such disputes. Hague Rules, in Introductory Note, state that the rules can be adopted either by way of an arbitration agreement or an arbitration clause inserted in an agreement before the dispute arises or thereafter by way of a submission agreement (*compromis*).[277] Due to the nature of FDL claims which is mentioned above, submission agreements are expected to become more common in practice. However, even this so-called 'open-offer' model of consent is considered problematic in practice, as MNCs refrain from taking any proactive position for remediation of liabilities.[278]

Another challenge for tort victims in business and human rights claims would be to cover the high costs of arbitration and fees of arbitrators, which would result especially high in transnational claims. In this respect, Hague Rules bring a deviation of the loser pays principle by stipulating that the arbitral tribunal may decide to apportion the costs between the parties if it deems it reasonable considering the circumstances of the case (such as public interest, financial burden on the parties, the parties' conduct during the arbitral proceedings).[279] Unfortunately, this rule would not suffice to relieve the concerns of the financially weaker claimants in business and human rights claims, as it provides a relief only at the end of the arbitration stage, hence leaving it to the claimants to cover the costs necessary to initate arbitral proceedings, e.g. administrative costs and lawyer's fees.[280] Hague Rules also refer to the possibility of receiving legal aid, contingency funding or an agreement on the asymmetric distribution of costs between the parties.[281] Third party funding and financial assistance are allowed to cover arbitration costs, provided that these are made transparently and by disclosing the required details concerning the funding or financial assistance.[282] *Tarman* suggests using different methods to ensure that arbitration proceedings under the Hague Rules are made more accessible for business and human rights claimants; namely, provision of pro-bono assistance to the victims by NGOs or lawyers, creation of a fund to cover arbitration costs by the PCA, insertion of clauses in contracts that the costs of arbitration of the victims

[277] Hague Rules, Introductory Note, pp. 3–4.

[278] Baykitch and Bao (2018), https://www.kwm.com/en/au/knowledge/insights/international-arbitration-of-business-related-human-rights-disputes-20181221.

[279] Hague Rules, Art. 53/1.

[280] Tarman (2020), p. 1557.

[281] Hague Rules, Introductory Note, p. 4.

[282] Hague Rules, Art. 55/1. This is a new provision compared to UNCITRAL Rules (Art. 55 Commentary).

would be compensated by the other party in case the proceedings result to the victims' favour.[283] If these mechanisms are applied in an appropriate manner, despite the clear unequality of arms, victims in business and human rights disputes might use arbitration as a viable dispute resolution mechanism to eventually reach an effective legal remedy.

Based on the concern of unequal standing of the parties in business and human rights disputes, the Hague Rules provides an obligation for the arbitral tribunal, that it will assist the party that faces barriers to access to remedy ("*including a lack of awareness of the mechanism, lack of adequate representation, language, literacy, costs, physical location or fears of reprisal*") to ensure that the relevant party can present its case in fair and efficient proceedings.[284] This is one of the rules that has been modified over the UNCITRAL Rules with a purpose to strike a balance between the unequal interests of the parties to the business and human rights claims.[285]

The Hague Rules refer to the possibility of the arbitral tribunal to make separate awards for different issues. Accordingly, an arbitral award may include monetary compensation, as well as non-monetary relief such as restitution, rehabilitation, satisfaction, specific performance and guarantees of non-repetition.[286] The remedies mentioned in this provision reflect the approach adopted in Pillar III of the UNGPs.[287]

Another issue with arbitration could be the clash between providing transparency, which is deemed essential in business and human rights claims, and confidentiality, which naturally comes with arbitration.[288] The importance of transparency in business and human rights disputes is explicitly recognised under the Preamble of the Hague Rules[289] and issues relating to transparency, such as public hearings, publication of documents, are regulated between Articles 38–43, which appear to promote a high level of transparency throughout arbitral proceedings, considering the specific public interest in business and human rights claims.

The enforcement of the arbitral awards under the Hague Rules regime will be made in line with domestic laws of the relevant countries, international conventions and the New York Convention on the Recognition and Enforcement of Foreign Arbitral Awards[290] (New York Convention). As per Article 1/2 of the Hague Rules, the disputes submitted to arbitration shall be deemed to have arisen from a commercial relationship or transaction for the purposes of the New York Convention.

---

[283] Tarman (2020), p. 1558. See also Baykitch and Bao (2018).

[284] Hague Rules, Art. 5/2.

[285] Hague Rules, Art. 5/2 Commentary.

[286] Hague Rules, Art. 45/2.

[287] Tarman (2020), p. 1559.

[288] Izzo (2019)

[289] Hague Rules, paragraph 6(d).

[290] New York Convention on the Recognition and Enforcement of Foreign Arbitral Awards, the UN Conference on International Commercial Arbitration (1958).

Considering that in majority of business and human rights cases the states might be involved or have certain interests, it might prove to be problematic to ensure enforcement of arbitral awards taken under the Hague Rules under the New York Convention regime. Indeed, states concerned might opt to reject enforcement on the basis that the award falls against public policy or contest the validity of arbitration agreement on other grounds.[291] For these reasons, it is recommended to establish a monitoring mechanism to check arbitral awards in these claims in order to increase the chances of enforcement.[292]

To conclude on private arbitration in business and human rights disputes, it would be reasonable to state that this method would certainly provide important advantages for the victims, especially ensuring specialised experience of arbitrators, eliminating challenges on jurisdiction, leaving aside other problems concerning unfair trials that the victims may face before domestic courts. The Hague Rules offer a well-considered and special focused approach in many aspects that are important for business and human rights claims, such as transparency, impartiality and ensuring access to effective remedy. There are, however, still some aspects that the Hague Rules remain insufficient in terms of these specific claims, such as the problem of choosing arbitration as a dispute resolution mechanism and enforcement of arbitral awards. Subject to the potential improvements that can be made on these points in near future, private arbitration might develop to finally constitute a viable alternative to litigation in business and human rights claims.

References

Online Sources

Davos Manifesto 2020: The Universal Purpose of a Company in the Fourth Industrial Revolution, World Economic Forum. https://www.weforum.org/agenda/2019/12/davos-manifesto-2020-the-universal-purpose-of-a-company-in-the-fourth-industrial-revolution/

Global Justice Now, 69 of the richest 100 entities on the planet are corporations, not governments, figures show (17.10.2018). https://www.globaljustice.org.uk/news/2018/oct/17/69-richest-100-entities-planet-are-corporations-not-governments-figures-show

Glossary for the European Union, Basic Terms, Secretariat General for the European Union Affairs, Ankara (December 2003) https://www.ab.gov.tr/files/Sozluk/Sozluk_Baski.pdf

Hague Rules for Business and Human Rights Arbitration (December 2019), available at Permanent Court of Arbitration (PCA), Other Conventions and Rules.

---

[291] Tarman (2020), p. 1560.

[292] Tarman (2020), p. 1560.

https://pca-cpa.org/en/documents/other-conventions-and-rules/the-hague-rules-for-business-and-human-rights-arbitration/

Holding Company – Definition, How it Works, Types, Corporate Finance Institute-CFI. https://corporatefinanceinstitute.com/resources/knowledge/strategy/holding-company/

Permanent Court of Arbitration (PCA), Other Conventions and Rules. https://pca-cpa.org/en/documents/other-conventions-and-rules/the-hague-rules-for-business-and-human-rights-arbitration/

Take Action for the Sustainable Development Goals – United Nations. https://www.unglobalcompact.org/sdgs

The Hague Institute for Global Justice, Active: Business and Human Rights Arbitration. https://www.thehagueinstituteforglobaljustice.org/portfolio/business-and-human-rights-arbitration/

United Nations Commission on Transnational Corporations – UIA Yearbook Profile – Union of International Associations. https://uia.org/s/or/en/1100059616

United Nations Sub-Commission Norms on business & human rights: Explanatory materials, Business & Human Rights Resource Centre. https://www.business-humanrights.org/en/united-nations-sub-commission-norms-on-business-human-rights-explanatory-materials

Legislation, Reports, Resolutions and Opinions

Communication from the Commission to the European Parliament, the Council, the European Economic and Social Committee and the Committee of the Regions (12.12.2012) Action Plan: European company law and corporate governance – a modern legal framework for more engaged shareholders and sustainable companies.

http://eur-lex.europa.eu/legal-content/EN/ALL/?uri=CELEX%3A52012DC0740

Winter J (2002) Final Report of the High Level Group of Company Law Experts on a Modern Regulatory Framework for Company Law in Europe, Brussels.

ILO Tripartite Declaration of Principles concerning Multinational Enterprises and Social Policy (March 2017) 5th edn. http://www.ilo.org/wcmsp5/groups/public/%2D%2D-ed_emp/%2D%2D-emp_ent/%2D%2D-multi/documents/publication/wcms_094386.pdf

"Norms on the Responsibilities of Transnational Corporations and Other Business Enterprises with Regard to Human Rights", approved August 13, 2003, by U.N. Sub-Commission on the Promotion and Protection of Human Rights resolution 2003/16, U.N. Doc. E/CN.4/Sub.2/2003/L.11 at 52 (2003).

The Modern Corporation Statement on Company Law, coordinated together with other disciplinary statement by Dr. Jeroen Veldman, Modern Corporation Project, which is hosted by Cass Business School, City University, London, the Purpose of the Corporation Project: purposeofcorporation.org - themoderncorporation.org

The Modern Corporation – Corporate Governance for the 21st Century. https://themoderncorporation.wordpress.com/

OECD Guidelines for Multinational Enterprises, 2011 edn. http://www.oecd.org/daf/inv/mne/48004323.pdf

OHCHR, Legally Binding Instrument to Regulate, in International Human Rights Law, the Activities of Transnational Corporations and Other Business Enterprises ("Zero Draft"), (16.07.2018). https://www.ohchr.org/documents/hrbodies/hrcouncil/wgtranscorp/session3/draftlbi.pdf

"Report on the first session of the open-ended intergovernmental working group on transnational corporations and other business enterprises with respect to human rights, with the mandate of elaborating an international legally binding instrument" of the Human Rights Council, dated 5 February 2016.

https://documents-dds-ny.un.org/doc/UNDOC/GEN/G16/018/22/PDF/G1601822.pdf?OpenElement

"Report on the second session of the open-ended intergovernmental working group on transnational corporations and other business enterprises with respect to human rights" of the Human Rights Council, dated 4 January 2017.

https://documents-dds-ny.un.org/doc/UNDOC/GEN/G17/000/94/PDF/G1700094.pdf?OpenElement

Report on the third session of the open-ended intergovernmental working group on transnational corporations and other business enterprises with respect to human rights" of the Human Rights Council, dated 24 January 2018.

https://documents-dds-ny.un.org/doc/UNDOC/GEN/G18/017/50/PDF/G1801750.pdf?OpenElement

United Nations Guiding Principles on Business and Human Rights – Implementing the United Nations "Protect, Respect and Remedy" Framework (2011) United Nations Human Rights Office of High Commissioner, New York and Geneva.

UN "Protect, Respect and Remedy" Framework for Business and Human Rights (7 April 2008) A/HRC/8/5.

UNDHR (1948) UNGA res. 217A (III), UN Doc. A/810, 71. https://www.un.org/en/universal-declaration-human-rights/

UN Global Compact.

https://www.unglobalcompact.org/

UN Global Compact – Making Global Goals Local Business. https://www.unglobalcompact.org/sdgs

UN Human Rights Council resolution 26/9 on the elaboration of an international legally binding instrument on transnational corporations and other business enterprises with respect to human rights (14 July 2014) A/HRC/RES/26/9

https://documents-dds-ny.un.org/doc/UNDOC/GEN/G14/082/52/PDF/G1408252.pdf?OpenElementCosimo Monteleone

Literature

Akın İ (2014) Şirketler Topluluğu Sorumluluk Hukuku (Law on Liability in Corporate Groups). Ankara

Amao O (2011) Human rights, ethics and international business: the case of Nigeria. In: Voiculescu A, Yanacopulos H (eds) The business of human rights – an evolving Agenda for corporate responsibility. Zed Books, pp 188–213

Anker-Sorensen L (2014) Parental liability for externalities of subsidiaries: domestic and extraterritorial approaches. University of Oslo Faculty of Law Legal Studies, Research Paper Series 2014/36

Antunes JE (1994) Liability of corporate groups. Kluwer Law

Arnold DG (2010) Transnational corporations and the duty to respect basic human rights. Bus Ethics Q 20(3):371–399

Arnold DG (2016) Corporations and human rights obligations. BHRJ 1:255–276

Bahtiyar M (2014) Ortaklıklar Hukuku, Kısa Karşılaştırma ve Değerlendirmeler, Dersler-Soru Örnekleri (Law of partnerships, short comparisons and analyses, classes-examples of questions), 8th edn. Istanbul

Bantekas I (2004) Corporate social responsibility in international law. Bost Univ Int Law J 22:309–347

Baykitch A, Bao E (2018) International arbitration of business related human rights disputes. King&Wood Mallesons. https://www.kwm.com/en/au/knowledge/insights/international-arbitration-of-business-related-human-rights-disputes-20181221

Bilchitz D (2016) The necessity for a business and human rights treaty. BHRJ 1:203–228

Buhmann K (2011) Integrating human rights in emerging regulation of corporate social responsibility: the EU case, International Journal of Law in Context, vol. 7(2). Cambridge University Press, pp 139–179

Buhmann K (2015) Business and human rights: understanding the UN guiding principles from the perspective of transnational business governance interactions. Transnatl Legal Theory 6(1): 399–434

Buhmann K (2016) Public regulators and CSR: the 'social license to operate' in recent United Nations instruments on business and human rights and the Juridification of CSR. J Bus Ethics 136:699–714

Cahn A, Donald DC (2018) Comparative company law – text and cases on the Laws governing corporations in Germany, the UK and the USA, 2nd edn. Cambridge University Press

Çakır Çelebi FB (2018) Şirketler Topluluğunda Hakim Teşebbüs (Dominant undertaking in group companies). TFM 4(1):19–32

Carrillo-Santarelli N (2018) A Defence of direct international human rights obligations of (all) corporations. In: Cernic JL, Carrillo-Santarelli N (eds) The future of business and human rights: theoretical and practical considerations for a UN treaty. Insersentia Publishers, pp 33–62

Cassel D (2018) The third session of the UN intergovernmental working group on a business and human rights treaty. BHRJ 3:273–283

Choudhury B (2005) Beyond the alien tort claims act: alternative approaches to attributing liability to corporations for extraterritorial abuses. Northwest J Int Law Bus 26:43–75

Choudhury B (2009) Serving two masters: incorporating social responsibility into the corporate paradigm. Univ Pa J Bus Law 11(3):631–674

Cragg W, Arnold DG, Muchlinski P (2012) Guest Editors' introduction human rights and business. Bus Ethics Q 22:(1):1–7

Crowe J (2012) Does control make a difference: the moral foundations of shareholder liability for corporate wrongs. Mod Law Rev 75:159–179

de Schutter O (2010) International human rights law. Cambridge University Press

Demir H (2008) Holding Şirketlerde Transfer Fiyatlandırmasının Esasları ve Uygulaması (Principles and Practice of Transfer Pricing in Holding Companies). Master's Thesis, Istanbul

Deva S (2018) Alternative paths to a business and human rights treaty. In: Jernej L, Carrillo-Santarelli N (eds) The future of business and human rights: theoretical and practical considerations for a UN treaty. Insersentia Publishers
Dine J (2005) Companies, international trade and human rights. Cambridge University Press
Dine J (2008) Democratization: the contribution of fair trade and ethical trading movements. Indiana J Glob Legal Stud 15(1):177–212
Dine J (2012) Jurisdictional arbitrage by multinational companies: a national law solution. J Human Rights Environ 3:44–69
Dine J, Koutsias M (2014) Company law, 8th edn. Palgrave Macmillan
Doğan İÜ (2014) 6102 Sayılı Türk Ticaret Kanunu'nun Şirketler Topluluğu Hükümleri ve 4054 Sayılı Rekabetin Korunması Hakkında Kanun Kapsamında "Kontrol" Kavramı ve Hukuki Sonuçları (The Concept of "Control" Under Turkish Commercial Code No. 6102 Provisions on Groups of Companies and the Law No. 4054 on the Protection of Competition and Related Legal Consequences). Master's Thesis
Dowling P (2020) Limited liability and separate corporate personality in multinational corporate groups: conceptual flaws, accountability gaps, and the case for profit-risk liability. In: Enneking L, Giesen I, Schaap AJ, Ryngaert C, Kristen F, Roorda L (eds) Accountability, international business operations, and the law: providing justice for corporate human rights violations in global value chains. Routledge, pp 219–239
Dündar E (2013) Yeni Türk Ticaret Kanunu Çerçevesinde Çok Uluslu Şirketler (Multinational Companies within Framework of the New Turkish Commercial Code). PhD Thesis, Istanbul
Embid I, José M (2005) Trends and realities in the law of corporate groups. EBOR 6:65–91
Eminoğlu C (2017) Kuram-Uygulama İkileminde Şirketler Topluluğu Hukuku ve (Normatif) Şirketler Topluluğu Meydana Getirmeyen Hakimiyet İlişkileri – TTK'nın Şirketler Topluluğuna İlişkin Hükümleri ve TSY m. 105 Bağlamında Bir İnceleme (Corporate Groups Law Under the Dichotomy of Theory-Practice and Relationships of Dominance that do not Form a (Normative) Corporate Group – An Analysis Within Scope of TCC Provisions on Corporate Groups and Art. 105 of Trade Registry Regulation) – Ticaret Hukuku ve Yargıtay Kararları Sempozyumu XXXI (Symposium on Commercial Law and Appeal Court Decisions XXXI). pp 9–55
Enneking L (2008) The common Denominatory of the Trafigura case, foreign direct liability cases and the Rome II regulation, an essay on the consequences of private international law for the feasibility of regulating multinational corporations through tort law. Eur Rev Priv Law 2:283–311
Eroğlu M (2008a) Multinational enterprises and tort liabilities, an interdisciplinary and comparative examination. Edward Elgar Publishing
Eroğlu M (2008b) Limited liability in Turkish law. Eur Bus Organ Law Rev 9:237–265
Forum Europaeum Corporate Group Law (2000) Corporate group law for Europe. EBOR 1:165–264
Göktürk K (2015) Şirketler Topluluğunda Sorumluluk Esasları – Anonim Şirketlerden Oluşan Topluluklar Bakımından (Liability Grounds in Corporate Groups – For Groups Formed of Joint Stock Companies). Ankara
Gürel M (2009) Türk Ticaret Kanunu Tasarısı'nda Şirketler Topluluğunda Hakimiyetin Hukuka Aykırı Kullanılmasından Doğan Sorumluluk (Liability for Unlawful Exercise of Dominance in Groups of Companies Under Draft Turkish Commercial Code). Master's Thesis, Ankara
Harsa T (2007) Şirketler Topluluklarında Tek Elden Yönetim ve Hakim Şirketin Tek Elden Yönetimden Kaynaklanan Sorumluluğu (Centralized Management in Corporate Groups and Liability of the Parent Company for Centralized Management). Master's Thesis, Istanbul
HC Lo S (2014) A parent company's tort liability to employees of a subsidiary. J Int Comp Law 117
Hopt KJ (2015) Groups of companies – a comparative study on the economics, law and regulation of corporate groups. ECGI, Law Working Paper No. 286/2015
Houben R, Straetmans G (2016) Shareholder rights and responsibilities in the context of corporate social responsibility. EBLR:615–637

Izzo ML (2019) A Further Step Towards Business and Human Rights Arbitration – The Hague Rules. Kluwer Arbitration Blog, http://arbitrationblog.kluwerarbitration.com/2019/09/13/a-further-step-towards-business-and-human-rights-arbitration-the-hague-rules/
Kara P (2018) The role of corporate social responsibility in corporate accountability of multinationals: is it ever enough without 'hard law'? Eur Comp Law J 15(4):118–125
Keay A (2010) Shareholder primacy in corporate law: can it survive – should it survive. ECFR 3(2010):369–413
Kershaw D (2012) Company law in context, text and materials, 2nd edn. Oxford University Press
Kırca İ, Şehirali Ç (2013) Feyzan Hayal/Manavgat, Çağlar, Anonim Şirketler Hukuku, Temel Kavram ve İlkeler, Kuruluş, Yönetim Kurulu (Law of Joint Stock Companies, Main Concepts and Principles, Incorporation, Board of Directors). Vol. 1, Ankara
Kraakman R et al (2009) The anatomy of corporate law, a comparative and functional approach, 2nd edn. Oxford University Press
Lopez C, Shea B (2016) Negotiating a treaty on business and human rights: a review of the first intergovernmental session. BHRJ 1:111–116
Macchi C (2018) A treaty on business and human rights: problems and prospects. In: Cernic JL, Carrillo-Santarelli N (eds) The future of business and human rights: theoretical and practical considerations for a UN treaty. Insersentia Publishers
Muchlinski P (2001) Human rights and multinationals: is there a problem? Int Aff 77(I):31–47
Muchlinski P (2011) The changing face of transnational business governance: private corporate law liability and accountability of transnational groups in a post-financial crisis world. Indiana J Glob Legal Stud 18(2):665–705
Muchlinski P (2012) Implementing the New UN corporate human rights framework: implications for corporate law, governance, and regulation. Bus Ethics Q 22:1; ISSN 1052-150X, pp. 145–177
Muchlinski P (2017) The development of human rights responsibilities for multinational enterprises. In: Sullivan R (ed) Business and human rights. Dilemmas & Solutions, New York, pp 33–51
Okutan Nilsson G (2009) Türk Ticaret Kanunu Tasarısı'na Göre Şirketler Topluluğu Hukuku (Corporate Groups Under Draft Turkish Commercial Code). XII Levha Yayıncılık, Istanbul
Okutan Nilsson G (2011) Şirketler Topluluğu (groups of companies). Bankacılar Dergisi (Bankers' Journal) 79:90–103
Okutan Nilsson G (2018) Türk Şirketler Topluluğu Hukukunun Hedefleri Bakımından İşlevsel Bir İnceleme ve Özellikle Hakim Şirketin Bilgi Alma Hakkı (A functional analysis on the targets of Turkish law on corporate groups and especially the parent company's right to obtain information). In: Okutan Nilsson G (eds) Karşılaştırmalı Şirketler Topluluğu Hukuku, 80. Yaş Gününde Prof. Dr. Ünal Tekinalp'e Saygı Konferansı (Comparative Corporate Group Law), Istanbul, pp 35–49
Petrin M, Choudhury B (2018) Group company liability. Eur Bus Org Law Rev 19:771–796
Pulaşlı H (2013) Şirketler Hukuku: Genel Esaslar. Updated 2nd edn. Ankara
Sağlam İ (1995) Tüzel Kişilik Örtüsünün Aralanması - Amerikan ve İngiliz Hukuku ile Karşılaştırmalı Olarak (Lifting the Corporate Veil – In Comparison with American and English Laws). Master's Thesis, Marmara University, Institute of Social Sciences, Civil Law, Istanbul
Sağlam İ (2020) Opinion on legal entity – sustainability Nexus. Marmara Univ Law Fac J Legal Res MÜFHD-HAD 26(2):1111–1125
Sjåfjell B (2011a) Why Law Matters: Corporate Social Irresponsibility and the Futility of Voluntary Climate Change Mitigation; Nordic & European Company Law. LSN Research Paper Series, No. 10-26
Sjåfjell B (2011b) If Not Now, When? European Company Law in a Sustainable Development Perspective. University of Oslo Faculty of Law Legal Studies Research Paper Series No. 2011-23
Sjåfjell B (2018) Redefining the corporation for a sustainable new economy. J Law Soc 45(1): 29–45

Starc-Meclejan F (2013) Groups of companies and environmental liability confronting. Perspect Bus Law J 2(1):234–246
Susuz K (2012) Şirketler Topluluğuna İlişkin Hükümlerin Uygulama Alanı Bakımından Hakim Teşebbüs Kavramı. MÜHFD-HAD 18(2):269–279
Tarman ZD (2020) İş Dünyası ve İnsan Hakları Uyuşmazlıklarında Tahkim (Arbitrating Business and Human Rights Disputes). Istanbul University Public and Private International Law Bulletin, Prof. Dr. Cemal Şanlı'ya Armağan 40(2):1535–1567
Tekinalp Ü (2013) Sermaye Ortaklıklarının Yeni Hukuku (New Law of Capital Partnerships), 3rd edn. Revised with Changes and Secondary Legislation, Istanbul
Uygun İD (2015) Şirketler Topluluğu Hukukunda Paysahipliği Haklarına Dayalı Hakimiyet (Dominance Through Shareholding Rights Under Group of Companies). Master's Thesis, Istanbul Bilgi University
van Tulder R, van Zanten JA (2018) Multinationals and the UN's Sustainable Development Goals: what do first steps reveal?. https://discovery.rsm.nl/articles/detail/351-multinationals-and-the-uns-sustainable-development-goals-what-do-first-steps-reveal/
Watson S (2015) How the company became an entity: a new understanding of corporate law. J Bus Law 2:120–141
Weber RH, Baisch R (2016) Liability of parent companies for human rights violations of subsidiaries. EBLR:669–695
Weller MP, Thomale C (2017) Menschenrechtsklagen gegen deutsche Unternehmen (Human rights lawsuits against German companies). ZGR 4:509–526
Werhane PH (2016) Corporate moral agency and the responsibility to respect human rights in the UN guiding principles: do corporations have moral rights. BHRJ 1:5–20
Woodroffe J (1999) Regulating multinational corporations in a world of nation states. In: Addo MK (ed) Human rights standards and the responsibility of transnational corporations. Kluwer Law International
Yıldırım AE (2015) Avrupa Birliği Müktesebatı ve Türk Hukuku'nda Şirketler Topluluğu (Regulations on Corporate Groups in European Union Acquis and Turkish Legislation). Master's Thesis, Istanbul
Zerk J (2014) Business and human rights: more reasons to "know and show". EnergySource 13:10–12
Zerk JA (2006) Multinationals and corporate social responsibility, limitations and opportunities in international law. Cambridge University Press

Chapter 4
Comparative Analysis of Substantive Legal Grounds for FDL

4.1 Analysis of FDL Under Tort Liability

The first pillar of the study is the analysis of FDL claims in terms of tort liability. For this purpose, focus will be firstly put on Turkish law, under which assessment will be made based on different elements of tort liability. Thereafter, English court judgments in relation to duty of care and more specifically the duty of care of the parent company will be analysed. An important Dutch court judgment will also be examined, as it successfully establishes parent company's duty of care in a Continental European jurisdiction. Finally some suggestions will be put forward for regulating parent company's liability under FDL in Turkish law.

4.1.1 Analysis of FDL in Tort Liability Under Turkish Law

A parent company's liability for the damage caused by its transnational subsidiary's actions will be analysed in this section in light of the current Turkish law provisions on tort liability (i.e. civil liability). Under Turkish law, the elements of tort liability are identified as fault, unlawful act (unlawfulness), causation and damage (Art. 49/1 TCO). In this section, FDL will be assessed in terms of each of these elements, firstly *de lege lata* and then *de lege ferenda*.

P. Kara, *Tort Liability in Multinational Corporate Groups*, Ius Gentium: Comparative Perspectives on Law and Justice 107,
https://doi.org/10.1007/978-3-031-29336-8_4

4.1.1.1 Fault

Turkish law on civil liability is based on fault.[1] In fact, as per the general principle in Article 49/1 of TCO, whoever causes damage to another through a faulty and unlawful act shall be obliged to compensate for the damage. The system based on fault is said to rest upon freedom of will, in the sense that law has dictated a consequence to any action committed by free will, which might also include faulty behaviour.[2]

While the law bases the system of civil liability on fault, it does not define this concept, leaving it instead to legal doctrine and judiciary to interpret. According to one opinion in Turkish legal doctrine, fault can be identified as a behaviour that is condemned by society, that is unlawful.[3] This opinion incorporates an ethical and moral evaluation of the individual's behaviour, which considers the element of fault to be a subjective element, while unlawfulness is considered an objective element of tort liability, which collectively results in the condemnation of the wrongdoer.[4] According to another opinion, the moral evaluation and condemnation aspects of fault should be abandoned, as liability should bear a legal assessment rather than a moral one.[5] There are several theories that have been adopted in legal doctrine which aim to interpret this concept, taking into consideration the different elements. The most well-known theories are the opinions supporting a subjective interpretation of fault and an objective one.

The subjective approach to fault focuses on the personal characteristics of the tortfeasor and assesses whether their subjective features—such as their abilities, physical and psychological condition, education and profession—justifies the commitment of the damaging act.[6] In other words, it takes as a basis any special circumstances and the state of mind of the wrongdoer. The objective approach, on the other hand, does not consider the subjective conditions of the wrongdoer, but instead focuses on a hypothetical person in the same time and place as the wrongdoer, bearing the same features, and assesses the existence of fault based on what that reasonable person would do in normal circumstances.[7] Supporters of the subjective approach assert that this theory is more appropriate for the concept of fault, while also noting that subjectivity should not be overemphasised in a way that

[1]Eren (2017), p. 540.

[2]Baysal (2019), p. 56.

[3]Eren (2017), p. 594; Karahasan (2003), p. 159. See also Widmer (2005), pp. 283–284. *Widmer* describes fault as a legal blame addressed towards the person who caused a damage acting either intentionally or negligently.

[4]Baysal (2019), p. 59.

[5]Atamer (1996), p. 31; Baysal (2019), p. 59.

[6]Antalya (2013), p. 424; Eren (2017), p. 595; Baysal (2019), pp. 60–61. Objective standard in negligence is also accepted in German law, under which the personal knowledge and abilities of the tortfeasor are not taken into account, but it is rather focused on the conduct of a typical professional (Van Dam 2007, pp. 190–191).

[7]Antalya (2013), p. 424; Eren (2017), p. 595; Baysal (2019), p. 61.

would make the establishment of fault impossible.[8] Moreover, objective theory is criticised by postulating that the failure to act in compliance with a standard behaviour cannot be considered faulty unless the person involved knew this; thus only those who knew that they should comply with the standard behaviour but have not done so can be deemed to have acted in fault.[9] In Turkish legal doctrine, the objective approach to fault is generally found to be more suitable in achieving legal certainty and equality, by moving away from engaging in a moral condemnation of the act based on the subjective qualities of the wrongdoer.[10]

The objective approach would be more appropriate for FDL cases, especially considering that every single subjective feature of the parent company could be used as an excuse to justify the damaging act. The standard in these claims should focus on what a legal entity would do acting reasonably under normal circumstances and then consider the defendant parent company's acts one by one to see how far they fall from the relevant standard. Otherwise, there is a risk that all the acts of the parent company will be deemed permissible. It is also quite unconvincing to impose a moral liability on MNCs by adopting the subjective approach to fault, and therefore, the objective approach seems more suitable in FDL claims. However, according to one view in Turkish legal doctrine, despite taking a reasonable person's behaviour as a standard, in cases where the wrongdoer has superior knowledge or ability, the reasonable person's standard will no longer apply.[11] In terms of FDL claims, this opinion might prove to be useful, as it could enhance the scope of the parent company's liability. On the other hand, it might also create confusion with the subjective theory, as it triggers a certain degree of subjectivity in the establishment of fault.

Differently from the Swiss Code of Obligations,[12] the law of reference, TCO does not stipulate different types of fault, but states that anyone who harms another through a faulty and unlawful act shall be obliged to compensate for the damage. Having said that, Turkish legal doctrine accepts the two main types of fault, which are referenced in the Swiss Code of Obligations. Intention (*dolus*), which is one of them, refers to an act that is committed willingly while desiring the unlawful result.[13] It is not necessary, however, for all damaging outcomes to be foreseen; it is sufficient

[8] Oğuzman and Öz (2013), p. 59.

[9] Nomer (2018), p. 170.

[10] Baysal (2019), p. 62. Principles of European Tort Law (PETL) also adopts the objective approach in Article 4:102(1) by setting out the factors surrounding the standard of conduct, allowing for certain subjective adjustments based on age, mental or physical disability and extraordinary circumstances in Article 4:102(2) (Koch 2009, p. 210).

[11] Eren (2017), p. 600.

[12] As per Article 41/1 of Swiss Code of Obligations, "*Any person who unlawfully causes damage to another, whether wilfully or negligently, is obliged to provide compensation.*" (Federal Act on the Amendment of the Swiss Civil Code of 30 March 1911, Part Five: The Code of Obligations, https://www.admin.ch/opc/en/classified-compilation/19110009/index.html).

[13] Antalya (2013), p. 426; Eren (2017), p. 559; Kılıçoğlu (2018), p. 415; Nomer (2018), p. 169; Oğuzman and Öz (2013), p. 55.

for the person to know that his act will cause damage.[14] The second type of fault is negligence (*culpa*), which refers to an act that is committed without knowing and wanting the unlawful consequences, yet failing to take the required precautions or acting in due care to prevent them.[15]

Intention and negligence have also been divided into sub-categories in Turkish legal doctrine. Accordingly, intention may take the form of (i) a direct intention where the damaging result is directly desired and the act is done willingly to achieve that result (*dolus directus*), and (ii) a potential or indirect intention where the damage is not directly wanted, but it is accepted and foreseen, and the damaging behaviour is nonetheless committed (*dolus eventualis*).[16] For the existence of an intention, the person who is committing the act should contemplate and desire or accept the respective unlawful result.

Negligence, on the other hand, is divided into categories according to the severity of the negligence. This sub-category is comprised of: (i) gross negligence (*culpa lata*), which is the failure to show the diligence of any reasonable person in the same circumstances, and (ii) slight negligence (*culpa levis*), which is the failure to show the diligence of an attentive and conscientious person.[17] It is important to note that this sub-categorisation has no impact on the establishment of tort liability, but merely affects the calculation of the amount of damages.[18]

In FDL claims, the parent company's tort liability would most likely occur in negligence, rather than intention. In fact, if the parent company were to instruct its subsidiary to carry out an act that would cause a human rights violation, this would be deemed an intentional act by the parent company, which would trigger its fault liability. However, what is seen to occur in most FDL cases is that the parent company fails to take action to prevent its subsidiary's human rights violations, which constitutes an omission on the parent company's side.[19] Accordingly, it would be difficult if not impossible to prove the parent company's intentions in these cases. Proving its negligence, on the other hand, seems conceivable.

---

[14] Atamer (1996), p. 31; Sanlı (2006), p. 221.

[15] Eren (2017), p. 601; Kılıçoğlu (2018), p. 415; Nomer (2018), p. 169; Oğuzman and Öz (2013), p. 56.

[16] Eren (2017), p. 600; Hatemi and Gökyayla (2017), p. 147; Oğuzman and Öz (2013), p. 55; Reisoğlu (2013), p. 172. *Baysal* also refers to a third type of intention, which is an intention where the damaging result is desired; Baysal (2019), p. 67. *Kılıçoğlu*, on the other hand, stipulates that there is one type and degree of intention; Kılıçoğlu (2018), p. 416.

[17] Hatemi and Gökyayla (2017), p. 147; Nomer (2018), p. 169; Oğuzman and Öz (2013), p. 57; Reisoğlu (2013), pp. 172–173; Baysal (2019), p. 70.

[18] According to Article 51/1 of TCO, the judge shall determine the scope of damages and payment method by taking into account the circumstances and especially the degree of fault. This provision is almost the same with Article 43/1 of Swiss Code of Obligations.

[19] van Dam (2011), p. 250. *Enneking* distinguishes in between the active and passive act as the misfeasance, which refers to when an omission is part of an activity, and nonfeasance, which is when it is not part of an activity, concluding that liability for nonfeasance imposes a greater liability on the tortfeasor's freedom of action by imposing a positive duty to act to prevent risks of damage to others (Enneking 2012, p. 238).

According to an opinion in legal doctrine, the superior knowledge and ability of the tortfeasor should be taken into account in assessing the existence of negligence, rather than taking the average reasonable person's behaviour as standard.[20] In this opinion, negligence will be deemed to exist in cases where due care has not been shown in a specific case upon consideration of the normal and reasonable behaviour of a person who lives in the same country and has the same profession.[21] It is, in fact, logical to consider the special conditions surrounding the negligent behaviour, such as the nature of the relevant work or operation, and the proficiency level of the relevant person. However, a very careful assessment should be made in order to distinguish this from the subjective approach, as it might be dangerous to depart completely from objective theory. The lack of clear criteria regarding the rules of 'showing the care of a reasonable and standard person' or 'requirement of showing additional care in activities with high risk' evidently poses a risk of arbitrary interpretation by judges, which might lead to legal uncertainty.[22] It is, therefore, crucial to create clear criteria or a method for determining and assessing the concept of care in the formation of the element of negligence.

To this end, it would be reasonable to assess whether the tortfeasor knew or ought to have known the risk pertaining to the relevant conduct and whether they could or ought to have avoided it. This approach reflects the 'reasonable person test' in objective theory (or in this case, 'reasonable corporation conduct'),[23] as opposed to the subjective one suggesting that the personal knowledge and ability of the tortfeasor to know and avoid the relevant risk should be taken into account.[24] If the parent company does detect risk—as a result of due diligence undertaken—then it will have to take measures for prevention. The seriousness of the expected harm and the likelihood of its occurrence shall be taken into account in determining the level of the expected risk, which will be assessed against the benefits of the company's conduct and the burden of preventive measures.[25]

---

[20] Eren (2017), p. 603.

[21] Antalya (2013), p. 428.

[22] Sanlı (2006), p. 229.

[23] van Dam (2011), p. 244. Within this approach, it might be considered that human rights due diligence constitutes a duty for companies as they should be aware of the risks pertaining to their group's operations and adopt measures to prevent potential harms (van Dam 2011, p. 245).

[24] Subjective theory in this sense is criticised for posing difficulties for the judge and for confusing the difference between liability and crime (Van Dam 2007, p. 219).

[25] van Dam (2011), pp. 245–246. van Dam refers to the duty to act positively to protect others from damage, regulated under Article 4:103 Principles of Tort Law (PETL), as in most cases a company's involvement in human rights violations takes place indirectly, especially through its subsidiaries (van Dam (2011), p. 246). As per this provision, a duty to act positively to protect others from damage may exist in the following circumstances: (i) if provided by law, or (ii) if the actor creates or controls a dangerous situation, or (iii) when there is a special relationship between parties or (iv) when the seriousness of the harm on the one side and the ease of avoiding the damage on the other side point towards such a duty (PETL, European Group of Tort Law (EGTL), http://www.egtl.org/petl.html).

The parent company's ownership of a majority shareholding in the subsidiary or having *de facto* control or having identical boards of directors could constitute the parent company's effective control over the subsidiary's policies and operations.[26] The parent company could be deemed to have *de facto* control over its subsidiary where it impacts the subsidiary's daily activities, or if it determines group policies on issues such as health, safety and environment and monitors compliance therewith, or if it has a right to approve or veto certain business decisions of the subsidiary, or if the subsidiary is financially dependent on the parent.[27] The assessment of each of these circumstances should be made on a case-by-case basis to determine if the parent company *de facto* controls the subsidiary. The crucial point in establishing parent company control in terms of building FDL is that the parent company's de facto control should effectively exist on the subsidiary's activities and operations that led to the relevant damage. Hence the control should relate to subsidiary's decisions, policies and/or practice concerning the relevant activities and operations that allegedly resulted in human rights abuses or environmental damages that harmed third parties. This constitutes a point of divergence between the concept of control in corporate groups and the one in FDL claims; in fact, the latter is referred to as "*de facto management of (subsidiary's) activities*" in the UKSC's recent Shell Nigeria judgment,[28] which serves to successfully distinguish these two concepts.

If we consider the given scenario in terms of the element of fault, different outcomes can be reached by making adjustments. For instance, if P has appointed health and safety advisors for S, has been actively involved in the formation of health and safety policies of S, has been in a position to know and foresee the relevant risks as it had superior knowledge of the relevant industry, and yet has failed to put in place any precautions to prevent them, then it may be concluded that P has acted in negligence. In fact, although it is hard to allege that P must have acted with a desire to attain the damaging result, P was certainly in a position to foresee it, but has failed to take any precautions. It is possible to say that potential intention and gross negligence might be quite similar to each other in practice. However, if the risk is higher, then the act might be deemed to be committed with potential intention, if it is lower with gross negligence.[29] In this case, P's liability might be based on gross or even slight negligence, which is easier to prove than intention. As previously mentioned, the degree of fault gains importance in the calculation of the amount of damages, which is left to the court's discretion. In other words, tort liability would be established regardless of the degree of fault.

On the other hand, if P has not been actively involved in the health and safety policies of its subsidiaries and more specifically, has not determined any group policy, or appointed any officers for checking compliance, or has put in place an effective monitoring mechanism, the analysis will be different. In such a case, P's

[26] van Dam (2011), p. 249.

[27] Enneking (2012), p. 236.

[28] Okpabi and others v Royal Dutch Shell Plc and another [2021] UKSC 3, para. 147.

[29] Oğuzman and Öz (2013), p. 58.

field of activity and position as parent company would be crucial. If P is involved in the same field of activity as S, namely gold mining in this scenario, has knowledge and experience of the field and is capable of foreseeing the risks pertaining to the relevant activity, then it might again be possible to speak of P's negligence, as P was in a position to recognise and prevent the risk, yet has not done so. This conclusion might appear to rely on subjective theory, which takes into account the personal capacities and superior knowledge of the tortfeasor in determining negligence. However, even though objective theory is adopted, this would also consider the typical knowledge and abilities of the group which P belongs to,[30] e.g. MNCs that operate gold mines worldwide. As suggested above, the reasonable corporation conduct test might also be applied to determine P's negligence, in which case, it shall be considered whether P's conduct (in this case failure to act) corresponds to the conduct expected by a reasonable corporation in the same circumstances and whether P has the reasonable corporation's knowledge and skills in the relevant case.[31] Accordingly, it might be possible to conclude that P has acted negligently by failing to put in place group policies or effective monitoring of its subsidiaries, and by failing to take precautions to prevent or mitigate potential risks.

In terms of substantive legal analysis of the parent company's negligence in the relevant scenario, it would also be significant to consider the impacts and risks of the use of cyanide in gold mining, which is an important activity in Turkey.[32] This study does not intend to discuss the technical aspects of using cyanide in gold mining, nor does it make any conclusive comments on the toxicity or potential harm of cyanide on the environment and consequentially on human health. The use of cyanide in gold mining has, nevertheless, become the subject of extensive analysis; this includes those discussing the detrimental effects of cyanide despite its wide use, and those focusing on the fact that it has not been legally restricted or banned under any law. The Turkish Council of State made a decision concerning the operations of a gold

---

[30] van Dam (2007), p. 191.

[31] This approach is also reflected in Article 4:102(1) of Principles of European Tort Law (PETL), which was prepared by the European Group on Tort Law as an unofficial source of comparative law: "*The required standard of conduct is that of the reasonable person in the circumstances, and depends, in particular, on the nature and value of the protected interest involved, the dangerousness of the activity, the expertise to be expected of a person carrying it on, the foreseeability of the damage, the relationship of proximity or special reliance between those involved, as well as the availability and the costs of precautionary or alternative methods*". In fact, instead of referring merely to a "*reasonable person in the (same) circumstances*", PETL has opted to state clearly the several factors of the standard of care, which will not all be sought collectively (Koch 2009, p. 208).

[32] According to the report of TEMA (Turkish Foundation for Combating Soil Erosion, for Reforestation and the Protection of Natural Habitats), on mining activities in Ida Mountains region, out of 1,697,062 hectare area, 1,294,335 hectares (76%) are subject to mining license and the relevant area is allocated to 1634 licenses. In the opinion of TEMA, the mentioned licensed mining activities will clearly destroy the ecological, cultural and economical structure of the Ida Mountains region (TEMA, Kaz Dağları Yöresi'nde Madencilik (Mining in Ida Mountains Region), (April 2020), https://www.tema.org.tr/basin-odasi/basin-bultenleri/kaz-daglari-yoresinde-madencilik-raporu).

mine in the Bergama-Ovacık district.[33] The Council of State did not discuss the technical aspects of the use of cyanide, but it decided that in view of the reports (including expert witness reports) on its environmental effects, using cyanide in the operation of a gold mine bears a potential risk and threat against the environment and human health.[34] The Council of State decided that there would be no public benefit in permitting the operation of the gold mine foreconomic reasons, knowing that it might pose risks for nature and human life. It was particularly noted in the judgment that the mere existence of trust towards the mine operator and its systems of supervision would not be enough to remove the risk probability in gold mining via the cyanide leaching method, and that priority should be given to the protection of human life and health. This decision caused concern amongst gold mines in Turkey, and finally, the Council of State issued a statement saying that its judgment did not constitute an absolute ban on the use of cyanide in gold mining and that special circumstances should be considered.[35]

The risks of cyanide exposure were also discussed by the Turkish Medical Association (TTB) in their Bergama report, whereby they contend that different levels of toxicity may occur as a result of cyanide exposure and that the long-term effects are not yet known.[36] Also TEMA (Turkish Foundation for Combating Soil Erosion, for Reforestation and the Protection of Natural Habitats) issued a report assessing the detrimental impacts and potential risks of the cyanide leaching method on the environment and on human health, where it gave examples of incidents of cyanide leakage in gold mines.[37] Having said that, this study does not set out to address any of the technical aspects of cyanide leaching. It aims, instead, to address the civil liability questions that may arise where a cyanide leakage occurs to soil and water sources.

For the purposes of this study, the important conclusion—in respect of the information given on the use of cyanide in gold mining—is that the risks and dangers of this method are acknowledged and known in the relevant industry. Therefore, any parent company that has subsidiaries operating gold mines by using cyanide should be expected to know and foresee the risks pertaining thereto. Consequently, any failure to carry out the required monitoring, impose the necessary policies and take

[33] Council of State 6th Chamber decision dated 13.05.1997 and numbered 1996/5477E., 1997/2312K.

[34] The Council of State based the judgment on the constitutional rights to life and to a healthy environment, regulated under Articles 17 and 56 of Turkish Constitution.

[35] The Council of State opinion dated 05.12.1999. For further details, see the decision of Conseil de l'Europe dated 10.10.2004 in Taşkın and others v Turkey (application no: 46117/99). In this decision, the Conseil de l'Europe decided that in continuing the use of cyanide in gold mining activities in Turkey (Bergama-Ovacık region), the right to respect for private and family life (Art. 8 ECHR) and the right to a fair trial (Art. 6 ECHR) were violated.

[36] Turkish Medical Association (TTB) – Bergama Raporu 2001, https://www.ttb.org.tr/eweb/bergama/.

[37] TEMA, Siyanür Liçi ile Altın Madenciliği (Gold Mining by the Method of Cyanide Leaching), https://cdn-tema.mncdn.com/Uploads/Cms/siyanur-lici-altin-madenciligi.pdf.

the required measures to prevent the risks would contribute to the establishment of negligence by the parent company. In fact, in certain cases, it might even be possible to speak of the intention of the parent company. For instance, if the home country legislation provides for restrictions on the use of cyanide in gold mining but the host country legislation does not, and the MNC is involved in the use of cyanide in the host country through its subsidiary without being subject to any restrictions, it might be possible to put forth that the parent company has acted with gross negligence or even with intention by engaging in these activities through its subsidiary with full knowledge of the risks. The different aspects of this example of unlawfulness will be evaluated in the following section.

Under any circumstances, the element of fault alone would not suffice for the establishment of tort liability, which should be accompanied by other elements which are discussed below.

4.1.1.2 Unlawfulness

4.1.1.2.1 General

Another compulsory element of tort liability is unlawfulness,[38] namely the commitment of an unlawful act. The concept of unlawfulness is not defined in law. The predominant opinion in legal doctrine views it as a behaviour that conflicts with mandatory legal norms that either prohibit harming others or dictate certain actions in order to prevent harm to others.[39] These legal norms might be written or unwritten, as long as they aim to protect personal rights or rights *in rem* and are mandatory.[40] In fact, the violation of non-mandatory legal norms will not, *per se*, constitute unlawfulness. The violation of the domestic laws of a foreign country would not, in principle, constitute unlawfulness; hence, any violated norm should form part of domestic law.[41]

---

[38]The term 'wrongfulness' is also used in legal doctrine as tantamount to 'unlawfulness' (e.g. for Swiss law, see Widmer 2005, p. 286). However, for the sake of consistency, the term 'unlawfulness' has been used throughout this study.

[39]Eren (2017), p. 611. This definition is also quite similar to the one written in the draft TCO, under Article 56: "Behaviours that do not comply with orders and prohibitions imposed by legal order with a purpose to protect property rights and personal rights are unlawful"; Baysal (2019), p. 90.

[40]Eren (2017), p. 611.

[41]Kılıçoğlu (2018), p. 376. *Enneking* propones, in the context of Dutch law, that the violation of directly applicable norms of public international law would lead to unlawfulness, in that, FDL claims can be based on legal norms that are applicable to parent companies in home countries, as long as the relevant norms aim to protect the interests of host country plaintiffs (see Enneking 2012, p. 230). The mentioned legal norms are those with extraterritorial scope of application. Enneking argues whether the violation of foreign law would constitute a violation of Dutch statutory law, and states that although there is no material ground to base such a claim, it might always be possible to allege violation of statutory norms under the breach of a duty of care (Enneking 2012, p. 231). This issue is further addressed in this section within scope of Turkish law.

An ‘act’ that constitutes unlawfulness involves both an active action of doing something and a passive action of not doing, namely an act of omission.[42] The establishment of unlawfulness in acts of omission requires the existence of a specific legal norm that regulates an obligation to behave in a certain manner.[43] This obligation may be a legal or a contractual one, and can be in written or unwritten form. As a matter of fact, omissions are the main type of liability in FDL claims, which mostly deal with whether a parent company owes a duty of care to third parties to prevent its subsidiary from causing harm.[44] Moreover, as per the principle of danger accepted by the Swiss Federal Court, anyone who creates a dangerous situation for someone else shall be responsible for taking the required measures to prevent any possible damage.[45]

On a further but related note, Turkish law recognises that there are certain factors that eliminate unlawfulness in torts: the consent of the victim to the damaging act; the exercise of an authority given by law; the existence of a superior private or public benefit; legitimate self-defence; defence of one’s own right by one’s own strength in cases where the authorised public authorities cannot intervene in time and the condition of necessity (Art. 63–64 TCO). However, it seems unlikely that any of these factors would be relevant in FDL claims and hence will not be reiterated hereunder.

Certain theories and opinions in legal doctrine will be considered hereunder in order to define the criteria of unlawfulness and provide a clearer interpretation of the concept within the scope of FDL claims.

---

[42] Oğuzman and Öz (2013), p. 13. This is also stated in the commentary of Principle 13 of UNGPs as “*a business enterprise’s “activities” are understood to include both actions and omissions*”; see UNGPs, https://www.ohchr.org/documents/publications/GuidingprinciplesBusinesshr_eN.pdf.

[43] Atamer (1996), p. 25; Baysal (2019), p. 87; Reisoğlu (2013), p. 176. Hatemi/Gökyayla discuss the act of omission under the element of causation. In their opinion, it is not possible to establish causation in a case where there is no active act, but only a failure to act, thus a passive act of omission (Hatemi and Gökyayla (2017), p. 120). The authors propound that tort liability in case of a passive act can be formed only if the actor has created a trust on the victim, by ensuring that it will act but it did not, or if there was a contractual or legal liability to prevent the relevant damage. The authors also distinguish between criminal aspects of passive act and tort liability. They put forward that while a passive act might lead to the formation of a crime under Article 98 of Turkish Criminal Code (concerning the obligation of aiding and notifying authorities), this is not possible for tort liability due to lack of causation, unless there is a liability due to trust (Hatemi and Gökyayla 2017, pp. 120–121, 137). However, this opinion appears to be related with the element of unlawfulness rather than causation, as the assessment on establishing tort liability based on a passive act concerns an analysis on unlawfulness. If a damage occurred due to an omission, thus if the damage could have been prevented if the tortfeasor had acted in a certain way, then there exists a causation between the relevant omission and the damage, which poses no difference than for active acts (see Koziol 2011, p. 131).

[44] van Dam (2011), p. 237.

[45] Eren (2017), p. 614.

4.1.1.2.2 Objective Unlawfulness: Subjective Unlawfulness

One of the sets of theories adopted in legal doctrine for interpreting unlawfulness concern objectiveness or subjectiveness of the concept.

According to subjective theory, all damaging acts are deemed unlawful, unless there is a norm that gives authority to engaging in the relevant act that led to damage.[46] In other words, where the damaging party has relied on a legal right in committing the relevant act, it will be deemed that there is a lawful cause and, therefore, the element of unlawfulness will not be present and no liability will arise.[47] Subjective theory is considered more favourable to the person committing the harmful act, as that person will be free to make their own evaluations within their own legal sphere and under their own authority, rather than having to consider the other party's rights and interests protected by law.[48] On the other hand, the victim might also have an advantage as in this theory the burden of proof will always rest with the person who committed the act, which is quite contradictory to the general principle of burden of proof which says that whoever claims a damage shall be liable to prove it.

As for the objective theory (also known as the normative theory), the element of unlawfulness is established where there is a damaging act and a legal norm forbidding it.[49] In other words, in this theory, the mere existence of an act that is harming others is not sufficient *per se* to constitute unlawfulness; it is necessary for that act to also violate a legal norm protecting the damaged interests.[50] In order to create unlawfulness, it would be required to violate a legal norm that is mandatory and specific to a certain behaviour.[51] Therefore, the relevant legal norm should be specifically aimed at protecting the interests that are damaged by the relevant act; *ratio legis* should be the protection of the relevant interests. These legal norms might appear as general norms that aim to protect absolute rights or as specific norms that aim to protect economic rights.[52] For the purposes of this study, the violation of absolute rights will be analysed.

To sum up, it is possible to say that in subjective theory everything is prohibited unless clearly permitted, while in objective theory everything that is not clearly prohibited is permitted.[53] The objective theory is the one predominantly adopted in Turkish legal doctrine, while the subjective theory is no longer supported. Regardless of which theory that is adopted, it might still prove difficult to identify which norms qualify as specific behavioural legal norms, whose breach could lead to

---

[46] Baysal (2019), p. 95; Kurtulan (2017), p. 468.

[47] Eren (2017), p. 609; Oğuzman and Öz (2013), p. 14.

[48] Koçyiğit (2016), p. 264; Çağlayan Aksoy (2016), p. 218.

[49] Eren (2017), p. 610; Oğuzman and Öz (2013), p. 14; Kurtulan (2017), p. 470.

[50] Antalya (2013), p. 432; Baysal (2019), p. 96.

[51] Sanlı (2006), p. 465.

[52] Çağlayan Aksoy (2016), p. 161.

[53] Baysal (2019), p. 97.

unlawfulness. For this purpose, a clarification is presented in legal doctrine concerning the different types of rights and the establishment of unlawfulness.

4.1.1.2.3 Theories of Unlawfulness in Behaviour and Unlawfulness in Result

A categorisation is acknowledged in respect of rights violated and establishment of unlawfulness, which consists of unlawfulness in behaviour and unlawfulness in result. The theory of unlawfulness in behaviour asserts that unlawfulness lies in human behaviour and therefore the assessment of unlawfulness should be focused on the behaviour of the person, rather than the damaging result.[54] Conversely, the theory of unlawfulness in result postulates that any violation of a third party's absolute right is, in itself, unlawful and the unlawfulness in behaviour can only be determined *ex post.*[55]

Unlawfulness in result is generally accepted for the violation of absolute rights. In Turkish legal doctrine, absolute rights are defined as *erga omnes* rights, that can be ascribed to anyone independently from any legal relationship.[56] It is acknowledged that personal rights (i.e. right to life and physical integrity, right to health as material personal rights, freedoms, honour, name etc. as moral personal rights), rights *in rem* (e.g. property rights, mortgage rights) and intellectual property rights (e.g. copyright, patent right) are absolute rights.[57] In these cases, any behaviour resulting in the violation of an absolute right shall be deemed unlawful, regardless of whether such behaviour contravenes a legal norm.[58]

On the other hand, any behaviour that results in damaging rights other than absolute rights requires a violation of a specific protective legal norm intended to protect the relevant interests.[59] These protective legal norms could be under public or civil law, written or unwritten, provided that they address an order or a prohibition; there is a sanction for their breach; they aim to protect not only general public interest but specifically the relevant tort victim's interest; and that they aim to prevent the damage incurred by the relevant act.[60] Ricochet damage, which occurs as a consequence of the aforesaid damage, is also considered under the theory of unlawfulness of behaviour. Where there is no legal protective norm forbidding the

[54] Eren (2017), p. 620.

[55] Eren (2017), p. 621.

[56] Çağlayan Aksoy (2016), p. 163.

[57] Kılıçoğlu (2018), p. 374.

[58] Baysal (2019), p. 97; Kurtulan (2017), p. 472.

[59] Kurtulan (2017), p. 473. PETL refers to "*the protective purpose of the rule that has been violated*" as a determining factor in establishling causation between the conduct and the damage occurred (Art. 3:201(e)).

[60] Çağlayan Aksoy (2016), pp. 176–178.

specific behaviour that resulted in the ricochet damage, tort liability will not be established.[61]

There is also a third opinion in legal doctrine, which brings together these two theories. According to this opinion, if an absolute right is violated, unlawfulness in the result would be sufficient to establish unlawfulness.[62] Therefore, unlike in violations of other rights, in cases of violation of absolute rights, there would be no need to assess whether the relevant legal norm aimed to protect the damaged interests.[63] An example given by *Baysal* on this issue is self-explanatory: If a bodily injury occurred because of an act falling within the scope of liability for dangerous activities (Art. 71 TCO), the unlawfulness would be deemed established, regardless of whether the damaging act was directed to such a result.[64] In fact, liability for dangerous activities is a form of strict liability. It is reasonable to suggest that in strict liability cases there are no acts contravening a specific legal norm, and therefore, it would not be possible to speak of unlawfulness in behaviour, as the more adequate approach would be to adopt unlawfulness in the result.[65]

Absolute rights are already protected by basic legal norms both under civil law and criminal law,[66] and therefore their violation would already result in a breach of the relevant norm, leading to unlawfulness in the behaviour as well as in the result. This reasoning led to the formation of a theory of unlawfulness in behaviour for the violation of absolute rights. According to the supporters of this theory, absolute rights are protected by basic protective legal norms, which demonstrates that unlawfulness in result is not *per se* sufficient to attain unlawfulness in case of violation of these rights.[67] Of course, the acceptance of this theory also leads to the theory of the protection scope of the violated norm in violations of absolute rights. Hence, in this case as well, it would be necessary to make an assessment of whether the violated interest and the relevant victim fall within the scope of protection of the violated norm that concerns an absolute right.[68] Although this theory might appear to reduce the importance given to the violation of absolute rights by the theory of unlawfulness in result, it also seems more logical and closer to reality. In any case, it might be said that supporting this theory for the violation of absolute rights would not give rise to any groundbreaking results for FDL claims, which would in any case be grounded upon the breach of duty of care and thus require assessment under the theory of the protection scope of the violated norm.

---

[61] Baysal (2019), p. 98; Nomer (2018), p. 154.

[62] Oğuzman and Öz (2013), p. 15.

[63] Sanlı (2006), p. 467.

[64] Baysal (2019), p. 101.

[65] Kurtulan (2017), p. 476.

[66] Çağlayan Aksoy (2016), p. 312. Legal norms that concern absolute rights aim to protect only the owners of such rights; Koçyiğit (2016), p. 276.

[67] Antalya (2013), p. 438; Çağlayan Aksoy (2016), p. 168.

[68] Çağlayan Aksoy (2016), p. 169.

In the event that rights other than absolute rights have been violated (e.g. pure economic loss), then the damaging act should also be unlawful, thus there should be a legal norm forbidding it. In this case, it would have to be assessed whether the relevant damage falls within the protection scope of the violated legal norm.[69] The same applies also to any ricochet damage that constitutes pure economic loss.[70] More specifically, in order to constitute unlawfulness, the damaging act should be committed against persons who are protected by the violated legal norm; the relevant violation must relate to the legal interests protected therein; the damage should have resulted from a prohibited act; and the conflicting interests and values of the victim should also be evaluated.[71] Hence the mere existence of a protective legal norm would not, in itself, be sufficient in the establishment of unlawfulness.[72] If it is determined that the relevant legal norm protects a right other than the violated one, then the element of unlawfulness would not be established. This is called the 'theory of the protection scope of the violated norm' or the 'link of unlawfulness'.

4.1.1.2.4 Liability Within the Scope of the Principle of Danger

There is also a theory in legal doctrine suggesting a general behavioural liability for cases where a dangerous situation is created. Accordingly, if a person creates a dangerous situation that might potentially harm others, then that person shall be liable to take the required measures to prevent such harm.[73] In the event that this person fails to take the required measures and an absolute right of a third person is then violated, then the principle of danger might constitute a grounds for imposing a general behavioural obligation on the person who committed the act.

In order to incur this liability, the aforementioned person who has omitted to act in a certain case would be conducting an operation that potentially creates danger and would have failed to take measures to prevent it. For instance, a gold mine operator who is using cyanide to search gold might be deemed to be obliged to foresee the risk of cyanide leaking into the soil and to take measures to prevent this danger. Although not regulated by law, this liability is deemed to arise as a general behavioural liability and might lead to the establishment of tort liability depending on other elements. Engaging in operations with dangerous materials is also

[69] Eren (2017), p. 620; Oğuzman and Öz (2013), p. 18.

[70] Koçyiğit (2016), p. 269. Having said that, pure economic loss is not covered by the scope of this study, as hereunder it is focused on corporate liability for human rights abuses only, which mostly concern absolute rights. Therefore, no detailed analysis will be given herein concerning pure economic loss.

[71] Atamer (1996), p. 105; Sanlı (2006), p. 466; Kurtulan (2017), p. 481.

[72] Özçelik (2016), p. 428.

[73] Karahasan (2003), p. 113; Sanlı (2006), p. 471; Çağlayan Aksoy (2016), p. 193.

considered an activity that requires measures to be taken to prevent any potential damage to third parties.[74]

This is especially the case in indirect violations of absolute rights or violations by way of omission, which require an assessment under the theory of unlawfulness in behaviour.[75] Thus, if an absolute right is violated by an indirect violation or by an omission due to the failure to prevent the danger created by a person, the victim can rely on the principle of danger to request compensation. Where it is not clear whether the violation of the absolute right has been direct or indirect, it would be prudent to check if there is a general security measure that could be taken as a grounds for justifying the relevant unlawfulness.[76]

The principle of danger might serve as a suitable basis for a successful FDL claim. At this point, the discussion will focus on whether P's failure to take measures regarding S's activities and P's failure to monitor and supervise S could be deemed to create a dangerous situation that could harm third parties. No specific written legal norm regulates this liability, hence it would be down to the judge's discretion to interpret this aspect. The judge will assess whether the victim has a just expectation of protection from the relevant danger and whether the tortfeasor is able to control the relevant danger.[77] Hence, in this case, the question to be considered is whether the victims had any trust in P's ability to protect them from any potential danger arising from S's operations. It should also be assessed whether P was actually in a position to actively prevent the occurring danger, in other words—if they had any kind of control over the dangerous situation. It is, however, important to note that these criteria should be established carefully by taking legal certainty into account. Therefore, the third opinion on unlawfulness, which concerns the duty of care, is worth exploring in respect of FDL.

4.1.1.2.5 Theory of the Duty of Care

There is a third theory concerning unlawfulness, which states that no distinction is required between the infringement of absolute rights and other rights in terms of unlawfulness. Instead, unlawfulness lies in the violation of a general behavioural obligation, which seems very similar to the duty of care in Common Law.[78] For this reason, this is also referred to as the 'theory of the duty of care'.

Turkish law provisions on general fault liability (Art. 49 et seq TCO) do not comprise any general obligation to act with reasonable care, as they only refer to an

[74] Karahasan (2003), p. 113.
[75] Atamer (1996), p. 35; Çağlayan Aksoy (2016), pp. 196–197.
[76] Atamer (1996), p. 37.
[77] Atamer (1996), pp. 76–78.
[78] Kurtulan (2017), pp. 477–478.

act by intention or negligence, as further explained above on the element of fault.[79] Hence, in principle, Turkish law recognises no duty of care to act in a certain manner to prevent potential damage on third parties.[80] Therefore, if the damage suffered by a third party occurred only due to the inaction of a person, then liability will not arise. Such a liability can only arise if there is a duty to prevent damage on third parties imposed on the relevant person by law.[81]

Sanlı highlights the importance of this theory referring to the kind of scenario where damage occurs due to the failure to act of a second person, which is not the person who has directly caused the damage. The author contends that the liability of the second person would be linked to the duty of care, which concerns the element of unlawfulness in tort liability.[82] In other words, this case involves a relationship between three parties: (i) the person who has committed the act that resulted in the direct damage, (ii) the victim who suffered the damage, and (iii) the person who has failed to act to prevent the damaging act from taking place, despite their knowledge and ability to act. Considering that FDL claims are also comprised of three parties (i.e. subsidiary, victim and parent company), the theory of the duty of care might be a viable legal basis for establishing the parent company's liability.

No distinction is made under the theory of the duty of care between different types of rights and violations to establish the element of unlawfulness, but rather this theory adopts a holistic approach focusing on the breach of a general behavioural obligation.[83] Even if there has been a violation of an absolute right, breach of duty of care will be sought under the given criteria. In other words, in this case, the mere existence of unlawfulness in result will not be deemed sufficient to establish unlawfulness. If the person in question has shown the expected duty of care but the damage has still occurred, then there will be no liability in tort as the element of fault will not be present. This aspect of the theory is similar to unlawfulness in behaviour. Having said that, it has been criticised for blurring the distinctions between the elements of fault and unlawfulness, considering that tort liability will not be established due to lack of fault if the person in question has shown the required duty of care.[84]

---

[79] In German law, for instance, a general obligation to act with reasonable care is regulated under Section 276(2) of German Civil Code (BGB), which stipulates that "*a person acts negligently if he fails to exercise reasonable care*". This is a general provision which is set to apply to all private law issues (Rühmkorf and Walker 2018, p. 13). On the flip side of the coin, the German legal concept of *Sorgfaltspflicht* (obligation of diligence decided case-by-case) also means that the person who caused the damage shall not be held liable if he/she acted with reasonable care (Rühmkorf and Walker 2018, pp. 13–14).

[80] Sanlı (2006), p. 470.

[81] Sanlı (2006), p. 470.

[82] Sanlı (2006), p. 473.

[83] Baysal (2019), p. 102.

[84] Kurtulan (2017), p. 479. It is, in fact, possible to state that breach of duty of care analysis is relevant both in terms of fault and unlawfulness. Therefore, its breach would also lead to the formation of fault and unlawfulness at the same time (Çağlayan Aksoy 2016, p. 232).

Requiring the existence of a specific legal norm to create unlawfulness in duty of care might be deemed to be in line with having the same requirement for omissions. In fact, it is widely accepted that there is no general duty to act in order to prevent others from impending harm.[85] According to one opinion that finds the theory of unlawfulness in result insufficient, in cases of violation by omission, there should be a specific legal norm requiring a person to act in a certain situation; the theory of unlawfulness in behaviour should therefore be adopted.[86] This would also apply to violation of absolute rights, where it would be necessary to demonstrate—in addition to the damaging outcome—that a specific legal norm protecting the victim from the relevant harm had in fact been violated.[87] A breach of a duty of care also mostly occurs as an omission. Therefore, it is also important to determine whether unlawfulness in behaviour, rather than unlawfulness in result, should be sought in cases of an indirect violation of rights. This debate is essential specifically to indirect violations of absolute rights. In *Atamer*'s opinion, in order to create unlawfulness in an indirect violation of absolute rights, a case of danger must exist, which would potentially violate the relevant absolute right, and there should be a legal norm imposing a duty of care on the defendant.[88]

There are several tests and criteria that have been proposed for the establishment of the duty of care and its breach in legal theory. According to an objective approach suggested under German law, a three-fold test shall be made for the evaluation of duty of care: (i) whether there is an objective duty of care violation, by considering reasonable standard behaviour, (ii) if a violation is detected, then whether the violating act can be attributed to the relevant person, by assessing if they had the required abilities to prevent the damage, and (iii) whether there was a cause justifying the relevant unlawfulness, being relied upon by the tortfeasor.[89] Accordingly, an objective protection and a type of duty of care is introduced, the breach of which may cause a damage that can be compensated for.[90] This test alone might not be sufficient to determine the parent company's liability for the damages incurred by the subsidiary's host country activities, as the test provides a framework but does not set any substantive criteria for assessing the breach of the duty of care.

Enneking, who analyses FDL under Dutch tort law, refers to four criteria in assessing whether the parent company has exercised sufficient care in the group's host country activities: (i) probability of the risk, (ii) seriousness of the damage, (iii)

---

[85] Koziol (2011), p. 131.

[86] Baysal (2019), p. 98. Koziol also points out to the need for a breach of duty (and, in fact, a duty of care) in order to establish liability in case of omissions (Koziol 2011, pp. 129–130).

[87] Çağlayan Aksoy (2016), p. 165.

[88] Atamer (1996), p. 14, 76 et seq.

[89] Çağlayan Aksoy (2016), pp. 228–229.

[90] Özçelik (2016), p. 433. There is also a theory that proposes a more subjective interpretation on the duty of care, which focuses on subjective conditions of the relevant event and the tortfeasor and suggests that duty of care be determined specifically case-by-case, especially for cases that create frequent damages (see Çağlayan Aksoy 2016, pp. 241–242). Based on its subjective focus, this theory appears to be closer to duty of care in Common Law.

character and benefit of the activities that allegedly led to the damage, and (iv) the burden of taking precautionary measures.[91] This fourth criterion refers to the existence of a burden on the parent company to act in a certain manner in order to prevent or mitigate potential damages pertaining to host country activities. This point is linked to the need to introduce a duty of care for the parent company in statutory law. Hence, it is crucial to have the duty of care regulated in statutory law in order to be able to impose a liability on the parent company for the respective breach. The remaining criteria serve to make substantive assessments in the establishment of the breach of duty of care. In terms of the first criterion, the probability of the materialisation of the relevant risk shall determine the standard of care that is expected from a parent company: the higher the probability of the risk, the higher will be the standard of care. The same is also applicable to the second criterion concerning the seriousness of the potential or materialised damage. The standard of care for the parent company would be higher where the relevant damage is serious, in that it would have a mass impact which would not be easy to recover from. The third criterion serves as a balancing element between the risk and damage pertaining to the relevant activities and the benefits expected by those activities. It appears to potentially create an advantage for parent companies in that their subsidiary's host country activities might have created significant benefits for the host country and therefore should not be deemed unlawful. This is a dangerous possibility for FDL claims, especially considering that host countries are usually developing countries in need of foreign investment, and this criterion might be used by parent companies to rebut plaintiffs' claims.

In the event that there is no specific legal norm imposing a certain obligation to act on the parent company, it might still be possible that there is a special pre-existing relationship between the parent company and the third party claimants. This might be the case when the parent company is involved in the subsidiary's activities at a certain level, so as to create a type of relationship with the involuntary creditors harmed by its subsidiary's activities. For instance, being involved in the design, management or operation of the buildings or equipment that created the relevant risk (e.g. factory, oil pipelines etc.) might be deemed to indicate the existence of this special pre-existing relationship.[92] As the last option, even in cases where there is no such special relationship between FDL claimants and the parent company, the parent company's liability might be tried based on the great danger posed by the subsidiary's operations, of which the parent company is informed – provided that this is limited to cases where there is a tangible threat of severe damage and the parent company has sufficient expertise and knowledge to put it in a better position to prevent the risk of damage compared to the potential victims.[93] Although these

[91] Enneking (2012), p. 233. Although Enneking refers to the mentioned criteria to determine the standard of care for parent company in FDL claims, it is noted that the relevant criteria is set for the element of wrongfulness (i.e. unlawfulness) under Dutch law (see Enneking 2012, p. 233, fn. 131).

[92] Enneking (2012), p. 239.

[93] Enneking (2012), p. 239.

options of special pre-existing relationship and/or situation of great danger might be employed to impose a duty of care on the parent company, it is still more advisable to have a special statutory norm regulating this liability in order to establish the element of unlawfulness in FDL claims.

Another example case scenario to discuss unlawfulness might be where the use of cyanide is restricted in the home country while being permitted without any restrictions in the host country. In such a case, the subsidiary's activities that caused the relevant damage (e.g. deterioration of health) would not be deemed unlawful, as there is no statutory law in the host country that would restrict these activities. However, the use of cyanide in the subsidiary's gold mining activities could still be deemed unlawful based on unlawfulness in result—i.e. violation of physical integrity and health, which is an absolute right. In fact, as discussed under the element of fault, in such a case the parent company would know the risks and effects of the use of cyanide on human health and the environment, given that this activity is restricted in the home country, and yet it chose to engage in the said activity in the host country where the laws permit it.

4.1.1.2.6 Interim Conclusion on Unlawfulness

In view of these theories and opinions, it is possible to draw a few conclusions from the previously given scenario, which involves different types of claims and different kinds of violations.

As most FDL claims focus on an alleged omission by the parent company to effectively monitor and supervise its transnational subsidiary, the position of omission in unlawfulness is important. As per the discussions held in Turkish legal doctrine, which are evaluated in the section above, in order to be able to deem an omission unlawful, there should either be a mandatory legal norm requiring an active act or there should be a situation of danger created by the parent company who failed to take measures to prevent harm to others. For liability arising from the duty of care, it is further required to have a mandatory legal norm, as unlawfulness in behaviour is accepted. Hence, as an important remark for the purposes of this study, unlawfulness in behaviour is more adequate for FDL claims, especially to construe the element of unlawfulness for omissions that are often the case in FDL and to establish the duty of care for the parent company.

The aforesaid legal norm should specifically identify the scope of protection, namely: (i) whose interests are protected, (ii) which interests are protected, and (iii) the type of violation that is thereby prevented. In the absence of such a norm, which is the current situation under Turkish law, the judge will have the discretion to make case-by-case evaluations.

The types of claims that are considered within this scope are as follows:

- **People living in the surrounding areas, who have been affected by the cyanide leaked into the soil and waters, and who claim that their physical integrity was violated, and that both S and P should have responsibility.**

Protection of physical integrity is an absolute right, under the category of material personal rights. Accordingly, as per the theory of unlawfulness in the result, the mere violation of absolute rights should *per se* suffice to the establishment of unlawfulness, with no need for a legal norm forbidding the relevant behaviour. However, at this point, it is important to distinguish between the acts of S and P that led to the damage. In the case of S, their operations involved the use of cyanide, which leaked into the soil and water, and caused the violation of third parties' absolute rights. Therefore, unlawfulness is established and, subject to the assessment of the other elements forming tort liability, S's tort liability might be successfully claimed.

As for P's role in this scenario, their involvement in the violation of absolute rights is their failure to take measures to prevent the foreseeable damage due to S's operations. In this case, the assessment should be made in consideration of duty of care, to see whether P actually had a duty of care towards the people living in the surrounding areas, and if so, whether they had breached it. In the case of duty of care, merely the violation of an absolute right would not be sufficient to establish unlawfulness, but it is necessary to breach a certain legal norm, either in statutory law or in case law, whichever is relevant. If there is such a legal norm, this should be interpreted under the theory of the protection scope of the violated norm to determine who and which interests are protected by the relevant norm, and against which actions. Therefore, in the absence of such a legal norm conferring on P a duty of care, unlawfulness and consequently P's tort liability will not be established. It is worth noting that under current Turkish law there is no such legal norm imposing a duty of care on the parent company against third parties affected by the operations of its subsidiary.

Another potential grounds for P's liability is the principle of danger. It is disputed in legal doctrine whether this principle should be written in statutory laws or not. As the failure to adopt measures to prevent harm to others (thus, a passive act) leads to unlawfulness, it would be more adequate to have this principle regulated in statutory law, to be in line with the theory of unlawfulness in behaviour, which is accepted for passive acts. For instance, if P knew the serious risks of cyanide leaching and yet failed to take any measures to prevent potential risks, with the high probability of this materialising, it might be argued that P has acted in breach of their duty of care. However, such an argument would be groundless if there is no statutory norm regulating such duty of care, or in this case, burden to take preventive measures.

There is a voluntary industry programme concerning the use of cyanide in gold and silver mining, which aims to create a standardised compliance mechanism in the sector within the scope of the 'International Cyanide Management Code For the Manufacture, Transport, and Use of Cyanide In the Production of Gold' ('Cyanide Code') developed by a multi-stakeholder steering committee under the guidance of the United Nations Environmental Program (UNEP) and the International Council on Metals and the Environment (ICME) at the time.[94] As mentioned, signing and

[94] International Cyanide Management Code for the Gold Mining Industry, About the Cyanide Code, https://www.cyanidecode.org/about-cyanide-code.

complying with the standards set out in the Cyanide Code is voluntary. The Cyanide Code sets basic standards for the use of cyanide, including the processes of transport and production, a monitoring mechanism checking compliance of the signatory companies, an auditing and certification mechanism, and a dispute resolution mechanism for the settlement of disputes arising in connection to the Cyanide Code.[95] However, the dispute resolution mechanism does not seem fit to accommodate FDL claims as it only addresses disputes arising from auditing and certification issues.

Nevertheless, the Cyanide Code might contribute to the evaluation of the element of unlawfulness in the parent company's alleged tort. If we assume that the parent company P is a signatory to the Cyanide Code, while the subsidiary S is not, and if P has been complying with the standards set out in the Cyanide Code while the operations of S mostly go against these standards, then P's omission in ensuring compliance with the same standards in the group's operations worldwide might be deemed unlawful. In fact, P, with their superior knowledge and experience of the relevant sector, would then be ignoring the standards adopted in S's operations that fall below the standards set by the Cyanide Code. This omission might be deemed a breach of the duty of care of the parent company P against the victims of the operations of S. On the other hand, if P were to ensure that the operations of S were in line with the standards set out in the Cyanide Code, even though S is not a signatory thereto, this would be seen as proof that P has been exercising the required due care as the parent company, and that the damage would have occurred despite P's efforts to prevent the risks. Therefore, in such a case, P could have had the required grounds to rebut the claims of breach of duty of care, as the damage would not be attributable to P, considering that despite its efforts it was not able to prevent the damage.

- **Employees of S who have suffered illnesses claim that their physical integrity was violated, for which S and P should have responsibility.**

For this claim, the element of unlawfulness in the claim brought towards P would again relate to duty of care. Accordingly, where P had a duty of care towards the employees of S and if they had breached such duty of care by not monitoring and supervising the health and safety policies of S, then the element of unlawfulness could be established in the relevant case. However, it is necessary to have a legal norm imposing such duty of care on P. In other words, the unlawfulness of the behaviour is required in respect of the duty of care.

The evaluations made above on the Cyanide Code for claims by people living in the surrounding areas are also valid for the claims of the employees of S.

- **Families of the employees who died due to illness claim compensation from S and P for the loss of support previously provided to them by these employees.**

[95]The dispute resolution mechanism aims to address disputes regarding auditor credentials, audit findings and certification issues, and it consists of an informal diolague, a mediation and finally a binding arbitration process (International Cyanide Management Code for the Gold Mining Industry, Dispute Resolution, https://www.cyanidecode.org/about-cyanide-code/dispute-resolution).

Article 53/3 of TCO regulates the compensation rights of those who have become deprived of the support of the deceased. Where the families of the deceased workers received regular, continuous and gratuitous support from the deceased, they would then qualify to request this compensation.[96] Accordingly, S's liability in tort might be established. It is worth noting that this type of damage is considered ricochet damage,[97] which is a secondary damage that arises due to the damage suffered directly by the tort victim, for which the tort liability should also be established.

In order to establish the element of unlawfulness in the claim against P, it would be required to determine a legal norm regulating this interest, as the claims of families of the deceased do not concern violations of absolute rights, but pure economic loss. It would be reasonable to consider that S, as the employer of the deceased, would be liable for the said damages sought by the families of the deceased employees. It is possible to have joint and several liability in terms of the compensation for support of loss.[98] However, the assessment of the duty of care of P might also be relevant to the purposes of this claim, to consider if P might also have a liability. Again, under the current Turkish law, there is no legal norm imposing such a duty of care on a parent company towards third parties harmed by the operations of its subsidiaries. It is worth noting that Turkish law does not recognise compensation of pure economic losses, unless they are protected by a specific legal norm, such as Article 53/3 of TCO. Therefore, it might be quite difficult for the families to establish a successful claim for compensation towards P in this case.

As an interim conclusion on unlawfulness, it seems that there is a pressing need to introduce a specific legal norm in Turkish law in order to invoke parent company liability for damages perpetrated by third parties due to the operations of its subsidiaries. The most viable form of this liability appears to be the duty of care, which has had an important role in Common Law jurisdictions. In order to establish unlawfulness in the violation of the duty of care, it would be necessary to have a

---

[96] It is, in fact, not a mandatory condition to be a family member or a close relative of the diseased in order to qualify for compensation under Article 53/3 of TCO, as long as the sought conditions are fulfilled; Çağlayan Aksoy (2016), pp. 313–315. It is also suggested in legal doctrine that generally close family members, those who live in the same house (regardless whether they have a familial link) and those who have been receiving regular support from the diseased (e.g. students receiving scholarship) will be deemed to fall within this scope; Çelik (2016), p. 16. Not only those who have lost support, but also those are deprived of the potential hypothetical support that they would most probably receive in future are also allowed to request for this compensation (such as parents of a child, a couple engaged to be married); Gökyayla (2014), p. 71.

[97] As per the dominant opinion in Turkish law, ricochet damage cannot be subject to compensation, the only exception being Article 53/3 of TCO. Having said that, according to *Çağlayan Aksoy*'s opinion, this is only an a contrario interpretation of Article 53/3 of TCO and there is, in fact, no specific provision in law stipulating that ricochet damage cannot be compensated (Çağlayan Aksoy 2016, p. 312). Therefore, this opinion suggests that as long as there is a special protective legal norm attributed to protecting the tort victim, pure economic losses that fall within scope of protection of such norm can be compensated (Çağlayan Aksoy 2016, p. 312).

[98] Gökyayla (2014), p. 82.

specific legal norm in statutory law, especially considering that Turkish law is not a case law regime.

4.1.1.3 Causation

Tort liability can arise only in cases where a causal connection exists between the tortious act and the damage. In other words, the damage should have arisen as a consequence of the respective unlawful act.[99] Therefore, causation is one of the mandatory elements of tort liability, in the absence of which no liability can be established.[100]

There are several theories in legal doctrine concerning causation in tort liability. As per the theory of natural causation, each event is a result of another one, and it is based on a logical approach in this sense.[101] However, it is not reasonable to impose liability on the tortfeasor for all the damages incurred by the committed act; in other words, a certain limitation should be accepted in establishing the aforementioned liability by assessing whether the act in question was capable of causing the relevant damage. The theory of equivalence of conditions sets forth that causation shall exist in cases where the relevant event constitutes a *conditio sine qua non* for the occurrence of the said damage.[102] Finally, according to the theory of adequate causation, which is mostly supported in Continental European and in Swiss-Turkish legal doctrine,[103] an act that is capable of causing the relevant damage in the normal course of events and life experience will be deemed to establish the causal connection.[104] This act should be capable of facilitating and increasing the occurrence of the damaging result in a general and objective way.[105] In this manner, the scope of liability is limited to those that are foreseeable in the course of normal life.[106] There are some theories that have been adopted in legal doctrine to further explain the application of the theory of adequate causation.

---

[99] Reisoğlu (2013), p. 175.

[100] Baysal (2019), p. 192; Eren (2017), p. 561; Oğuzman and Öz (2013), p. 44. Causation also serves to determine the scope of the damage. Hence, liability shall cover the extent of damage that has occurred as a result of the relevant unlawful act (Baysal 2019, p. 193).

[101] Baysal (2019), p. 194.

[102] Baysal (2019), p. 195; Eren (2017), pp. 563–564; Oğuzman and Öz (2013), p. 44; Koşar (2019), p. 118. This test refers to a condition without which the damage would not have occurred, which is called as "but for" test in Anglo-American system (van Dam (2007), pp. 268–269). The theory of equivalence of conditions is criticised for unreasonably extending the scope of liability, as it serves to delimit the liability only by way of degree of fault of the tortfeasor (Baysal 2019, p. 197).

[103] Baysal (2019), p. 198; Eren (2017), p. 565.

[104] Atamer (1996), p. 33; Eren (2017), p. 565; Kılıçoğlu (2018), p. 407; Koşar (2019), p. 118; Nomer (2018), p. 166; Oğuzman and Öz (2013), p. 45.

[105] Atamer (1996), p. 41.

[106] Eren (2017), p. 566; see also Turkish Court of Appeal General Assembly of Civil Chambers decision dated 22.11.2018 and numbered E.2017/115 K.2018/1756.

Atamer, who considers the theory of adequate causation to be a cause for limitation of tort liability, identifies a point of convergence between these theories, which is to accept no liability for behaviours that are not *conditio sine qua non* for the occurrence of the damaging outcome.[107] Therefore, in order to impose a liability for damage caused by tort, it is necessary that the relevant act has been the effective cause of the aforesaid damage. This may, in fact, be considered a focal point of tort liability. It is worth noting that causation is affected by the type of damage caused, as it is more easily established in cases of personal injury or death compared with pure economic losses.[108]

As per the objective *ex post* theory, the issues that are specific to the case, regardless of whether these can be foreseen by the tortfeasor or a third party or whether they were actually present at the time of the act, shall also be taken into account.[109] For instance, in the case of a sudden death of someone—living in the vicinities of the gold mine—due to cyanide exposure having triggered his heart disease, the tort liability will be assessed by taking into account the specific case of a person with heart disease, instead of just a regular healthy person, and might lead to the establishment of causation. In this case, the fact that the deceased person had a heart condition would not affect the establishment of liability, but it may lead to a

[107] Atamer (1996), p. 42. PETL also adopts the *conditio sine qua non* test for establishing causation, which requires the existence of certain factors (Art. 3:201): "*a) The foreseeability of the damage to a reasonable person at the time of the activity, taking into account the closeness in time or space between the damaging activity and its consequence, or the magnitude of the damage in relation to the normal consequences of such an activity; b) the nature and the value of the protected interest; c) the basis of liability; d) the extent of the ordinary risks of life; and e) the protective purpose of the rule that has been violated.*" See also Magnus (2014), p. 235. A similar approach is adopted in Dutch tort law, which applies a two-stage causation test: (i) conditio sine qua non test, to see whether the relevant act has contributed to the materialization of the damage (no exclusivity is sought), and (ii)legal causation test, to see the extent of damage that can be imputed on the tortfeasor, by using factors of foreseeability, remoteness, as well as the degree of fault of the tortfeasor (Enneking 2012, pp. 241–242).

[108] van Dam (2007), p. 268, 270. Climate change litigation, concerning claims for compensation arising from losses incurred due to the alleged participation of companies in climate change, holds a peculiar position in terms of causation. In Lliuya v RWE, a Peruvian farmer sued the German energy company RWE claiming compensation to cover the restitution costs to mitigate the risks of flood in his village posed by the melting glacier due to the climate change (Landgericht Essen (Az. 2 O 285/15) (16.12.2016)). The compensation amount requested by the claimant is pro rata to RWE's share in total greenhouse gas emissions (0.47%). The German court of first instance rejected the lawsuit on the lack of certainty of the claim and the lack of causation between the alleged damage and RWE's activities. The claimant has appealed the decision and German Appeal Court has decided to hear the case, which is currently pending. Although not decided upon, the case is important in the sense that the court accepted at least a potential liability of a company due to the negative consequences of climate change (Luciano Lliuya v. RWE AG, Climate Change Litigation, http://climatecasechart.com/non-us-case/lliuya-v-rwe-ag/). Also see Choudhury and Petrin (2019), p. 262; Hösli and Weber (2020), jusletter.weblaw.ch, p. 11 et seq.

[109] Nomer (2018), p. 167; Atamer (1996), p. 53; Baysal (2019), p. 200. Accordingly, no liability will incur in case of a damage occurred accidentally due to several extraordinary events that could not have been objectively foreseen by anyone (Eren (2017), p. 567).

decrease in compensation.[110] Furthermore, the tortfeasor will also be liable for all consequential events that are expected in the normal course of life or that are specifically facilitated by the tortfeasor's act.[111] This is the theory that is predominantly accepted in Swiss-Turkish legal doctrine.[112] The subjective *ex ante* theory, on the other hand, considers only the conditions that the tortfeasor knew or ought to have known at the time of committing the act.[113] According to this theory, the example given would have a different outcome. It would be considered whether the tortfeasor was in any position to know that the victim had a heart condition, thus making an *ex ante* assessment. If the answer to this question is negative, then liability might not arise due to the lack of adequate causation. A third theory was put forward, the objective *ex ante* theory, which considers the conditions that would be foreseen by an 'ideal' person—in other words, someone who has the utmost ability to comprehend the aforementioned condition and any other conditions that are known to the tortfeasor at the time of the occurrence.[114] This theory creates a middle ground between the subjective *ex ante* and objective *ex post* theories. In fact, in this theory, *ex post* conditions would not be considered, while the subjective assessment—based on the knowledge of the tortfeasor—would be objectivised in a way, by taking into account the knowledge of an 'ideal' person.

Baysal highlights, most accurately, the requirement that the assessment of adequate causation should be made based on an objective approach. According to the author, the subjective approach that takes into account the tortfeasor's position on the foreseeability of the damage would bring causation closer to the element of fault, as the assessment on foreseeability is actually part of the analysis on fault.[115] Hence, the analysis of adequate causation should be based on the objective approach, whereby causation would be established in those cases where the damage is objectively a consequence of that chain of events in the normal course of life. Therefore, the tortfeasor might be liable even though he did not foresee the damage that occurred as an adequate result of his own act.[116]

The above-mentioned theories are crucial in discussing the role of foreseeability in the formation of adequate causation. There are, in fact, certain causes which break the chain of causation when they occur, mostly because they step out of the foreseeable chain of events in that specific case. These causes that break the chain of causation are *force majeure*, victim's fault and third party's fault. In order to break

[110] Nomer (2018), p. 168; Koşar (2019), p. 120; Oğuzman and Öz (2013), p. 46.

[111] Eren (2017), p. 568. The author gives the example of breaking the windows of a house. In such a case, the tortfeasor should be held liable for the harms occurred due to heavy rain passing through the broken windows, as well as the loss incurred due to the burglary that was facilitated by the same act.

[112] Eren (2017), pp. 567–568.

[113] Atamer (1996), p. 52; Baysal (2019), p. 200.

[114] Atamer (1996), p. 55; Baysal (2019), p. 201.

[115] Baysal (2019), p. 204. See also Koşar (2019), p. 120 in this respect.

[116] Baysal (2019), p. 204.

the chain of causation, the victim's fault and the third party's fault should be in the form of intention or gross negligence, otherwise—in the case of a slighter type of fault—the chain of causation will not be broken.[117] It is worth noting here that these causes should be assessed on a case-by-case basis to determine whether the specific cause was sufficiently effective to render the tortfeasor's act unessential in the occurrence of the relevant damage, thus whether they constituted the exclusive cause of the damaging result.[118]

In the event that one of the actual causes of the damage has such a strong link with the damage that the other causes are considered unessential, then it will be deemed that the causal connection is cut between the damage and the other causes.[119] If these causes are not effective enough to discontinue the chain of causation, then they could be considered as a reason for a decrease in compensation.[120] The burden to prove the existence of any of the causes breaking the causation shall rest on the alleged tortfeasor, who wishes to rebut the liability claims.[121]

Force majeure, as one of the causes breaking the chain of causation, is defined as an extraordinary event that has occurred outside the scope of the tortfeasor's activities or enterprise, that inescapably led to the violation of a legal norm or obligation, and that was unforeseeable and unpreventable.[122] Accordingly, a *force majeure* has to be an external event, taking place outside the territory of the tortfeasor, which is not possible to foresee nor to prevent.[123] The factor of inevitability is interpreted objectively in legal doctrine, in that it refers to an event that would have resulted in a violation despite taking all the required measures, using all available options and showing the required due care.[124] Therefore, the personal characteristics of the tortfeasor are not taken into account in this respect. The factor

[117] Kılıçoğlu (2018), p. 413.

[118] Baysal (2019), p. 212; Koşar (2019), pp. 121–122.

[119] Nomer (2018), p. 168.

[120] Hatemi and Gökyayla (2017), p. 168. Nomer is in the opinion that third party's severe fault will not constitute a reason for decrease in compensation; Nomer (2018), p. 169.

[121] Turkish Court of Appeal, General Assembly of Civil Chambers decision dated 22.11.2018 and numbered E.2017/115 K.2018/1756.

[122] Eren (2017), p. 582.

[123] Baysal (2019), p. 212. Having said that, Baysal supports the opinion that exteriority should no longer be considered as a factor of force majeure (Baysal 2019, p. 213).

[124] Eren (2017), p. 585. In fact, the factors of unforeseeability and inevitability are considered together, as an event that was foreseen led to a damaging result despite all measures taken due to its inevitability would not create any liability (Baysal 2019, p. 214). Although taking into account the possibility to take required measures would resonate the analysis on fault, it would be only reasonable to assess this as part of attributability, which is a wider concept than fault and it serves to determine the spheres of influence of the tortfeasor and the tort victim (Baysal 2019, p. 214). By the same token, causation will be deemed broken if the force majeure event occurred outside the tortfeasor's sphere of influence, thus outside his control, which should be seen as part of attributability, rather than fault (Baysal 2019, p. 215). The close relationship between the factors establishing fault and causation is considered to make it challenging to design a general concept for causation in statutory law (van Dam (2007), p. 267).

of unforeseeability, on the other hand, refers to the results of the relevant event, as the event itself could be foreseen.[125]

Another cause to potentially break the chain of causation is the victim's fault. There are different opinions in legal doctrine as to the degree of fault of the victim that would be capable of breaking the chain of causation. According to one opinion, this should be an intention or at least gross negligence, otherwise the causation might continue.[126] This opinion is criticised for requiring an analysis of fault in determining the chain of causation.[127] The supporters of the second opinion suggest that no fault analysis should be required in determining whether there is a cause to break the chain of causation and, therefore, it would be sufficient if the victim's act were to constitute the exclusive cause of the relevant damage.[128] The victim's fault has not been a commonly tried grounds for breaking the chain of causation in FDL claims, as in these cases the victims usually have no control over the damaging event. For instance, if an employee of a subsidiary acted against the occupational rules and safety standards in which he was trained, and caused a leakage of toxic gas which resulted in a massive explosion that caused serious injury to the relevant employee, it might not be possible for this employee to seek the parent company's liability, as the chain of causation would be discontinued. However, as previously mentioned, this situation presents itself very rarely in FDL claims.

The last cause for breaking the chain of causation is the case where the damaging event occurs because of a third party's action. It is not essential to establish whether the third party has acted in fault or not, as long as his action is the exclusive cause of the damaging event.[129] If the third party's action was sufficient to cut the causation with the primary cause of the damaging result, then the first tortfeasor's liability could be challenged. However, dangerous activities such as those involving oil facilities, mines, airplanes, should be kept outside the scope of the aforementioned case, as in these cases the act of a third party would result in the characteristic danger posed by the relevant activity, which would not lead to the discontinuation of the chain of causation.[130] In the case of the example given above regarding the victim's

[125] Eren (2017), p. 586.

[126] According to this opinion, in case the victim's fault is not sufficient to cut the chain of causation, liability will be established but it might be possible to decrease the compensation (Eren 2017, p. 588). On the other hand, in certain cases such as risks pertaining to a dangerous activity (strict liability) or employer's liability, the victim's faulty act might not be sought to break the chain of causation, as long as the relevant act constitutes the main cause of the damage (Eren 2017, pp. 589–590).

[127] Baysal (2019), p. 216.

[128] Baysal (2019), pp. 216–217; Koşar (2019), p. 124.

[129] Baysal (2019), p. 219; Eren (2017), p. 591; Koşar (2019), p. 124. See also the decisions of the Turkish Court of Appeal, General Assembly of Civil Chambers, dated 22.11.2018 and numbered E.2017/115 K.2018/1756, dated 16.09.2015 and numbered E.2014/2058 K.2015/1768, whereby the court stated that the third party's act should be objectively intense and efficient enough to cut the causation.

[130] Eren (2017), pp. 591–592.

fault, people living in the vicinities of the relevant factory would be able to seek the liability of the corporate defendant despite the third party's fault. In fact, in such a case, gas leakage and explosion can be deemed characteristic risks of the relevant enterprise and the employee's faulty behaviour would not be considered sufficient to break the causation.

To give some examples, if an explosion occurs in an oil pipeline because of third party sabotage and local people wish to hold the operator company (and its multinational parent company) accountable for the health problems they have encountered as a result of the pollution, then at first glance it might seem that the explosion took place within the scope of the activities and operations of the alleged tortfeasor, and therefore, that the chain of causation would continue.[131] On the other hand, as the explosion happened as a result of third party sabotage, the corporate defendants would be able to argue, perhaps successfully, that a third party caused the damage through its intentional or grossly negligent act, which would normally break the chain of causation. Having said that, it would still be worth considering whether the relevant third party sabotage that led to the said damage was foreseeable by the corporate defendant. If the corporate defendant is operating in a region where terrorist acts and acts of sabotage are quite common, then one might argue that the sabotage was in fact a foreseeable and even preventable cause and, therefore, the chain of causation was not broken. In fact, the corporate defendant should have carried out all the required research and investigation in order to operate in the relevant region and, knowing that there was a risk of sabotage, could have employed security officers to guard the oil pipelines or make a different arrangement (such as burying the pipelines in the ground) that could effectively prevent any potential sabotage. As this example shows, the assessment of the element of causation should be made case-by-case by taking into consideration all the specifics of each case.

Similar to the previous example, we can also consider our previously given scenario of gold mining, but this time with an earthquake causing the leakage of cyanide due to damage done to the cyanide pool. In such a case, it would again be necessary to consider the external, the unforeseeable and the inevitable elements of the event. Earthquakes are normally seen as *force majeure* events. However, in modern technology, earthquake zones are well known, although the earthquakes themselves cannot be accurately predicted. Therefore, it would be reasonable to expect that a multinational gold mine operator would be well informed about the area where it operates and the risks of operating in an earthquake zone, and that it should therefore take the necessary precautionary measures to prevent any potential earthquake damage. In other words, the elements of unforeseeability and inevitability

[131] According to an opinion in Turkish legal doctrine, an event that takes place within the sphere of influence of the alleged tortfeasor can be an unexpected event in any case, but it cannot be a force majeure to affect the element of causation, due to the lack of the factor of exteriority. Unexpected event is deemed to differentiate from force majeure by having a relative character, which concerns the alleged tortfeasor, while force majeure is of an absolute and objective character (Eren 2017, p. 585). See Baysal (2019), p. 213, for further discussions on this issue, who supports an opposite view.

should be deemed to be lacking in such a case, which would lead to the continuation of the chain of causation.[132]

4.1.1.4 Damage

Damage is another mandatory element in the establishment of tort liability, which—like the other elements of tort liability—is not defined in statutory law. Tort liability may only arise where there are damages.[133] This is a reflection of the concept of civil liability, which only aims to cover the actual loss, without any further aim to punish the tortfeasor.[134] Under Turkish law, the principle consists of compensation for actual losses, rather than for future or potential losses.[135] In fact, as in comparative law, Turkish law also considers the primary aim of the law of liability and damages as obtaining compensation for the actual loss that occurred,[136] while the aim of prevention comes as secondary.[137] The burden to prove the amount of damage rests on the tort victim (Art. 50/1 TCO).

Although the general provision on fault liability under Turkish law (Art. 49 TCO) refers to the term 'damage', it left the term undefined. For this reason, the term damage has been subject to several different interpretations in legal doctrine and jurisprudence. Damage may be defined as a detriment to someone's assets, rights or person, without the consent of the owner.[138] Damage in the narrower sense refers only to pecuniary (material) losses, while damage in a broader sense covers non-pecuniary (immaterial) losses alongside pecuniary (material) ones.[139] Damage in the broader sense is defined as a deficit occurring in one's assets or person outside of one's own will; namely, the difference between the state of legally protected

---

[132] For an opposite opinion, see Eren (2017), p. 586. Eren deems earthquakes as a natural disaster, which would break the causation and thus create no liability. The author gives an example of an employee who is injured due to the building of the workplace being destroyed because of an earthquake, in which case, the author finds no liability for the employer or the owner of the building. It would be more appropriate to argue the specifics of the case, such as whether the workplace was in an earthquake zone or whether the building was built in accordance with earthquake standards, in order to determine if the factors of foreseeability and inevitability were present and consequently if the chain of causation would indeed be broken in the relevant case.

[133] As opposed to criminal liability, which punishes the risk of damage as well (Eren 2017, p. 544).

[134] This principle in compensation of damages is also accepted in majority of EU countries; see Eren (2017), p. 544; Kılıçoğlu (2014), p. 37; Kılıçoğlu (2018), p. 396; Magnus (2001), p. 185; Oğuzman and Öz (2013), p. 84.

[135] Antalya (2013), p. 465.

[136] Magnus (2001), p. 185.

[137] Magnus (2001), pp. 186–187.

[138] Antalya (2013), p. 455.

[139] In comparative legal doctrine, the pecuniary and non-pecuniary losses are also referred to as patrimonal and non-patrimonial losses (see Magnus (2001), p. 3, question 7 of the Questionnaire on the Law of Damages). For the sake of consistency, the terms of pecuniary and non-pecuniary losses (and damages) have been used hereunder, as these terms are more commonly used in Turkish law.

pecuniary and non-pecuniary assets before and after an act of infringement on them.[140]

Pecuniary damage is defined as a deficit (the decrease) occurring in the value of one's assets outside of one's own will.[141] A person's assets consist of both active elements (i.e. rights and receivables) and passive elements (i.e. debts and obligations), that carry an economic and monetary value.[142] The concept of assets is interpreted widely in civil liability law, in the sense that it covers not only rights *in rem*, rights of receivables, intellectual property rights, but also the economic future of the person (i.e. potential income).[143] Personal rights, in principle, do not form a part of assets, but violations of right to life, physical integrity and health might cause detriments to one's assets.[144] For instance, damage to one's physical integrity would usually result in medical and recovery costs and loss of income if the person can no longer work, which all have a negative economic impact on the person's assets. On the other hand, if a violation of personal rights does not result in any decrease in the relevant person's assets, this would not be seen as pecuniary damage, but might constitute non-pecuniary damage depending on the circumstances.[145]

Types of damages are also categorised in terms of legal right or value that is harmed by an action, such as damage inflicted to person or to property. For the purpose of FDL claims that are analysed within the scope of this study, the damage inflicted on a person is relevant, as this type of damage involves a decrease in one's assets as a result of the violation of physical integrity (e.g. death, physical injury, deterioration of health).[146] This damage results in a material loss on the victim's rights and person, and is universally recognised as deserving the highest degree of legal protection and priority when it comes to compensation.[147]

Another categorisation of damages in tort law is based on the consequential aspects of the damaging act, namely direct or indirect damage. Direct damage relates to damages occurring as a primary and adequate consequence of the related tort, such

[140] Baysal (2019), p. 156; Eren (2017), p. 545; Nomer (2018), p. 98.

[141] Eren (2017), p. 545; Nomer (2018), p. 164; Karahasan (2003), p. 80; Reisoğlu (2013), p. 170; Baysal (2019), p. 156. Theory of normative damage, as opposed to the deficit theory, adopts a wider approach to the scope of damage. According to the supporters of this theory, there may be cases where although not having a deficit in one's assets, it would still be just and equitable to compensate the damage, by appreciating an economic value to the occurred loss (Baysal 2019, p. 163).

[142] Eren (2017), pp. 545–546.

[143] Antalya (2013), p. 456; Eren (2017), p. 546.

[144] Eren (2017), p. 546.

[145] Eren (2017), p. 546.

[146] Eren (2017), p. 552; Kılıçoğlu (2018), p. 397. Pure economic loss, which consists of a decrease in a person's assets without violation of an absolute right (such as personal rights or rights in rem) (Baysal (2019), p. 175), is not relevant in terms of FDL claims, and therefore, is not within scope of this study.

[147] Baysal (2019), p. 179; Koch (2009), p. 109. Having said that, the relevant damage might also affect personal values that would result in an immaterial loss (Kılıçoğlu 2018, p. 397). In such a case, non-pecuniary damages might be claimed depending on the circumstances of the case.

as physical treatment expenses in case of a bodily injury.[148] Indirect damage, on the other hand, relates to additional damages occurring that are linked to the direct damages inflicted on the same victim, such as financial losses incurred by being unable to work because of bodily injury.[149]

The case of death as a direct damage is specifically regulated in Article 53 of TCO. According to this provision, losses occurring in the case of death are identified as (i) funeral expenses, (ii) if it is not an immediate death, treatment expenses and losses incurred due to the loss or decrease in the ability to work, and (iii) losses incurred by people who were dependent on the support of the deceased. These are all pecuniary losses that can be claimed due to a death as a result of a tort. In principle, it is not possible to claim any type of pecuniary loss other than the ones expressed in this provision.[150] According to Article 54 of TCO, losses incurred in cases of bodily injury are identified as (i) treatment expenses, (ii) loss of profit, (iii) losses due to the decrease or loss of the ability to work, and (iv) losses arising due to the negative impacts on future economic prospects. As it is evident from the wording of this article ('particularly'), the aforementioned types of damages are not *numerus clausus*.

Ricochet damage is a type of damage incurred by a third person who was not the addressee of the relevant tortious act, but who suffered losses due to their relationship with the tort victim, such as those who lose the financial support of the deceased person.[151] While some scholars consider the loss of support of the deceased as a kind of ricochet damage,[152] another opinion in legal doctrine stipulates that this is actually a direct damage, as it relates to a loss of support arising from death.[153] However, considering that the damaging act has impacted the physical integrity of the deceased and caused the relevant damage, the loss of support appears as a fairly typical example of ricochet damage, which affects a third person in response to the direct damage caused by the tort. It is, therefore, possible to say that compensation for the loss of support constitutes an exception to the principle of compensating only direct damage.

In principle, only direct damage can be compensated in civil liability law. Having said that, when establishing adequate causation, it is accepted that indirect damage can also be compensated.[154] Ricochet damage can only be compensated where there is a specific legal norm in statutory law.[155] To be able to claim ricochet damages, it would be necessary for the victims and their interests to fall within the protection

---

[148] Antalya (2013), p. 461; Eren (2017), p. 553; Kılıçoğlu (2018), p. 400.

[149] Antalya (2013), p. 461.

[150] Reisoğlu (2013), p. 220.

[151] Antalya (2013), p. 462; Baysal (2019), p. 183; Kılıçoğlu (2018), p. 401.

[152] Gökyayla (2014), p. 69.

[153] Çelik (2016), p. 12.

[154] Antalya (2013), p. 462.

[155] Art. 53 of TCO on compensation for the loss of support of the diseased and Art. 56/2 on compensation for close relatives of a person who is dead or severely injured are examples of

scope of the legal norm; otherwise, the element of unlawfulness would not be present.[156]

In FDL claims, an example of direct damage could be personal injuries or deaths occurring due to an activity of the subsidiary, also including occupational diseases (e.g. *Chandler v Cape*). Indirect damage, on the other hand, might be the loss of income by tort victims living in the vicinities of the area polluted by the subsidiary's activities (e.g. Shell Nigeria cases). An example of ricochet damage would be the losses suffered by the close relatives and families of the deceased individuals as a result of the toxic gas leaked from the factory (e.g. in the Bhopal case).

Apart from pecuniary losses, FDL claims might also effectively lead to non-pecuniary losses for the direct or indirect victims of the corporate tort. Immaterial loss, non-pecuniary loss or moral damage (*pretium doloris*) is defined in legal doctrine as a decrease in one's person (being) outside his own will, consisting of objective losses resulting from a violation of legal values that form his personal being.[157] There are two main theories interpreting the concept of moral damage. According to the objective theory, any violation of personal values and personal rights (such as right to life, physical integrity, health, honour etc.) shall cause an objective loss for the relevant person, which would constitute moral damage.[158] As for the subjective theory, the mere violation of the aforementioned personal rights would not be sufficient to cause a moral damage, but it would also be necessary to have a subjective aspect as a consequence, such as a feeling of pain and suffering, loss of mental balance or loss of joy of living (*joie de vivre*) due to such damage.[159] Supporters of the objective theory also do not completely eliminate the element of pain and suffering, but place it secondarily to the objective loss and decrease in one's personal values, which is considered as the main component of moral damage.[160] Regardless of which theory is supported, under Turkish law, moral damages can be

statutory exception, which allow compensation in case of a ricochet damage (Baysal 2019, p. 184; Kılıçoğlu 2018, p. 401).

[156] Baysal (2019), p. 184.

[157] Eren (2017), p. 556.

[158] Antalya (2016), p. 228; Baysal (2019), p. 570; Eren (2017), p. 556. Both Baysal and Eren are supporters of the objective theory in the definition of non-pecuniary loss. Antalya supports a mix theory by complementing objective theory with subjective factors, in that a subjective (inward) factor should be present in order to claim non-pecuniary damages, which should be assessed objectively by checking whether the relevant loss would normally be expected to create the alleged moral damage (Antalya 2016, pp. 229–230).

[159] Antalya (2016), p. 227; Eren (2017), p. 556; Nomer (2018), p. 164. For detailed discussions concerning criticisms made on subjective theory, see Antalya (2016), p. 228; Baysal (2019), p. 571; Eren (2017), pp. 559–560.

[160] Eren stipulates that pain and suffering would negatively impact mental integrity and health of a person, which would cause the violation of physical integrity and result in non-pecuniary loss (Eren 2017, pp. 558–559).

claimed in cases of violation of personal rights (Art. 58/1 TCO, Art. 25 CC) and of physical integrity (Art. 56/1 TCO).[161]

There are several theories that have been adopted to explain the purpose of moral damages, which are also helpful, in practice, in determining the appropriate amount of compensation; these are satisfactory purpose, rectifying purpose, punishing purpose and disincentivising purpose. Amongst these theories, the one that is most closely related to objective theory would be the rectifying purpose, which proposes that the main aim of moral damages is to rectify the loss and decrease suffered by one's personal being.[162] The Turkish Court of Appeal, in a recent decision concerning a mine accident that killed over 300 employees in the Soma region of Manisa, Turkey, praised the disincentivising purpose of moral damages, stating that in developed countries legal systems began considering the disincentivising aspect of moral damages in addition to simply rectifying the losses.[163] This approach of the Turkish Court of Appeal could be particularly important in those FDL claims that mostly concern extensive damages impacting not only individual victims but also wider society. In fact, the Turkish Court of Appeal referred to Soma case's as "*it has created deep sadness not only on the victims of the work accident or on their relatives, but in general on the whole society*", and for this reason it emphasised the significance of determining moral damages by considering the disincentivising purpose thereof.

Only moral damage occurring because of a violation of personal rights can be compensated.[164] Compensation for moral damage does not constitute compensation for a pecuniary damage, thus the main aim is not to compensate the losses affecting the victim's assets, but rather to provide the possibility of recovering the moral damages suffered by the victim.[165] In principle, it is acknowledged that moral damage can be successfully claimed by the person who has suffered a direct violation of personal rights. Hence, any other person who has incurred ricochet damage (as pain and suffering) due to the physical damage perpetrated on another

[161] Article 58/1 of TCO is the general rule on non-pecuniary damages, while Article 56/1 of TCO is a special rule concerning violation of physical integrity. Accordingly, Article 58/1 of TCO, as the general rule on this issue, shall apply to non-pecuniary damages in case of violation of personal rights where this is not specifically regulated elsewhere (Antalya 2016, p. 224). In the event that an unlawful act has resulted in the violation of both physical integrity and other personal rights, then both Article 56/1 and 58/1 shall apply to the relevant claim (Baysal 2019, p. 559). In the opinion of Antalya, Article 58/1 considers both the objective and subjective aspects by stipulating that the victim may claim non-pecuniary damages for the "violation of personal rights" and "for the moral damage the victim suffered" (Antalya 2016, p. 225).

[162] Baysal (2019), p. 550. For detailed explanations on each one of the mentioned theories on the purpose of moral damages, see Baysal (2019), pp. 545–550; Eren 2017, pp. 809–812.

[163] Turkish Court of Appeal, 21st Civil Chamber decision dated 03.10.2017 and numbered E.2017/4601 K.2017/7189, also quoted in Baysal (2019), p. 547. Also in the same opinion, decision of the Turkish Court of Appeal, General Assembly of Civil Chambers, dated 23.06.2004 and numbered E.2004/13-291 K.2004/370.

[164] Nomer (2018), p. 164; Antalya (2013), p. 494.

[165] Reisoğlu (2013), p. 228.

person cannot, in principle, claim moral damages. However, the TCO has introduced an exception to this general rule in Art. 56/2, which stipulates that in cases of severe bodily injury or death, those who are close to the victim may be granted an adequate amount in moral damages.[166] This type of compensation is different to the one concerning loss of support, which can be claimed by those who are close to the deceased and who were receiving regular financial support from that person, as the latter is a type of pecuniary damages, while the one under Art. 56/2 of TCO constitutes non-pecuniary damages. The term ‘being close’ in this respect is interpreted widely, so as to cover not only the immediate family of the victim, but also those who are relatively close, who have a regular relationship with the victim and who would feel pain and suffering due to the fatal or severe injury.[167] The injury suffered by the victim should be severe, so as to affect the relationship between the victim and those who are closest to that person in a permanent and serious way or to change the relevant relationship radically and completely.[168] The amount of non-pecuniary damages that may be granted within the scope of Article 56/2 of TCO is left to the discretion of the judge.[169]

[166] Before the enactment of the TCO in 01.07.2012, Turkish Court of Appeal had ruled in its settled precedents that non-pecuniary damage can be incurred by more than one people directly, especially in cases where a close relative (e.g. wife, husband, parent, child, sibling) of the severely injured victim claims compensation for damage caused due to nervous breakdown (Turkish Court of Appeal General Assembly of Civil Chambers, numbered 4-214/894, dated 2.12.1987; Turkish Court of Appeal 11th Civil Chamber, numbered E. 2004/8414 K. 2005/6326, dated 16.06.2005; Turkish Court of Appeal 11th Civil Chamber, numbered E. 1193 K. 4118, dated 08.03.2007; Turkish Court of Appeal 11th Civil Chamber, numbered E. 2009/3142 K. 2010/9750, dated 05.10.2010.). In these cases, Turkish Court of Appeal deemed the losses incurred by close relatives as a type of direct damage, rather than richocet damage. PETL also bears a similar provision in Art. 10:301(1): “*Non-pecuniary damage can also be the subject of compensation for persons having a close relationship with a victim suffering a fatal or very serious non-fatal injury*”. The type of damages requested by those who are close to a diseased or severely injured person is referred to as damages for bereavement, which are considered as an exception to the rule that only directly affected victims are able to request damages from the tortfeasor (Magnus 2014, p. 231).

[167] Erlüle (2016), p. 1090.

[168] Erlüle (2016), p. 1103. In Swiss legal doctrine, which serves as basis to the mentioned provisions under Turkish law, it is accepted that in order for those who are close to the victim to successfully claim non-pecuniary damages, it is necessary that the victim’s injury is highly severe. Some examples are being in a state of coma, becoming severely disabled, having severe brain damage. Impotence is also recognized as severe injury in this sense, allowing the wife to claim non-pecuniary damages (see Erlüle 2016, pp. 1093–1094).

[169] The judge shall decide on the amount of non-pecuniary damages in view of principles of justice and equity, under Article 4 of CC: “*In cases where the judge is given a discretion authority by law or where the law ordered that the judge shall consider the specifics of the case or just causes, the judge shall decide in view of law and principle of equity*”. Antalya refers to a Swiss Federal Court practice in the appreciation of non-pecuniary damages, whereby the amount of non-pecuniary damages is reduced in view of the lower local purchasing power and cost of living of the country where the victim resided. As Antalya also points out, such an approach would fall against the principle of social equality, which serves as a limitation to the judge’s discretion in determining the amount of non-pecuniary damages (Antalya 2016, p. 241). Needless to say, the mentioned practive

In light of the foregoing analysis, it is possible to conclude with respect to the element of damage in FDL claims that the damage occurring in these cases would generally be recognised as a pecuniary loss related to physical damage on the life, physical integrity or health of the tort victims, which all constitute violations of absolute rights. Although pure economic loss is also conceivable in certain cases of FDL (e.g. loss of farmers due to the oil spills that pollute the land and harm agriproducts), this aspect is not covered in this study. While some of the aforementioned pecuniary losses are directly incurred by the victims (such as occupational diseases), the majority of these claims concern environmental damage due to corporate activities causing detrimental effects on people's health and physical integrity, where the environment could be deemed to be the primary direct victim and the affected people the indirect victims. It is worth noting that environmental damage is extremely challenging and complex to deal with, as it not only has widespread effects on an often unidentifiable group of people, but also has the potential to create unforeseeable harm for an indeterminable period of time. For these reasons, it has become necessary to impose a type of strict liability for the civil aspects of environmental damage, which are discussed in detail under Sect. 4.2.3 of this study.

As for non-pecuniary damages, it would be reasonable to expect that victims of FDL claims, and those close to them in the case of fatal incidents, would be eligible to receive these damages, where they are able to establish their case against parent companies in MNCs.

4.1.2 Analysis of FDL in English Law

English law might be viewed as a pioneer in defining the parent company's duty of care, as English case law has made decisions addressing the parent company's liability and it has also become a persuasive influence on other countries.[170] For this reason, the specific English case law on the duty of care in general and the parent company's duty of care will be analysed in this section. The first cases presented are related to the duty of care, then will follow the cases on the duty of care for parent companies and finally a closer look at the duty of care of parent companies for their transnational subsidiaries, which form FDL.

---

of Swiss Federal Court poses a significant danger for the victims of FDL cases, who might face unjust results in their claims of non-pecuniary damages.

[170] Palombo (2020), pp. 38–39.

4.1.2.1 The Concept of the Duty of Care in English Law

'Duty of care' is defined in legal doctrine as the amount of care that a reasonable, prudent person would show in respect of the decisions he would make under similar circumstances.[171] The concept of the duty of care was first discussed and decided upon in the *Anns v Merton London Borough Council* judgment of the House of Lords.[172] This case concerned the claims of various residents in the borough, who alleged that the council owed them a duty of care, which was breached by the structural defects in their buildings arising from the incorrect depth of the foundations. The claimants alleged that the council, who approved the plans of the buildings that were then built by a third party contractor, was responsible for checking and ensuring that the buildings were constructed on adequate foundations. The House of Lords determined a test of duty of care in this judgment, which consisted of two elements: (i) a relationship of proximity or neighbourhood between the alleged wrongdoer and the claimant that may reasonably cause damage to the claimant in the case of careless acts by the other (referred to as '*prima facie* duty of care'), and (ii) a consideration of whether there may be any causes that would reduce or delimit the relevant duty of care.

Under English law, the currently applicable criteria for duty of care in tort of negligence were set in *Caparo Industries Plc v Dickman,*[173] which revised the criteria set by the *Anns v Merton* judgment. The case was brought by Caparo Industries, which had become a shareholder of Fidelity Plc, against Dickman, who were the auditors of the company and who allegedly breached their duty of care in relation to checking and certifying the company's accounts, which did not reflect the real values of the shares. The House of Lords identified a three-step test to establish the duty of care, which are:

(i) foreseeability, namely that the damage resulting from the breach of duty of care should be reasonably foreseeable,
(ii) proximity, namely that there must be a relationship of proximity or neighbourhood between the parties, and
(iii) fairness, justness and reasonableness, meaning that imposing liability for the damage incurred should be fair, just and reasonable.

Based on these criteria, the House of Lords decided that in this case there was no proximity between Caparo and Dickman, and therefore ruled that there was no duty of care imposed on Dickman against Caparo. The concept of proximity has been interpreted so as to cover those relationships existing prior to the relevant tort. With this judgment, the House of Lords adopted a different interpretation of assumption of responsibility—by deeming it a grounds for proximity between the perpetrator and

---

[171] Weber and Baisch (2016), p. 685.

[172] Anns v Merton London Borough Council [1978] AC 728. See also Ulfbeck and Ehlers (2016), p. 168; Cassel (2018), p. 190.

[173] Caparo Industries Plc v Dickman [1990] UKHL 2.

the tort victim—and left the door open to other potential grounds on which proximity could be established, other than a relationship existing prior to tort.[174] Although this case does not relate to an FDL claim, it is the leading case where the criteria for the duty of care is established.

4.1.2.2 The Parent Company's Duty of Care in English Law

The concept of parent company's duty of care is not regulated in statutory law in Common Law jurisdictions, including English law. Therefore, consideration should be given to case law which gradually defined the concept of duty of care and a parent company's duty of care towards stakeholders for the actions of its subsidiaries. In light of the above-mentioned case law it is observed that the duty of care is described as a parent company's direct liability towards a stakeholder and covers the parent company's due diligence obligation to monitor its subsidiaries' activities.[175] The interpretation of duty of care could be different for the parent company and for the subsidiary in a corporate group. In fact, while duty of care for the subsidiary could be interpreted as compliance with local legislation and human rights, this could instead refer to putting in place monitoring, checking and reporting mechanisms for the parent company.[176] The duty of care of the parent company does not extend to all persons who suffered damages due to the subsidiary's actions, nor does it arise in all cases where the parent company exercises control over an integrated economic unit.[177] Given the diverse criteria used to establish this liability and the complexity of corporate structures and relations, the conditions of the parent company's duty of care must be analysed on a case-by-case basis.

4.1.2.2.1 Connelly v RTZ

The *Connelly v RTZ Corporation Plc and Others*[178] case concerned the claims of Mr. Connelly, who worked in a uranium mine in Namibia, operated by Rossing Uranium Ltd., who was disagnosed with cancer of the larynx because of being exposed to uranium. Rossing Uranium Ltd. was a wholly owned subsidiary of the English company, Rio Tinto Zinc Corporation Plc (RTZ). After obtaining legal aid, the plaintiff initiated legal proceedings against RTZ before the English courts. Mr. Connelly claimed that RTZ had an active participation in its subsidiary's environmental, health and safety policies, which led to its duty of care towards its

[174] Palombo (2015), p. 465.

[175] Palombo (2019), p. 270.

[176] Weber and Baisch (2016), p. 685.

[177] Nygh (2002), p. 65.

[178] Connelly v RTZ Corporation Plc and Others [1997] UKHL 30 (24th July, 1997).

subsidiary's employees. It was also alleged that RTZ supervisors were effectively supervising the implementation of the policies in Rossing's uranium mine.

The defendant applied to the High Court in London who decided to stay proceedings, stating that the claim was closely and substantially connected with Namibia. The case was then brought to the House of Lords, which accepted that the lawsuit should be heard in England. This was based on the fact that the plaintiff received legal aid in England, while this was not provided in Namibia, thus justice could not be served there. However, the High Court Queen's Bench Division finally dismissed Mr. Connelly's claims based on the lapse of statute of limitations.[179] Therefore, this particular case that could have been an important landmark in FDL unfortunately does not provide any analysis of the substantive legal aspects of the matter.

4.1.2.2.2 Lubbe v Cape

The *Lubbe and others v Cape Plc*[180] case concerned damages incurred by the activities of an asbestos mine operated by South African companies with an English parent holding company. There was an unusual situation concerning the corporate structure of the group. In fact, the defendant and parent company, Cape Plc (an English company), had divested its shares in its South African companies and had no link to them as of 1989. The plaintiffs were thousands of people either working or living in the vicinities of the mine, who alleged to have been negatively affected by the mine's operations. The main question in this judgment was whether a parent company, which exercised *de facto* control over the operations of a subsidiary and knew that their operations involved health risks to workers and/or persons in the vicinity, would owe a duty of care to these people.

The House of Lords considered it important to clarify the role of the parent company in controlling the operations of the group and also what the directors and employees knew or ought to have known, what actions were taken or not taken and, accordingly, if the parent company did owe a duty of care, whether this was in fact breached. In answering these questions, the House of Lords stated that various forms of evidence, such as meeting minutes and director reports, would be considered. Although the case was not decided on substantive grounds, the House of Lords made it clear in this judgment that both a subsidiary's employees and third parties—such as the people living in the vicinities of the mine—could be considered involuntary creditors within the meaning of FDL claims, enabling claims to be addressed against the duty of care of the parent company.

---

[179] Connelly v RTZ Corporation Plc and Others, Queen's Bench Division (04.12.1998).

[180] Lubbe and others v Cape Plc [2000] UKHL 41.

4.1.2.2.3 Chandler v Cape Plc

The *Chandler v Cape Plc*[181] case concerned a former worker of a subsidiary of Cape Plc who claimed that the parent company had breached its duty of care by failing to ensure a safe work environment for the employees of its wholly owned subsidiary. The plaintiff suffered from asbestosis caused by the exposure to asbestos throughout the period of employment. The subsidiary had since ceased its activities, therefore the former employee initiated legal action against the parent company before the English courts.

The English High Court[182] referred to the *Adams v Cape*[183] judgment and confirmed that the mere fact that the parent company held shares in the subsidiary did not *per se* mean that it owed a duty of care towards the employees of its subsidiary, and held that this case would not qualify for piercing the corporate veil, as it was not proven that the subsidiary was a sham covering the parent's activities. The court decided that the parent company owed a duty of care towards the employees of its subsidiary by applying the three-fold test of the *Caparo v Dickman*[184] judgment, stating that the parent company was aware of the working conditions of its subsidiary's employees, that it had appointed an officer responsible for health and safety issues, and also held the responsibility for ensuring that its subsidiaries' employees were not harmed. The case was then appealed by Cape.

The Court of Appeal[185] examined the High Court's judgment in detail in comparison also with previous judgments on the matter and stated that: "*The parent company is not likely to accept responsibility towards its subsidiary's employees in all respects but only for example in relation to what might be called high level advice or strategy.*" (para. 66). The Court of Appeal confirmed the High Court's decision that the case did not constitute a piercing of the corporate veil, but was a case of the direct duty of care of the parent company towards its subsidiary's employees (para. 69–70). The Court of Appeal finally found it reasonable to impose liability on a parent company for the health and safety of its subsidiary's employees in the following circumstances (para. 80):

1. the business of the parent company and the subsidiary are in a relevant respect the same,
2. the parent has, or ought to have, superior knowledge on some relevant aspect of health and safety in the particular industry,
3. the subsidiary's system of work is unsafe as the parent company knew, or ought to have known, and
4. the parent knew or ought to have foreseen that the subsidiary or its employees would rely on its using that superior knowledge for the employees' protection.

---

[181] Chandler v Cape Plc [2012] EWCA Civ 525.

[182] Chandler v Cape Plc [2011] EWHC 951 (QB).

[183] Adams v Cape Industries plc [1990] Ch 433.

[184] Caparo Industries Plc v Dickman [1990] UKHL 2.

[185] Chandler v Cape Plc [2012] EWCA Civ 525.

In respect of criterion (4) mentioned above, the Court of Appeal deemed it sufficient to establish that the parent was intervening in the trading operations of the subsidiary (e.g. production, funding) by clarifying that it was not necessary to prove that the parent was intervening specifically in the subsidiary's health and safety policies. In this case, the Court of Appeal found that Cape Plc controlled its subsidiary in relation to health and safety policies. The concept of 'control' here does not refer to control as understood in company law (i.e. controlling the general meeting and management board), but to an actual control on the subsidiary's operations that caused the relevant damage.[186]

This case established the basis for a parent company's duty of care towards the employees of its subsidiary. Therefore, the element of proximity is interpreted as a relationship between the parent company and its subsidiary, rather than that between the perpetrator and the tort victim. According to this judgment, a parent company (a holding company in this case) that exercises full control over its subsidiary's operations is deemed to be aware of the risks pertaining to the relevant industry and therefore to have duty of care. This refers to a broad assumption of responsibility by the parent company.[187] It is possible to say that with this judgment the Court of Appeal transformed the assumption of responsibility by the parent company from being a voluntary act to a legal imposition, which would apply in cases where the parent company knows or ought to know about the damages affecting the employees of its subsidiaries.[188]

As the above-mentioned case concerns only the claims of the employees of the subsidiary, it might raise questions about whether the outcome would also cover claims brought by third party tort victims, such as the people who live in the vicinities of the subsidiary's operations where the damage occurred. However, the employees of a subsidiary are also third party creditors for a parent company, as there is no direct relationship between these two. Furthermore, as the subsidiary—allegedly, the primary wrongdoer—had been involved in this case, it became necessary to have recourse to the parent company, which is said to present similarities to the legal policy of the piercing the corporate veil cases.[189] In fact, the judgment is often criticised for only being based on tort law grounds rather than company law principles, even though it circumvents company law principles.[190] On the other hand, as the case does not involve a piercing of the corporate veil but instead the direct liability of the parent company for its own conduct, the judgment might also be seen as not affecting the separate legal personality of parent companies and subsidiaries in corporate groups.[191] In time, as case law developed, further

[186] Kershaw (2012), p. 154.

[187] Petrin and Choudhury (2018), p. 776.

[188] Palombo (2015), pp. 465–466.

[189] Jones (2019), p. 2, fn. 6.

[190] Ulfbeck and Ehlers (2016), p. 168.

[191] Rühmkorf (2015), p. 177.

criteria were presented for the purpose of identifying a parent company's duty of care and its breach.

Another point of concern, if the *Chandler v Cape* judgment were able to serve as a legal basis for multinational tort claims, is that in this case there was no extraterritoriality, as both the parent and the subsidiary were companies established in the UK. In legal doctrine, this aspect of the judgment is interpreted along with other cases on this subject, including *Lubbe v Cape,*[192] concluding that in the absence of a clear decision by the court that the case would not apply to multinational tort claims, it would cover situations where the parent and subsidiary are located in different countries.[193]

Furthermore, it is considered rather unlikely that the criteria set in the *Chandler v Cape* case would apply to cases where parent companies are not involved, to any degree, in the operations of their subsidiaries.[194] In fact, this judgment does not clearly present the type and level of control that is sought for establishing the duty of care of the parent company.[195] The judgment shows that the general involvement in a subsidiary's trading operations is sufficient to create the duty of care, regardless of whether the relevant interventions concerned the operations that caused the alleged damage.[196] *Petrin* and *Choudhury* criticise this aspect of the *Chandler v Cape* judgment as being over-inclusive, given almost all parent companies in every corporate group become involved in their subsidiaries' operations, and also under-inclusive, given the parent company's failure to exercise control should not lead to the rejection of a duty of care.[197] The latter is a crucial aspect of the parent company's duty of care in corporate groups, considering that such an approach could incentivise structuring corporate groups as pure holdings with no intervention in subsidiaries' activities. This would not prevent the occurrence of transnational torts but would only disqualify any claims against the parent company, which would in no way be desirable.

4.1.2.2.4 Thompson v Renwick

David Thompson v The Renwick Group plc[198] involved claims brought by Mr. David Thompson, who was employed by two companies within the Renwick Group as a labourer and driver. Throughout his employment he was exposed to direct contact with asbestos, which caused him to develop several diseases including lung cancer. Mr. Thompson claimed that the parent company, Renwick Group plc

[192] Lubbe and others v Cape Plc [2000] UKHL 41.
[193] Palombo (2015), p. 468.
[194] Rühmkorf (2015), p. 178.
[195] Petrin and Choudhury (2018), p. 778.
[196] Petrin and Choudhury (2018), p. 778.
[197] Petrin and Choudhury (2018), p. 778.
[198] David Thompson v The Renwick Group plc [2014] EWCA Civ 635.

(the holding company of the group), had breached its duty of care towards him as an employee. The Manchester County Court held in favour of Mr. Thompson, stating that the parent company's appointment of a director responsible for health and safety issues sufficiently established a duty of care on the parent company's side towards its employees.

The Court of Appeal, however, reversed this judgment by holding that the director was not acting on behalf of the parent company, but was merely exercising his fiduciary duties, and therefore the parent company cannot be deemed to have exercised control and assumed duty of care in this respect. The Court of Appeal applied the *Chandler v Cape* criteria, by comparing and distinguishing between the two cases. First of all, the court stated that while in the *Chandler v Cape* case the parent company had not only appointed a health and safety team for the whole group but also got involved in the production process of its subsidiary, in the *Thompson v Renwick* case the parent company had only appointed a director for health and safety issues. Secondly, the court stated that the parent company in *Chandler v Cape* had superior expertise and knowledge of the nature of the industry, while in *Thompson v Renwick* the parent company was only a holding company, mainly operating in the leisure field, and with no specific expertise on the business of its subsidiary or its implications. In light of these, the Court of Appeal rejected the claim of duty of care of the parent company, by stating that the facts in *Chandler v Cape* was in this case 'far removed' from the facts of the relevant case (para. 29).

The judgment of the Court of Appeal in this case is interpreted by some scholars as casting a shadow over the positive environment created by the *Chandler v Cape* case in FDL claims, as it further restricts the criteria of duty of care in practice and confines it to very exceptional circumstances, to be decided on a case-by-case basis.[199] The judgment also implied that a parent company of a corporate group which is acting as a pure holding would not normally face any risk of prosecution for duty of care violations against the tort victims of its subsidiary's activities.[200]

4.1.2.2.5 AAA v Unilever

The *AAA & Others v Unilever*[201] case concerned claims brought by employees, former employees and residents of a tea plantation run by Unilever's Kenyan subsidiary, Unilever Tea Kenya Limited (UTKL) for violent acts committed by tribes in Kenya following the 2007 Presidential elections. It appears that the employees of UTKL working in the tea plantations were not from the majority tribe of the surrounding area and therefore this led to conflicts and acts of violence against the employees during times of unrest. The plaintiffs claimed that both Unilever Plc, the English parent company, and UTKL had breached their duty of

[199] Grušić (2015), p. 33.

[200] Petrin and Choudhury (2018), pp. 776–777.

[201] AAA & Others v Unilever [2017] EWHC 371 (QB) (04.07.2018).

care towards them for their failure to take appropriate steps to protect them. Unilever Plc was the indirect parent company of UTKL with an 88.2% shareholding; the remaining percentage was held by its sister company incorporated in the Netherlands, Unilever NV. As it is acknowledged by the court, Unilever exercised control over its Kenyan subsidiary. However, despite this control exercised via shareholding, the court noted that the parent company had no superior knowledge or expertise in local politics or ethnic issues, and also did not exercise any control over its subsidiary regarding the running of the tea plantation. The court also examined the Crisis Management Process policy of Unilever for the Region of Africa, Middle East and Turkey, which stipulated that local managers would be responsible for taking measures against risks in crisis situations. It is also noted in UTKL's Crisis and Emergency Management policy that UTKL managed the crisis situation itself, without taking any advice or assistance from Unilever group, which was also supported by the submitted evidence.

Applying the test on the establishment of duty of care from the *Chandler v Cape* judgment, the Court of Appeal concluded that even though the relevant violent acts could be deemed foreseeable, there was no proximity to allow the claimants to have an arguable case against Unilever. The court based its reasoning on the separate legal entity principle, stating that there was no special doctrine in tort law suggesting that a parent company should be vis-à-vis responsible for people affected by the activities of its subsidiary. The court went on, stating that the criteria set out in the *Chandler v Cape* judgment do not constitute a separate legal test distinct from the general principle for the imposition of duty of care on the parent company. It identified the two grounds for duty of care for the parent company, based on previous case law, as (i) the parent company's taking over of the subsidiary's management, or (ii) the parent company's giving advice to the subsidiary in respect of management of a particular risk. Accordingly, the court decided that none of these two grounds were present in this case and thus rejected the claimants' arguments.

Although both the first instance court and the Appeal Court reached the same conclusion, they evidently did so by relying on different grounds. Laing J at the first instance court held that there was no foreseeability and that it was therefore not fair, just and reasonable to impose a duty of care on Unilever in this case; the Court of Appeal, on the other hand, approached the claim from the aspect of proximity, deciding that the current state of operational structure and control did not justify the imposition of a duty of care on the parent, without disturbing the previous grounds relied upon by Laing J.[202] Hence the analysis implies the rationale that if the parent had acted as it is claimed, would it then be reasonable to expect that the relevant damage would be avoided? This was answered in the negative in Unilever's case.[203]

[202] Jones (2019), p. 4.

[203] Jones (2019), p. 5.

Unilever has been criticised for having 'fought hard' on every aspect of this case.[204] Several NGOs have come together to write a letter to the then CEO of Unilever, Paul Polman, expressing their concerns about Unilever's approach to this case. In summary, they put forward that Unilever's strong defence in this case contradicted with its usual care for responsible business action, its enthusiasm for human rights and its due diligence obligations under the UNGPs. This criticism brings about an interesting consequence for MNCs. While it is unreasonable to expect that MNCs would not oppose claims and allegations which they can possibly rebut and disprove, it seems that any attempt by MNCs to defend their positions in FDL claims could be interpreted as an attempt by them to ignore corporate accountability. There should be clear criteria for determining the duty of care of parent companies against the creditors of their subsidiaries, which can be easily applied by any court in any jurisdiction. In the absence of such criteria, not only will court decisions be open to criticism but also the defences of MNCs will face public reaction, which at times can be too extreme. The lack of clear criteria would eventually result in a vicious circle for MNCs. Under normal circumstances, interfering in the delicate politics of the host country where its subsidiary is located should not be an obligation which creates a liability for the parent when unmet. Such could be seen as imposing extensive obligations on corporations and blurring the line between respect for human rights and political interference in a country's affairs.[205]

4.1.2.2.6 Lungowe v Vedanta

The *Lungowe v Vedanta*[206] case involved allegations of damage to the land and waterways, as well as loss of income, in the city of Chingola in Zambia by the citizens against the operator of Nchanga copper mine, Konkola Copper Mines Plc (KCM), a Zambian company, and its parent company in the UK, Vedanta Resources Plc (Vedanta). The majority of KCM's shares (79.42%) were held by Vedanta, while the remaining shares were owned by the Zambian state. The mining operations were carried out under a Zambian mining licence that was held by KCM. Vedanta was a holding company with many subsidiaries all over the world. The plaintiffs (1826 Zambian citizens) argued that both Vedanta and KCM were aware of the damaging activities which polluted the waterways and environment. The plaintiffs stated that Vedanta owed a duty of care to them, as it had assumed responsibility for KCM's operations by exercising a high level of control and direction on KCM, including

[204] NGOs Call on Unilever CEO to Match Rhetoric with Action – CORE, 19.04.2018, https://corporate-responsibility.org/ngos-call-unilever-ceo-match-action-rhetoric/.

[205] *Werhane* makes this remark with respect to Shell's non-interference with the assassination of Ken Saro-Wiwa and others within scope of Shell Nigeria case; see Werhane (2016), p. 18.

[206] Lungowe and Ors. v Vedanta Resources Plc and Konkola Copper Mines Plc [2017] EWCA Civ 1528.

ensuring its compliance with health, safety and environmental standards. The plaintiffs based their claims on the three-part test set by the House of Lords in *Caparo v Dickman,*[207] which are (i) foreseeability, (ii) proximity and (iii) fairness, justness and reasonableness.

The Court of Appeal acknowledged that the mere fact of Vedanta being the holding company of a group, which included KCM, would not show that Vedanta owed a duty of care to the plaintiffs and that this issue needed to be further supported to have any arguable claim (para. 69). The judge, after delving into detailed analysis of the previous judgments on parent company's duty of care, determined certain conditions regarding when a parent company would owe a duty of care towards those harmed by its subsidiary's actions (para. 83):

1. The three-part test under *Caparo* case (i.e. foreseeability, proximity and fairness, justness and reasonableness) shall be firstly applied;
2. The parent company may owe a duty of care to those affected by its subsidiary's operations under certain circumstances, which are: (a) where the parent has taken direct responsibility regarding health and safety policies, which is subject to the claim, or (b) where the parent controls the subsidiary's operations which are subject to the claim;
3. One of the criteria expressed in *Chandler v Cape* is important to analyse if a duty of care is owed by the parent company: in cases where the parent and subsidiary have similar knowledge and expertise, and they make decisions jointly about the subsidiary's actions that are made subject of the claim, then they may both owe a duty of care to the affected persons, which may include the employees and also other people affected by the subsidiary's actions.

The judge evaluated the following evidence in arguing whether there was a duty of care on Vedanta's side in this case and reached the conclusion that there was a "serious question to be tried" (paras. 84, 90):

- A report showing that the oversight of the subsidiaries rested with the board of Vedanta.
- An agreement whereby Vedanta assumed the obligation to provide KCM with a number of services that included mining, employee training, financial support and strategic planning.
- Vedanta's provision of environmental and technical information, as well as health, safety and environmental training across the group.
- Vedanta's financial support for KCM—which the judge found to be "*considerably beyond a conventional parent–subsidiary relationship*".
- Vedanta's public statements stipulating that it was committed to addressing the environmental risks of KCM's mining infrastructure.
- A former KCM employee's witness statement referring to the high degree of control Vedanta exercised over KCM.

[207] Caparo Industries Plc v Dickman [1990] UKHL 2.

In reaching the conclusion, the judge also reasoned: "*The English common law confines a duty of care because otherwise (…) a defendant may be exposed to an indeterminate class, for an indeterminate amount, for an indeterminate time.*" (para. 68).

Following the UK High Court's rejection of Vedanta's obligations on filing the lawsuit before London courts, Vedanta appealed the case, which again resulted in the Court of Appeal upholding the UK High Court's decision. Thereafter, Vedanta brought the case to the UK Supreme Court.

On 10 April 2019, the UK Supreme Court issued its decision[208] rejecting the objections of Vedanta and accepting the case of the claimants to proceed to trial before the UK courts. The judgment explicitly recognised that filing the lawsuit before the Zambian courts would be risky for the claimants in terms of achieving 'substantial justice' (paras. 88 et seq). The court also declared that in this case there was a basis for successfully claiming that the parent company owed a duty of care, based on Vedanta's intervention and assumption of responsibility for the environmental policies of its Zambian subsidiary (para. 61). It was, in fact, argued throughout the proceedings that while Vedanta had a group-level policy in place for health and safety, it also exercised control over its subsidiaries by way of supervision and monitoring.[209] The UK Supreme Court's judgment was solely about the jurisdiction and did not delve into the merits of the case. The case will now be decided upon by the UK courts, which will look into the parent company's duty of care in FDL cases. There is no doubt that the UK Supreme Court's recognition of the duty of care is of utmost importance and signals a positive approach by the English courts.

In applying the criteria required for duty of care under tort liability of the parent company towards third parties harmed by the activities of its subsidiary, the UK Supreme Court stated that the criteria set under *Chandler v Cape* and in *AAA v Unilever* judgments were not necessarily decisive in every case of foreign tort liability, but instead, the parent company's liability should be decided on a case-by-case basis. The court also rejected the arguments of Vedanta and KCM that the imposition of a duty of care on the parent company for the activities of its subsidiary would form a novel duty of care, which would lead to a positive duty on the parent to intervene in its subsidiary's business to ensure implementation of human rights and environmental standards. Vedanta submitted that this was a novel duty, based on novel principles that would result in a far-reaching and unprecedented duty on MNCs, and that it would thus constitute a matter for the parliament.[210] The court declared that this was not a novel duty of care, as it was still based on previous judgments in common law. The UK Supreme Court stated that the types of

---

[208] Lungowe and Ors. v Vedanta Resources Plc and Konkola Copper Mines Plc [2019] UKSC 20.

[209] Lopez and Croser (2019), http://opiniojuris.org/2019/01/22/the-uk-supreme-court-considers-whether-parent-company-vedanta-has-a-duty-of-care-and-so-may-be-held-legally-responsible-for-the-harm-caused-by-its-zambian-subsidiary/.

[210] Lopez and Croser (2019), http://opiniojuris.org/2019/01/22/the-uk-supreme-court-considers-whether-parent-company-vedanta-has-a-duty-of-care-and-so-may-be-held-legally-responsible-for-the-harm-caused-by-its-zambian-subsidiary/.

management and control effectively present in MNCs were not limited; while a parent company might act as only a passive investor, another one might arrange a reorganisation of the group structure so that it operates as a single entity in terms of management (para. 51). However, it seems that by reducing the criteria set in previous judgments, the UK Supreme Court introduces stricter criteria for parent company liability, which can be used in favour of FDL claimants. It states that parent company liability based on duty of care could be claimed in those cases where the parent company has no declared group policies but has taken active steps to have them implemented by its subsidiaries (by way of training, supervision and enforcement). On the other hand, it stipulates that the parent company could have a duty of care in those cases where it has declared, in published materials, that it exercises a degree of supervision and control over its subsidiaries, even if it does not actually do so. In the opinion of the UK Supreme Court, either one of these cases might lead to an effective claim on a breach of duty of care by the parent company against third party victims (para. 53). In this specific case, the court decided that Vedanta has both declared its responsibility in relation to environmental standards in the operations of its subsidiaries, particularly of the mine, and also has conducted training, supervision and enforcement for the implementation of these standards, thereby concluding that a sufficient level of intervention by Vedanta in the operation of the mine could be demonstrated at trial (para. 61). Although the interveners to the case cited the international standards, treaties and comparative jurisprudence to the court, the UK Supreme Court did not refer to any of these, which was marked as a disappointing point of this judgment.[211]

The *Lungowe v Vedanta* decision is important to the discussion on whether parent companies can be held liable along with their foreign subsidiaries in respect of damages caused by their operations, as it concludes that this liability may occur in certain circumstances. With this approach, both the Court of Appeal and the Supreme Court have paved the way for the acknowledgement of a duty of care for a parent company towards third parties. If such a duty of care is indeed acknowledged at trial, this would be the first case where this is set towards a person who has been harmed by a subsidiary's operations, rather than the employees. It is also worth noting that the court's approach to the traditional separate entity of parent and subsidiary seems to have been modified. Although it has not explicitly acknowledged the single entity concept, it has referred to the financial situation of the subsidiary as raising legitimate concerns and decided on the jurisdiction over the parent company, which might seem as a shift away from the traditional approach.[212] This decision may also lead to concerns on the side of MNCs, in the sense that the parent company's active involvement in the transnational subsidiary's health and safety policies—or a direct control or assumption of responsibility by the parent

---

[211] McCorquodale (2019), http://opiniojuris.org/2019/04/18/symposium-duty-of-care-of-parent-companies/.

[212] Aristova (2016), http://conflictoflaws.net/2016/uk-court-on-tort-litigation-against-transnational-corporations/.

company over the relevant operations of its transnational subsidiary—may result in the parent company's liability for these actions. The flip side of the coin is that the MNC would normally need to organise its group operations and policies in line with UNGP rules, by ensuring a certain level of supervision by parent companies over their subsidiaries, which, within the context of this judgment, might be deemed an act of assumption of responsibility or control by the relevant parent company. This situation might be referred to as a Catch 22: any attempt to involve the parent company in the subsidiary's operations or policies could increase the likelihood of duty of care, while, at the same time, this is required to ensure the compliance of the group with the UNGP.[213] Moving the responsibility of compliance with the UNGP to the operating subsidiary level is suggested as a viable solution, considering that the subsidiaries might be in a better position to foresee the human rights risks involved in their activities compared to their parent companies.[214]

This decision, without any doubt, will prove to be challenging for MNCs. In fact, as the UK Supreme Court judges unanimously agreed, the parent company of an MNC could be deemed to incur a duty of care towards third parties for its subsidiaries' activities, where it is effectively involved in these activities by way of supervision and monitoring, to check if they comply with the environmental or health and safety standards imposed by the parent company. The same liability might also be deemed to exist where the parent company was not effectively involved in any such supervision regarding implementation of these standards but had declared that it assumed responsibility in this respect. It is possible to conclude that this approach by the UK Supreme Court might have undesirable consequences, such as certain changes in the companies' activities and legal structures aimed at avoiding responsibility, e.g. through a wilful avoidance of supervision of their subsidiaries' actions and their implementation of the human rights and environmental standards.[215] In light of this judgment, it seems that the way for a parent company to avoid any liability would be either to stay completely out of the operations of its subsidiaries, in which case there might still be a risk of incurring liability by way of omission, or to ensure without any doubt that it has identified sufficient standards and that its subsidiaries are effectively implementing them. In the latter scenario, the parent company who faces FDL claims could at least prove that (i) it has addressed all adequate standards to eliminate environmental and health and safety-related risks in the operations carried out within the group, including by its transnational subsidiaries, and (ii) it has also effectively and actively supervised, monitored and controlled its subsidiaries in implementing these standards. Only in this manner, it seems, can a parent company successfully rebut the claimants' claims.

[213] Hughes-Jennett and Hood (2017), https://www.law.ox.ac.uk/business-law-blog/blog/2017/10/how-should-english-domiciled-multinationals-manage-their-human-rights.

[214] Hughes-Jennett and Hood (2017), https://www.law.ox.ac.uk/business-law-blog/blog/2017/10/how-should-english-domiciled-multinationals-manage-their-human-rights.

[215] McCorquodale (2019), http://opiniojuris.org/2019/04/18/symposium-duty-of-care-of-parent-companies/.

Given the detailed decision of the UKSC on the conditions for imposing parent company liability in FDL claims, it comes as no surprise that the parties have reached a settlement without any admission of liability by Vedanta and KCM.[216] Nevertheless, it seems fair to conclude that the *Lungowe v Vedanta* judgment still represents an important step forward in FDL claims as it has departed from the dichotomy that existed in UK case law on the criteria required to establish a parent company's duty of care for the activities of its subsidiaries, by seeking a link between the parent company, its subsidiary and the tort victim.[217]

4.1.2.2.7 English Shell Nigeria

The *Okpabi v RDS* case concerned the claims of Ogale community citizens in Nigeria against Shell Petroleum Development Company of Nigeria Ltd. (SPDC) and its parent company established in the UK, Royal Dutch Shell Plc (RDS). Plaintiffs argued that SPDC and RDS were jointly and severally responsible for the damages caused by the oil spills from the pipelines operated by SPDC, and that the liability of RDS was based on a breach of duty of care for the failure to control the operation and infrastructure in Nigeria.

The High Court, in its judgment of 26 January 2017,[218] decided that it had jurisdiction to hear the case against RDS, but not against SPDC, and rejected the plaintiffs' claims on the grounds that there was no arguable case for RDS owing the plaintiffs a duty of care. The judge proclaimed that there was no proximity in this case as (i) RDS was not directly SPDC's parent company, (ii) there were only two RDS officers who were in the Executive Committee of the Shell Group, (iii) RDS was only a holding company, with no involvement in the oil operations in Nigeria, (iv) imposing a duty of care on RDS would be too broad as Shell had numerous subsidiaries around the world. Hence, the High Court adopted a very conservative and strict approach on separate legal personality between RDS and SPDC.[219] The plaintiffs appealed the decision claiming that RDS owed a duty of care because it controlled the operation of the pipelines and infrastructure involved in the oil leak or because it assumed direct responsibility to protect the plaintiffs against environmental damages caused by the leaks (para. 3). The plaintiffs based their claims of duty of care on the following arguments: (1) that RDS controlled and directed SPDC's management in respect of pollution, environmental compliance and infrastructure operation, (2) RDS knew about the environmental damage in Niger Delta, (3) RDS

---

[216] Leigh Day, Legal claim by more than 2500 Zambian villagers in a case against Vedanta Resources Limited (19.02.2021), https://www.leighday.co.uk/latest-updates/news/2021-news/legal-claim-by-more-than-2-500-zambian-villagers-in-a-case-against-vedanta-resources-limited/.

[217] Palombo (2019), p. 274.

[218] Okpabi and others v Royal Dutch Shell Plc and Shell Petroleum Development Company of Nigeria Ltd., [2017] EWHC 89 (TCC).

[219] Aristova (2018), p. 15.

had superior expertise, knowledge and resources on health, safety and environmental protection issues, and (4) RDS knew that SPDC would rely on RDS's superior expertise, knowledge and resources on these issues (para. 37).

The English Court of Appeal ruled on 14 February 2018,[220] with a majority, to uphold the decision of the High Court, that the English courts are not authorised to hear the case against SPDC due to a lack of personal jurisdiction. The Judge, Simon LJ, emphasised the need to "*distinguish between a parent company which controls, or shares control of, the material operations on the one hand, and a parent company which issues mandatory policies and standards which are intended to apply throughout a group of companies in order to ensure conformity with particular standards*" (para. 89). Simon LJ concluded that the mere issuance of mandatory policies would not imply any control of the subsidiary's operations by the parent in a way that would lead to a duty of care, and once again emphasised the criteria sought for the establishment of duty of care as follows: (1) foreseeability of the damage incurred, (2) proximity between the party owing the duty of care and the party to whom this is owed, (3) fairness, justness and reasonableness in imposing the relevant duty of care (para. 58). Within the scope of the evaluations made under the criterion of 'proximity', it is stated that the plaintiffs failed to show any degree of proximity that would suggest any kind of control by RDS over the operations of SPDC or any direct responsibility in this respect. Simon LJ considered for this purpose that there was no indication that the parent company exercised specific control or took responsibility for SPDC and also that the supervision and guidance in the implementation of group standards did not constitute exercising control over the operations of the subsidiaries, but merely ensured that the subsidiaries exercised control in accordance with the policies (paras. 118–129).[221] As for the criterion of fairness, justness and reasonableness, Simon LJ rejected the claimants' arguments for corporate social responsibility, stating that this was an abstract principle that provided a doubtful basis for duty of care (paras. 130–131).[222] Accordingly, Simon LJ concluded "(. . .) *this is not a case in which the claimants can demonstrate a properly arguable case that RDS owed them a duty of care on the basis either of an assumed responsibility for devising a material policy the adequacy of which is the subject of the claim, or on the basis that it controlled or shared control of the operations which are the subject of the claim*" (para. 132).

This judgment made direct and clear reference to the holding structure of the Shell group stating that RDS, as a holding company, could not bear any responsibility for the failures taking place due to the operations of its subsidiaries (para. 138). English Court of Appeal made a distinction between a parent company which exercises control over the operations of its subsidiary and one which issues group policies subject to mandatory compliance. According to the court's decision, in the event that

---

[220] Okpabi and others v Royal Dutch Shell Plc and Shell Petroleum Development Company of Nigeria Ltd. [2018] EWCA Civ 191.

[221] See also Bergkamp (2018), p. 115.

[222] See also Bergkamp (2018), p. 115.

the parent has only issued mandatory guidelines, without engaging in the subsidiary's material operations, then there would be no duty of care on the part of that parent company. Apparently, the Court of Appeal sought evidence to show that RDS was significantly involved in and controlled the day-to-day operations of its subsidiary, which included imposing and enforcing mandatory design and engineering practices.[223] The court also referred to the analysis made under *Chandler v Cape* and *Lungowe v Vedanta,*[224] stating that where a parent company has taken control of the subsidiary's operations in a direct and substantial way, then a duty of care may arise. The case was interpreted as a significant barrier for human rights claims against MNCs, as it asserted that even though one of the companies in the group might be deemed to have a duty of care, as long as the relevant court lacks jurisdiction, the corporate group would be able to successfully avoid liability.[225]

The judgment of the UK Appeal Court was then brought to the UK Supreme Court,[226] which allowed the appeal to go forward in light of the *Lungowe v Vedanta* judgment.[227] On 23 June 2020, the UK Supreme Court heard the oral pleadings of the parties.[228] During the hearing, the plaintiffs contended that Shell's top-down management structure proved its high-level intervention in the operations of its subsidiaries. There was evidence in addition to the mandatory group-wide policies that RDS exercised a substantial and *de facto* control over its subsidiaries – in fact the accountability of the CEO of RDS was stipulated in a company document of group operations. The defendant, RDS, argued in its defence that its parent company did not get involved in its subsidiaries' operations, that each subsidiary had its own board of directors which was accountable for the relevant subsidiary's operations, and that the Appeal Court's approach was right in deeming the existence of group-wide policies as not sufficient to establish the parent company's duty of care.

The UK Supreme Court has issued its final judgment on the matter on 12.02.2021, holding that the parent company RDS can be sued before English courts by tort victims who suffered harms due to the Nigerian subsidiary's activities and hence there is a real issue to be tried in terms of the parent company's duty of care in the relevant case.[229] The judgment is remarkable in the court's diligent analysis through Shell's corporate documents that were submitted as legal evidence, which

---

[223] Aristova (2018), p. 16.

[224] Lungowe and Ors. v Vedanta Resources Plc and Konkola Copper Mines Plc [2017] EWCA Civ 1528.

[225] Ryerson (2018), https://corpaccountabilitylab.org/calblog/2018/7/5/shell-in-nigeria-the-case-for-new-legal-strategies-for-corporate-accountability.

[226] Okpabi and others v Royal Dutch Shell Plc and another, Case ID: UKSC 2018/0068.

[227] Lungowe and Ors. v Vedanta Resources Plc and Konkola Copper Mines Plc [2019] UKSC 20.

[228] The hearing was broadcasted live on the website of the Supreme Court, Okpabi and others (Appellants) v Royal Dutch Shell Plc and another (Respondents), https://www.supremecourt.uk/cases/uksc-2018-0068.html.

[229] Okpabi and others v Royal Dutch Shell Plc and another [2021] UKSC 3.

are plenty and variable.[230] The judgment also referred in detailed to expert witness statements that explained the corporate management structure of the group, mainly describing the parent company's direct control over its subsidiaries, as well as promulgation of mandatory standards by them, making it clearer that although subsidiaries were separate legal entities, they actually had limited autonomy.[231]

It is crucial to note that the judgment made a distinction between the concept of 'control' of a parent company over its subsidiaries in a corporate group and the parent company's management of subsidiary's activities that led to the damaging outcome.[232] In doing so, the UK Supreme Court emphasised the normality of a parent company controlling its subsidiaries, while clearly distinguishing this type of control from *de facto* management of a subsidiary's certain activities, and finally held that the key issue for the purposes of the case was "*the extent to which the parent did take over or share with the subsidiary the management of the relevant activity (here the pipeline operation)*".[233] Based on all these analysis and reasoning, the court took into account the specifically vertical organisational structure of Shell group, where the whole group functions as a single commercial undertaking, and concluded that there was a real issue to be tried in this case.[234] The judgment will surely remain as a landmark judgment for FDL claims, which will most certainly create significant outcomes, leading perhaps even to MNCs reconsidering their organisational structures.

4.1.3 Parent Company's Duty of Care in Light of Dutch Court Judgments

The *Dutch Shell Nigeria* cases[235] are renowned as they are the only cases that concluded with a court judgment on FDL in the EU, other than the UK. The cases concerned the litigation brought against Shell Petroleum Development Company of

[230] According to the judgment, Shell group has many different types of documents concerning corporate management, led by RDS Control Framework, which organises the group along Business and Function lines that are directly accountable to RDS (paras. 37–44). The judgment also refers to certain mandatory policies, standards and technical requirements, which are all imposed and promulgated on the subsidiaries (paras. 41–50).

[231] See paras. 60–69 of the judgment.

[232] See para. 147 of the judgment.

[233] See para. 147 of the judgment.

[234] See paras. 157–159 of the judgment.

[235] Oguru, Efanga, Milieudefensie v Royal Dutch Shell Plc and Shell Petroleum Development Co Nigeria Ltd. (District Court of The Hague, C/09/330891/HA ZA 09-0579, 2013); Friday Alfred Akpan v Royal Dutch Shell Plc and Shell Petroleum Development Co Nigeria Ltd. (District Court of The Hague, 337050/HA ZA 09-1580, 2013); Barizaa Manson TeteDooh v Royal Dutch Shell Plc and Shell Petroleum Development Co Nigeria Ltd. (District Court of The Hague, C/09/337058/HA ZA 09-1581, 2013).

Nigeria Ltd. (SPDC) and Royal Dutch Shell Plc (RDS), the Dutch parent company located in the Hague. This case is significant for the reason that it is the first FDL claim where a Dutch court accepted jurisdiction.[236] In this case, four Nigerian farmers from the Goi, Ikot Ada Udo and Oruma villages and the Dutch NGO Milieudefensie sued SPDC and RDS before the District Court of the Hague in 2008, with the allegation that certain damages had occurred in Niger Delta due to oil spills from the pipelines operated by SPDC, and RDS and SPDC were held jointly and severally liable in this respect. The plaintiffs requested that the damages be compensated, pipelines be repaired and maintained properly by Shell and the oil spills be cleaned up. RDS argued in its defence that the Dutch courts had no jurisdiction in a claim that regarded alleged damages caused by its Nigerian subsidiary SPDC, that the oil spills happened because of a sabotage on the pipelines, and finally, that RDS itself had no responsibility in respect of the alleged oil spills from the pipelines operated by SPDC.[237]

One of the key points of this litigation was access to evidence. Throughout the proceedings, the plaintiffs requested access to certain documents that were in Shell's possession, which would serve in proving their claims. The District Court of the Hague only partially accepted this request of the plaintiffs, stating that they could access certain reports drafted by subcontractors concerning the village of Goi only. In its decision dated 30 January 2013, the court decided that SPDC was responsible for the damages occurring in one of the villages, Ikot Ada Udo, and that it had to compensate these damages, while no liability was found for RDS for the activities of its Nigerian subsidiary, on the basis that Nigerian tort law did not impose an obligation on the parent company to prevent its subsidiaries from causing damages to third parties.[238] In this respect, the court also considered the circumstances of the *Chandler v Cape* case and found that the parent company's duty of care towards the employees of its subsidiary comprised a limited number of people, while its alleged duty of care towards the people living in the vicinity of the oil pipelines operated by its subsidiary concerned an unlimited number of people, which cannot be deemed equal. The court further argued that the case in question did not involve any superior knowledge of the parent company operating in the same field as its subsidiary nor did it involve any expectation that the parent company should have intervened to prevent the damage, like it was the case in *Chandler v Cape*. Thus the court concluded that there was not a sufficient connection between RDS and the victims to establish a duty of care for RDS.[239] The court also accepted Shell's defences that the other oil spills occurred due to a sabotage and Shell, therefore, was not responsible for the damages that occurred.

---

[236] Muchlinski (2011), p. 689; Enneking (2013), p. 136.

[237] RDS admits in its annual report (for fiscal year 2017) that in addition to cases of theft and sabotage, there are instances where oil spills occur due to operational reasons (Strategic Report, Shell Annual Report and Form 20-F 2017, p. 60).

[238] Enneking (2013), p. 136.

[239] Cambou (2015), pp. 356–357.

Both Shell and the plaintiffs appealed this decision on different grounds. The plaintiffs then gained access to certain internal documents of Shell, obtained during the litigation proceedings before the UK courts, which were useful in proving some degree of negligence on the part of Shell regarding the oil spills that occurred in other villages.

On 18 December 2015, the Hague Court of Appeal decided that the Dutch courts had jurisdiction in the relevant case concerning alleged damages occurring in Niger Delta and also ruled that Shell would provide the plaintiffs access to all documents related to the claims.

In this case, the Hague Court of Appeal referred to the *Chandler v Cape* criteria, which shows that the court effectively engaged in a comparative analysis of the matter and also that a mutual influence exists between different state courts in this specific area. The Hague Court of Appeal has, however, interpreted it rather restrictively, by stating that the parent company's duty of care would not extend to cover third parties other than the employees of its subsidiary. Therefore, although the *Dutch Shell Nigeria* judgment paved the way for other jurisdictions to recognise parent company liability based on *Chandler v Cape*, it has failed to provide a flexible interpretation of duty of care. *Bergkamp* interprets this as a policy decision as well as a legal one, considering the Dutch government's abolishment of the dividend tax to keep the corporate groups headquartered in the Netherlands.[240]

The Hague Court of Appeal, which heard the two appealed cases,[241] decided on 29.01.2021 that SPDC has acted in negligence in failing to protect its pipelines from sabotage and hence it is liable for the harms occurred as a result of the oil spillage.[242] Although no direct liability is envisaged for RDS in relation to the relevant damages, the court held both RDS and SPDC responsible to put in place warning systems to detect oil spills. This judgment might be considered hopeful for the future of FDL cases and also in terms of comparative law, as the Dutch court has specifically referred to the UKSC judgment in *Lungowe v Vedanta*[243] in assessing the parent company liability.[244]

[240] Bergkamp (2018), p. 116.

[241] Cases numbered C / 09/337058 / HA ZA 09-1581 and C / 09/365482 / HA ZA 10-1665.

[242] Dooh and Milieudefensie v Royal Dutch Shell Plc and Shell Petroleum Development Co Nigeria Ltd, The Hague Court of Appeal, Civil Chamber, no. 200.126.843 and 200.126.848, court cases numbered C / 09/337058 / HA ZA 09-1581 and C / 09/365482 / HA ZA 10-1665 (29.01.2021).

[243] Lungowe and Ors. v Vedanta Resources Plc and Konkola Copper Mines Plc [2019] UKSC 20.

[244] See the judgment of the Hague Court of Appeal in Shell Nigeria, para. 3.29.

4.1.4 Suggestions on Regulating the Parent Company's Duty of Care Under Turkish Law

As previously stated, Turkish law does not accommodate any specific legal grounds on the duty of care of the parent company towards third party victims of human rights abuses arising from its subsidiaries' actions. The cases of piercing the corporate veil are extremely rare under Turkish law and there are no court precedents that resemble FDL claims. Under any circumstances, piercing the corporate veil requires the satisfaction of a much stricter set of criteria than duty of care, which would go against the interests of FDL claimants. In jurisdictions where this doctrine is accepted, it is usually required that claimants show that the subsidiary was a mere façade, a sham, a shell company, that it was established to avoid the legal obligations of the parent company.[245] Meanwhile, the threshold for establishing a duty of care might be much lower. The challenge of duty of care is that there are no clear criteria providing legal certainty for both the claimants and the defendants. Therefore, a statutory regulation would be in the interests of both parties.

It is worth noting that the distinction between a subjective and objective approach to fault, which was discussed above, is important in establishing the element of fault in negligence. In fact, in cases where the tortfeasor has acted with intent, it would be assumed that he has already shown his will to act against the reasonable care expected of him in these particular circumstances, and hence, fault will be established without the need for further assessment.[246] On the other hand, in cases where the tortfeasor has acted in negligence, an assessment will be necessary to determine if fault can be established, which will be made in accordance with objective or subjective factors. Subjective assessment takes into account the tortfeasor's personal state—such as his capabilities, professional abilities and experience—while the objective assessment is based on the normal behaviour of an average reasonable person who is in the same position as the tortfeasor in the relevant circumstances (*diligens pater familias*).[247] It can be observed, based on the criteria accepted in the relevant case law for the parent company's duty of care, that the objective assessment of fault seems to be the one most often adopted, rather than the subjective one.

Based on the analysis made under the elements of fault liability in Turkish law, this study will now be focused on the factors that might affect the establishment of the parent company's duty of care in FDL claims.

[245] Aristova (2018), p. 8.

[246] Baysal (2019), p. 60.

[247] Baysal (2019), p. 61.

4.1.4.1 Shareholding

As it is also discussed in relation to the relevant case law, the mere fact of holding shares in a subsidiary does not, *per se*, create a duty of care for the parent company towards the tort victims affected by its subsidiary's actions. Therefore, a parent company which is a holding company, with the sole purpose of holding the shares in the other companies within the corporate group, would not be deemed to have any duty of care towards third parties, subject to certain conditions.

At this point, it would be significant to make a distinction between 'pure holding' and 'mixed holding', considering that the assumption of duty of care as a parent company for pure holdings and mixed holdings might not be the same. A pure holding, whose activity consists of making investments in other companies, might not have sufficient knowledge and experience in the work field of its subsidiaries and, therefore, might not reasonably be expected to have a duty of care towards FDL claimants.[248] On the other hand, mixed holdings generally operate in the same field as their subsidiaries. Therefore, these holdings would have superior knowledge and practical experience in the field, which would allow them to foresee the relevant risks and in many cases they would also be monitoring and controlling the activities of their subsidiaries that resulted in the relevant damaging outcome. Accordingly, it might be reasonable to expect that mixed holdings that were involved in the management of the activities of their subsidiaries that led to a certain damage would have a duty of care towards third party creditors for the harms they suffered due to the relevant activities of the subsidiaries. However, the sole presence of a mixed holding, without any other factors (e.g. an effective *de facto* control over the subsidiary's operations), would be insufficient to establish the parent company's duty of care.

The assessment of the parent company's duty of care might seem more problematic in cases of whole ownership, where the subsidiary will most likely follow the parent company's instructions and orders, which would be in line with the group interest. Moreover, in most whole ownership cases, the parent company will have a majority of the subsidiary's voting rights in its management body. In such a case, a presumption of liability might be recognised, which would be rebuttable if the parent company were able to prove that the level of *de facto* control exercised over the subsidiary were not sufficient to impose a duty of care on the parent company.[249] For instance, in a case where the parent company can prove that it was not effectively managing the activities of its wholly owned subsidiary that resulted in the relevant

[248] Affirming this stance, see David Thompson v The Renwick Group plc [2014] EWCA Civ 635. Also see Choudhury and Petrin (2019), p. 102. However, it is not an absolute fact that pure holdings cannot be held liable for the damage caused by their subsidiaries' operations, as the liability analysis depends on several factors (Choudhury and Petrin (2019), p. 106).

[249] Atamer and Willi (2020a), p. 12; Dowling (2020), p. 229. It is also an economic case to disregard limited liability in case of wholly owned groups, as the investments in such cases do not represent a diversification of risk and therefore do not require limited liability (Choudhury and Petrin (2019), p. 111).

damage, it might then be able to rebut the liability claims based on the breach of its presumed duty of care.

This presumption of liability might be based upon the cases of control stipulated under Article 195/1 of TCC for corporate groups. Accordingly, in cases where there is an ownership of the majority of the voting rights, or a right to procure the appointment of the decision-making majority of the members of the management body, or an ownership of the majority of voting rights (individually or collectly) based on an agreement, or a control based on an agreement or otherwise on another company, a presumption of liability might be imposed on the relevant parent company. Therefore, in cases mentioned in Article 195/1 of TCC, it might be presumed that the parent company not only had control over its subsidiary within the meaning given under corporate groups, but it had also managed the relevant activities and operations of its subsidiary, which eventually resulted in damage to third parties. In the event that the parent company will be able to prove that despite its control over its subsidiary, it had no intervention in the management of the operations and activities of the subsidiary, and for this reason it cannot be deemed to owe a duty of care towards third party tort victims. This distinction between the concept of control within a corporate group and the concept of management of subsidiary's activities was made in the UKSC's judgment in Shell Nigeria case, where the UKSC sought the existence of management of activities in order to accept a duty of care of the parent company. It is, therefore, important to note that even a presumption of liability were to be assumed under the criteria for control in corporate groups, it will still be required that the parent company would be involved in the management of the subsidiary's relevant activities. Needless to say, a presumption of liability would bring advantages to plaintiffs for purposes of burden of proof.

4.1.4.2 Control Over a Subsidiary's Operations

A parent company who exercises direct and substantial control over its subsidiary's material operations will be deemed to have assumed a duty of care towards third party creditors. In other words, what is important is the presence of a *de facto* control over the subsidiary's operations that led to the relevant damage.

Burgess, who interprets the existence of substantial control as a potential ground to pierce the corporate veil, states that the degree of control is expected to be more than participating in the subsidiary's affairs in a normal and usual manner, which might be in the form of exercising dispositive and proprietary power over the subsidiary's assets.[250] It may, however, be challenging to prove the participation in the subsidiary's affairs in an unusual manner in practice. Such a condition would also significantly deprive the FDL claimants from the possibility to pursue their claims. UKSC's judgment in Shell Nigeria case distinguishes the concept of control and invovlement in the management of the subsidiary's activities that led to the

[250] Burgess (1963), p. 182.

relevant damage. In doing this, the UKSC referred to the parent company's taking over, intervening in, controlling, supervising or advising the management of the relevant operations of the subsidiary.[251] The exercised control should not be on an *ad hoc* basis but should be regular and structured.[252] In light of these explanations, it appears to be crucial to have a case-by-case analysis to assess the nature of parent company's interference in its subsidiary's operations, where it will surely be necessary to consider the group's management and organizational structure to observe the decision making mechanisms.

4.1.4.3 Operating in the Same Business Line

One of the grounds for a parent company's duty of care is whether it is aware or if it should be aware of the risks pertaining to its subsidiary's operations, which can be argued within the framework of several factors.

A parent company and subsidiary operating in the same line of business is accepted as a grounds for creating a duty of care for the parent company. In fact, in such a case, the parent company will normally have a certain degree of control over the operations of its subsidiary, as well as knowledge and experience regarding the risks pertaining to the relevant operations and industry. In other words, the parent company's actions as if it were the owner and controller of its subsidiary—especially in those cases where it is aware of the dangerous operations run by its subsidiary—might lead to the imposition of a duty of care.[253] In these cases, the element of proximity from the three-fold test of *Caparo v Dickman*[254] would be satisfied, establishing a neighbour relationship between the parent company and third party tort victims.

4.1.4.4 Appointment and Supervision of a Subsidiary's Directors

The parent company's power to appoint and supervise the managers or directors of the subsidiary, who are in charge of the day-to-day business, might be another way of exercising control over the subsidiary.[255] Furthermore, if the parent company

[251] UKSC also referred to the UKSC's judgment in Lungowe v Vedanta (Lungowe and Ors. v Vedanta Resources Plc and Konkola Copper Mines Plc [2019] UKSC 20), analysed under Sect. 4.1.2.2.6 hereunder; see para. 146 of Okpabi and others v Royal Dutch Shell Plc and another [2021] UKSC 3.

[252] Witting (2009), p. 130.

[253] Villiers (2008), p. 95.

[254] Caparo Industries Plc v Dickman [1990] UKHL 2. See the explanations on this case under Sect. 4.1.2.1 (The Concept of the Duty of Care in Common Law).

[255] For an opinion to the contrary, claiming that the potential influence on the subsidiary's board by appointing nominees would also not be sufficient to create a duty of care by itself, see Nygh (2002), p. 77.

makes operational decisions for its subsidiary—for example on supply, production or capital expenditure—or if the subsidiary's management body acts in line with the parent company's instructions on these issues, then the parent company will be deemed to have a substantial degree of control.

4.1.4.5 Binding Group Policies

Most parent companies issue mandatory compliance policies to the whole corporate group and put mechanisms in place to train their subsidiaries and monitor and supervise their compliance. On the one hand, it is reasonable to ensure group-wide compliance to mandatory policies, but on the other hand, this could be interpreted as exercising control over the operations of the subsidiaries and thus leading to the assumption of a duty of care. A solution suggested after the Bhopal case to avoid imposing liability for duty of care on parent companies was to give as much autonomy as possible to subsidiaries regarding operational matters, thus maintaining strategic control from afar.[256] This issue was the subject of dissenting opinion in the *Okpabi v Shell* case, where Sales LJ agreed that the mere existence of group standards was not sufficient *per se* to impose a duty of care on the parent company; he regarded the existence of a "*mechanism for the projection of real practical executive control by RDS*" as evidence for the imposition of duty of care.[257] This view might be interpreted as an advantage for the victims of corporate abuse, as it implies that the existence of an effective control mechanism over the subsidiary—in addition to group standards on health and safety—might trigger the establishment of the duty of care of the parent company.[258]

Having said that, the mere existence of binding group policies should not be deemed sufficient by itself to impose a duty of care on the parent company. If the damage arose due to the inadequacy of the health and safety policies imposed by the parent company (rather than due to their enforcement by the subsidiary), the element of proximity may be deemed to exist between the parent company and the third party who suffered the damages.[259] Sufficient proximity will also be deemed to exist where the parent company is familiar with the subsidiary's operations and its health and safety risks and also if it exercises a degree of control over the subsidiary's operations in a way that influences the manner in which they are carried out.[260]

---

[256] Zerk (2006), pp. 222–223.

[257] Aristova (2018), p. 16.

[258] It is also said that the situation is delicate for parent companies which strive to define a CSR strategy in balance of their public responsibilities and the risks of liability (Hennchen (2015), p. 13). This situation also shows the importance of regulating parent company's duty of care in law for purposes of legal certainty.

[259] H C Lo (2014), p. 11.

[260] Zerk (2006), p. 217.

4.1.4.6 Dangerous Technology or Process

Parent companies that are creators of a hazardous technology or process, in the sense that they take part in the design, manufacture and testing of substances such as pharmaceuticals or pesticides, can be attributed with duty of care towards the subsidiaries' employees or third parties who were exposed to the relevant substance or who suffered damage due to a fault in the relevant design—even if the parent companies do not exercise control over the relevant technology.[261] The rationale for this opinion is explained by the similarity of the liability for 'process' with product liability, which was tried in the Bhopal case.[262]

As can be seen, it is not easy to make a clear identification in each case based on the currently available criteria arising from the relevant international case law.[263]

4.1.4.7 Evaluation of the Criteria for a Parent Company's Breach of the Duty of Care

Based on the foregoing analysis, it appears that the potential imposition of the duty of care on a parent company for its substantial control and active involvement in its subsidiaries' policies and operations might provide an incentive for the parent company to refrain from engaging in any kind of involvement, supervision or control over its subsidiaries. In this way, by refraining from exercising any direct and substantial control over its subsidiary, by not getting involved in its subsidiary's policies, by not engaging in any kind of monitoring or control over the subsidiary, and by not getting involved in its subsidiary's operations that led to the relevant damage on a regular and *de facto* basis and acting merely as a shareholder, the parent company might try to avoid the duty of care.[264] However, such an approach could create undesirable results in terms of corporate group liability, as parent companies would then be unwilling to get involved in the health and safety issues of their transnational subsidiaries, or to exercise any kind of supervision or control over them, which would definitely reduce the possibilities of positive consequences for tort victims. Furthermore, the courts considering the aforementioned risk may decide that it would not be fair or reasonable to impose a duty of care on the parent company, based on the concern that the parent companies' less active control over their subsidiaries might bear broader risks for the victims of corporate abuse.[265]

[261] Zerk (2006), p. 219.

[262] Zerk (2006), p. 219.

[263] In *Chandler v Cape* ([2012] EWCA Civ 525), the court refused to provide a standard test that considers what are normal incidents of a parent-subsidiary relationship, as there are several different formations of corporate groups, thus it would not be possible to state that a certain event is normal for all of those relationships (see H C Lo 2014, p. 10; Rühmkorf (2015), p. 177).

[264] Witting (2009), p. 130.

[265] Kershaw (2012), p. 155.

On this point, *de Schutter* makes a distinction between two approaches. The first approach is the derivative liability approach, which would create a disincentive for the parent company to control the activities of its subsidiaries, even in those cases where it is able to do so. In such a case, *de Schutter* argues, the piercing of the corporate veil will take place only when the subsidiary has no existence on its own, which would result in the separate legal personalities being disregarded, potentially causing the parent company to not monitor its subsidiary's operations and instead to leave it to the subsidiary to implement the group policies.[266] The second one is an integrated enterprise approach, which is based on the presumption of liability on the parent company or that the parent company would be held directly liable for failing to monitor its subsidiaries' activities.[267] In such situation, the parent company would be incentivised to effectively monitor its subsidiaries' activities and to exercise due diligence. It is clear that the integrated enterprise approach would create a beneficial outcome for tort victims and might, in the long run, overcome the majority of the risks posed by MNCs in their transnational operations. In fact, in determining the method for parent company liability, it should be considered that MNCs might tend towards decentralising their transnational activities in order to escape liability by providing an impression that the subsidiaries are autonomously operating companies, while the MNC continues to engage in dangerous activities transnationally.[268] As a combined method for striking a reasonable balance, *Choudhury/Petrin* suggest adopting enterprise liability for traditional corporate groups, whereby not only the parent company but all members would be liable for damage caused to tort victims, while for 'network' companies (defined as companies with a strong contractual relationship, without any equity or voting rights) a modified vicarious liability could be adopted.[269] However, an acceptance of enterprise liability for the whole corporate group might bring undesired consequences, such as MNCs refraining from forming corporate structures to engage in transnational activities and using small local companies instead. It is difficult to say if such an outcome would eventually be to the benefit or detriment of tort victims.

In light of all these potential concerns, it is crucial to identify clear criteria for addressing the parent company's duty of care towards third parties for the harm they suffered due to the subsidiary's activities. Imposing a direct liability on the parent company to monitor the activities of the subsidiaries under its control would be beneficial for both sides of the case, i.e. parent companies of MNCs and tort victims in FDL claims. *Zerk* summarises the relevant criteria for the parent company's direct liability as follows[270]:

[266] de Schutter (2016), pp. 51–52.

[267] de Schutter (2016), p. 52.

[268] Dowling (2020), p. 231.

[269] Choudhury and Petrin (2019), pp. 120–121.

[270] Zerk (2006), p. 222.

- The parent company having detailed knowledge of the health and environmental risks related to the subsidiary's activities, processes or technology that are subject to the claim,
- The parent company having been closely involved in the day-to-day operations of the subsidiary,
- The parent company failing to exercise the appropriate level of due diligence in the relevant case, and
- The aforementioned failures giving rise to damages on the third party.

The parent company's close involvement in its subsidiary's operations is determined by the actual knowledge of the parent company, through its directors and officers, in the subsidiary's operations, for example—if they were aware of the risks involved regarding the health and safety of employees, and of the potential environmental impacts. Furthermore, in line with the judgment made in *Lungowe v Vedanta*, a parent company might be deemed to have assumed the duty of care in cases where (i) it has taken direct responsibility in relation to the relevant health and safety policy, or (ii) it exercises control over the operations of the subsidiary that allegedly caused the damage. In other words, it is acknowledged that the parent company's direct and substantial oversight of the subsidiary's operations, while the parent company was effectively aware of the risks, would likely lead to the imposition of duty of care.[271]

In order to suggest a wording to regulate the liability of MNCs under Turkish law, it would be beneficial to consider the ongoing process of drafting a legally binding instrument on business and human rights by the UN.[272] The scope of the UN draft is quite extensive, covering—among other things—state responsibility to provide access to remedy for victims, applicable law, jurisdiction, as well as the statute of limitations. Considering that the suggested regulation would form part of Turkish law (if it is signed and ratified upon being finalised), these procedural law matters would already be covered by the relevant Turkish law provisions and, therefore, the scope of parent company liability could be determined accordingly.

The draft UN legally binding instrument imposes duties and obligations on the contracting states to regulate corporate responsibility for human rights violations within their domestic laws. The Third Revised Draft[273] adopted a more extensive approach in setting the scope of corporate responsibility compared to the previous drafts. Accordingly, state parties shall ensure that corporations within their jurisdiction, territory or control shall human rights and prevent or mitigate human rights abuses throughout their business activities and relationships, including those of a

[271] Aristova (2018), p. 13.

[272] For more information on the UN's draft of legally binding instrument, see 2.2.3.2 (A UN Treaty on Business and Human Rights) of this study.

[273] Open-Ended Intergovernmental Working Group on Transnational Corporations and Other Business Enterprises With Respect to Human Rights (OEIGWG), Third Revised Draft Legally Binding Instrument to Regulate, in International Human Rights Law, the Activities of Transnational Corporations and Other Business Enterprises (17.08.2021), https://www.ohchr.org/EN/HRBodies/HRC/WGTransCorp/Session7/Pages/Session7.aspx.

transnational nature.[274] While business activities cover any type of economic or other activity carried out by any natural or legal person, business relationships extend to cover any relationship between natural or legal persons to conduct business activities, including those conducted through different structures such as affiliates, subsidiaries and suppliers.

Turkish law, on the other hand, defines the concept of a corporate group in TCC, which can be formed by way of a control held through shareholding, majority of voting rights, contract or in any other manner. This issue was further dealt with in Chap. 3, however it is worth noting here that as the relevant provisions of TCC effectively regulate the context and scope of corporate groups, it would be sufficient to provide a wording for the parent company's liability for its subsidiaries' activities without having to describe in detail which entities would fall hereunder. Accordingly, a provision such as the following one may be suggested for this purpose, to be inserted as an additional provision within the provisions on corporate groups under TCC:

> The parent company of a corporate group that is engaged in business activities, transnational or otherwise, shall bear responsibility for harms occurring in relation to the business activities of its subsidiaries, provided that:
>
> – It exercises substantial control, management or supervision over the operations of the relevant subsidiary that allegedly caused the harm,
> – There is a strong and direct connection between its subsidiary's conduct and the damage suffered by the victim, and
> – It has foreseen or should have foreseen the relevant risks of human rights violations in the conduct of the group's business activities, but has failed to carefully monitor and instruct its subsidiary, to put adequate measures or appropriate organisation in place to prevent or mitigate the aforementioned risks.
>
> In the event that there is a type of control under Article 195/1 of TCC, the parent company will be deemed *prima facie* liable for the damages referred to in the preceding paragraph, unless it is able to prove that it had no intervention in the management of its subsidiary's operations that led to the alleged damage. The parent company will not be held liable under this provision if it is able to prove that it has carefully monitored and sufficiently instructed its subsidiary in relation to the risks, has arranged the appropriate organisation to determine the relevant risks and obtain preventive measures, and yet the risks still materialised.
>
> The legal consequences of the parent company's liability as per the above paragraph shall be subject to the general provisions of tort of negligence under the Turkish Code of Obligations.

Although the main concern of this study is to look into the liability issues arising due to harms perpetrated on third parties due to transnational business activities in a corporate group, the suggested provision has been drafted purposefully in a manner to also cover domestic business activities with the aim to address the liability of parent companies within a domestic context as well as transnationally.

The criteria for parent company liability in this context work together as a whole. In fact, the mere existence of substantial control over the activities of the subsidiary should not be deemed sufficient to lead to the imposition of duty of care within the

[274] Third Revised Draft, Article 6/2 (Prevention).

meaning of Turkish law. The second criterion related to a connection between the relevant conduct and the damage caused satisfies the element of causation.[275] The first two criteria also reflect the element of proximity, which might be considered part of the element of causation under Turkish law. Meanwhile, the last criterion provides foreseeability, which might correspond to the element of fault or unlawfulness under Turkish law, as it contributes to the analysis of the duty of care.

Based on the foregoing suggested provision, any plaintiff claiming compensation from the parent company for damages it has suffered due to a subsidiary's actions will have the burden to prove that all three criteria are satisfied in the given case. Likewise, a parent company who faces such a claim will have to rebut the plaintiff's allegations based on the relevant criteria, thus either by proving that there was no substantial control over the operations of the subsidiary or no direct link between the subsidiary's operations and the damage or no foreseeability in the relevant case. The parent company should also be able to rebut liability claims where it can effectively prove that it has exercised due diligence and closely monitored its subsidiary's operations, issued group policies and supervised compliance, showed best efforts to obtain information on the subsidiary's conduct, but still could not avoid the risky behaviour of the subsidiary which led to the damage.[276]

The liability discussed under the suggested provision is a liability in tort of negligence. Therefore, it will be subject to legal consequences attributed thereto under the general provisions of the TCO (Art. 49 et seq.), which is reflected in the second paragraph of the suggested provision. In this manner, any claims for compensation or issues related to proof and evidence will be dealt with under the relevant provisions of the TCO.

The parent company's failure to act as envisaged in this provision would lead to a breach of duty of care, which results in unlawfulness and the assumption that the parent company has acted in negligence. This approach is in line with the theory of the protection scope of the violated norm. In fact, with the adoption of such a provision, the discussions concerning the unlawfulness in result or in behaviour in the case of the violation of absolute rights would become redundant, as there would be a specific legal norm to create such unlawfulness if breached. The theory of danger under the element of unlawfulness would support this provision, considering that the parent company—by failing to act as envisaged—would be failing to take the required measures to prevent the danger created by its subsidiaries' operations

[275] The causation under this provision refers to the subsidiary's activities and the human rights violation that harmed third party victims. The proximity and causation of the parent company's involvement (in an active or passive manner) in the operations of its subsidiary would be established by the satisfaction of the third criterion suggested here.

[276] *De Schutter* proposes that a presumption of liability for the parent company might be a viable method, whereby the parent company would be liable for the actions of the subsidiaries under its control, while it can rebut such presumption by proving that it took the required measures but still was not able to prevent the damaging actions of its subsidiary (De Schutter 2016, p. 53). Such a provision would result in a reversal of the burden of proof and it would resonate strict liability.

and its own conduct. Therefore, the breach of the aforementioned provision would eventually constitute a breach of the duty of care of the parent company.

In addition to the criteria given in the suggested provision, mHRDD might also serve as grounds for a parent company's tort liability. This issue will be discussed under Sect. 3.3 (Mandatory Human Rights Due Diligence) below.

4.2 Parent Company's Strict Liability

Other than fault liability, which might be based on a breach of the parent company's duty of care as analysed in the previous section, Turkish law also regulates several different types of mild causal or strict liability that can be useful in imposing the parent company's liability in FDL claims. Strict liability is regulated in addition to the liability in tort of negligence for purposes of social justice to create a liability that does not require any fault on the wrongdoer's side.[277] In other words, in cases falling within the scope of a strict liability, the person who has committed the relevant act shall be held liable regardless of whether he/she has acted in fault or not. Therefore, strict liability is liability without fault, which will be established in cases where there is an act, unlawfulness, damage and causation.

There are three types of strict liability under the TCO: liability based on fairness, mild causal liability (related to due care) and strict causal liability (related to risk).[278] For the purposes of this study, mild causal liability and strict causal liability might be relevant in defining a parent company's strict liability.[279]

The mild causal liability arises in cases where the person who has committed the wrongful act has not fulfilled his/her liability to act with due care and thus is held responsible for the damages that have occurred.[280] The employer's mild causal liability for its employee's actions is a liability based on care, which will be analysed in detail below.

Finally, the strict causal liability concerns a type of liability that arises due to dangerous activities or materials and substances that may significantly harm others. This liability is based on the understanding that anyone who is benefiting from the operations of an enterprise that is engaged in dangerous activities, which may cause

[277] Kılıçoğlu (2018), p. 421.

[278] Baysal (2019), p. 98; Nomer (2018), pp. 241–242; Eren (2017), p. 639; Kılıçoğlu (2018), pp. 422–423; Ersöz (2017), p. 2897; Başoğlu (2015), p. 37.

[279] In fact, liability based on fairness refers to cases where the person who committed the relevant act is held liable for purposes of fairness and justice, even though it has not acted in fault. The typical example for this type of liability is the liability of a person with a mental disability who has caused a damage, which might be necessarily compensated as per fairness and justice (Art. 65 TCO). Therefore, this type of strict liability does not appear to be relevant for FDL claims and thus will not be reiterated hereunder.

[280] Kılıçoğlu (2018), p. 422.

damages that are difficult to prevent, should be held liable in this respect.[281] Unlike mild causal liability, strict causal liability does not carry any escape clause to avoid liability. Therefore, the only way to escape liability in this case would be to prove that the causal connection is absent in the relevant case.[282] There are several provisions of strict causal liability under Turkish law, one of which is the general provision on strict liability due to dangerous activities, regulated under Article 71 of TCO, which will be analysed hereunder. As the scope of this study covers environmental damages within the scope of FDL claims, the liability of the polluter, which is regulated under Article 28 of Environmental Law, will also be assessed.

4.2.1 Mild Causal Liability of the Employer

Turkish law regulates the employer's liability for its employees' acts or actions that result in damages to third parties as a type of mild causal liability[283] (Art. 66 TCO). According to this article, the employer shall be responsible for compensating the damages to others due to its employee's acts during the course of work (Art. 66/1 TCO). The employer shall not be held responsible if he can successfully prove that he has shown the required due care in choosing the employee, giving instructions regarding the work, and supervising and monitoring the employee in order to prevent any damage (Art. 66/2 TCO). If the employment takes place within a business enterprise, the employer shall be responsible for compensating the damages occurred due to the relevant enterprise's activities, unless he can prove that the work organization was suitable to prevent the occurrence of the relevant damage (Art. 66/3 TCO).

The most important element in this type of causal liability is the breach of the due care regulated in law, which is based on principles of causing the relevant result, as well as having control on the relevant employees and benefiting from their actions.[284] The employer's liability due to its employees' actions is based on the due care expected by the employer in exercising the required diligence, monitoring and supervision of its employees to prevent any harm to third parties.[285] In this liability, the employer can avoid liability by proving that it has shown the required

[281] Ersöz (2017), p. 2897.

[282] Kılıçoğlu (2018), p. 424.

[283] The term of 'mild causal liability' is used in Swiss legal doctrine concerning Article 55 of Swiss Code of Obligations, which is the basis for Article 66 of TCO. This type of causal liability is interpreted differently than strict liability, such as liability for dangerous activities (Art. 71 TCO). In fact, in this case, if the tort victim proves the criteria sought under Article 55 of Swiss Code of Obligaitons, the employer might avoid liability by proving that it has exercised due care to avoid damage or that the damage would have occurred even if it had exercised due care (Koch and Koziol 2002, p. 323–324; Atamer and Willi 2020a, p. 14).

[284] Başoğlu (2015), p. 39.

[285] Eren (2017), p. 643.

due care or even in case it were to show the required due care the relevant damage would still have occurred (and thus there was no causation).[286] Taking into consideration the criteria to escape employer's liability cited under Article 55 of Swiss Code of Obligations, if the employer is able to show that it has chosen the employee correctly, that it has carefully monitored and instructed the employee, and that appropriate organisation is in place to assess risks and take measures, it might successfully escape liability under this clause.[287]

In order to invoke the employer's causal liability, it is first necessary for there to be an employer–employee relationship, based upon an employment contract or otherwise,[288] regardless of whether there is a corresponding pay or not.[289] The relationship requires the existence of work under the instructions and orders of the employer, thus a state of subordination. This subordination is considered as *conditio sine qua non* of the employer–employee relationship. In other words, even in the absence of an employment contract, Article 66 of TCO may apply if there is subordination between the parties.[290]

The employer is defined as a natural or legal person who requires and benefits from a third party's services, and who has the authority to exercise supervision and monitoring on the said third party, within the scope of a relationship of dependence.[291] In light of this definition, in order to be considered an employer, there should be an aim of having work or service performed, seeking another person's service for this purpose, being in a relationship of dependence, having a duty to supervise and monitor the employee, and giving orders and instructions.[292]

On the other hand, the employee is a person who performs the work given by another person under this person's instructions and supervision, within a relationship of dependence.[293] Even though the employee might have knowledge and expertise in the relevant work, he/she will apply these in a limited manner, in line with the instructions of the employer.[294] Under Turkish law, in the traditional approach, the term employee under Article 66 of TCO is interpreted to cover only real persons, and not legal entities.[295] It is, in fact, difficult to consider a relationship of subordination

---

[286] Eren (2017), p. 642; Kılıçoğlu (2018), p. 423; Başoğlu (2015), p. 39.

[287] Atamer and Willi (2020a), p. 14.

[288] It is accepted under Turkish law that an employer-employee relationship might arise from an employment contract or on a de facto basis (Okyar Karaosmanoğlu 2019, p. 93).

[289] Eren (2017), pp. 647–648; Kılıçoğlu (2018), p. 434.

[290] Baysal (2019), p. 98; Nomer (2018), p. 244. Employment contract is not deemed as a crucial factor to establish employer's liability. In other words, it is not important to have a valid contract in order to form an employer-employee relationship within the meaning under Article 66 of TCO (Çelik 2015, pp. 19–20).

[291] Eren (2017), p. 647; Çelik (2015), p. 18; Okyar Karaosmanoğlu (2019), p. 70.

[292] Çelik (2015), p. 19.

[293] Eren (2017), p. 649; Ünlütepe (2015), p. 260.

[294] Kara Kılıçarslan (2016), p. 70.

[295] Çelik (2015), p. 22.

between independent companies.[296] However, there are also opinions in legal doctrine that legal entities may also act as employees within the scope of this article.[297] *Ünlütepe* puts forth, on this point, that the employer's organisational liability under Article 66/3 TCO shall apply in corporate groups in respect of the parent company liability for damage caused by its subsidiary's operations.[298] According to this opinion, a relationship of subordination may exist between a parent company and its subsidiary in a corporate group, which might trigger the basis for applying organisational liability whereby the parent company would be deemed liable for the operations of its subsidiary as the entity responsible for organisation.[299] However, this opinion does not explicitly specify which types of damages (caused by the subsidiary's operations) would be covered by the parent company's organisational liability. It would seem quite ambitious to include FDL claims within this framework, as there is no stipulation in law concerning a parent company's liability in this respect.

To apply the provision of Article 66 of TCO, the damage caused to the third party should take place while the employee is doing the relevant work and the employee's conduct should be related to that work. It is also necessary for the employee's act to be unlawful. It is, however, debated whether the employee should have acted in fault or not in order to invoke this liability. The Turkish Court of Appeal's approach to this point is that no fault is sought for this type of liability for the employer and for the employee, thus the employer's liability might be established regardless of whether the employee has acted in fault or not.[300] As the liability under this provision concerns the employer's mild causal liability based on a failure to act with due care, it would be redundant to seek the employee's fault in the relevant action.[301] Therefore, employer's liability under Article 66 of TCO may be imposed regardless of whether the employee has acted in fault or not.

The employer's mild causal liability provides the employer with the opportunity to avoid liability by proving that it has shown the required diligence in choosing the relevant employee, providing instructions and supervising the work done. This proof is based on the objective criteria that the employer has shown the required diligence and care to prevent the relevant damage and it is not an attempt to prove that the employer had no fault in the relevant case.[302] In other words, it is accepted that the employer has acted in fault and is liable for the relevant damage, unless it can

[296] Atamer and Willi (2020a), p. 12.

[297] Okyar Karaosmanoğlu (2019), p. 90; Ünlütepe (2015), p. 261.

[298] Ünlütepe (2015), p. 261.

[299] Ünlütepe (2015), p. 296. Ünlütepe stipulates that the acceptance of parent company's responsibility within organization liability for its subsidiary's activities would also be in line with piercing the corporate veil.

[300] Baysal (2019), p. 98; Nomer (2018), p. 244.

[301] Çelik (2015), p. 43.

[302] Kılıçoğlu (2018), p. 422.

effectively prove that it has complied with its duty of care, which constitutes an escape clause.[303]

An additional type of causal liability was introduced by the TCO upon its enactment in July 2012, referred to as the employer's organisational liability (Art. 66/3 TCO). Accordingly, in cases where the employer is operating a business, it shall also prove that the work organisation of the relevant business is satisfactory and capable of preventing the rise of such damage; otherwise, even though the employer has proven that it has shown due care in choosing, instructing and supervising the employee, it would still be held responsible.[304] Having said that, one opinion in Turkish legal doctrine puts forward that the obligations under TCO Art. 66/2 and 66/3 are independent of each other and, accordingly, an employer who could successfully prove that it has either shown diligence or that the organisation was adequate to prevent the damage could avoid liability.[305]

There are several different opinions in Turkish legal doctrine as to the legal character of this new provision. Some scholars argue that employer's liability and organisational liability constitute a type of fault liability whereby the onus of proof has shifted to the tortfeasor. In this opinion, the employer's liability and organisational liability concern the breach of a duty of care and are therefore closer to fault liability, which can be avoided by the tortfeasor on proving that he has acted with due care.[306] The predominant opinion in Turkish legal doctrine, on the other hand, contends that the employer's liability and organisational liability are types of mild causal liability, whereby the employer shall be responsible regardless of its fault with the possibility of escaping liability by proving that it has shown the required due care.[307]

As a general principle, the employer can avoid liability by proving that the chain of causation was broken in the relevant incident. The employer would need to show that there was a *force majeure*, or the third party's gross negligence, or the victim's gross negligence in the occurrence of the damage. It is possible to state that the assessments concerning causation are less stringent than the strict liability for

---

[303] Kara Kılıçarslan (2016), p. 86.

[304] Kılıçoğlu (2018), p. 440. The term of 'business' within the meaning of Article 66/3 of TCO is to be interpreted broadly, so as to include but not be limited to commercial enterprises (Kara Kılıçarslan 2016, p. 154; Okyar Karaosmanoğlu 2019, pp. 128–129). Factors such as the type of operation, size of business or whether the business carries out a one-time-only operation or a continuous one are not decisive in the formation of a 'business' under Article 66/3 of TCO (Kara Kılıçarslan 2016, p. 154; Okyar Karaosmanoğlu 2019, pp. 130–131).

[305] Ünlütepe (2017), p. 30.

[306] Ünlütepe (2015), p. 145.

[307] Antalya (2013), p. 548; Kılıçoğlu (2018), p. 423; Ünlütepe (2015), pp. 147–148. The wording of the TCO is also in line with the dominant opinion, as the employer's liability is regulated under the section of strict liability and liability for due care. Also, Turkish Court of Appeal has a joint chambers' judgment whereby it has decided that the employer's liability (then regulated under Article 55 of the Code of Obligations no. 818) constitutes a type of causal liability (Turkish Court of Appeal, General Assembly of Joint Chambers decision dated 27.03.1957 and numbered 1957/1E. 1957/3K.) (see also Ünlütepe 2015, p. 149).

dangerous activities, which are analysed in detail in the following section, considering that this type of liability is a mild causal liability. In other words, the employer has a higher chance of proving the discontinuation of the chain of causation than the operator or owner of the dangerous enterprise, within the meaning of Article 71 of TCO.

In respect of FDL claims, the most likely scenario is that the employees of the subsidiary would be involved in the alleged human rights abuse, in which case the parent company cannot be held responsible under the liability of the employer, as the employer in that case would be the subsidiary. It would be too far-fetched to argue that the relationship between a parent company and its subsidiary could be deemed a type of employer–employee relationship within the meaning of Article 66 of TCO. In fact, in order to speak of employer's strict liability, it is required that there be a relationship of dependence, which is unlikely to be present in the parent company–subsidiary relationship, which are two separate legal personalities.[308] Although in certain instances, especially where there is full dominance, it might be put forth that the employee's actions are completely under the order and instructions of the parent company, but such a relationship should not be covered by the correct interpretation of the relevant article. It would also be difficult to effectively prove that the parent company is the ultimate beneficiary of the subsidiary's activities,[309] considering that in most cases the subsidiaries are operating their enterprises in their name and account, and bearing any benefits and costs arising. This liability aims to hold employers accountable for any damaging acts committed by their employees during the course of their employment, based on the assumption that the employer has breached its duty of care to supervise and monitor the acts of its employees.[310] Therefore, it would be quite challenging to prove that an independent legal entity, the subsidiary in this case, has acted in complete subordination and under the instruction of its parent company.[311] Moreover, under Turkish law it would be problematic to consider the subsidiary of a corporate group an employee within the meaning of Article 66 of TCO, as this term aims to cover only real persons.[312] It might be acceptable to make a comparison to the employer's liability in certain cases

[308] Harsa (2007), p. 170.

[309] The employer's condition of receiving benefits from the work performed is considered as an element in establishing the employer-employee relationship within the meaning given under Article 66 of TCO (Kara Kılıçarslan 2016, p. 81; Okyar Karaosmanoğlu 2019, p. 94).

[310] Eren (2017), p. 643.

[311] It is stated that the more extensive the scope of autonomy in giving decisions, the less is the possibility of being defined as an employee under Article 66 of TCO (Kara Kılıçarslan 2016, p. 73; Okyar Karaosmanoğlu 2019, p. 95). The mere fact that there is a subordination between two persons does not lead to the conclusion of an employee-employer relationship; it will be considered whether the relevant subordination eliminates the employee's discretion in performing the relevant work (Okyar Karaosmanoğlu 2019, p. 95).

[312] Çelik (2015), p. 22.

concerning the damages incurred by the subsidiary's employees.[313] However, it still proves to be challenging to impose the same liability on a parent company as if it were the employer of its subsidiaries. In fact, these two relationships are very different in nature.

Enneking, who has analysed the same issue under Dutch law, has also come to the conclusion that it would not be possible to designate the subsidiaries (in the host countries) as the employees of the parent companies, considering that these are separate legal entities.[314] The same is also thought to be applicable to the currently available provisions of Turkish law. In fact, even in whole shareholding structures, it would be difficult to effectively prove that a subsidiary with a separate legal personality to the parent company would be dependent on the parent company in the sense required for employer's liability. Furthermore, even in cases where the relationship between the parent company and its subsidiary is misused in a manner that would harm third parties, the doctrine of piercing the corporate veil might be considered as a viable option, to the extent that the required criteria are present. Under any circumstances, it seems both challenging and redundant to apply Article 66 of TCO in FDL claims.

4.2.2 Strict Liability for Dangerous Activities

Under Turkish law, there are several grounds for strict causal liability related to risk. These are by nature different to the simple causal liability grounds related to due care, such as the liability of the employer. Strict causal liability related to risk arises when there is a causal connection between the occurrence of the typical risk linked to the liability and the damage.[315] Unlike other strict liability types under Turkish law, liability for dangerous activities does not include any escape clause for the wrongdoer, and therefore is generally accepted as the most severe type of strict liabilities.[316]

Liability concerning dangerous activities is linked to the operation of an enterprise,[317] be it commercial or otherwise, which carries out dangerous activities, or where the element of danger is posed by a particular substance or subject. There are

---

[313]Morgan (2015), p. 287. *Morgan* refers the employer's liability whereby the employer has the duty to select and monitor its employee and which constitutes a direct claim addressed by the victim to the employer.

[314]Enneking (2012), p. 246.

[315]Tiftik (1997), p. 34; Eren (2017), p. 501; Akartepe (2012), p. 169.

[316]Ersöz (2017), p. 2899; Başoğlu (2015), p. 44.

[317]Although this type of liability concerns the activities of an enterprise, it is not similar to the enterprise liability under Article 4:202 of PETL, which establishes a liability due to the harms caused by a defect of an enterprise or of its output, unless the operator proves that it has complied with the required standard of conduct. This is considered as a negligence based liability based on an objective notion of fault and a reversal of the burden of proof in cases where the victim is unable to

several examples of this type of liability under Turkish law, deriving from a range of sources from motor vehicles to oil tankers. While some of these are regulated under specific legislation, others are based on the general provision on liability for dangerous activities (Art. 71 of TCO) and recognised by the Court of Appeal judgments. The predominant opinion in legal doctrine suggests that it is not necessary to introduce specific provisions into statutory law in the presence of the said general provision, which in any case aims to cover different types of dangerous activities, as they may arise with the development of technology.[318] Therefore, it is accepted that both the cases covered by the general provision under Article 71 of TCO and those covered by special provisions shall constitute liabilities for dangerous activities, which are a type of strict liability.[319]

As per the general provision on the liability for dangerous activities (i.e. Art. 71 TCO), in the event that damage has occurred due to the activities of an enterprise which pose an abnormally high degree of danger, the owner of the enterprise and its operator (if any) shall be jointly and severally liable in respect thereof. The criteria sought for imposing strict liability under this provision is (i) the existence of an enterprise (not necessarily commercial), (ii) the significantly dangerous nature of the activity carried out by the relevant enterprise, (iii) damage and causal link between the activity and the damage that has occurred.

Accordingly, in order to apply liability under this provision, first of all, the existence of an enterprise is sought. This aspect of the provision is criticised by *Atamer*, based on the rationale that it delimits the scope of the liability.[320] In the first draft of TCO, the term used was liability for a "dangerous activity" without requiring the existence of an enterprise. As the provision does not refer to a "commercial enterprise", which is defined in the TCC, different interpretations have arisen in Turkish legal doctrine as to how this concept should be understood. *Arkan* defines the concept of 'enterprise' as "*bringing together labour and capital independently, with an aim to create economic interest by an entrepreneur*".[321] In the opinion of *Sanlı*, the enterprise is any unit which carries out economic activities, and the

---

base its claims on any other type of strict liability regulated in PETL (Koch 2009, p. 211; Choudhury and Petrin 2019, p. 161).

[318] Eren (2017), p. 523.

[319] There is an opinion in Turkish legal doctrine suggesting that this type of liability does not constitute a liability in tort (Eren 2017, p. 524). According to this opinion, damage in tort claims arises from the act of a person, while in liability for dangerous activities the damage is linked to the operations of an enterprise or an action which is considered dangerous by itself, and even if a person's act could be involved, this could only be secondary. Furthermore, the element of unlawfulness, which should be present in tort, might be absent in liability for dangerous activities, considering that at times, these activities are conducted based on a legal license or permission. Nevertheless, as much as this opinion seems well-grounded, it does not affect the analysis to be made hereunder in relation to FDL claims.

[320] Atamer (2006), p. 22. Article 5:101 of PETL on strict liability for abnormally dangerous activities, which is similar to Article 71 of TCO, also does not bring any requirement for the existence of an enterprise to call this liability (See İkizler 2014, p. 3253).

[321] Arkan (2012), p. 26.

concept of 'enterprise' within the context of Article 71 of TCO is closer to the commercial enterprise, but with a wider scope.[322] Therefore, it is possible to conclude that for the purposes of Article 71 of TCO, the aim of earning profit is not crucial for an enterprise and even in the absence of such an aim, it might still be possible to define an enterprise by taking into account its economic activities and organisational structure.[323] Having said that, enterprises operated by independent merchants, such as doctor's or lawyer's offices, are not considered enterprises that should fall within the scope of this article, as it is unlikely that these would create any serious danger.[324] In general, the usual trend of FDL claims shows that the enterprises operated by subsidiaries would likely satisfy the criteria for being defined as an 'enterprise' for the purposes of this provision.

The second criterion for liability for dangerous activities is that the operations of the enterprise should pose a significant danger. Article 71/2 of TCO regulates which activities might be considered to be significantly dangerous. Accordingly, an enterprise will be deemed to pose a significant danger where it is likely to create frequent or serious damages in consideration of the nature of the enterprise or the material, tools or power used in its operations, even where the due care expected by an expert is shown in this respect. As a general note, taking into account that the main purpose of this clause which regulates a general liability based on danger is to create a catch-all provision that could be adapted to new conditions posing significant danger, the types of enterprises and activities that pose a significant danger will also naturally change over time. In other words, a certain activity that is deemed significantly dangerous in today's world may not be deemed so in future, and vice versa. The provision is not clear on the concept of posing significant danger. This concept is interpreted as a general condition of the enterprise or activity to create a significant danger, rather than a condition to be evaluated based on a specific case.[325] However, as the provision does not exemplify any cases that would fall within its scope, the interpretation is basically left to the discretion of the judiciary. Activities such as nuclear energy production, mining, electricity production and distribution, hazardous material production and distribution, oil drilling and distribution might be considered significantly dangerous for the purpose of Article 71 of TCO.[326]

Another criterion for establishing liability for dangerous activities is that the danger posed should be frequent or serious. Hence, this liability may only arise in cases where the characteristic risk or danger has occurred.[327] The characteristic risk

[322] Sanlı Kerem (2012), p. 77.

[323] Saraç (2013), p. 32.

[324] Büyüksağiş (2006), p. 6.

[325] Oğuzman and Öz (2013), p. 192.

[326] See Turkish Court of Appeal, General Assembly of Civil Chambers decision dated 29.11.2017 and numbered 2017/439E. 2017/1463K. (operation of oil pipelines). See also Sarıhan (2014), p. 1183.

[327] Eren (2017), pp. 501–502; Erdem (2012), p. 220; Tiftik (1997), p. 23; Akartepe (2012), p. 170; Saraç (2013), p. 61. The requirement for the occurrence of a characteristic risk or damage is also sought under PETL (İkizler 2014, p. 3252).

for the purposes of this provision is the frequency or severity of the damage, which constitutes the objective element of the concept of posing significant danger.[328] This objective element covers two circumstances: (i) the frequency of the probability of the occurrence of damage, and (ii) the severity of the damage that has occurred.[329] The presence of either one of these two conditions will suffice to constitute a dangerous activity within the scope of Article 71 of TCO. Activities dealing with nuclear energy or explosives are considered dangerous, as the damage arising from these activities is usually severe and powerful enough to have a mass impact. Radio stations or base stations are also considered to fall within the scope of dangerous activities in the sense of this provision.[330] However, it might not always be simple to decide whether an activity ought to be deemed dangerous or not. For instance, shipbuilding may be considered an activity that poses a serious risk of damage for workers, while the detrimental effects are often limited to the workers rather than being a threat for the wider public. Similarly, the ships that carry cargo might pose a significant risk of damage for seamen, while not carrying a public risk, unless they were to carry chemicals or explosives, in which case this could constitute a dangerous activity. Mining is another activity that could cause severe damages to both the employees and the people living in the vicinities, and therefore might be deemed a dangerous activity within the meaning under Article 71 of TCO.

The subjective element of 'posing significant danger' is that the relevant danger cannot be avoided even in cases where the due care expected by an expert is shown. The concept of due care mentioned here is different to the duty of care concept under tort liability. Within the context of this article, due care refers to the reasonable care expected from a person with expertise in the relevant field.

In order to speak of a liability for dangerous activity, it is necessary for the significantly dangerous activity of the enterprise to have caused a damage. This implies that a chain of causation should exist between the activities or operations of the relevant enterprise and the damage that occurred. Under Turkish law, the chain of causation will be broken in cases where there is a fault of the victim, a *force majeure*, or a fault or gross negligence of a third party. Where the victim's faulty behavior caused the relevant damage, then it is only reasonable to accept that no liability for dangerous activities should arise. However, where it is a *force majeure* or a third party's fault or gross negligence causing the damage, it might still be argued whether the purpose of Article 71 of TCO would still be to cover the resulting damage.[331] In fact, considering the severity of this type of strict liability, it might be worth arguing that the defendant should be responsible for taking the required measures to prevent the occurrence of damage in cases of *force majeure* or a third party's wrongful act.

[328] Tiftik (1997), p. 115; Yılmaz (2010), p. 572; Erdem (2012), p. 218; Saraç (2013), pp. 36–37; Antalya (2008), p. 80.

[329] Eren (2017), p. 503; Akkayan Yıldırım (2012), p. 210.

[330] Uygur (2012), p. 521.

[331] Eren (2017), p. 528.

The effect of *force majeure* in breaking the chain of causation in strict liability has been interpreted less stringently than general fault liability. While in general terms, *force majeure* would be deemed to exist in cases where an event is external, unavoidable, unforeseeable and extraordinary, in strict liability cases this is not a straightforward conclusion.[332] In fact, the extraordinary and unforeseeable nature of a *force majeure* might be relative. The main aim of the strict liability under Article 71 of TCO is to impose liability for damage that has occurred despite all the measures and precautions that were taken within the scope of a dangerous activity, which is permitted despite the significant danger it poses to society. Hence, the occurrence of the typical risk of the relevant activity due to an external event which causes the damage should be deemed to fall within the scope of strict liability regulated under Article 71 of TCO.[333] It would, therefore, be reasonable to assess, case-by-case, whether the *force majeure* event is of an extraordinary nature that would break the chain of causation between the typical risk and the damage that occurred.[334]

As for a third party's fault, it is suggested that the fault should amount to gross negligence and have a primary role in the occurrence of the relevant damage.[335] In the case of a third party's fault, the approach of the Turkish Court of Appeal has been to assess whether the relevant damage would have arisen in the absence of the third party's wrongful act.[336] In a more recent decision by the General Assembly of Civil Chambers of Turkish Court of Appeal, concerning damages taking place due to the explosion of the oil pipelines operated by the defendant company, it was held that the chain of causation was broken due to the third party's fault, which was a terrorist attack.[337] In the reasoning of this decision, the court also referred to a previous decision by the Turkish Court of Appeal, where the issue was elaborated and discussed in more detail.[338] The court, in this previous decision, acknowledged that the operation of oil pipelines would constitute a significantly dangerous activity presenting significant danger to the environment, and therefore the operator's or owner's liability under Article 71 of TCO should be more severe than other types of strict liability. The court also stated that the element of causation, required to establish strict liability under Article 71 of TCO, might not be broken in all cases

[332] Alper (2018), pp. 202–203.

[333] Alper (2018), p. 204.

[334] Alper (2018), p. 204. In Swiss law, force majeure events that eliminate strict liability for dangerous activities are restricted with natural disasters and war. For instance, operation of air vehicles is considered as an activity for which strict liability cannot be eliminated due to force majeure (see Sarıhan 2014, p. 1189).

[335] Sarıhan (2014), pp. 1188–1189.

[336] Turkish Court of Appeal, General Assembly of Civil Chambers decision dated 03.02.2010 and numbered 2010/21-36 E. 2010/67 K.

[337] Turkish Court of Appeal, General Assembly of Civil Chambers decision dated 29.11.2017 and numbered 2017/439E. 2017/1463K.

[338] Turkish Court of Appeal, General Assembly of Civil Chambers decision dated 16.03.2016 and numbered 2014/3-841E. 2016/321K.

where a third party acted in gross negligence. The court further admitted that in the area where the pipelines were located, terrorist acts were quite common and even expected, therefore the defendant company was obliged to take precautions to prevent the relevant terrorist attacks, but failed to do so. However, the majority of the General Assembly of Civil Chambers rejected the suggestion that in these circumstances the chain of causation should be deemed to exist and ruled that the defendant company could not be held liable under Article 71 of TCO due to the third party's fault, which broke the chain of causation.

In light of these decisions, it is possible to conclude that the Turkish Court of Appeal's most recent approach has unfortunately been quite restrictive in terms of establishing strict liability under Article 71 of TCO. In fact, the *rationae legis* of this provision is to regulate a general liability for significantly dangerous activities that have the potential to inflict extensive damages on people. Therefore, delimiting the relevant liability's scope in the aforementioned manner would go against the main aim of this regulation. Especially in the case of abnormally dangerous activities by an enterprise that are expected to create widespread damage or harm to others, a third party's intervention should not be seen to affect the relevant strict liability.[339] In fact, in these cases, the operator or owner of the enterprise should be reasonably expected to have effectively ensured that third party risks are eliminated.

It is important to note that to speak of liability for dangerous activities, the damage should have occurred due to the occurrence of a typical danger arising from the enterprise's operations. The occurrence of a typical danger should be assessed on a case-by-case basis, taking into account the features of the relevant activity and enterprise, which shall be proven by the victim.[340] For instance, environmental damages and health issues arising from the explosion of an oil pipe should be deemed a typical or characteristic danger for an oil company. On the other hand, a bodily injury caused by tripping over a hose that was lying on the floor of a gas station cannot be deemed a characteristic danger and therefore should not lead to any liability for dangerous activities.

It is clear from the wording of Article 71 of TCO that the parties who can be held accountable for dangerous activities within the scope of this clause are the owner and/or operator of the relevant enterprise. This is a joint and several liability under which each one of the liable parties are responsible for the whole debt and the victim is free to request damages from either one of them.[341] The owner of the enterprise is the natural or legal person who has organisational or economic control over the relevant enterprise, who is not necessarily the owner of all the assets.[342] The operator

[339] Sarıhan (2014), p. 1189.

[340] Baysal (2019), p. 98; Nomer (2018), p. 325.

[341] Ersöz (2017), p. 2922.

[342] Ersöz (2017), p. 2923; Baysal (2019), p. 98; Nomer (2018), p. 330. Alper, who disagrees with this definition, states that the owner of the enterprise is the person who is the owner of the right subjects and rights that form the relevant enterprise and that are part of the assets of the relevant enterprise (Alper 2018, pp. 210–211).

of the enterprise can be a natural or legal person who operates the enterprise in his/her own name and account, bearing both the benefits and expenses arising therefrom,[343] based on a lease or management contract.[344] Moreover, anyone who operates the enterprise based on a right of usufruct or superficies can also be deemed an operator.[345]

FDL claims involve harms caused by a transnational subsidiary's activities which therefore concern an enterprise owned or operated by the relevant subsidiary. In cases where the parent company may be the owner or the operator of the enterprise, its liability under this clause could be disputed; in usual circumstances, however, it would be challenging to assert the parent company's liability for the damaging activities of an enterprise owned or operated by its subsidiary. Accordingly, by way of a literal interpretation of this clause, it seems difficult to assert the parent company's liability under this provision.

Nevertheless, there are some theories which support a broader interpretation of the scope of this liability. If it could be proven that the parent company is the ultimate beneficiary of the activities carried out by its subsidiary in its enterprise, then it could be argued that the parent company is in fact the 'owner' of the relevant enterprise, as it is the one receiving the benefits.[346] In other words, being the party who is receiving the benefits, the parent company should also be held liable for the consequences of such activities.[347] In economic theory this is explained as a method of loss shifting. In cases concerning liability for dangerous activities, it is either the owner or the operator of the enterprise who would be in the best position to bear the responsibility and then to reflect the costs to society, and should therefore be held liable for the damages.[348] It is accepted in Turkish legal doctrine that while the operator of the enterprise is a person who exercises *de facto* and direct control over the business and its employees, and who receives the benefit and bears the risk arising from the operations, the owner of the enterprise is the person who controls the enterprise economically or from an organisational perspective.[349] In terms of ownership within

[343] Alper (2018), p. 224.

[344] Oğuzman and Öz (2013), p. 193.

[345] Akkayan Yıldırım (2012), p. 211; Nomer (2018), p. 121.

[346] Erişgin (2013), p. 72; Antalya (2008), p. 74; Alper (2018), p. 208.

[347] This principle is also accepted in Turkish legal doctrine as one of the grounds for strict liability under Article 71 of TCO. Accordingly, whoever receives the benefits of a certain thing or operation shall also bear the negative consequences and damage arising thereof (Yücel 2013, p. 33).

[348] Gordley (2006), p. 206, 208; Vandall (1989), p. 20; Başoğlu (2015), p. 45.

[349] Alper (2018), p. 208; Ersöz (2017), p. 2923; Başoğlu (2016), p. 200; Ünlütepe (2017), p. 20–21; Yücel (2013), p. 232. It is worth noting that in the majority of European jurisdictions, strict liability for dangerous activities is addressed to the keeper or operator of the relevant enterprise or vehicle, rather than the owner. The justification for this approach is stated as holding liable the person who is taking advantage of the activity and who might be in the best position to internalise the costs (Koch and Koziol 2002, pp. 418–419). However, in German law, ownership is considered as a decisive element in establishing strict liability. The conditions of strict liability are determined as (i) having free disposition over the relevant object and (ii) using or operating it on one's own account (Koch and Koziol 2002, p. 161). Also, in Swiss law, the tendency is to hold liable the person who has the

the meaning of Article 71 of TCO, it is also stated that the crucial factor in determining ownership would be who has the disposal of the relevant enterprise in practice, the ability to monitor it and the authority to decide on economic terms.[350] This can be the case in situations where the level of control and dominance within the integrated structure of the corporate group is so high that the subsidiary is in fact acting as an organ of the parent company. Another potential grounds for questioning the position of parent companies in strict liability for dangerous activities is the principle of danger, which stipulates that whoever carries out a dangerous operation shall be obliged to take all the required precautions to prevent the potential harms.[351] In case of FDL claims, it might be argued that the parent company that is receiving the benefits and economically controlling the activities of its subsidiary, knowing the risks pertaining thereto, should also be liable for any harms incurred by such activities. Having said that, the specific case of group companies (i.e. whether a parent company could be deemed, under certain circumstances, the owner of the enterprise operated by its subsidiary) has so far not been assessed under the liability for dangerous activities in Turkish legal doctrine.

In light of the discussions concerning the definition of the operator and owner of the enterprise within Article 71 of TCO, it appears to be rather unlikely that liability would be successfully imposed on the parent company, as the enterprise in question would most usually be owned and operated by the subsidiary. In fact, in corporate groups, each subsidiary and the parent company have functional independence, although they might be economically dependent, and it will be challenging to therefore consider the whole corporate group as the owner or operator of the enterprise with dangerous activities.[352] It could be argued that it might be possible under certain circumstances to claim that the parent company had economic and organisational control over the enterprise, knew the risks and failed to take measures to prevent them. However, in most cases this argument would be difficult to prove in practice. Therefore, this provision does not seem to provide an effective legal grounds to accommodate FDL claims.

As per the third paragraph of Article 71, the provisions of law on special cases of liabilities are reserved. Therefore, any type of liability for danger that is already regulated in statutory laws will continue to be subject to the relevant provisions. This principle is in line with the nature of the liability regulated under Article 71, as this is considered an umbrella clause that would cover cases that are not already subject to

---

effective organizational and economic control of the relevant object (Koch and Koziol 2002, p. 336). The approach under Swiss law might be useful in FDL cases, if it can be proven that parent company holds the effective organizational and economic control over the enterprise and activities of its transnational subsidiary.

[350] Yücel (2013), p. 229. *Yücel* also states that the ownership rule usually applies in cases where the liability concerns the use of a certain material or thing, rather than the operations or activities of an enterprise (Yücel 2013, p. 226).

[351] Yücel (2013), p. 36.

[352] Alper (2018), p. 103, fn. 463.

any specific provision.[353] One of the aforementioned liabilities which is already regulated in statutory law is the polluter's liability for environmental damages (Art. 28 of Environmental Law).[354] This is also another type of strict liability, which will be further explained in the following section. As per the provision of Article 71/3, the polluter's liability will continue to be subject to this provision.

4.2.3 Strict Liability for Polluting the Environment

A good number of FDL cases concern claims for damages arising due to the deterioration or pollution of the environment, which allegedly results in harming the people living in the vicinities of the transnational subsidiary. In fact, companies play a big role in the pollution of the environment and the exploitation of natural resources,[355] and especially in some industries (e.g. mining, energy, oil) where impacting the environment lies at the core of their operations.[356] Yet the position of environmental rights within human rights is still under debate.[357] It is, therefore, important to examine liability for environmental damage, which is regulated as a type of strict liability under Turkish law.

Article 28 of Environmental Law stipulates that "*Those who pollute and harm the environment are liable for the damages arising from the pollution and harm they caused, without need to prove any fault*", making it clear that liability for causing environmental damage is a type of strict liability. As the provision reserves compensation liability of the polluter within the general principles (Art. 28/2), it may be possible to recover the losses and damages caused by pollution based on Article

[353] On a further note, Article 71/4 of TCO stipulates that even in cases where the activity of the significantly dangerous enterprise has been legally permitted, the victims may still request a reasonable amount of set-off for the losses caused by the relevant enterprise's activities. This is considered as a much controversial provision. The article's wording shows the legislator's attempt to distinguish between the activities that were not permitted by law, which would be subject to strict liability under the first three paragraphs of Article 71, and activities that were permitted by law, which would be subject to the last paragraph. For thorough discussions on the interpretation of this provision, and particularly on the legal nature of the term 'set-off', see Tandoğan (1981), p. 28; Sanlı Kerem (2012), pp. 79–80; Yavuz (2008), pp. 32–33; Yücel (2013), pp. 201–203. In terms of FDL claims, it would be sufficient to state that this provision should be interpreted teleologically by taking into consideration the protective purpose thereof, so as to allow the victims of a legally permitted enterprise activity falling within scope of this provision to obtain a reasonable amount of damages.

[354] Uygur (2012), p. 522.

[355] For further information and real life examples on the continous effects of corporate activities on the environment, see Choudhury and Petrin (2019), pp. 239–240.

[356] Choudhury and Petrin (2019), p. 242.

[357] ECHR does not regulate an independent right to a clean, healthy and sustainable environment. However, in its decisions after mid 90'ies, the European Court of Human Rights has considered the right to a healthy environment under Article 8 of ECHR, which protects the right to respect for private life, family life and home (Grosz 2017, pp. 982, 984).

28 or based on general tort liability under the Turkish Code of Obligations.[358] This article provides a general liability for environmental damages and therefore enterprises that do not carry out a significantly dangerous activity (as sought under Art. 71 of the TCO) may fall within the scope of this provision. The type of liability under this provision is considered to be strict objective liability in Turkish legal doctrine, as it provides for no escape clause while it refers to compensation under general provisions.[359] Consequently, unless the polluter proves that the chain of causation was broken, it will be responsible for the environmental damage caused in view of the 'polluter pays' principle,[360] without any possibility to escape liability by proving that it had taken all measures required to prevent the relevant environmental pollution.[361]

Environmental pollution refers to all damage to the environment, including any deterioration of ecological balance and environmental values.[362] Environmental damage, by its very nature, can continue to generate negative effects for some time which might not always be recognised throughout the whole process of such damage. In the words of *Öztekin Gelgel*:

> In this manner, damage that occurs during production, which is not known and acknowledged at the time of granting of disposal permit might in future become knowingly dangerous with the development of science and become effective. The lack of information and equipment in relation to the mentioned damage might be arising from the lack of knowledge on the impacts related to the type and amount of the relevant materials. However, it will also take time to determine that these disposed wastes created a deep and slow impact on the environment after a certain time or a certain use. In such a case, the damage will neither be a sudden one nor will it be possible to determine it.[363]

The above-mentioned characteristic of environmental damage makes it difficult to determine the responsible parties or to prevent potential environmental damage in most of the cases, even when due care is shown, which justifies adopting a strict liability regime for environmental damage.[364] Furthermore, environmental pollution affects not only specific individuals, but society as a whole, and thereby gains a

---

[358] In the act of polluting the environment, although the activity that leads to pollution is not always unlawful, the result is considered unlawful, and therefore, the act of polluting the environment is deemed as a tort liability in the wide sense (Oğuz 1991, p. 33).

[359] Oğuz (1991), p. 33. For further discussions on the nature of liability for environmental pollution see Güdük (2017), pp. 200–201. The type of liability under Article 28 of Environmental Law is criticised as referring only to civil liability for damage occurred on the material or immaterial assets of persons, as opposed to a liability also due to general environmental harm that might affect public in general (Güdük 2017, p. 222; Turgut 1995, p. 616).

[360] 'Polluter pays' principle constitutes an allocation of cost and it requires that the polluter pays the external costs arising due to the environmental pollution caused (Choudhury and Petrin 2019, p. 245).

[361] Güdük (2017), p. 201; Oğuz (1991), p. 33.

[362] Güdük (2017), p. 205.

[363] Öztekin Gelgel (2006), p. 159.

[364] *Öztekin Gelgel* has made a brief comparative study throughout certain European legislations and determined that the majority of domestic laws impose strict liability regime for environmental

public character.[365] The mere existence of environmental pollution has therefore been found sufficient to assert the strict liability of the polluter, as the element of unlawfulness is deemed established since the pollution itself goes against the provisions of Environmental Law.[366]

The type of liability under Article 28 of Environmental Law is considered to be the polluter's liability for primary environmental damage; while the primary environmental damage is the pollution of the environment, the secondary one is the resulting damage suffered by the victim.[367] The Turkish Court of Appeal has also acknowledged this feature of polluter's liability, stating that it concerns the damage arising from environmental pollution, which occurs in violation of the right to live in a healthy environment.[368] Accordingly, the damages suffered by the victims of the environmental pollution shall be subject to compensation claims under general provisions of tort liability (Art. 28/2 Environmental Law).

As per the definition made under Article 2 of Environmental Law, the polluter is a real person or legal entity[369] who directly or indirectly causes environmental pollution, harming the ecological balance and the environment, throughout its activities or thereafter. Nevertheless, the interpretation of the term 'polluter' is made rather widely, so as to cover not only activities by an enterprise, but also acts of pollution that may be deemed to occur continuously or as a single act.[370] Needless to say, this view should not lead to the conclusion that a one-time act by an enterprise—such as a leakage of oil from an oil tanker—is not to be deemed pollution within the meaning of this provision. In fact, the aforesaid interpretation aims to widen the scope of the term 'polluter', rather than to delimit it to those involving continous acts of pollution. On a further note, Article 2 also applies to foreigners who pollute the environment and, therefore, transboundary environmental pollution might be deemed to fall within the scope of Environmental Law.[371]

---

damage (including Swiss, German, Portuguese and English law) (Öztekin Gelgel 2006, p. 159). See also Oğuz (1991), p. 34.

[365] Yücel (2013), p. 164.

[366] Güdük (2017), p. 205; Turgut (1995), p. 625. Violation of the pollution standards determined under the secondary legislation of Environmental Law also is also considered unlawful and leads to polluter's liability (Güdük 2017, p. 206). In terms of causes lifting unlawfulness, *Güdük* opines that this should be interpreted quite restrictively for environmental damage, as pollution has negative impacts on public rather than a specific individual, and therefore, the victim's consent cannot be considered as a reasonable cause to lift unlawfulness in environmental pollution claims (Güdük 2017, p. 208).

[367] Yücel (2013), p. 165.

[368] Turkish Court of Appeal 4th Civil Chamber decision dated 01.06.2004, numbered 2003/12540E. and 2004/7006K.; Yücel (2013), p. 166.

[369] In legal doctrine and practice, the definition of polluter is interpreted widely, so as to cover public legal entities alongside private ones (Güdük 2017, p. 203).

[370] Başoğlu (2016), p. 196.

[371] Oğuz (1991), p. 42.

The definition of the term 'polluter' brings to mind the same concerns as Article 71 of TCO in which the entities forming part of an MNC (thus, the parent company or the subsidiary which is operating the enterprise) could be deemed to be the polluter. Neither Environmental Law nor Turkish legal doctrine bring any strict interpretation of the term 'polluter', in the sense that it should be interpreted as the owner of the relevant enterprise or vehicle.[372] Hence, it might be possible to adopt a wider interpretation of the term, covering not only the operator but also whoever is receiving economic benefit from the operation of the relevant enterprise.[373] Generally speaking, the polluter would typically be deemed the subsidiary, whose operations give rise to the relevant environmental damage. However, in *Başoğlu*'s opinion, where environmental damage is caused by the operations of an enterprise engaged in significantly dangerous activities, it might be possible to adopt an interpretation similar to Article 71 of the TCO, thereby creating a joint liability for the owner and the operator of the enterprise.[374] It might, in fact, be possible in certain cases to successfully establish that it is the parent company who is ultimately benefiting from the operations of its transnational subsidiary.

For interpretation purposes, the regulation under the EU acquis could be taken into consideration. In the EU acquis, the nature of strict liability for environmental damages is mandated by Directive 2004/35/EC of the European Parliament and of the Council of 21 April 2004 on environmental liability with regard to the prevention and remedying of environmental damage,[375] which stipulates that the member states should provide in their domestic laws a strict liability for compensating damages arising from environmental pollution.

According to Article 2/6 of the Directive, an 'operator' means "*any natural or legal, private or public person who operates or controls the occupational activity or, where this is provided for in national legislation, to whom decisive economic power over the technical functioning of such an activity has been delegated, including the holder of a permit or authorisation for such an activity or the person registering or notifying such an activity*". In light of this definition, it is possible to put forth that parent companies that exercise a high level of operational control over their subsidiaries may be deemed to be operators.[376] In fact, a parent company in an MNC might have decisive economic power over the activities of its subsidiary that are subject to environmental concerns. It is worth noting, however, that this decisive economic power should be demonstrated in the technical functioning of the activity,

[372] Güdük (2017), p. 204.

[373] Güdük (2017), p. 204.

[374] Başoğlu (2016), pp. 199–200. *Yücel* correctly states that Article 28 of Environmental Law shall apply priorly to Article 71 of TCO, as the former is a special law provision and the latter has clearly reserved the application of other provisions concerning risk liability (Yücel 2013, p. 171).

[375] OJ L 143, 30.4.2004, pp. 56–75. The Directive establishes an administrative law regime, whereby the public authorities shall ensure that the polluter will pay for the environmental damages, mostly on a strict liability basis (See Bergkamp 2016, p. 183). Therefore, there are no provisions concerning civil liability in the Directive.

[376] Bergkamp (2016), pp. 184–185.

which would in most cases belong to the subsidiary itself. Still, the definition of 'operator' under the Directive is considered wide enough to cover not only primary but also secondary actors and, in this sense, a parent company with a subsidiary that carries out the activities mentioned within the Directive can be deemed the 'operator' as long as it controls the activity of its subsidiary or has the decisive economic power to do so.[377] This point requires a case-by-case analysis. For instance, the parent company's supervision of the subsidiary's environmental management practices, the enforcement of corporate standards beyond the requirements of national law, and the verification of actual compliance and follow-up procedures are deemed to be examples of a high level of control for this purpose.[378] This interpretation might be beneficial also in terms of Turkish law.

In light of the foregoing analysis, if the environmental damage arose due to the operations of an enterprise carrying out a dangerous activity, which is operated by the subsidiary of an MNC, it should be assessed whether the parent company might be deemed the owner of the relevant enterprise. This will be the case if the parent company exercises control over the enterprise from an organisational and economic point of view. The interpretation of control in this sense could also include receiving benefits from the operations of the relevant subsidiary.[379] For instance, where a parent company controls the economic activities of its subsidiary and especially where it is involved in funding issues, it might be deemed to have an economic control, which might lead to the imposition of a liability hereunder. In other words, different companies in a group might be deemed to form a single entity in cases where there is a unity between them from technical, functional or organisational aspects.[380] This is not the same as 'enterprise liability', which suggests that if the parent company exercises control over the whole group to a degree that would lead to the impression that they form a single enterprise, then the whole group can be sued simultaneously as an enterprise.[381] As can be seen, the theory of enterprise liability goes beyond what can be achieved by way of the extensive interpretation made under Environmental Law and might be deemed to be too straightforward and far-fetched in certain cases. Nevertheless, considering the parent company as the 'operator' and the 'polluter' based on the above-mentioned theories might pave the way for environmental liability in FDL claims.

---

[377] Muchlinski (2007), p. 560.

[378] Bergkamp (2016), p. 185.

[379] It is worth noting that *Oğuz* considers receiving benefits from the operations of an enterprise as a reason to justify strict liability for environmental damage arising therefrom (Oğuz 1991, pp. 34–35).

[380] Enneking (2012), p. 247.

[381] Dine and Koutsias (2014), p. 29.

4.3 Mandatory Human Rights Due Diligence

As a recent and growing trend, regulations are being introduced that are bringing in certain due diligence obligations for MNCs. This due diligence mostly relates to non-financial matters, including specifically human rights concerns and environmental issues. This type of regulation is, therefore, of crucial importance to FDL claims, as it can serve as legal ground to improving the feasibility of these claims. In this section, we will firstly look at the international legal instruments regulating this subject. We will then analyse the current domestic laws that are in force or in the process of being legislated, which introduce mHRDD requirements for MNCs.

The current state of the regulation of mHRDD might be described to be constituted of different stages. There are those countries, like Turkey, where this issue is not yet regulated by law. There are regulations like EU's Non-Financial Reporting Directive[382] that introduce due diligence obligations on companies, but on a 'comply or explain' basis, which diminuishes the impact of the regulation significantly. There are also countries that are in the way of regulating mHRDD in their domestic laws, such as Germany (Act on Corporate Due Diligence Obligations for the Prevention of Human Rights Violations in Supply Chains)[383] and Switzerland,[384] with no reference to civil liability provisions, and therefore, posing a great challenge to ground FDL claims. There is French Law on Duty of Vigilance,[385] which has regulated mHRDD in detail with specific reference to civil liability provisions in case of breach. Finally, there is the Dutch Bill on Responsible and Sustainable International Business Act[386] (the "Dutch Bill"), where the duty of care is also regulated alongside mHRDD. The French law and the Dutch Bill pave the way for reaching out to tort of negligence in terms of parent company liability, while in other laws it remains to be challenging to successfully address this liability in the absence of a clear reference. Further analysis on this issue will be made under this Sect. 4.3 after examining the different types of regulations on HRDD.

[382]Directive 2014/95/EU of the European Parliament and of the Council of 22 October 2015 amending Directive 2013/34/EU as regards disclosure of non-financial and diversity information by certain large undertakings and groups.

[383]Act on Corporate Due Diligence Obligations for the Prevention of Human Rights Violations in Supply Chains (Lieferkettensorgfaltspflichtengesetz—LkSG) of 16 July 2021 ("German Act").

[384]Counter-proposal of the National Council of Parliament, Anträge der Kommission für Rechtsfragen des Nationalrates (RK-N) Eidgenössische Volksinitiative 'Für verantwortungsvolle Unternehmen – zum Schutz von Mensch und Umwelt': Indirekter Gegenentwurf.

[385]Loi no. 2017-399 du 27 Mars 2017 relative au devoir de vigilance des sociétés mères et des entreprises donneuses d'ordre.

[386]Responsible and Sustainable International Business Act (Wet Verantwoord en Duurzaam Internationaal Ondernemen), 11.03.2021, Tweede Kamer, vergaderjaar 2020–2021, 35 761, nr. 2.

4.3.1 International Legal Instruments for HRDD

Some forms of HRDD, although mostly voluntary, have been regulated in international legal instruments issued by authorities like the UN, the OECD and the EU. These regulations have greatly influenced and served as starting points for the current trend of regulations in domestic laws. In fact, the regulation of mHRDD in domestic laws is quite recent, but the the concept itself has been in the legal arena for some time now, albeit as a voluntary mechanism set under international instruments. While the UN has been actively engaged in setting voluntary mechanisms and recommendations regarding HRDD, the OECD has also taken an efficient step in providing guidance to the relevant parties on this issue.

4.3.1.1 UN Instruments for HRDD

The UN Global Compact dated 2000 provided for a voluntary reporting mechanism for companies regarding their conduct under the principles of human rights. The UNGPs also regulated an HRDD requirement for companies. As *Ruggie* also mentioned in the 2008 Report to the Human Rights Council, the companies that do not comply with human rights may become subject to "*the courts of public opinion*", which may include consumers, employees, society and investors.[387] This is referred to as the social licence to operate. In fact, due to several different reasons – such as pressure from investors, reactions by consumers, and even concerns to mitigate the risk of liability for human rights abuses in their supply chains—companies have begun to adopt HRDD mechanisms, even where these are not mandatory. In this way, companies set out to identify, respond to and disclose issues that concern human rights abuses within their supply chain, before they incur any liability in this respect.[388] Due diligence reporting on human rights issues might be considered an effective method to ensure that a company is respecting human rights while providing transparency. This type of due diligence should include a human rights policy, periodic assessments, and checking and reporting mechanisms.[389] The requirement of a HRDD mechanism is also mentioned under the OHCHR's Zero Draft. As per Article 9 thereof, states shall introduce a due diligence mechanism in their domestic laws for businesses of a transnational nature, which includes—among others—monitoring its subsidiaries and other connected companies, identifying the risks, taking measures to prevent the risks, and reporting publicly and periodically. In light of these improvements, it is hopeful that while only a few years ago the incorporation of a HRDD mechanism into domestic law was only a suggestion in

[387] UN Special Rep. Of the Secretary-General, Protect, Respect and Remedy: a Framework for Business and Human Rights, UN Doc. A/HRC/8/5 (7 April 2008); Conway (2015), pp. 754–755.

[388] Conway (2015), p. 755.

[389] Muchlinski (2011), p. 691.

light of the UNGPs,[390] now countries have already begun to implement this mandatory mechanism in their laws.

4.3.1.2 OECD Due Diligence Guidance for Responsible Business Conduct

The OECD Due Diligence Guidance for Responsible Business Conduct (the OECD Guidance on HRDD) was adopted by the Council at Ministerial level on 30 May 2018.[391] The OECD Guidance on DD aims to provide practical support to companies in the implementation of the OECD Guidelines on Multinational Enterprises and also to reach a common understanding between governments and various stakeholders on due diligence for responsible business conduct. The OECD Guidance on DD is seen as a useful tool to assist companies to implement due diligence for responsible business conduct, which is now being subject to mandatory legislation in some domestic laws, such as in France, and which are 'hardening' expectations into compliance requirements.[392]

The OECD Guidance on DD covers all multinational enterprises, SMEs, and the members of their corporate groups, including subsidiaries. The topics covered by the OECD Guidance on DD are human rights, employment and industrial relations, the environment, combating bribery, consumer interests and disclosure, which would be subject to a due diligence process carried out by the relevant multinational enterprise in determining adverse impacts or potential adverse impacts related thereto (identified as 'risks'). The OECD Guidance on DD clarify the concept of adverse impact in an "*outward-facing approach*" as "*the likelihood of adverse impacts on people, the environment and society that enterprises cause, contribute to, or to which they are directly linked*".[393]

The due diligence process and the relevant measures are identified as follows[394]: (1) embedding responsible business conduct into the enterprise's policies and management systems, (2) identifying actual or potential adverse impacts, (3) ceasing, preventing or mitigating these impacts, (4) tracking implementation and results, (5) communicating how impacts are addressed, and (6) enabling remediation. The OECD Guidance on DD provides extensive information and specific examples from practice to clarify how to conduct due diligence, which stakeholders to consult, how to monitor compliance and how to make this process sustainable.

---

[390] Muchlinski (2012), pp. 160–162.

[391] OECD Due Diligence Guidance for Responsible Business Conduct (2018) ("OECD Guidance on HRDD").

[392] Shavin (2019), p. 142.

[393] OECD Guidance on DD (2018), p. 15.

[394] OECD Guidance on DD (2018), p. 21.

4.3.1.3 EU Instruments on Non-Financial Reporting and Corporate Due Diligence

The EU's Non-Financial Reporting Directive[395] provides a legal basis for a mandatory due diligence reporting mechanism for 'public-interest companies' that satisfy the criteria required thereunder. The Directive 2013/34/EU,[396] which is further amended by the Non-Financial Reporting Directive, sets out the entities that are covered. Accordingly, the types of companies referred to under Annex I, which are limited liability companies,[397] as well as those listed under Annex II, provided that their direct or indirect shareholding structure leads to a limitation of liability, shall fall within the scope of the Directive. Public-interest companies also fall within the given scope, which are defined as companies that either (i) have transferable securities traded on a regulated market, (ii) are credit institutions, (iii) are insurance undertakings, or (iv) are designated as similar to these under a Member State legislation. Amongst the aforementioned types of companies, those employing at least 500 people shall be obliged to report on environmental, social and employee-related matters, human rights and anti-corruption. The main purposes of the Directive are proclaimed to be to foster long-term sustainability and profitability, and to increase transparency for improving corporate social responsibility (CSR) practices.[398] The reporting mechanism under the Directive is criticised because of the unavailability of any control over the reported information, as the audits are limited to whether a report is submitted or not.[399] Furthermore, as the compliance to the Directive is sought on a 'comply or explain' basis, allowing companies to comply with the reporting requirements or to explain their reasons for not doing so, it might be questionable whether the desired compliance would in fact be achieved amongst Member States.

Following the growing momentum on mHRDD in EU Member States, the European Parliament took a resolution on 10 March 2021 with recommendations to the Commission on corporate due diligence and corporate accountability, with an annex on the proposed text of the EU Directive on Corporate Due Diligence and

[395] Directive 2014/95/EU of the European Parliament and of the Council of 22 October 2015 amending Directive 2013/34/EU as regards disclosure of non-financial and diversity information by certain large undertakings and groups.

[396] Directive 2013/34/EU of the European Parliament and of the Council of 26 June 2013 on the annual financial statements, consolidated financial statements and related reports of certain types of undertakings, OJ L 182, 29.6.2013, pp. 19–76.

[397] For example: la société anonyme, la société en commandite par actions, la société à responsabilité limitée, la société par actions simplifiée in France; public companies limited by shares or by guarantee, private companies limited by shares or by guarantee in the UK; la società per azioni, la società in accomandita per azioni, la società a responsabilità limitata in Italy.

[398] Quinn and Connolly (2017), p. 15.

[399] Kara Pınar (2018), p. 122.

Corporate Accountability ("Proposed EU Directive on Corporate DD").[400] The Proposed EU Directive on Corporate DD aims to bring HRDD obligations for companies operating in the internal market, taking into consideration the legal instruments that are already in force, with reference to OECD Guidelines for MNEs, UNGPs, ILO Tripartite Declaration, as well as domestic legislations in certain EU Member States.

The personal scope of the Proposed EU Directive on Corporate DD is determined in Article 2 as (i) large undertakings, (ii) publicly listed SMEs, (iii) and SMEs operating in high-risk sectors, either governed by the law of a Member State or established within the EU, or operating in the internal market.

The obligations covered by the Proposed EU Directive on Corporate DD are focused on potential or actual adverse impact on human rights, on environment and on good governance.

The Proposed EU Directive on Corporate DD provides a corporate responsibility for the adverse impacts on human rights, environment and good governance that the relevant undertaking has caused or contributed to in its value chain or through its business relationships.[401] The term 'business relationships' is defined as subsidiaries and commercial relationships throughout the value chain, which include suppliers and sub-contractors that are directly linked to business operations, products or services.[402] The definition of 'value chain' is made so as to cover both upstream and downstream, direct and indirect business relationships.[403] In terms of identifying contribution to an adverse impact, factors such as the extent to which an undertaking encourages or motivates an adverse impact by another entity, the extent to which an undertaking could or should have known about the adverse impact (foreseeability), and the degree to which an undertaking's activities mitigated the adversed impact or decreased the risk of its occurrence can be taken into consideration.[404]

The Proposed EU Directive on Corporate DD regulates a detailed mHRDD strategy involving the following stages: (1) specifying the potential or actual adverse impacts on human rights, environment and good governance arising from an undertaking's own operations and throughout its business relationships, (2) value chain mapping, which will be publicly disclosed, (3) adopting policies and measures to cease, prevent or mitiage adverse impacts, and (4) implementing a prioritisation strategy for the adverse impacts in line with Principle 17 of the UNGPs.[405] It is also regulated that stakeholders engagement will be ensured both at the stage of

[400] European Parliament Resolution of 10 March 2021 with Recommendations to the Commission on Corporate Due Diligence and Corporate Accountability (2020/2129(INL)) and Annex to the Resolution: Recommendations for Drawing Up a Directive of the European Parliament and of the Council on Corporate Due Diligence and Corporate Accountability.

[401] Proposed EU Directive on Corporate DD, Art. 1(1)-1(3).

[402] Proposed EU Directive on Corporate DD, Art. 3(2).

[403] Proposed EU Directive on Corporate DD, Art. 3(5).

[404] Proposed EU Directive on Corporate DD, Art. 3(10).

[405] Proposed EU Directive on Corporate DD, Art. 4(4).

establishing and implementing the due diligence strategy, as well as at the stage of annual evaluation and revision thereof.[406]

The undertakings are also obliged to establish a grievance mechanism both as an early-warning for risks and as a mediation system by involving the stakeholders, and to provide a remediation process for adverse impacts that they have caused or contributed to.[407] The supervision of the application of the Proposed EU Directive on Corporate DD shall be under the discretion of a national competent authority, which will be independent and have a staff with the required expertise.[408] The relevant authority shall be entitled to carry out investigations, checks, examination of the due diligence strategy or of the grievance mechanisms put in place by the undertakings as well as on-the-spot checks.[409]

The Proposed EU Directive on Corporate DD envisages sanctions for failure to comply with the obligations set out therein, such as monetary fines, exclusion from public procurement, from state aid, from public support schemes, seizure of commodities and other administrative sanctions.[410] It also stipulates that a civil liability regime should be provided in national law, according to which the undertakings could be held liable for remedying the harms arising from adverse impacts that they have caused or contributed to, unless they are able to prove that they took all due care to avoid the harm or that the harm would have occurred regardless of the due care taken.[411]

Although the publishing of the proposed legislation by the European Commission was delayed indefinitely, which halted the entry into force of the directive,[412] the overall process has encouraged certain EU Member States to issue national laws or improve the existing laws on mHRDD.

4.3.2 Emergence of mHRDD and a Case of Reform in Corporate Law

A trend has been recently observed in the regulation of business and human rights issues in statutory laws. The trend started with regulations on sustainability reporting in the US, the UK and other EU countries like the Netherlands and Denmark, where the obligations addressed a specific issue, such as child labour, human trafficking or

---

[406] Proposed EU Directive on Corporate DD, Art. 5, 8.

[407] Proposed EU Directive on Corporate DD, Art. 9–10.

[408] Proposed EU Directive on Corporate DD, Art. 12.

[409] Proposed EU Directive on Corporate DD, Art. 13.

[410] Proposed EU Directive on Corporate DD, Art. 18(2).

[411] Proposed EU Directive on Corporate DD, Art. 19.

[412] European Parliament, Corporate Due Diligence, Legislative Train Schedule, https://www.europarl.europa.eu/legislative-train/theme-an-economy-that-works-for-people/file-corporate-due-diligence.

slavery. This then extended to a wider horizon with the French Law on Duty of Vigilance, the Swiss Responsible Business Initiative and the German Act. These laws cover the obligations of companies (especially MNCs) to assess, report and take measures against any violations of human rights and environmental damages that are under risk within their corporate group, supply chains and even their business partners. Needless to say, the shift to mandatory laws for business and human rights concerns face significant criticism from companies, who express their concerns regarding competition and the lack of means to ensure that these rights are fully respected throughout their global supply chains. There are even views that the mandatory approach fails to ensure a full compliance, which is better achieved by way of soft law instruments, as companies are already struggling under the burden to protect their reputation and survive the competition. However, none of these criticisms seem to suggest an alternative method that would ensure compliance as effectively as mandatory laws.

In the UK, reporting of non-financial information was first regulated by a reform to the UK Companies Act 2006,[413] introducing the Operating and Financial Review, which put in place a mandatory non-financial reporting requirement. The requirements under the Operating and Financial Review were detailed – including environmental issues, employees, social and community issues. However, this system was found to impose an unnecessary burden on companies and replaced by the Business Review, which required reporting on the same issues but to the extent that directors deemed relevant in the context of their business.[414] In 2013, some elements of the Business Review were changed to create the Strategic Report, which covers the same reporting elements but where compliance is only voluntary.[415] Moreover, the UK Modern Slavery Act 2015[416] also sets out certain reporting requirements in respect of slavery and human trafficking that may occur within a company's business and supply chain.[417] Four years after its enactment, the UK Modern Slavery Act was the subject of an independent review,[418] which looked into its implementation and efficiency in practice. It was recommended in this report that the UK government act urgently to adopt mHRDD in statutory laws. However, neither the EU Non-Financial Reporting Directive nor the aforementioned legislation in the UK provide for a duty of due diligence for the parent companies of MNCs or set conditions for liability for these companies.[419] Therefore, the more recent

[413] UK Companies Act 2006, 2006 c 46.

[414] Quinn and Connolly (2017), p. 18.

[415] Quinn and Connolly (2017), p. 19.

[416] The Modern Slavery Act 2015 (2015) c. 30.

[417] Modern Slavery Act 2015, Chapter 30, http://www.legislation.gov.uk/ukpga/2015/30/contents.

[418] Independent Review of the Modern Slavery Act 2015: Final Report, Presented to Parliament by the Secretary of State for the Home Department by Command of Her Majesty, May 2019, https://assets.publishing.service.gov.uk/government/uploads/system/uploads/attachment_data/file/803406/Independent_review_of_the_Modern_Slavery_Act_-_final_report.pdf.

[419] Bueno (2020), p. 245.

improvements in French, German, Dutch and Swiss laws provide a stronger basis for FDL claims.

It is possible to say that the mentioned developments in domestic laws are supported by the actions of EU institutions, which give a positive signal in terms of regulating mHRDD under the EU acquis.[420] In January 2020, the European Commission published a study on due diligence requirements in supply chains,[421] which focuses on "*due diligence requirements to identify, prevent, mitigate and account for abuses of human rights, including the rights of the child and fundamental freedoms, serious bodily injury or health risks, environmental damage, including with respect to climate*".[422] This study covers case studies of due diligence in major supply chains, as well as reports on a number of countries which regulate due diligence requirements in their domestic laws. The study points to the due diligence regulations in place for corporate groups in domestic laws and emphasises that in most of these laws the concept of 'corporate group' is defined broadly, in some cases even covering certain types of supply chains.[423] It is worth noting that this aspect of the study is similar to the Turkish law provisions on corporate groups. The study stipulates that the general practice across EU member states is to include the subsidiaries within a corporate group in the due diligence on human rights and environment.[424]

Later on, in January 2021, the European Parliament has issued a legislative initiative calling the Commission to regulate corporate responsibility for human rights abuses and environmental harms committed contributed to by companies.[425] In this legislative initiative the European Parliament has stressed the pressing need for mandatory regulation on mHRDD obligations, in view of the proven insufficiency of voluntary soft law mechanisms. Different options of regulating mHRDD are suggested in the legislative initiative, referring to the material and personal scope, monitoring, severity of violations, penalties for non-compliance and liability, where civil liability is mentioned alongside criminal one. The mentioned legislative initiative was then followed by the European Parliament Resolution of 10 March 2021 with Recommendations to the Commission on Corporate Due Diligence and Corporate Accountability (2020/2129(INL)) and the Proposed EU Directive on Corporate DD in the Annex, which was addressed under Sect. 4.3.1.3 herein above. This process surely signals a new era for the EU in terms of regulating mHRDD. In fact, if the European Commission would agree to proceed in line with

[420] It is worth noting that there are certain EU regulations concerning due diligence requirements in supply chains limited to specific high-risk industries; such as Conflict Minerals Regulation (2017/821 of 17.05.2017) and Timber Regulation (995/2010 of 20.10.2010).

[421] European Commission, Study on due diligence requirements through the supply chain – Final Report, January 2020, B-1049 Brussels ("Commission Study on DD").

[422] Commission Study on DD (2020), p. 7.

[423] Commission Study on DD (2020), pp. 207–208.

[424] Commission Study on DD (2020), p. 209.

[425] European Parliament, Committee on Legal Affairs, Towards a mandatory EU system of due diligence for supply chains, 27.01.2021.

the European Parliament's suggestions, the Member States will soon be required to have this issue regulated in their domestic laws.

Regulation of mHRDD, *per se*, should also be supported by an overall reform in corporate law and especially in corporate governance. Such a reform is required to successfully integrate environmental concerns and human rights issues within the decision-making mechanisms of companies. The Sustainable Companies Project,[426] which investigates the barriers and potential actions that may be taken in this respect, have proven through research that a reform in company law is required in order to achieve environmental sustainability in the operation of companies; a shift, therefore, from shareholder primacy is needed to realise this reform.[427]

The traditional corporate law approach is based on the norm of shareholder primacy, which takes as reference the maximisation of profits—that would benefit the shareholders—as the main purpose of a company and also holding the directors responsible for ensuring this outcome. The grounds of the profit maximisation for shareholders' interest lies on the nexus of contracts theory, which sees the company as a bundle of various contracts. According to this view: (1) the company has a fictional nature, which prevents it from assuming social and moral duties, and makes the profit of shareholders its main purpose, (2) being the contractual agents of the shareholders, the directors owe a fiduciary duty to maximise profits, and (3) profit maximisation is required to reduce agency costs.[428] This may be deemed a social norm, based on the legal myth that the shareholders are the owners of the company and that the directors are acting as agents of the shareholders with the ultimate aim of maximising profits.[429] In fact, shareholders are not the owners of the company, as they merely hold the shares of stock, which provides them with certain rights, such as the right to dividends and right to vote.[430] Furthermore, from a different perspective, it is possible to suggest that adopting shareholder primacy by seeing the shareholders and the company as a single unit (considering that the company's main purpose is to protect shareholders' interests) conflicts with the usual consequence of this approach, which is to regard the principles of separate legal entity and limited liability in the context of tort claims by arguing that shareholders (parent company) should not be held liable for the torts committed by the company (subsidiary).[431]

In corporate groups, shareholder primacy is considered to be a powerful obstacle to achieving corporate sustainability.[432] On the other hand, in order to achieve

[426] Sustainable Companies Project by the Department of Private Law of the University of Oslo, https://www.jus.uio.no/ifp/english/research/projects/sustainable-companies/.

[427] Sjåfjell (2018), p. 37.

[428] Choudhury and Petrin (2018), pp. 386–387.

[429] Sjåfjell (2018), p. 39.

[430] The Modern Corporation Statement on Company Law, 6 October 2016, https://papers.ssrn.com/sol3/papers.cfm?abstract_id=2848833.

[431] The Modern Corporation Statement on Company Law.

[432] Sjåfjell (2017), p. 5.

corporate sustainability, shareholder primacy in company law should be revised as a broader stakeholder approach, which would entail that the company would not only provide benefit to its shareholders, but also to its stakeholders in the general sense. The scope of stakeholders could be kept wide, covering the company's employees, subsidiaries' employees, customers and, in general, society. The reason for this approach is that a company's operations and actions have the capacity to impact not only those with whom it has a relationship (either contractual or otherwise) but also those who are not directly connected to the company but yet are affected by its actions.

It is, however, important that the aforementioned corporate reform—from a shareholder approach to a stakeholder approach—be made in statutory law, and therefore mandatory. In this manner, all issues related to environmental, social and human rights can be integrated into the internal decision-making of companies, by 'internalising the externalities' and thus deeming the costs for compliance a cost for doing business.[433] A reform has already begun with the enactment of domestic laws on mHRDD in EU Member States, which may eventually lead to a wider reform in company law to change the main pillars that may result in a concept of a sustainable company.

4.3.3 Regulations on mHRDD in Europe: France, Germany, Switzerland and the Netherlands

Although the concept of the parent company's duty of care is yet to be regulated in statutory law, there is a trend of imposing due diligence and reporting obligations on parent companies with respect to the human rights abuses and environmental damages that have arisen or may arise within the scope of the activities of their subsidiaries, as well as other companies within their global supply chains subject to certain conditions, such as the existence of a certain level of control or an established business relationship between them. Even though mHRDD is a completely different concept from the parent company's duty of care, the failure to comply with mHRDD obligations might lead to a breach of the duty of care or the duty of care might already entail an mHRDD obligation on the parent company's side.[434] It is therefore possible to say that these two separate concepts are intertwined with each other in a certain sense.

[433] Sjåfjell (2011a, b), p. 17.

[434] *Palombo* points out that while in the UK a parent company's due diligence obligation is a consequence of its duty of care towards stakeholders for its subsidiaries' operations, the French law on duty of vigiliance and Swiss legislative proposals aim to establish an obligation for the parent company to monitor their subsidiaries' compliance with human and environmental rights. Palombo (2019), p. 270, 278.

There is a dynamic trend in terms of imposing mandatory regulations on companies for mHRDD throughout the world, and especially within the European countries. While some countries have already enacted legislation on mHRDD, some of these countries are still in the process of legislating and others have taken government commitments for this purpose.[435] Amongst these, there are countries that opt to impose a general reporting obligation, without making any distinctions regarding the subject matter of such reporting (e.g. France, Germany, Switzerland, the Netherlands).

It is worth mentioning that mHRDD obligations have an important role in the assessment of the parent company's duty of care. As it will be detailed further below, according to the French Law on Duty of Vigilance, any parent companies that fail to comply with their obligations are liable under the provisions of general tort law. The French law imposes the onus of proof on the parent company to prove that, under the relevant circumstances, it took the required due care, or otherwise it would be held liable.[436] This approach under the due diligence obligation reflects a different one to the UK's on the parent company's duty of care, where it is mostly accepted that parent companies who owe a duty of care towards third party tort victims will also have a due diligence obligation to supervise their subsidiaries' activities to prevent any potential damages.[437] Despite this difference, the main issue remains that the duty of care and mHRDD are strictly connected to each other, regardless of which one comes as a consequence of the other. Hence the mHRDD does not result in any secondary and indirect liability of the parent company (as in the case of piercing the corporate veil), but instead it leads to a direct liability of the parent company (as in the case of a breach of the duty of care) due to its failure to exercise the required due diligence.[438]

4.3.3.1 French Law on Duty of Vigilance

France has taken an innovative step in imposing a duty of care on corporate groups for the failure to comply with reporting obligations, which constitutes the first law ever to regulate this issue. The French Law on Duty of Vigilance,[439] regulates mHRDD by identifying the risks, mitigating them and putting in place monitoring

---

[435] Gilligan, Elaine, Mandatory human rights due diligence: an issue whose time has come, CORE, https://corporate-responsibility.org/issue-whose-time-come/.

[436] This is a presumption of liability that can be rebutted by the parent company (Choudhury and Petrin 2019, p. 114).

[437] Palombo (2019), p. 282.

[438] Cassel (2016), p. 181.

[439] Loi no. 2017-399 du 27 Mars 2017 relative au devoir de vigilance des sociétés mères et des entreprises donneuses d'ordre, https://www.legifrance.gouv.fr/affichTexte.do?cidTexte=JORFTEXT000034290626&categorieLien=i.

mechanisms and civil liability for the breach of this obligation for parent companies of a specific criteria.[440]

The French Law on Duty of Vigilance introduces a duty of vigilance on companies incorporated or registered in France for two consecutive fiscal years, that (i) employ at least 5000 people together with their French subsidiaries, or (ii) employ at least 10,000 people together with their French and foreign subsidiaries. Therefore, French companies, as well as MNCs whose headquarters are in France or at least one of the subsidiaries are located in France would fall within the scope of this requirement.[441] In other words, the duty of vigilance has an extraterritorial reach by creating an obligation for the parent company to monitor the activities of its transnational subsidiaries.[442]

The concept of 'duty of vigilance' seems to have been chosen on purpose to distinguish this duty from the duty of care under Common Law, as the duty of vigilance is based on specific and codified criteria which relates to mHRDD combined with civil liability.[443]

The duty of vigilance has been designed in a three-part process: elaboration, disclosure and effective implementation of the vigilance plan.[444] Accordingly, every company that satisfies the required criteria would be obliged to prepare a regular report on the human rights and environmental issues that may potentially arise from their own operations or from the operations of their subsidiaries, including those located abroad, as well as the subcontractors and suppliers with whom the company has an established relationship. Under French law, an established relationship is interpreted as a stable, regular commercial relationship, based on a contract or otherwise, providing a certain volume of business and with a reasonable expectation of that relationship continuing.[445] As can be seen, the scope of duty of vigilance is kept quite broad so as to include not only the subsidiaries but also closely linked subcontractors and suppliers, thus extending beyond control via shareholding. This provides a more extensive approach compared to other legislation; for instance, the business relationships that fall within the scope of this law may not satisfy the proximity requirement under English law.[446]

The obligations of vigilance determined for companies that fall within the scope of this requirement are set as (i) preparing a vigilance plan, (ii) effectively implementing the plan and (iii) making the plan public and reporting on its implementation in the company's annual management report.[447] The details of the vigilance plan are not regulated in detail in the Law, but it has been referred to the

[440] Soudain (2019), p. 58.

[441] Weller and Pato (2018), pp. 411–412.

[442] Palombo (2019), p. 276.

[443] Rühmkorf and Walker (2018), p. 5.

[444] Cossart et al. (2017), p. 320.

[445] Bueno (2020), p. 250.

[446] Rühmkorf and Walker (2018), p. 39.

[447] Brabant and Savourey (2017b), p. 5.

Conseil d'État for further improvements to the details of the requirement. It is also important to note that the Law stipulates that the vigilance plan will be prepared in collaboration with the stakeholders of the company, thus adopting a multi-stakeholder approach. However, in addition to the details of a monitoring plan, there are also other issues that are not sufficiently regulated in the Law. For instance, the Law is criticised for its vagueness concerning the extent of liability, as to whether a parent company who sets up an effective monitoring plan could be held responsible for its failure to ensure its effective implementation, in case the subsidiaries do not implement it.[448] These ambiguities might render the Law difficult to apply in practice. Moreover, the burden of proof set for the victims—which requires the establishment of causation between the parent company's failure to set up an effective monitoring plan and the damage created by the subsidiary's act—is quite high.[449]

The Law on Duty of Vigilance sets sanctions for non-compliance with the requirements regulated therein. However, the law was brought to the Constitutional Council by business-supported organisations and politicians with claims of legal uncertainty in respect of civil fines and harm on transparency which would arguably have a negative impact on competition. The Constitutional Council, with its decision, dated 23 March 2017, has taken a balanced approach by upholding its majority with the exception of civil fines, which were struck out.[450] The Constitutional Court, on the other hand, has not touched upon the periodic penalty payments (*astreintes*), which are defined as injunctive fines payable on a daily or per-event basis until the defendant satisfies a given obligation, and civil liability action (*responsibilité civile*) under Articles 1240 and 1241 of French Civil Code[451] for the damages resulting from the failure to comply with legal obligations,[452] which regulate extra-contractual liability. Article 1240 sets the general extra-contractual liability, as anyone who causes a damage to another by fault is obliged to compensate it. Article 1241 takes this general liability further by stating that everyone will be responsible for the damages he/she caused, not only for fault, but also for negligence and imprudence. The standard of care is not defined in French statutory law, thus this will be decided upon by courts; however, a general standard is *bon père de famille* (*bonus pater familias*), which is seen as an equivalent to the Common Law standard of reasonable person.[453]

Therefore, the removal of civil fines does not render the French Law on Duty of Vigilance inefficient, as anyone who has standing may ask the court to order the company to establish and implement a vigilance plan and those who are damaged by

[448] Palombo (2019), p. 282.

[449] Palombo (2019), p. 284.

[450] Cossart et al. (2017), p. 323.

[451] French Civil Code (*Code Civil*), in force as of 21.03.1804, https://www.legifrance.gouv.fr/codes/id/LEGITEXT000006070721/.

[452] Brabant and Savourey (2017a), p. 1.

[453] Rühmkorf and Walker (2018), pp. 38–39.

the company's non-compliance with its legal obligations can always ask the court for compensation. Furthermore, the court may also deem it appropriate to order for penalty. The protection offered by civil liability provisions is questioned on the point that the claimants would be under the burden to prove that the parent company acted negligently and that the damages they suffered were caused by such negligent behaviour, which might be a heavy burden.[454] Having said that, the clear reference to civil liability renders the French Law on Duty of Vigilance the one and only domestic law, for the time being, regulating mHRDD that links the non-compliance with the obligations to civil liability.

There has also been significant criticism regarding the lack of coordination between the French law and the conflict of law rules. *Weller* and *Pato* questioned if French law could be applicable to FDL cases in light of the provisions of the Rome II Regulation, which refer to the law applicable at the place where the damage occurred (*lex loci damni*).[455] This point on applicable law, and whether French law could be seen manifestly as the more closely connected law applicable under Article 4/3 of Rome II Regulation, will be discussed further in the next chapter. It might be possible to successfully argue that the place where the tortious act occurred should be deemed the place where the parent company held the decisions regarding the relevant activity of its subsidiary (based on the assumption that the parent company has effective control over the subsidiary's operations). This argument might be logical especially in cases where the parent company's act or omission has led to a misconduct in the subsidiary's operations, which has caused the relevant damage. On the other hand, there is also the opposite opinion arguing that the event giving rise to the damage cannot be interpreted merely as the decisions of the parent company, and that this should be understood as the immediate cause of the aforesaid physical damage.[456] If this view is adopted, then it would be harder to claim that French law would be applicable as the home country law in FDL claims. In such a case, there might be another way to argue the applicability of the French law: if the claim relates to an incident of environmental damage, the claimants would be allowed to choose between the law of the place where the damage occurred or the law of the place where the event giving rise to the damage occurred (*lex loci delicti commissi*), which might result in French law being applied depending on the circumstances. It is also stated that Article 16 of the Rome II Regulation might force the application of French law on the basis that it is an overriding mandatory provision, but the French legislator did not make any comments in this respect.[457]

As the first of its kind to regulate mHRDD for companies, French Law on Duty of Vigilance has already begun to have an impact on the business and legal realms. In October 2019, Total SA, a French company with subsidiaries all around the world, was brought to court by six NGOs claiming that Total SA was in breach of its

[454] Weller and Pato (2018), p. 412.

[455] Weller and Pato (2018), p. 413.

[456] Mansel (2018), p. 461.

[457] Weller and Pato (2018), p. 413.

obligations under the duty of vigilance law by failing to revise its vigilance plan (which was published as required by the duty of vigilance law) and to implement it for the oil project operating in Uganda, alleging that the project would confiscate people's private properties without adequate compensation and create environmental damages in the Great Lakes region where the project was operating.[458] The High Court of Nanterre found that it lacked the competence to hear the case on 30.01.2020 and therefore referred the case to a commercial court.[459] The decision was appealed by the plaintiffs in March 2020.[460] Versailles Court of Appeal has approved the decision of the High Court of Nanterre, confirming that the case should fall within competence of commercial courts as the issue of vigilance plan was directly related to the management of commercial companies.[461]

Having said that, the issue of competent court in relation to the claims concerning the vigilance plan appears as an enduring problem of the French system for now, as the law is not clear on this much important point; namely, if the civil court or the commercial court would be competent to hear these cases. In a second lawsuit initiated against Total SA by several associations and local authorities with allegations of the company's contribution to climate change caused by the insufficient measures it took to prevent environmental damage and human rights abuses, Nanterre Civil Court discussed this issue in detail byevaluating whether the obligation regarding vigilance plan would concern shareholders of the relevant company or the whole public, and reached the conclusion that the core of this obligation exceeds the limits of corporate activity.[462] The court has come to the conclusion that the duty of vigilance plan was indeed directly linked with the company management, as the

---

458 Total au Tribunal, Les Amis de La Terre France, https://www.totalautribunal.org/amisdelaterre; "Oil company Total faces historic legal action in France for human rights and environmental violations in Uganda", Friends of the Earth International, 23.10.2019, https://www.foei.org/news/total-legal-action-france-human-rights-environment-uganda.

459 Total Ouganda: le TGI se déclare incompétent au profit du tribunal de commerce (30.01.2020), Business & Human Rights Resource Centre, https://www.business-humanrights.org/fr/derni%C3%A8res-actualit%C3%A9s/total-ouganda-le-tgi-se-d%C3%A9clare-incomp%C3%A9tent-au-profit-du-tribunal-de-commerce/.

460 Les ONG font appel dans l'affaire du manquement présumé de Total à la loi sur le devoir de vigilance dans ses activités en Ouganda (30.03.2020), Business & Human Rights Resource Centre, https://www.business-humanrights.org/fr/les-ong-font-appel-dans-laffaire-du-manquement-pr%C3%A9sum%C3%A9-de-total-%C3%A0-la-loi-sur-le-devoir-de-vigilance-dans-ses-activit%C3%A9s-en-ouganda.

461 Les Amis de la Terre France, The National Association of Professional Environmentalists, Africa Institute for Energy Governance C/ SA Total, Cour d'Appel de Versailles, N° RG 20/01692 N ° Portalis DBV3-V-B7E-T2A7 (10.12.2020); also see "French Court of Appeal remands case against Total over alleged failure to respect Duty of Vigilance law in Uganda to commercial court", Business & Human Rights Resource Centre, https://www.business-humanrights.org/fr/derni%C3%A8res-actualit%C3%A9s/french-court-of-appeal-remands-case-against-total-over-alleged-failure-to-respect-duty-of-vigilance-law-in-uganda-to-commercial-court/.

462 Tribunal Judiciare de Nanterre 1ère Chambre, Ordonnance de mise en Etat, N. RG 20/00915 – N. Portalis DB3R-W-B7E-VQFM (11.02.2021); also see "First court decision in the climate litigation against Total: A promising interpretation of the French Duty of Vigilance Law", Sherpa

findings would require the management to take measures, mitigate risks and take the strategic decisions by considering the relevant human rights risks. However, the court declared, taking into account that the main purpose of the duty of vigilance is beyond the management of a company, as it affects the society as a whole, civil courts would have competence to hear cases in this respect. Although the decision is still pending at the stage of appeal, it surely constitutes a favourable step for FDL cases and the discussions held thereunder will surely contribute to the future of the question of competent court.

4.3.3.2 German Act on mHRDD in Supply Chains

The German Federal Ministry for Economic Cooperation and Development issued a 'draft law regulating human rights and environment-related duties of care in global value chains' in February 2019,[463] which included amendments to be made to the Commercial Code on the duty of due diligence for certain companies and their liabilities in this respect. It is possible to say that the draft law presented a fairly ambitious approach to ensuring compliance with human rights and environmental standards throughout supply chains, as its scope extends to more companies compared with the French Law on Duty of Vigilance and the sanctions for non-compliance are much stronger. The draft law was seen as an effective reaction following the German National Action Plan on Business and Human Rights of 2017,[464] where the government had undertaken to adopt legislative measures in case by 2020 less than 50% of German companies with more than 500 employees would have introduced an effective HRDD mechanism.[465] On 15.02.2021, the German government has declared its approval on the draft law in a milder version, by leaving out reference to civil liability and delimiting the scope,[466] the German Bundestag adopted the act on 11.06.2021, which was followed by the authorisation of the German Bundesrat on 25.06.2021, and the Act on Corporate Due Diligence Obligations for the Prevention of Human Rights Violations in Supply Chains

(26.03.2021), https://www.asso-sherpa.org/first-court-decision-in-the-climate-litigation-against-total-a-promising-interpretation-of-the-french-duty-of-vigilance-law.

[463] Entwurf Eines Gesetzes zur Regelung Menschenrechtlicher und Unweltbezogener Sorgfaltspflichen in Globalen Wertchöpfungsketten, Stand 01.02.2019.

[464] The National Action Plan on Implementation of the UN Guiding Principles on Business and Human Rights (2016–2020), https://www.auswaertiges-amt.de/blob/610714/fb740510e8c2fa83dc507afad0b2d7ad/nap-wirtschaft-menschenrechte-engl-data.pdf.

[465] Wilks and Blankenbach (2019), https://www.business-humanrights.org/en/will-germany-become-a-leader-in-the-drive-for-corporate-due-diligence-on-human-rights.

[466] Commentary: "The German Supply Chain Due Diligence Act in the Making – What to Expect", Business & Human Rights Resource Centre, 15.02.2021, https://www.business-humanrights.org/en/latest-news/commentary-by-robert-grabosch-the-german-supply-chain-due-diligence-act-in-the-making-what-to-expect/.

(Lieferkettensorgfaltspflichtengesetz—LkSG) (the "**German Act**") was finally published on the Federal Law Gazette on 22.07.2021.

The German Act will be applicable to enterprises of any legal form that have their central administration, principle place of business or statutory seat and have at least 3000 employees in Germany, including those posted abroad, as well as to enterprises of any legal form that have their branch office and have at least 3000 in Germany.[467,468] As can be seen, the scope of the German Code is wider than its French counterpart and a good number of companies are expected to fall thereunder.

The German Act provides detailed descriptions of human rights risks covered by the HRDD obligation, including but not limited to the prohibition of child labour, health and safety at workplace, forced labour, slavery, unequal treatment at work and also different types of environmental harm, which it classifies as human rights related obligations and environment related obligations.[469]

The German Act's approach to HRDD is similar to the UNGPs, as they both comprise risk analysis, risk prevention and remedial measures.[470] The companies that fall within the scope of the German Act shall have the obligation to make assessments and identify risks pertaining to human rights violations and environmental damages caused by the operations within their supply chain, which is said to cover an enterprise's own actions in its business area, as well as the actions of their direct and indirect suppliers.[471] In group companies, subsidiaries that are under the 'decisive influence'[472] of the parent company are also deemed to be within the

---

[467] German Act, Section 1(1) (Scope of Application). From 2024, the German Act will also apply to enterprises with at least 1000 employees in Germany; see Federal Ministry of Labour and Social Affairs, Act on Corporate Due Diligence in Supply Chains, https://www.csr-in-deutschland.de/EN/Business-Human-Rights/Supply-Chain-Act/supply-chain-act.html.

[468] The draft law of German Development Ministry on mandatory human rights due diligence for German companies had a lower threshold for number of employees (250 employees), but it required also an annual turnover of at least 40 million Euros or a balance sheet total of at least 20 million Euros, or operating in high-risk sectors (e.g. mining, energy, textiles) or in areas with weak security conditions (such as areas of armed conflict). For more information, see Business & Human Rights Resource Centre, German Development Ministry drafts law on mandatory human rights due diligence for German companies, https://www.business-humanrights.org/en/german-development-ministry-drafts-law-on-mandatory-human-rights-due-diligence-for-german-companies#:~:text=In%20February%202019%2C%20the%20German,global%20business%20partners%2C%20including%20suppliers.

[469] German Act, Section 2(2) (Definitions).

[470] Rühmkorf and Walker (2018), p. 38.

[471] German Act, Section 2(5) (Definitions).

[472] Although the term of 'decisive influence' is not defined in the German Act, the summary of questions published by the Federal Ministry of Labour and Social Affairs states that decisive influence shall be determined by considering all economic, personnel-related, organisational and legal ties between the parent company and the subsidiary. Having a significant majority shareholder, a compliance system throughout the group, responsibility for controlling the core process of the subsidiary, similar business areas and having the same employees in the same roles in both companies are set out as examples of the existence of a decisive influence. See Federal Ministry of

business area of the parent company.[473] HRDD obligations set out under the German Act are (1) establishing a risk management system, (2) designating responsible person(s) in the company, (3) carrying out regular risks analyses, (4) issuing a policy statement, (5) setting preventive measures in its own business area and for direct suppliers, (6) taking remedial action, (7) establishing a complaints procedure, (8) implementing HRDD obligations with regard to risks concerning indirect suppliers,[474] and (9) documenting and reporting.[475] It is also mandated that the companies document their compliance to HRDD obligations, prepare an annual report and make it publicly availabe on their website.[476]

Federal Office for Economic Affairs and Export Control (*Bundesamt für Wirtschaft und Ausfuhrkontrolle*) ('BAFA') is appointed as the competent authority to monitor and check compliance with the HRDD obligations regulated under the German Act.[477] The enterprises that fall within scope of the German Act shall submit their reports concerning HRDD obligations to BAFA within 4 months as of the end of their financial year. BAFA is also authorized to carry out random checks, enter and inspect business premises, summon people and access documents.[478]

The sanctions for non-compliance with the requirements under the German Act are set as financial and administrative fines, and exclusion from public contracts.[479] Any liability arising from civil law is left outside the scope of the HRDD obligations under the German Act, as it is stipulated that violating any provision of the German Act would not give rise to any civil liability, while any liability under civil law arising independently remains unaffected.[480] In this manner, it has been made clear that the violation of the obligations under the German Act cannot, *per se*, give rise to any tort liability. Having said that, as it is stipulated that the other grounds for civil liability will remain unaffected, the compliance with the German Act should also not be deemed as a ground to escape tort liability for enterprises. For instance, if a parent company faces claims of breach of duty of care concerning human rights abuses occurred due to the actions of its subsidiary, it should not be able to rebut these claims merely by showing that it has complied with its HRDD obligations under the

---

Labour and Social Affairs, Act on Corporate Due Diligence in Supply Chains, https://www.csr-in-deutschland.de/EN/Business-Human-Rights/Supply-Chain-Act/supply-chain-act.html.

[473] German Act, Section 2(6) (Definitions).

[474] In case an enterprise has substantiated knowledge, thus indications that a human rights or environment related violation is possible due to the action of its indirect supplier, then it shall be obliged to carry out a risk analysis and identify preventive measures or a mitigation plan for violations that have already occurred (German Act, Section 9(3)).

[475] German Act, Section 3(1) (Due Diligence Obligations).

[476] German Act, Section 10(1) and 10(2) (Documentation and Reporting Obligation). The provision sets out that the protection of business and trade secrets will be taken into consideration (Section 10 (4)).

[477] German Act, Section 19(1) (Competent Authority).

[478] German Act, Sections 14–18.

[479] German Act, Sections 22–24.

[480] German Act, Section 3(3) (Due Diligence Obligations).

German Act; it should, instead, try and rebut the relevant claims based on the available grounds under civil law.

The German Act has no specific provisions concerning the applicable law issue in claims concerning alleged human rights or environment related obligations of transnational subsidiaries.[481] Therefore, in case of any such claim, it will be required to apply the rules of the conflict of laws to determine whether German law, as the law of the home country, or foreign law, as the law of the host country would apply.[482]

4.3.3.3 Swiss Initiative's Proposal and the Counter-Proposal on mHRDD

In Switzerland, three alternative proposals to regulate the corporate responsibility for human rights violations and environmental damages have so far been issued and debated. To explain the chain of events chronologically, firstly, a coalition of NGOs has filed a popular initiative[483] with the Parliament on 16 October 2016. The so-called Responsible Business Initiative proposed to introduce a duty of HRDD on companies established in Switzerland by way of amending the Swiss Federal Constitution. The initiative was submitted to the Federal Council, which recommended rejection. After discussions held at the Parliament, the National Council of the Parliament accepted a counter-proposal in June 2018.[484] With the the acceptance of the counter-proposal by the National Council of the Parliament in June 2018, the Council of States decided not to enter into deliberations concerning the counter-proposal. In June 2020, the Council of States decided to abide by the counter-proposal, which was then followed by an evaluation by a parliamentary conciliation committee which decided to continue with the due diligence requirements concerning conflict minerals and child labour with no liability provisions. The renewed and delimited version of the counter-proposal was then approved by the National Council of the Parliament and the Council of States. However, as the

[481] This is a step backwards from the previous draft law, which set out that in terms of non-contractual liability claims, the draft law provisions regarding mHRDD obligations would apply as overriding mandatory norms, without regard to the applicable law determined under private international law.

[482] According to the information given by the Federal Ministry of Labour and Social Affairs, in case of a transnational claim, the law of the country where the alleged damage has occurred shall apply. See Federal Ministry of Labour and Social Affairs, Act on Corporate Due Diligence in Supply Chains, https://www.csr-in-deutschland.de/EN/Business-Human-Rights/Supply-Chain-Act/supply-chain-act.html.

[483] Popular initiatives under Swiss law are tools that allow Swiss citizens to request amendments on the Swiss Federal Constitution. A popular initiative that is supported by 100,000 signatures from the Swiss electorate will be submitted to the Federal Council and the Parliament, which will decide on whether to accept or reject the amendment or to issue a counter-proposal, and the initiative will then be put to a popular vote. See Swiss Coalition for Corporate Justice (SCCJ), About the Initiative, https://corporatejustice.ch/about-the-initiative/.

[484] SCCJ, https://corporatejustice.ch/about-the-initiative/.

counter-proposal is considered to have been significantly weakened, the popular initiative of the Responsible Business Initiative was put to referendum on 29 November 2020, which was rejected due to not gaining majority of the cantonal vote, despite having achieved popular vote by 50.7%.[485] Finally, the parliamentary counter-proposal has entered into force in January 2022. Although at first the result of the referendum might seem like a narrow loss for business and human rights defenders, the consequence is at least the enactment of new legislation imposing corporate liability.

According to the popular initiative by the Responsible Business Initiative, an additional Article 101a would be inserted into the Constitution, which would regulate the responsibility of business. The proposed text began with a general duty imposed on the Swiss Confederation to strengthen respect for human rights and the environment through business. The scope of this legal duty was described as companies that had their registered office, central administration, or principal place of business in Switzerland. Therefore, not only companies that were established in Switzerland but also those that had their management and decision-making there, as well as those that had their business focus or their staff and resources in Switzerland, would fall within the scope of the proposed law.[486]

The initiative stipulated that companies must respect internationally recognised human rights and international environmental standards, which would be defined in accordance with UNGPs and other related international instruments, and that companies would also ensure that any companies under their control also respect these rights and standards.[487] The concept of 'control' was defined broadly here, including *de facto* control that might cover the exercise of power in business relationships. Therefore, the interpretation of this concept would be left to the discretion of the legislative and the judiciary to be clarified in practice.[488]

The scope of the obligation of due diligence was set as identification of the impacts on human rights and the environment, taking measures to prevent the same, ceasing existing violations and bearing responsibility for actions. The due diligence obligations extended to subsidiaries and controlled companies within the meaning given in the previous paragraph. The position of SMEs was left to the discretion of the legislator. In the explanations on the text, the Coalition stated that in general these companies were exempt from human rights due diligence, unless they

[485] Switzerland: Responsible Business Initiative rejected at ballot box despite gaining 50.7% of popular vote, Business & Human Rights Resource Centre, https://www.business-humanrights.org/en/latest-news/swiss-due-diligence-initiative-set-for-public-referendum-as-parliament-only-opts-for-reporting-centred-proposal/.

[486] See the explanations on the proposed text at Swiss Coalition for Corporate Justice (SCCJ), The Initiative Text with Explanations, available at https://corporatejustice.ch/about-the-initiative/.

[487] *Hofstetter* criticised the initiative text as covering an undefined category of rights, which provides for a wide liability on corporations (Hofstetter 2019, p. 277).

[488] Bueno (2020), p. 243. *Hofstetter* argues that the scope that covers companies in control is too extensive and vague, but instead it should be limited to subsidiaries (Hofstetter 2019, p. 277).

operated in a high-risk sector, which would be determined periodically by the Federal Council.[489]

The text of the initiative stated that companies would be liable for the damages caused by the companies under their control, in cases where these had committed violations of human rights and environmental standards during the course of business. It is worth noting that, as also mentioned in the explanations of the initiative,[490] controlled companies are usually subsidiaries of parent companies, but it might also be possible to exercise *de facto* control over a company that is not within the corporate group structure, for instance in an exclusive supply relationship.[491]

The article also included an escape clause, stating that no liability would occur if the companies could prove that they took all due care to prevent the damage or that the damage would have still occurred even if all due care had been taken. This was based on Article 55 of the Swiss Code of Obligations, which concerns the employer's responsibility for the acts of its employees,[492] and it differentiated the initiative text significantly from the French Law on Duty of Vigilance that does not offer such an escape clause. The clause was interpreted as beneficial in motivating compliance with the requirements of due diligence, in the sense that compliance would eliminate the risk of liability.[493] At the same time, it was considered reasonable to enable companies to avoid liability where they are able to prove that they have conducted all required human rights due diligence, tried to mitigate the risks of violations, and yet the damage still occurred. These types of clauses concerning the escape of liability are common in strict liability provisions, such as the employer's liability.[494] This escape clause was also interpreted as a reversal of the burden of proof, namely a shift from the victims to the parent company, which in the end benefits the victims.[495] In fact, it is possible to state that reversing the burden of proof in this manner effectively makes the relevant provision more like strict liability, which usually accepts the existence of liability under specific circumstances, unless the allegedly liable party can prove that it has acted diligently to eliminate the risks

---

[489] SCCJ, The Initiative Text with Explanations. See also Atamer and Willi (2020a), pp. 5–6.

[490] SCCJ, The Initiative Text with Explanations.

[491] Hence, although the name of the initiative text is '*Konzernverantwortungsinitiative*', the scope is not exclusively limited to corporate groups, but it covers all relationships with sufficient power and control (a "control relationship") (Atamer and Willi 2020a, p. 6).

[492] Weller and Pato (2018), p. 414. Article 55 of the Swiss Code of Obligations is parallel to Article 66 of TCO, concerning employer's strict liability for the actions of its employees, with the only difference being that Article 66 of TCO regulates also organizational liability, which stipulates that if the employment is within an enterprise, then the employer shall be responsible for the damage caused due to the operations of the relevant enterprise unless it proves that the work organization is suitable to prevent the occurrence of the relevant damage.

[493] Soudain (2019), p. 62.

[494] Soudain (2019), p. 62.

[495] Palombo (2019), p. 278. *Petrin* and *Choudhury* interpret this provision as 'presumption of liability' on the parent company's side, as the parent company would be responsible unless it is able to prove that it has acted with due care (Petrin and Choudhury 2018, p. 785).

and yet the risks have nonetheless occurred. Having said that, a presumption of liability might also be addressed, where, for instance, the parent company holds the majority of the voting rights in its subsidiary. In this case, it would be deemed to have sufficient control, although it may prove that it does not *de facto* exercise any control, and the parent company should not be able to rebut liability claims.[496]

Finally, the initiative text stipulated that Swiss law would apply irrespective of the law applicable under private international law. This clause created an imperative nature to these provisions, ensuring that they would apply extraterritorially.[497] This aspect of the Swiss initiative was also different to the French Law on Duty of Vigilance, which apparently failed to provide the substantive law's link to the conflict of law principles.

Resulting from the rejection of the initiative's proposal for an amendment to the Swiss Federal Constitution, the National Council of Parliament approved the milder version of the counter-proposal suggesting amendments to the Swiss Code of Obligations and Swiss Criminal Code,[498] with the majority of the provisions regulated in the Swiss Code of Obligations.[499] The mentioned counter-proposal regulates non-financial reporting obligations and due diligence obligations. The scope of the non-financial reporting under the counter-proposal seems similar to the EU's Non-Financial Reporting Directive,[500] as it covers employee rights, social and environmental issues, human rights abuses and anti-corruption.[501] On the other hand, due diligence obligations are set only relating to child labour and conflict minerals.

According to the counter-proposal, non-financial reporting obligations apply to public companies and financial institutions with at least 500 full-time employees and with a balance sheet total of 20 million CHF, or a turnover of 40 million CHF within two consecutive financial years.[502] The scope of the non-financial reporting is wide enough to cover the companies, either Swiss or foreign, that are under sole or collective control of the relevant company subject to the non-financial reporting obligation. In the absence of a definition of 'control', it remains important to be seen how it will be interpreted by the judiciary. The non-financial reporting in the counter-proposal is regulated on a 'comply or explain' basis,[503] which has already

[496] Atamer and Willi (2020a), p. 6.

[497] Weller and Pato (2018), p. 414.

[498] Swiss Federal Office of Justice, Code des Obligations: Contre-projet indirect à l'initiative populaire "Entreprises responsables – pour protéger l'être humain et l'environnement", https://www.parlament.ch/centers/eparl/curia/2016/20160077/Texte%20pour%20le%20vote%20final%202%20NS%20F.pdf.

[499] Swiss Code of Obligations, Chapters VI and VIII (Art. 964a-964l).

[500] Directive 2014/95/EU of the European Parliament and of the Council of 22 October 2015 amending Directive 2013/34/EU as regards disclosure of non-financial and diversity information by certain large undertakings and groups.

[501] Atamer and Willi (2020b), pp. 686–687.

[502] Swiss Code of Obligations, Art. 964a.

[503] Swiss Code of Obligations, Art. 964b(5).

been proven to be ineffective in ensuring compliance, as the liberty given to companies in this sense results in incompliance and negatively affects legal certainty.[504]

Due diligence obligations, on the other hand, apply to companies that have registered office, central administration or principal place of business in Switzerland and that have activites concerning minerals and metals in conflict-affected and high-risk zones or that provide good or services with a reasonable suspicion to have been produced by using child labour.[505] There are certain exceptions to the regulated due diligence obligations. As for the conflict minerals part, import and processing of recycled metals is left outside the scope of due diligence.[506] As for the child labour related due diligence, SMEs (defined as companies that satisfy two of the three given criteria: (i) a balance sheet of a total of CHF 30 million, (ii) turnover of CHF 40 million, and/or (iii) 250 employees) are exempted from due diligence obligation, unless they produce goods or provide services with a confirmed use of child labour.[507] Companies that procure goods and services only from countries with a low risk of child labour, determined in accordance with UNICEF's Children's Rights in the Workplace Index,[508] are outside the scope of the relevant due diligence obligations.[509] Moreover, companies that implement and comply with the international standards concerning conflict minerals and child labour are also exempt from these obligations.[510]

The companies that fall within the mentioned scope are obliged to prepare a due diligence policy for their supply chain, to establish a tracking mechanism, to identify and evaluate the risks arising from their supply chain, to prepare a detailed management plan and to take measures to prevent or mitigate the relevant risks.[511] The management of the company shall be responsible to report annually on the fulfilment of due diligence obligations, which will be made accessible to public.[512]

The failure to fulfil the obligations concerning non-financial reporting, conflict minerals or child labour related due diligence is subject to a fine of up to CHF

[504] Atamer and Willi (2020b), p. 693.

[505] Swiss Code of Obligations, Art. 964j. The details of the due diligence obligations are regulated in the Swiss Federal Ordinance on Due Diligence and Transparency on Conflict Minerals and Child Labour (03.12.2021).

[506] Swiss Federal Ordinance on Due Diligence and Transparency on Conflict Minerals and Child Labour, Art. 2–3.

[507] Swiss Federal Ordinance on Due Diligence and Transparency on Conflict Minerals and Child Labour, Art. 6, 8.

[508] UNICEF, Children's Rights in the Workplace Index, https://www.childrensrightsatlas.org/country-data/workplace/.

[509] Swiss Federal Ordinance on Due Diligence and Transparency on Conflict Minerals and Child Labour, Art. 7.

[510] Swiss Federal Ordinance on Due Diligence and Transparency on Conflict Minerals and Child Labour, Annex 2.

[511] Swiss Code of Obligations, Art. 964k.

[512] Swiss Code of Obligations, Art. 964l.

100,000.[513] There is no clear enforcement mechanism nor any reference to civil liability for failure to comply with these obligations, which significantly weakens the efficiency of this new legislation.[514] The lack of reference to civil liability and to a standard of duty of care leaves the French Law on Duty of Vigilance in its unique position to impose civil liability to parent companies in case of their failure to comply with the relevant obligations.[515]

4.3.3.4 The Dutch Bill on Responsible and Sustainable International Business Conduct

Following the enactment of the Child Labour Due Diligence Law,[516] the Netherlands has also adopted the Dutch Bill,[517] which offers a wide scope mHRDD obligations on companies over a certain scale, as well as specific provisions on the duty of care. The Dutch Bill was submitted to parliament on 11.03.2021 and is expected to enter into force in 2023,[518] when the Child Labour Due Diligence Law will be abolished.[519]

The Dutch Bill adopts a different approach than its equivalents in other jurisdictions by distinguishing between the mHRDD obligations and the duty of care for human rights violations arising from business activities. This distinction shows a clear preference of the legislator to impose mHRDD obligations to companies over a certain size, while imposing the duty of care to all companies that have transnational operations. The mHRDD obligations apply to companies that satisfy at least two of the following: (i) having a balance sheet total of €20 million, (ii) having a net turnover of €40 million, and (iii) having at least 250 employees in average in a financial year.[520] Only companies that have operations outside the Dutch territory fall within scope of the mentioned mHRDD obligations; hence, the Dutch Bill excludes all those companies that carry out business activities only in the Netherlands. According to the relevant provisions,[521] companies that fall within scope of

---

[513] Swiss Criminal Code, Art. 325ter.

[514] Bueno and Kaufmann (2021), p. 547.

[515] On French Law on Duty of Vigilance, see the explanations under Sect. 4.3.3.1 hereunder.

[516] Child Labour Due Diligence Law (Wet van 24 oktober 2019 houdende de invoering van een zorgplicht ter voorkoming van de levering van goederen en diensten die met behulp van kinderarbeid tot stand zijn gekomen), Staatsblad (2019), 401.

[517] Responsible and Sustainable International Business Act (Wet Verantwoord en Duurzaam Internationaal Ondernemen), 11.03.2021, Tweede Kamer, vergaderjaar 2020–2021, 35 761, nr. 2.

[518] While the majority of the provisions of the Dutch Bill will enter into force on 01.01.2023, the provisions on sanctions (Art. 3.2–3.5) will enter into force on 01.07.2023 and Art. 3.6 on 01.01.2024.

[519] Dutch Bill, Art. 4.1.

[520] Dutch Bill, Art. 2.1.

[521] Obligations concerning mHRDD are regulated under Articles 2.2–2.8 of the Dutch Bill, based on the OECD Guidance on HRDD.

the mHRDD obligations shall (i) publish a policy document setting out their mHRDD plan and the process of implementation, (ii) conducting a risk analysis on their own business activities and those of their business relationships, and preparing an action plan with measures to prevent and mitigate the relevant risks, (iii) terminating their own activities if they cause or contribute to negative impacts, (iv) monitoring the application and effectiveness of their measures concerning mHRDD, (v) reporting annually, and in a form accessible to everyone, on their mHRDD policy, their measures and results of the monitoring (vi) establishing a remediation mechanism for complaints, and (vii) remediating any negative impacts caused.

The duty of care, on the other hand, is applicable to all companies domiciled in or operating in the Netherlands or in the Carribean Netherlands, and to large foreign companies that operate in the Netherlands or sell products to the Netherlands. Accordingly, a company that knows or that can reasonably suspect that its business activities may create an adverse impact on human rights, labour rights or the environment[522] is obliged to (a) take all measures that can be reasonably be expected to prevent the harming result, (b) if the result cannot be prevented, to mitigate, reverse and where possible remedy the harms, and (c) if the harms cannot be sufficiently mitigated, then to terminate and refrain from engaging in the relevant activity in so far that it can reasonably be expected.[523]

As for the supervision of compliance, the Dutch Bill stipulates that a public regulator will be designated that will be authorised to order compliance with mHRDD obligations and to impose an administrative penalty for the breach thereof.[524] The fines and penalties to be ordered by the public regulator will be made public.[525] There is also a criminal offense in case of repeated violation of mHRDD obligations,[526] which would surely have a deterrent impact on companies.

Based on the foregoing explanations, the Dutch Bill might be considered to offer a logical and sufficient ground for mHRDD obligations and the duty of care of companies for violations of human rights resulting from the business activities throughout their supply chains. Separately regulating the two main points of liability, namely the mHRDD obligations and the duty of care, creates the opportunity to

[522]The Dutch Bill sets out a non-exhaustive list of adverse impacts on human rights, labour rights and the environment in Art. 1.2(2), whereby focus appears to be on labour rights: restriction of freedom of association and collective bargaining, discrimination, forced labour, child labour, unsafe working conditions, slavery, exploitation, environmental damage.

[523]Dutch Bill, Art. 1.2(1).

[524]Dutch Bill, Art. 3.1–3.3. There is also a hardship clause, whereby the regulator may decide to rule out the penalty in case it deems that the penalty will result in extreme unfairness for the relevant enterprise (Art. 3.4).

[525]Dutch Bill, Art. 3.5.

[526]The third time violation of the mHRDD obligations under the Dutch Bill is considered a criminal offense under the Dutch Economic Offenses Act (Dutch Bill, Art. 3.6), which is punishable by up to six years' imprisonment, community service or a fine of €87,000 (art. 6.1(1°) Dutch Economic Offences Act) (See Hoff 2021, https://voelkerrechtsblog.org/a-bill-for-better-business/).

access civil liability in case of non-compliance. The administrative fines, reinforced by criminal offense in case of repeated violation, will surely be effective to ensure compliance. Yet, without any clear reference to civil liability, it would still be challenging to create a decisive and continuing influence on corporate actors. For all these reasons, the Dutch Bill should create a significant difference in the future of FDL cases, which will be strengthened by the promising case law of Dutch courts on this field.

4.3.4 Suggestions for Regulating mHRDD in Turkish Law

Turkish tort law requires the existence of a legal norm to establish the element of unlawfulness, and consequently tort liability, especially in the case of an omission (a passive action) that led to a damage. Accordingly, the provision that will be suggested under this section on mHRDD would also contribute to the formation of unlawfulness in establishing the parent company's liability due to the breach of the duty of care under Turkish law. Hence the provision suggested hereunder is related and complementary to the provision suggested for the parent company's duty of care.

Despite being complementary to civil liability, mHRDD might be deemed to provide a wider scope of protection for the victims of FDL claims. In fact, as *Atamer* and *Willi* point out, while tort liability concerns an *ex post* compensation of the damage occurred, mHRDD provides an *ex ante* prevention of the relevant abuse that might cause damage.[527] Therefore, mHRDD not only constitutes a viable legal basis for imposing a liability in tort on a parent company, but it also serves as potentially the most efficient way to protect the interests of tort victims in a precautionary manner.

As analysed in Chap. 3 of this study, Turkish law provides an extensive statutory regulation on corporate groups under the TCC and the Trade Registry Regulation. According to these provisions, a corporate group might in certain cases extend to include foreign subsidiaries, supply chains, sub-contractors as well as other types of relationships, provided that these satisfy the criteria regulated therein.[528] It is therefore considered that Turkish law provides suitable legal grounds for regulating mHRDD. In elaborating on the suggestions given herein below, the previously analysed legislation in France, Germany, Switzerland and the Netherlands are taken into account, together with OHCHR's Third Revised Draft, the Proposed EU Directive on Corporate DD, as well as the relevant considerations in legal doctrine. It is considered that for the purposes of regulating this obligation, it would be adequate to create *de lege ferenda* either by inserting an additional provision into the provisions on corporate groups under the TCC or by adopting

---

[527] Atamer and Willi (2020a), p. 4.

[528] See the explanations made under Sect. 3.1.2 in this respect.

secondary legislation on this specific subject that would apply in support of the corporate groups provisions under the TCC.

In addition to the above, in October 2020, an amendment was made in the Turkish Capital Markets Board's Communiqué on Corporate Governance No. II-17.1 ('Communiqué No. II-17.1'),[529] which introduced new obligations concerning sustainability principles on public companies.[530] Accordingly, public companies that are obliged to submit a compliance report for corporate governance principles shall also include explanations on their compliance to sustainability principles. These companies shall provide information on their compliance with corporate governance principles and sustainability principles in their annual activity reports on a 'comply or explain' basis, and they shall also identify consequences of non-compliance with these principles in terms of environmental and social risk management.[531] The Communiqué No. II-17.1 also stipulates that compliance with sustainability principles is voluntary.[532] The Capital Markets Board published a Compliance Framework for Sustainability Principles,[533] which sets out in detail what should be done by public companies that wish to be abided by sustainability principles. Within this framework, the relevant companies shall mainly (i) set a strategy and policy concerning environmental, social and corporate governance issues, (ii) appoint committees for applying these principles and set action plans, (iii) report on these issues within their annual activity reports, and (iv) declare to public their sustainability performance measures. Specific requirements are also set in the Compliance Framework for Sustainability Principles for environmental compliance, social compliance (comprising human rights, employee rights, multiple stakeholders, international standards and initiatives) and corporate governance principles. UN's SDGs for 2030[534] are also mentioned as part of companies' reporting requirements, stipulating that the companies shall identify which SDG is relevant in terms of their activities. The recognition of the UN's SDGs for this purpose might be seen as a positive improvement for sustainability reporting, even though it concerns public companies

[529] OJ 03.01.2014/28871, in force as of 03.01.2014; the amendments concerning sustainability principles entered into force on 02.10.2020 (OJ 02.10.2020/31262).

[530] The provisions on corporate governance of the Communiqué on Corporate Governance No. II-17.1 do not apply to (a) public companies whose shares are not traded in stock exchange, (b) companies whose shares are traded in markets or platforms other than National Market, Second National Market or Corporate Products Market, (c) companies that applied to the Capital Markets Board for initial public offering and/or trading in stock exchange whose shares will be traded in markets or platforms other than National Market, Second National Market or Corporate Products Market and (d) companies that are considered as located abroad in accordance with Decision No. 32 on the Protection of the Value of Turkish Lira (in force by the decision of the Council of Ministers dated 07.08.1989 and numbered 89/14391).

[531] Article 8/1 of Communiqué No. II-17.1.

[532] Article 8/3 of Communiqué No. II-17.1.

[533] Compliance Framework for Sustainability Principles (*Sürdürülebilirlik İlkeleri Uyum Çerçevesi*), Capital Markets Board of Turkey, https://www.spk.gov.tr/Sayfa/Dosya/1332.

[534] Take Action for the Sustainable Development Goals – United Nations, https://www.unglobalcompact.org/sdgs.

only. As a general remark, the amendments made in the Communiqué No. II-17.1 concerning sustainability and the Compliance Framework for Sustainability Principles might be considered as an initial phase for the road leading to introducing mHRDD in domestic law. The suggestions *de lege ferenda* on regulating mHRDD under Turkish law are given herein below.

4.3.4.1 The Personal Scope of the Suggested Regulation

The main purpose of regulating mHRDD in statutory law is to place an obligation on companies, including MNCs, to make assessments and report on the potential risks to human rights and the environment that may arise due to their own activities, as well as the activities of their subsidiaries, sub-contractors and others in their global supply chains. It is noted that all of the regulations in force or under discussion to be enforced have set a scope that would mostly cover all of the above-mentioned entities.

As discussed previously, the OEIGWG's Third Revised Draft[535] has set a wide scope for the subject of mHRDD obligations. As per Article 3/1, the draft legally binding instrument shall apply to all business activities, including but not limited to those of a transnational character. As previously explained,[536] the transnational character of business activities has also been defined widely in the Third Revised Draft.[537] Therefore, it is possible to suggest that the personal scope of application of the Third Revised Draft is wide enough to cover all business activities of any kind, including those with a transnational nature that are subject to FDL claims.

The range of companies that would fall within the mHRDD requirement is stipulated under Article 6/3(b) of the Third Revised Draft, covering not only the relevant companies conducting business activities but also entities or activities that are under their control or management. The legal liability in respect of mHRDD is regulated under Article 8, which indicates the exact scope of companies that should be included in the mHRDD. According to this provision (Art. 8/6), the legal liability of natural or legal persons conducting business activities shall occur where they fail to prevent others, with whom they have business relationships, from causing harm to third parties, provided that they control, manage or supervise such persons or the

[535] Open-Ended Intergovernmental Working Group on Transnational Corporations and Other Business Enterprises With Respect to Human Rights (OEIGWG), Third Revised Draft Legally Binding Instrument to Regulate, in International Human Rights Law, the Activities of Transnational Corporations and Other Business Enterprises (17.08.2021), https://www.ohchr.org/EN/HRBodies/HRC/WGTransCorp/Session7/Pages/Session7.aspx.

[536] See Sect. 3.2.3.2. of this study.

[537] As per Article 1/4 of the Third Revised Draft, a business activity shall be deemed to have transnational character if (a) it is undertaken in one or more jurisdiction or state, or (b) the most substantial part of its preparation, planning, direction, control, design, processing, manufacturing, storage or distribution took place through any business relationship in another state or jurisdiction, or (c) creates significant effect in another state or jurisdiction.

relevant activity that caused or contributed to the human rights abuse, or should have foreseen the risks of human rights abuses in the conduct of their business activities, including those of a transnational nature, or in their business relationships, but failed to put adequate measures in place to prevent the abuse.

The legislative instruments regulating mHRDD in France, Switzerland, Germany and the Netherlands, which are analysed above, have a common approach in terms of the personal scope of mHRDD provisions. In fact, all these cover the business activities of the company that is the main subject of the relevant obligations, including the activities of its affiliates and subsidiaries, as well as others with whom the company has a specific relationship, albeit an established commercial relationship or a *de facto* control by exercise of decisive influence over the latter. This appears to be based on the logic that in order to include the activities of the relevant companies within its HRDD policy and plan, a company needs to have a certain level of control and leverage over those companies; otherwise, expecting an action towards others and suggesting a liability for non-compliance would be unrealistic.

As analysed in detail under Chap. 3, the scope of corporate groups is kept wide under Turkish law, which can be realised through obtaining control over another company by way of shareholding, voting rights, contract or in any other manner. Here, the concept of 'dominance in any other manner' is not defined in the relevant provision of the TCC. As further detailed in Sect. 3.1.2.4.5 above, this concept is open to interpretations of a wider scope, where control might be deemed to exist in case of exercising a decisive influence on business and finance policies of another company, such as decisions concerning production, sale, marketing, budget and financial planning.[538] Accordingly, although it has not yet been subject to a court decision, this type of control could under certain circumstances be interpreted so as to cover suppliers that are dependent on the purchasing company, especially economically; for instance where the majority of the goods manufactured by the supplier is allocated to a specific company. Therefore, the provisions on mHRDD need not address in detail the entities that should fall within its scope, but it might refer sufficiently to corporate groups as described under Turkish law. In this manner, both the subsidiaries and any other entities that are under the control of a company shall fall within the scope of this obligation. Hence in the proposed regulation it would be sufficient to refer to the concept of corporate groups within the meaning given under TCC and Trade Registry Regulation as the personal scope of mHRDD.

It is also important to set the complete criteria regarding which companies would fall within the scope of the mHRDD obligation. French law provides stricter criteria, covering a rather small number of companies, while the Dutch Bill provides broader criteria which would result in a good number of companies falling within the scope of the legislation. The criteria sought in these regulations are dependent on the size of companies—based on the number of employees, the turnover figure and the balance sheet total. Providing such criteria for the purposes of mHRDD is a reasonable

[538] Okutan Nilsson (2009), p. 98.

approach, considering that the said obligation could be a big burden for SMEs. Therefore, the same approach could also be adopted in Turkish law. On the other hand, it might be considered that the definition of a corporate group under Turkish law already requires a certain number of companies to be linked to the parent company: i.e. three subsidiaries where the parent is an undertaking (who can be a real person or a legal entity), and two subsidiaries where the parent is a company. It is possible to state that this definition would already cover companies of a certain size and thus there would be no need to also include a criterion based on the number of employees or the annual turnover as is done in exemplary legislation. At first glance, this scope could seem insufficient to cover all types of global supply chains, as it requires a minimum number of entities to constitute a corporate group in the first place. However, considering the extraterritorial reach of corporate groups under Turkish law (where a corporate will be deemed to exist if the parent company or one of the subsidiaries is based in Turkey)[539] and also that global supply chains have mostly an MNC at the top of the chain, the relevant provision would provide a sufficient legal framework to regulate mHRDD. It would, nevertheless, still be prudent to also include a clear exemption for SMEs,[540] by specifying certain circumstances where SMEs should also be included within the scope of mHRDD considering the probability of human rights abuses within business activities and the pressing need to prevent or mitigate the same: i.e. when these are operating in high-risk sectors,[541] or when they are operating in high-risk areas, such as areas of armed conflict, or when their line of work has a high risk of child labour.[542]

4.3.4.2 The Material Scope of the Suggested Regulation

The general obligation of the companies under the suggested regulation will be to respect international human rights and environmental standards in their operations, ensure that these are respected by the companies under their control and take measures for compliance in their supply chains.[543] Accordingly, the content of the mHRDD report should mainly be the potential and actual impacts on human rights

[539] Art. 195/1 of TCC.

[540] As per the Regulation on Definition, Qualifications and Classification of Small and Medium Sized Enterprises (No. 2005/9617), the medium and small sized enterprises are economic units or enterprises that employ less than 250 employees and that have either net sales or financial balance sheet total of maximum 25 million Turkish Liras and which are defined in the Regulation as micro enterprise, small enterprise and medium enterprise.

[541] Similar to the provision of Art. 2(3) of the EU Directive Draft. Also see European Coalition for Corporate Justice (ECCJ) Position Paper (2018), p. 3, http://corporatejustice.org/documents/publications/eccj/2018eccj-position-paper-mhrdd-final_june2018.pdf.

[542] Similar to the provision of Art. 964j of the Swiss Code of Obligations.

[543] European Coalition for Corporate Justice (ECCJ), EU Model Law on Corporate Accountability in Global Value Chains, Legal Brief, January 2022, https://corporatejustice.org/wp-content/uploads/2022/01/ECCJ_Model_Law_Redesigned_final.pdf.

and environmental standards that arising due to the operations of the companies that are subject to the mHRDD obligation. In other words, the material scope of this obligation should cover internationally recognised human rights, labour rights, international environmental standards, other types of environmental impacts and stakeholders' rights to the extent that these are relevant.[544] The concepts of human rights and environmental damages should be defined in accordance with the relevant international legal instruments and available domestic law on these matters. German Act sets out a non-exhaustive list of human rights, amongst which there are labour-related rights such as the prohibition of child labour, elimination of modern slavery and forced labour, occupational safety and health, freedom of association and union, as well as prevention of discrimination and right to a clean environment.[545] This rather casualistic approach that enlists not all but perhaps the most frequently infringed human rights might be helpful, but it is surely not mandatory to ensure an extensive scope of human rights that fall within the mHRDD obligations. Making clear references to internationally recognised human rights, labour rights and environmental standards could instead be sufficient.

The human rights to be covered by due diligence should be interpreted to include the ones mentioned in the International Bill of Human Rights, ILO's Declaration on Fundamental Principles and Rights at Work, and EU Charter of Fundamental Rights for EU Member States, while environmental standards shall cover the norms adopted through international processes or by international organisations.[546] The Third Revised Draft of the UN's legally binding instrument also refers to internationally recognised human rights and fundamental freedoms, including environmental rights (Art. 1/2). Making reference to international legal instruments concerning especially human rights, labour rights and environmental issues in the relevant regulation would in fact ensure that the scope of mHRDD is kept wide enough to cover all crucial elements of sustainability.[547]

---

[544] The scope of the sustainability reporting is kept quite wide under Compliance Framework for Sustainability Principles of the Capital Markets Board of Turkey, which might be taken as reference in determining the material scope of mandatory human rights due diligence. Accordingly, risks pertaining to environmental damage, human rights abuses, employee's rights' infringements as well as other stakeholders' rights' infringements might be put within this scope. See Compliance Framework for Sustainability Principles (*Sürdürülebilirlik İlkeleri Uyum Çerçevesi*), Capital Markets Board of Turkey, https://www.spk.gov.tr/Sayfa/Dosya/1332.

[545] German Act, Art. 2(2).

[546] European Coalition for Corporate Justice (ECCJ) Position Paper, Key Features of Mandatory Human Rights Due Diligence Legislation, June 2018, p. 2, http://corporatejustice.org/documents/publications/eccj/2018eccj-position-paper-mhrdd-final_june2018.pdf.

[547] It is worth noting that Compliance Framework for Sustainability Principles, based on Communiqué No. II-17.1 of Capital Markets Board of Turkey (although setting voluntary principles on reporting), has made specific reference to the main international legal instruments on this subject, such as UN's Global Compact, UN's SDGs, as well as global reporting standards such as Global Reporting Initiative (GRI). It is possible to say that by making such reference the relevant soft law mechanism acquires a hard law character.

In light of the exemplary legislation and international legal instruments that were analysed previously, the proposed scope of mHRDD under Turkish law might be described as identifying and analysing the impacts and potential risks on human rights and environment[548] due to the activities of the relevant entities. Within this context, the relevant companies shall be obliged to fulfil the following[549]: (1) issuing an mHRDD policy statement, mapping their global supply chain and establishing a risk management system to identify the actual and potential risks arising from business activities, (2) proposing and implementing measures to mitigate or prevent these risks, (3) documenting and reporting the risks and the measures taken publicly and regularly, (4) performing regular risk analysis on the relevant activities, (5) appointing a responsible person or unit within the company to check and monitor compliance, (6) establishing an internal grievance mechanism to handle complaints from various stakeholders, and (7) ceasing existing abuses and taking remedial actions.

Furthermore, in line with the UN's Third Revised Draft, it would also be adequate to provide a requirement that the proposed measures and remedial actions will be discussed and consulted with groups of stakeholders other than shareholders, such as employees, workers' unions and local people living in the vicinities of the subsidiary's operations, which is crucial to ensure the adequacy and efficiency of the relevant measures.[550] Such a provision would also allow the inclusion of the NGOs that represent the interests of the victims of potential or actual human rights abuses and it would also be in support of moving from shareholder primacy towards multi-stakeholder approach in terms of corporate legal theory.

4.3.4.3 Monitoring Compliance

The German Act adopts an ambitious approach on monitoring compliance with mHRDD obligations. First of all, it provides for a monitoring mechanism within the company, by appointing an officer to check compliance and by creating a complaint mechanism.[551] It further stipulates that a governmental authority will be authorised to check compliance by companies.[552] This is similarly arranged in the Dutch Bill, whereby it is regulated that a public authority will be designated to monitor

[548]As *Choudhury* and *Petrin* most accurately note, environmental damage may not always be sufficiently 'material' to be foresee, to set out in due diligence report and to mitigate by way of precautionary measures, and might be ignored by companies. Therefore, environmental issues must be a part of the decision-making process in companies and must be taken into account together with corporate interests (Choudhury and Petrin 2019, p. 273).

[549]The mHRDD obligations set out herein are mostly based on the Draft EU Directive on Corporate DD and the German Act, which provide the most extensive scope amongst all other legislative instruments on mHRDD.

[550]Third Revised Draft, Art. 6.5(d).

[551]German Act, Art. 8.

[552]German Act, Art. 12–21.

compliance, handle complaints and issue administrative fines for non-compliance.[553] The Third Revised Draft of the UN legally binding instrument also regulates that state parties shall arrange for effective national procedures to ensure that business enterprises comply with the due diligence requirements set out therein and that there will be sanctions for non-compliance along with the criminal, administrative and civil liability (Art. 6/7). However, in its capacity as a framework treaty, the Third Revised Draft does not stipulate in detail the types of sanctions that might be triggered for non-compliance with due diligence obligations, but leaves this issue to the discretion of the state parties to regulate in their domestic laws.

Appointing a committee or an officer within the company to check compliance with the mHRDD requirements is an effective monitoring tool. The relevant committee or officer should be obliged to report periodically to the board of directors, as the management body of the company. It should also handle complaints from internal and external stakeholders through a process that is accessible to everyone and that is conducted confidentially, impartially and transparently.

Designating an authorised public authority to monitor compliance with mHRDD requirements might also be considered an important method to track and ensure compliance. However, it should be noted that such a mechanism could also fail to reach just and effective consequences if not properly built. First of all, in order to be able to grant such wide powers to an authority, including checking whether the proposed measures are effective or remedial actions are implemented properly, it will be necessary to ensure that the appointed officers are experts in this field, which will not be easy considering the enhanced scope. Another issue would be to procure the independent and unbiased character of the relevant authority, which would require a separate personality detached from the state and accountability for actions supported by full transparency. Taking into account the wide authorities provided in German Act,[554] under which the relevant public body is authorised to carry out investigations, inspect documents and summon people, it seems quite unlikely that corporate actors would accept to be under such control of a non-public entity. It would also be problematic to appoint such a national public authority to check compliance through the whole global supply chain – i.e. the national legal character of such an authority would be incompatible with the extraterritorial scope of mHRDD obligations.[555] Finally, check of compliance by the relevant authority might also create a potential ground of defense for companies that face claims of non-compliance. For instance, a company whose due diligence report is checked and approved by the relevant authority might rely on this approval for proving it has complied with the mHRDD obligations at a potential legal action filed by those alleging to have their human rights violated due to its business activities. This is dangerous as it creates a risk that the mHRDD becomes a superficial and formalistic

[553] Dutch Bill, Art. 3.1–3.3.

[554] German Act, Art. 13–17.

[555] Sherpa (2021), https://www.asso-sherpa.org/wp-content/uploads/2021/05/2021.05-Position-Paper-DV-Public-Enforcement.pdf.

tick-box exercise[556] and it greatly hinders potential claims of FDL victims by presenting a fairly easy ground of defense to companies.

4.3.4.4 Sanctions for Non-Compliance

The efficiency of the mHRDD obligations greatly depends on the availability of adequate and proportionate sanctions and liability set for non-compliance. In the absence thereof, it will be difficult to effectively implement these obligations in practice and the relevant provisions would lose their hard law character as they would move closer to non-mandatory soft law instruments. In order to ensure compliance by regarding legal certainty, the relevant sanctions and references to liability provisions should be addressed clearly in law. Accordingly, in order to ensure compliance, sanctions and liability should be addressed for non-compliance with the HRDD obligations, and also for non-implementation of the relevant remedies or preventive measures set out in the HRDD plan.

Potential sanctions for non-compliance with mHRDD obligations may consist of a fixed administrative or judicial monetary fine,[557] a fine calculated on the basis of the relevant company's turnover[558] and/or a periodic monetary fine to be applied throughout the period of non-compliance.[559] Exclusion from public procurement,[560] state aid or from public support schemes could also be alternative sanctions that would be effective to provide compliance.[561] As the Draft EU Directive on Corporate DD also emphasises, the designated sanctions should take into account the severity of the violations and whether or not there is a repeated violation.[562] To this end, criminal liability could also be foreseen for repetitive violations as a stringent sanction that would surely contribute to ensuring compliance.

Although administrative and criminal sanctions would certainly create a disincentivising impact on companies to engage in any breach of mHRDD obligations, they would not be sufficient to ensure a complete mechanism whereby the victims of human rights abuses arising from business conduct are compensated for their losses in a fair manner, as the payment in such a case would be made to the public authority.[563] A clear reference to civil liability is, therefore, of paramount importance. More specifically, a company's failure to comply with mHRDD obligations which eventually results in damage to the environment and/or to tort victims

---

[556] Sherpa (2021), https://www.asso-sherpa.org/wp-content/uploads/2021/05/2021.05-Position-Paper-DV-Public-Enforcement.pdf.

[557] German Act, Art. 23.

[558] Draft EU Directive on Corporate DD, Art. 18/2; German Act, Art. 24.

[559] French Law on the Duty of Vigilance, Art. 1; French Commercial Code, Art. L. 225-102-4.-II.

[560] German Act, Art. 22.

[561] Draft EU Directive on Corporate DD, Art. 18/2.

[562] Draft EU Directive on Corporate DD, Art. 18/1.

[563] Commission Study on DD, p. 212.

in general should trigger civil liability of the relevant company to compensate the damage occurred. Moreover, it should also be clarified that a company's compliance with its mHRDD obligations shall not *per se* absolve the undertaking of civil liability under national law.[564]

Therefore, in addition to the suggested sanctions, non-compliance with mHRDD obligations should also trigger the civil liability of the parent company under the general provisions of Turkish tort law (Art. 49 et seq TCO). Furthermore, even when a company has fulfilled its mHRDD obligations, its own activities or the activities of the companies under its control might have still caused human rights violations or environmental harms, in which case the joint and several civil liability of the parent company and its subsidiary should be assessed. As explained in detail under Sect. 4.1.1, Turkish tort law requires the existence of the elements of fault, unlawfulness, causation and damage in order to successfully establish fault liability. In cases of a breach of duty of care, which constitutes the main type of liability for FDL claims, it is particularly challenging to establish the element of unlawfulness. More specifically, these cases usually involve an act of omission by the parent company, which needs to be based on a special legal norm to be considered unlawful; thus there would be no breach of the duty of care unless this is specifically regulated by law. Therefore, regulating the parent company's obligation for mHRDD and linking it to civil liability would constitute the required legal ground for establishing the parent company's fault liability under Turkish law. This legal method would have great potential to satisfy tort victims in FDL claims, as the failure of companies to satisfy their obligations on mHRDD might lead to successfully proving that they have breached their duty of care against third parties or have acted in negligence. Therefore, it is crucial to have a clear regulation that would create a link between mHRDD and general civil liability to enforce the practice of mHRDD and to provide legal certainty.[565]

4.4 Interim Conclusion on Substantive Legal Analysis of FDL

In light of the foregoing analysis presented in this chapter through liability in tort, strict liability and liability for mHRDD, it is possible to conclude that all of these different legal grounds could be relevant for FDL claims.

Tort liability of negligence, as it is currently regulated under Turkish law, might be used in addressing FDL claims provided that the elements of tort are present in the relevant case. The main point of focus in tort liability is the breach of duty of care, for

[564] Draft EU Directive on Corporate DD, Art. 19/1.

[565] European Coalition for Corporate Justice (ECCJ) Position Paper, Key Features of Mandatory Human Rights Due Diligence Legislation (2018), p. 2, http://corporatejustice.org/documents/publications/eccj/2018eccj-position-paper-mhrdd-final_june2018.pdf.

which the view of unlawfulness of the behaviour seems more adequate under Turkish law. In fact, parent company's role in terms of FDL usually takes place in the form of omission, which requires the existence of a legal norm regulating an obligation to act in order to establish the element of unlawfulness. Liability for the breach of the duty of care should also be possible where there is a duty of care is regulated by law. Referring to the arguments in Turkish legal doctrine and comparative law, it is possible to state that it would be both necessary and adequate to include a provision in statutory law addressing the parent company's duty of care in MNCs for the damage incurred by third parties due to their transnational subsidiaries' operations. To this end, the analysed cases in international case law can be useful in determining the criteria for the establishment of the parent company's duty of care and any breaches thereof. In this manner, under the theory of the protection scope of the violated norm, FDL claims might be accommodated within a legal framework under Turkish law.

Types of strict liability in Turkish law also present some alternative grounds for FDL claims. Although the employer's mild causal liability does not appear to be fit for this purpose, liability for dangerous activities under the TCO and liability of the polluter under the Environmental Law constitute two viable legal grounds. In both of these options, how to position the parent company within an MNC would be important. As for the liability for dangerous activities, it might be argued that the parent company could be considered the owner of the relevant enterprise, as a consequence of its effective control over the subsidiary's activities. As for the liability of the polluter, it might be argued that the indirectly polluting party might be deemed to be the parent company, in comparison with the discussions in EU law on the definition of the 'operator' which, according to some, may cover parent companies that exercise a certain level of control over their subsidiaries.

Finally, an alternative legal basis for FDL claims might be regulated under corporate law by imposing mHRDD obligations on parent companies of MNCs that satisfy a certain criteria. This is a growing trend in the world, initially adopted in France and now in the process of being legislated in Switzerland, Germany and the Netherlands. Turkish law, with a special chapter on corporate groups regulated in TCC, might also accommodate provisions concerning mHRDD. In fact, the current Turkish law does not provide for any such obligation. If regulated, the failure to conduct mHRDD, as well as any failure to adopt the required measures or exercise the necessary monitoring over the subsidiaries, might constitute a breach of the duty of care of the parent company, which would be considered under the umbrella of tort liability, by clarifying that the fulfilment of mHRDD obligations will also not *per se* absolve the potential tort liability of the relevant companies. Therefore, it is possible to say that the obligations concerning mHRDD and the duty of care under tort liability are intertwined with each other, as the former could trigger the latter. Introducing mHRDD in Turkish law would complement any provision regulating the parent company's duty of care within the scope of tort liability and it would also contribute to the discussions concerning the element of unlawfulness in establishing the aforementioned liability.

References

Online Sources

European Coalition for Corporate Justice (ECCJ), The compromise on a counter-proposal to the Swiss Responsible Business Initiative sinks in the Council of State.
https://corporatejustice.org/news/13372-the-compromise-on-a-counter-proposal-to-the-swiss-responsible-business-initiative-sinks-in-the-council-of-state

"First court decision in the climate litigation against Total: A promising interpretation of the French Duty of Vigilance Law", Sherpa (26.03.2021). https://www.asso-sherpa.org/first-court-decision-in-the-climate-litigation-against-total-a-promising-interpretation-of-the-french-duty-of-vigilance-law

Gilligan E, Mandatory human rights due diligence: an issue whose time has come, CORE
https://corporate-responsibility.org/issue-whose-time-come/

International Cyanide Management Code for the Gold Mining Industry, About the Cyanide Code.
https://www.cyanidecode.org/about-cyanide-code

International Cyanide Management Code for the Gold Mining Industry, Dispute Resolution
https://www.cyanidecode.org/about-cyanide-code/dispute-resolution

Luciano Lliuya v. RWE AG, Climate Change Litigation. http://climatecasechart.com/non-us-case/lliuya-v-rwe-ag/

NGOs Call on Unilever CEO to Match Rhetoric with Action – CORE (19.04.2018).
https://corporate-responsibility.org/ngos-call-unilever-ceo-match-action-rhetoric/

"Oil company Total faces historic legal action in France for human rights and environmental violations in Uganda", Friends of the Earth International (23.10.2019).
https://www.foei.org/news/total-legal-action-france-human-rights-environment-uganda

Swiss Coalition for Corporate Justice.
http://konzern-initiative.ch/initiativtext/?lang=en

Switzerland: Responsible Business Initiative rejected at ballot box despite gaining 50.7% of popular vote, Business & Human Rights Resource Centre. https://www.business-humanrights.org/en/latest-news/swiss-due-diligence-initiative-set-for-public-referendum-as-parliament-only-opts-for-reporting-centred-proposal/

Take Action for the Sustainable Development Goals – United Nations. https://www.unglobalcompact.org/sdgs

Total au Tribunal, Les Amis de La Terre France. https://www.totalautribunal.org/amisdelaterre

Total Ouganda: le TGI se déclare incompétent au profit du tribunal de commerce (30.01.2020) Business & Human Rights Resource Centre. https://www.business-

humanrights.org/fr/derni%C3%A8res-actualit%C3%A9s/total-ouganda-le-tgi-se-d%C3%A9clare-incomp%C3%A9tent-au-profit-du-tribunal-de-commerce/
UK Supreme Court, Okpabi and others (Appellants) v Royal Dutch Shell Plc and another (Respondents).
https://www.supremecourt.uk/cases/uksc-2018-0068.html

Legislation, Reports, Resolutions and Opinions

European Commission (January 2020) Study on due diligence requirements through the supply chain – Final Report. B-1049 Brussels
European Coalition for Corporate Justice (ECCJ) Position Paper (June 2018) Key Features of Mandatory Human Rights Due Diligence Legislation. http://corporatejustice.org/documents/publications/eccj/2018eccj-position-paper-mhrdd-final_june2018.pdf
Independent Review of the Modern Slavery Act 2015: Final Report, Presented to Parliament by the Secretary of State for the Home Department by Command of Her Majesty (May 2019). https://assets.publishing.service.gov.uk/government/uploads/system/uploads/attachment_data/file/803406/Independent_review_of_the_Modern_Slavery_Act_-_final_report.pdf
The Modern Corporation Statement on Company Law, coordinated together with other disciplinary statement by Dr. Jeroen Veldman, Modern Corporation Project, which is hosted by Cass Business School, City University, London, the Purpose of the Corporation Project: purposeofcorporation.org - themoderncorporation.org
The Modern Corporation – Corporate Governance for the twenty-first Century. https://themoderncorporation.wordpress.com/
OECD Due Diligence Guidance for Responsible Business Conduct (2018). https://mneguidelines.oecd.org/OECD-Due-Diligence-Guidance-for-Responsible-Business-Conduct.pdf
TEMA (April 2020) Kaz Dağları Yöresi'nde Madencilik (Mining in Ida Mountains Region).
https://www.tema.org.tr/basin-odasi/basin-bultenleri/kaz-daglari-yoresinde-madencilik-raporu
TEMA, Siyanür Liçi ile Altın Madenciliği (Gold Mining by the Method of Cyanide Leaching)
https://cdn-tema.mncdn.com/Uploads/Cms/siyanur-lici-altin-madenciligi.pdf
Turkish Medical Association (TTB) – Bergama Raporu 2001. https://www.ttb.org.tr/eweb/bergama/
UN Global Compact – Making Global Goals Local Business. https://www.unglobalcompact.org/sdgs
UN Special Rep. Of the Secretary-General, Protect, Respect and Remedy: a Framework for Business and Human Rights (7 April 2008) UN Doc. A/HRC/8/5.

Literature

Akartepe A (2012) Türk Borçlar Kanunu'nun Haksız Fiilden Doğan Borç İlişkileri Alanında Getirdiği Yenilikler ve Değişiklikler (Novelties and changes that the Turkish code of obligation brings in tort liability). EÜHFD 16(1–2):159–190

Akkayan Yıldırım A (2012) 6098 Sayılı Türk Borçlar Kanunu Düzenlemeleri Çerçevesinde Kusursuz Sorumluluğun Özel Bir Türü Olarak Tehlike Sorumluluğu (Liability for dangerous activities as a special type of strict liability within scope of Turkish code of obligations No. 6098). İÜHFM 70:203–220

Alper G (2018) İşletme Nedeniyle Tehlike Sorumluluğu (TBK m. 71) (Ultrahazardous Activity Liability of Enterprises). PhD thesis

Antalya G (2008) Sorumluluk Hukukunda yeni Gelişmeler (new improvements in the law of liabilities). Liability from roman law to modern law – symposium special issue, MÜHFD-HAD 14(4):63–83

Antalya G (2013) 6098 Sayılı Türk Borçlar Kanunu'na Göre Borçlar Hukuku Genel Hükümler (Law of obligations general provisions under Turkish code of obligations No. 6098), 2nd edn. Istanbul

Antalya G (2016) Manevi Zararın Belirlenmesi ve Manevi Tazminatın Hesaplanması -Türk Hukukuna Manevi Zararın İki Aşamalı Olarak Belirlenmesine İlişkin Bir Model Önerisi (Determination of moral damages and evaluation of damages for pain and suffering proposal for the evaluation of moral damages in two stages in Turkish law). MÜHF-HAD 22(3):221–250

Aristova E (2016) UK Court on Tort Litigation Against Transnational Corporations. http://conflictoflaws.net/2016/uk-court-on-tort-litigation-against-transnational-corporations/

Aristova E (2018) Tort litigation against transnational corporations in the English courts: the challenge of jurisdiction. Utrecht Law Rev 14(2):6–21

Arkan S (2012) Ticari İşletme Hukuku. Banka ve Ticaret Hukuku Araştırma Enstitüsü, 17th edn. Ankara

Atamer YM (1996) Haksız Fiillerden Doğan Sorumluluğun Sınırlandırılması, Özellikle Uygun Nedensellik Bağı ve Normun Koruma Amacı Kuramları (Limitation of liability for damages caused by torts – especially the theories of adequate causality and the protection scope of the violated norm). İstanbul

Atamer YM (2006) Revize Edilmiş Türk Borçlar Kanunu Tasarısı'na İlişkin Değerlendirme ve Teklifler (Evaluations and proposals regarding the revised draft turkish code of obligations). Hukuki Perspektifler Dergisi (J Legal Perspect) 6:9–36

Atamer YM, Willi F (2020a) Konzernverantwortungsinitiative: Was ändert sich bei einem JA? SZW/RSDA 4(2020):435–448

Atamer YM, Willi F (2020b) CSR-Berichterstattung Ante Portas: Indirekter Gegenvorschlag zur Konzernverantwortungsinitiative. SZW/RSDA 6(2020):686–701

Başoğlu B (2015) Sözleşme Dışı Kusursuz Sorumluluk Hukuku ve Özellikle Tehlike Sorumluluğuna İlişkin Değerlendirmeler (Thoughts on strict tort liability, especially on liability for abnormally dangerous activities). J Fac Law Inonu Univ 6:29–56

Başoğlu B (2016) Çevre Zararlarından Doğan Hukuki Sorumluluk (Civil liability arising from environmental damages). Vedat Kitapçılık

Baysal B (2019) Haksız Fiil Hukuku – BK m. 49–76 (Tort Law – TCO Art. 49–76). Istanbul

Bergkamp L (2016) The environmental liability directive and liability of parent companies for damage caused by their subsidiaries ('Enterprise Liability'). Eur Comp Law 13(5):183–190

Bergkamp PA (2018) Parent company liability after Okpabi v. Shell. Eur Comp Law J 15(4): 112–117

Brabant S, Savourey E (2017a) Law on the Corporate Duty of Vigilance – A Contextualised Approach, Revue Internationale de la Compliance et de L'Éthique des Affaires – Supplément À La Semaine Juridique Entreprise et Affaires N° 50 du Jeudi 14 Décembre 2017, pp 1–7

Brabant S, Savourey E (2017b) A Closer Look at the Penalties Faced by Companies, Revue Internationale de la Compliance et de L'Éthique des Affaires – Supplément À La Semaine Juridique Entreprise et Affaires N° 50 du Jeudi 14 Décembre 2017, pp 1–5
Bueno N (2020) The Swiss popular initiative on responsible business: from responsibility to liability. In: Enneking L, Giesen I, Schaap AJ, Ryngaert C, Kristen F, Roorda L (eds) Accountability, international business operations, and the law: providing justice for corporate human rights violations in global value chains. Routledge, pp 239–259
Bueno N, Kaufmann C (2021) The Swiss human rights due diligence legislation: between law and politics. BHRJ 6(3):542–549
Burgess RH (1963) Liability of parent corporation for tort of subsidiary. Cleveland-Marshall Law Rev:176–184
Büyüksağiş E (2006) Tehlike Esasına Dayanan Genel Sorumluluk Kuralı Üzerine Eleştirel Değerlendirmeler (Critical analyses on general liability rule on dangerous activities). Dokuz Eylül Üniversitesi Hukuk Fakültesi Dergisi (J Dokuz Eylül Univ Law Fac) 8(1):1–19
Çağlayan Aksoy P (2016) Hukuka ve Ahlaka Aykırılık Unsurları Çerçevesinde Salt Malvarlığı Zararlarının Tazmini (Compensation of Pure Economic Loss with Regard to Unlawfulness and Immorality). Istanbul
Cambou D (2015) The Dutch Shell case: foreign direct liability claims as an avenue for holding multinational corporations accountable for human rights violations. In: Cernic JL, Van Ho T (eds) Human rights and business: direct corporate accountability for human rights. Wolf Legal Publishers, pp 347–365
Cassel D (2016) Outlining the case for a common law duty of care of business to exercise human rights due diligence. BHRJ 1:179–202
Cassel D (2018) The third session of the UN intergovernmental working group on a business and human rights treaty. BHRJ 3:273–283
Çelik ÇA (2016) Ölüm Nedeniyle Destekten Yoksunluk (Loss of Support Due to Death). Revised 2nd edn. Ankara
Çelik NH (2015) Adam Çalıştıranın Sorumluluğu (The responsibility of an employer). PhD thesis, Istanbul
Choudhury B, Petrin M (2018) Corporate governance that 'works for everyone': promoting public policies through corporate governance mechanisms. J Corp Law Stud 18(2):381–415
Choudhury B, Petrin M (2019) Corporate duties to the public. Cambridge University Press
Conway M (2015) A new duty of care - tort liability from voluntary human rights due diligence in global supply chains. Queen's Law J 40:741–786
Cossart S, Chaplier J, Beau de Lomanie T (2017) The French law on duty of care: a historic step towards making globalization work for all. BHRJ 2:317–323
de Schutter O (2016) Towards a new treaty on business and human rights. BHRJ 1(1):41–68
Dine J, Koutsias M (2014) Company law, 8th edn. Palgrave Macmillan
Dowling P (2020) Limited liability and separate corporate personality in multinational corporate groups: conceptual flaws, accountability gaps, and the case for profit-risk liability. In: Enneking L, Giesen I, Schaap AJ, Ryngaert C, Kristen F, Roorda L (eds) Accountability, international business operations, and the law: providing justice for corporate human rights violations in global value chains. Routledge, pp 219–239
Enneking L (2012) Foreign direct liability and beyond. Eleven International Publishing
Enneking L (2013) Multinationals and transparency in foreign direct liability cases. Dovenschmidt Quarterly 3:134–147
Erdem M (2012) Türk Borçlar Kanunu Uyarınca Tehlike Sorumluluğu (Liability for Dangerous Activities Under Turkish Code of Obligations). 6098 Sayılı Türk Borçlar Kanunu Hükümlerinin Değerlendirilmesi Sempozyumu (Symposium on Analyses on Turkish Code of Obligations No. 6098), 26 June 2011, Symposium No: III, Prof. Dr. Cevdet Yavuz'a Armağan, 2nd edn. Istanbul, pp 213–222
Eren F (2017) Borçlar Hukuku Genel Hükümler (General provisions of law of obligations), 21st edn. Ankara

Erişgin N (2013) Türk Borçlar Kanunu Madde 71: Genel Tehlike Sorumluluğu (Article 71 of Turkish Code of Obligations: General Liability for Dangerous Activities). Yeni Türk Borçlar Kanunu ve Yeni Türk Ticaret Kanunu Sempozyumu, Makaleler, Tebliğler, TOBB Ekonomi ve Teknoloji Üniversitesi Hukuk Fakültesi (Symposium on New Turkish Code of Obligations and New Turkish Commercial Code, Articles and Presentations, TOBB Economy and Technology University Law Faculty). In: Kırca Ç (eds) Istanbul, pp 59–93

Erlüle F (2016) 6098 Sayılı Türk Borçlar Kanunu'nun Yürürlüğe Girmesinin Ardından Yargıtay'ın Bedensel Zararlarda Yakınların Manevi Tazminat Talebine İlişkin Uygulaması (Supreme Court of Appeal Practices in Case of Spiritual Damage Claim of Kinsmen of the Injured after 6098 Numbered Turkish Code of Obligations Coming into Operation). MÜHF-HAD 22(3): 1087–1117

Ersöz O (2017) 6098 Sayılı Türk Borçlar Kanunu'nda Tehlike Sorumluluğu (The Liability for Danger Under Turkish Code of Obligation No: 6098). Legal Hukuk Dergisi 15(174):2895–2938

Gökyayla EK (2014) Destekten Yoksun Kalma Tazminatı (Compensation for Loss of Support). Prof. Dr. İsmet Sungurbey'e Armağan, Borçlar Kanunu Genel Hükümler Konferansları II, Istanbul, pp 68–84

Gordley J (2006) Foundations of private law, property, tort, contract, unjust enrichment. Oxford University Press

Grosz M (2017) Menschenrechte als Vehikel für ökologische Unternehmensverantwortung. Aktuelle Juristische Praxis:978–987

Grušić U (2015) Responsibility in groups of companies and the future of international human rights and environmental litigation. Cambridge Law J:30–34

Güdük Z (2017) Türk Mevzuatında Çevreyi Kirletenin Hukuki Sorumluluğu (civil liability of the polluter in the Turkish legislation). TBB Dergisi 130:187–224

H C Lo S (2014) A parent Company's tort liability to employees of a subsidiary. J Int Comp Law 117

Harsa T (2007) Şirketler Topluluklarında Tek Elden Yönetim ve Hakim Şirketin Tek Elden Yönetimden Kaynaklanan Sorumluluğu (Centralized Management in Corporate Groups and Liability of the Parent Company for Centralized Management). Master's Thesis, Istanbul

Hatemi H, Gökyayla E (2017) Borçlar Hukuku Genel Bölüm (law of obligations general provisions), 4th edn, Istanbul

Hennchen E (2015) Royal Dutch Shell in Nigeria: where do responsibilities end? J Bus Ethics 129: 1–25

Hoff A (2021) A Bill for Better Business - Dissecting the new Dutch Mandatory Human Rights Due Diligence Initiative, Völkerrechtsblog. https://voelkerrechtsblog.org/a-bill-for-better-business/

Hofstetter K (2019) Konzernverantwortungsinitiative und Geschäftsherrenhaftung. Schweizerische Juristen-Zeitung 115:271–282

Hösli A, Weber RH (2020) Klimaklagen gegen Unternehmen. Jusletter, jusletter.weblaw.ch

Hughes-Jennett J, Hood P (2017) How Should English Domiciled Multinationals Manage their Human Rights Risk in Light of the Judgment in Lungowe v Vedanta?. Oxford Law Faculty, Business Law Blog. https://www.law.ox.ac.uk/business-law-blog/blog/2017/10/how-should-english-domiciled-multinationals-manage-their-human-rights

İkizler M (2014) Strict liability in principles of European Tort law and a short comparison of PETL and Turkish law on strict liability. Dokuz Eylul Universitesi Hukuk Fakultesi Dergisi 16: 3241–3260

Jones G (2019) It's not easy being a parent: AAA v. Unilever and the control conundrum – when a controlling shareholder may owe a duty of Care in Respect of the acts or omissions of a subsidiary. Bus Law Rev 40(1):2–6

Kara Kılıçarslan S (2016) Adam Çalıştıranın Sorumluluğu (Employer's Liability). PhD thesis, Ankara

Karahasan MR (2003) Sorumluluk Hukuku (Law of Liability). Enhanced, 6th edn

Kershaw D (2012) Company law in context, text and materials, 2nd edn. Oxford University Press

Kılıçoğlu AM (2018) Borçlar Hukuku Genel Hükümler (Law of Obligations General Provisions), 22nd edn. Ankara

Kılıçoğlu M (2014) Özel Durumlar (Ölüm ve Bedensel Zarar, Kişilik Hakkının Zedelenmesi (Special Cases (Death and Physical Damage, Infringement of Personal Rights)). Prof. Dr. İsmet Sungurbey'e Armağan, Borçlar Kanunu Genel Hükümler Konferansları II, Istanbul, pp 37–44

Koch BA (2009) Principles of European tort law. King's Law J 20(2):203–214

Koch BA, Koziol H (eds) (2002) Unification of tort law: strict liability, principles of European tort law, vol 6. Kluwer Law International

Koçyiğit P (2016) Türk Hukukunda Yansıma Zarar ve Yansıma Zararın Tazmin Edilebilirliği (Ricochet losses and compensating ricochet losses under Turkish law). In: Baysal B (eds) Sorumluluk Hukuku Seminerleri. Istanbul, pp 253–286

Koşar G (2019) Haksız Fiil Sorumluluğunda Kusur ve Etkisi (Fault and Its Effect in Tort Liability). PhD thesis, Ankara

Koziol H (2011) Liability for omissions - basic questions. J Eur Tort Law 2(2):127–134

Kurtulan G (2017) Haksız Fiilde Hukuka Aykırılık Unsuru (Unlawfulness in Turkish Tort Law). MÜHF – HAD 23(1):465–503

Lopez C, Croser M (2019) The UK Supreme Court considers whether parent company Vedanta has a duty of care and so may be held legally responsible for the harm caused by its Zambian subsidiary. OpinioJuris, http://opiniojuris.org/2019/01/22/the-uk-supreme-court-considers-whether-parent-company-vedanta-has-a-duty-of-care-and-so-may-be-held-legally-responsible-for-the-harm-caused-by-its-zambian-subsidiary/

Magnus U (ed) (2001) Unification of tort law: damages, principles of European tort law, vol 5. Kluwer Law International

Magnus U (2014) Damages rules in the common European sales law and in the principles of European tort law. Int Trade Bus Law Rev 17(1):224–240

Mansel HP (2018) Internationales Privatrecht de lege lata wie de lege ferenda und Menschenrechtsverantwortlichkeit deutscher Unternehmen (international private law *de lege lata* as well as *de lege ferenda* and human rights responsibility for German companies). ZGR 2–3:439–478

McCorquodale R (2019) Vedanta v. Lungowe Symposium: Duty of Care of Parent Companies. Opinio Juris, http://opiniojuris.org/2019/04/18/symposium-duty-of-care-of-parent-companies/

Morgan P (2015) Vicarious liability for group companies: the final frontier of vicarious liability? Prof Negl 31(4):276–299

Muchlinski P (2007) Multinational enterprises and the law, 2nd edn. Oxford University Press

Muchlinski P (2011) The changing face of transnational business governance: private corporate law liability and accountability of transnational groups in a post-financial crisis world. Indiana J Glob Legal Stud 18(2):665–705

Muchlinski P (2012) Implementing the New UN corporate human rights framework: implications for corporate law, governance, and regulation. Bus Ethics Q 22:1; ISSN 1052-150X, pp 145–177

Nomer HN (2018) Borçlar Hukuku Genel Hükümler (Law of obligations general provisions), 16th edn. Istanbul

Nygh P (2002) The liability of multi-national corporations for the torts of their subsidiaries. Eur Bus Org Law Rev 3:51–81

Oğuz A (1991) Sınırlarötesi Çevre Kirlenmelerinden Doğan Kanunlar İhtilafı (conflict of laws arising from transboundary environmental pollution). Türkiye Barolar Birliği Dergisi 1:23–46

Oğuzman K, Öz T (2013) Borçlar Hukuku Genel Hükümler (Law of obligations general provisions), vol 2, Revised 10th edn. Istanbul

Okutan Nilsson G (2009) Türk Ticaret Kanunu Tasarısı'na Göre Şirketler Topluluğu Hukuku (Corporate Groups Under Draft Turkish Commercial Code). XII Levha Yayıncılık, Istanbul

Okyar Karaosmanoğlu D (2019) Adam Çalıştıranın Sorumluluğu (TBK m. 66) (Liability of Employer Under Article 66 of Turkish Code of Obligations). PhD thesis, Ankara

Özçelik N (2016) Salt Malvarlığı Zararı ve Bu Zararın Tazmin Edilebilirliği (Pure economic loss and compensation of pure economic loss). In: Baysal B (ed) Sorumluluk Hukuku Seminerleri. Istanbul, pp 413–443

Öztekin Gelgel G (2006) Akit Dışı Borç İlişkilerine Uygulanacak Hukuk Hakkındaki Avrupa Birliği Düzenlemesi (EU Regulation on Applicable Law in Non-Contractual Obligations). Istanbul

Palombo D (2015) Chandler v. Cape: An Alternative to Piercing the Corporate Veil beyond Kiobel v. Royal Dutch Shell. Br J Am Legal Stud 4:453–472

Palombo D (2019) The duty of care of the parent company: a comparison between French law, UK Precedents and the Swiss Proposals. BHRJ 4:265–286

Palombo D (2020) The case for legal reform - business and human rights: the obligations of the European home states. Hart Publishing, Oxford

Petrin M, Choudhury B (2018) Group company liability. Eur Bus Org Law Rev 19:771–796

Pınar K (2018) The role of corporate social responsibility in corporate accountability of multinationals: is it ever enough without 'hard law'? Eur Comp Law J 15(4):118–125

Quinn J, Connolly B (2017) The non-financial information directive: an assessment of its impact on corporate social responsibility. Eur Comp Law J 14(1):15–21

Reisoğlu S (2013) Türk Borçlar Hukuku Genel Hükümler (Turkish law of obligations general provisions). 24th edn. Istanbul

Rühmkorf A (2015) Corporate social responsibility, private law and global supply chains. Edward Elgar Publishing

Rühmkorf A, Walker L (2018) Assessment of the concept of 'duty of care' in European legal systems for Amnesty International. European Institutions Office

Ryerson C (2018) Shell in Nigeria: The Case for New Legal Strategies for Corporate Accountability. Corporate Accountability Lab, https://corpaccountabilitylab.org/calblog/2018/7/5/shell-in-nigeria-the-case-for-new-legal-strategies-for-corporate-accountability

Sanlı KC (2006) Hukuk ve Ekonomi Öğretisi ve Haksız Fiil Hukukunun Ekonomik Analizi (Discipline of law and economics and economic analysis of tort law). Istanbul

Sanlı Kerem (2012) Kusursuz Sorumluluk Halleri (Strict Liability Cases). Türk Borçlar Kanunu Sempozyumu, Makaleler-Tebliğler (Symposium on Turkish Code of obligations, articles-presentations), Istanbul, pp 61–81

Saraç S (2013) Türk Borçlar Kanunu'nda Tehlike Sorumluluğu (Liability for dangerous activities in Turkish code of obligations). Istanbul

Sarıhan BB (2014) Türk Borçlar Kanunu'nda Genel Bir Kural Olarak Tehlike Sorumluluğu (Risk liability as a general principle in the Turkish obligations law). Prof. Dr. Ali Rıza Okur'a Armağan, MÜHFD-HAD 20 (1):1177–1195

Shavin C (2019) Unlocking the potential of the new OECD due diligence guidance on responsible business conduct. BHRJ 4:139–145

Sjåfjell B (2011a) Why law matters: corporate social irresponsibility and the futility of voluntary climate change mitigation. Nordic & European Company Law. LSN Research Paper Series, No. 10-26

Sjåfjell B (2011b) If not now, when? European company law in a sustainable development perspective. University of Oslo Faculty of Law Legal Studies Research Paper Series No. 2011-23

Sjåfjell B (2017) Dismantling the legal myth of Shareholder primacy: the corporation as a sustainable market actor. University of Oslo Faculty of Law Legal Studies Research Paper Series No. 2017-03

Sjåfjell B (2018) Redefining the corporation for a sustainable new economy. J Law Soc 45(1): 29–45

Soudain T (2019) La mise en oeuvre des obligations de due diligence en matière de droits de l'Homme par les entreprises - Etude à l'aune de l'initiative sur les entreprises responsables et de son contre-projet (The implementation of human rights due diligence obligations by companies –

A study in light of the initiative on responsible companies and its counter-proposal). Gesellschafts – und Kapitalmarketrecht, pp 52–64
Tandoğan H (1981) Kusura Dayanmayan Sözleşme Dışı Sorumluluk Hukuku (Law on Strict Non-Contractual Liability). Ankara
Tiftik M (1997) Tehlike Sorumluluğunun Ayırıcı Özellikleri ve Türk Hukukunda Tehlike Sorumluluklarının Genel Kural ile Düzenlenmesi Sorunu (Distinctive features of liability from dangerous activities and the problem of regulation by general rule under Turkish law). Revised and Enhanced 2nd edn. Erzurum
Turgut N (1995) Kirleten Öder İlkesi ve Çevre Hukuku (Polluter pays principle and environmental law). AÜHFD 44:607–654
Ulfbeck V, Ehlers A (2016) Tort law, corporate groups and supply chain liability for workers' injuries: the concept of vicarious liability. Eur Comp Law 5:167–174
Ünlütepe M (2015) Organizasyon Sorumluluğu (TBK m. 66/III) (Organisation Liability (TCO Art. 66/III)). PhD thesis, Istanbul
Ünlütepe M (2017) Organizasyon Sorumluluğu (TBK m. 66/III) ve Tehlike Sorumluluğu (TBK m. 71) İlişkisinin Değerlendirilmesi (Assessment of the Relation Between Liability for Organization (TCO Art. 66/III) and Liability for Danger (TCO Art. 71). ERÜHFD 12(2)
Uygur T (2012) 6098 Sayılı Türk Borçlar Kanunu Şerhi (Explanations of Turkish Code of Obligations No. 6098) Vol. I, Ankara
van Dam C (2007) European tort law. Oxford University Press
van Dam C (2011) Tort law and human rights: brothers in arms on the role of tort law in the area of business and human rights. J Eur Tort Law 2(3):221–254
Vandall FJ (1989) Strict liability legal and economic analysis, Connecticut USA
Weber RH, Baisch R (2016) Liability of parent companies for human rights violations of subsidiaries. EBLR:669–695
Weller M, Pato A (2018) Local parents as 'anchor defendants' in European courts for claims against their foreign subsidiaries in human rights and environmental damages litigation: recent case law and legislative trends. Unif Law Rev 23(2):397–417
Werhane PH (2016) Corporate moral agency and the responsibility to respect human rights in the UN guiding principles: do corporations have moral rights. BHRJ 1:5–20
Widmer P (ed) (2005) Unification of Tort law: fault, principles of European Tort law. Kluwer Law International
Wilks S, Blankenbach J (2019) Will Germany become a leader in the drive for corporate due diligence on human rights?. Business & Human Rights Resource Centre. https://www.business-humanrights.org/en/will-germany-become-a-leader-in-the-drive-for-corporate-due-diligence-on-human-rights
Witting C (2009) Liability for corporate wrongs. Queensl Law J, pp 113–142
Yavuz C (2008) Türk Borçlar Kanunu Tasarısı'na Göre "Kusursuz Sorumluluk" Halleri ve İlkeleri (Strict Liability Cases and Principles Under Draft Turkish Code of Obligations). Liability from Roman Law to Modern Law – Symposium Special Issue, MÜHFD-HAD 14(4):29–61
Yılmaz S (2010) Türk Borçlar Kanunu Tasarısında Sebep Sorumluluklarına İlişkin Yeni Hükümler (New Provisions in Draft Turkish Code of Obligations on Strict Liability). AÜHFD 59(3)
Yücel Ö (2013) Türk Borçlar Kanunu'na Göre Genel Tehlike Sorumluluğu (General Clause for Strict Liability According to Turkish Code of Obligations). PhD Thesis, Ankara
Zerk JA (2006) Multinationals and corporate social responsibility, limitations and opportunities in international law. Cambridge University Press

Chapter 5
A Comparative Analysis of FDL Under Private International Law

5.1 Jurisdiction in FDL Claims: A Comparative Analysis of Turkish Law, EU and US Law

One of the issues concerning the private international law aspects of FDL claims is determining the jurisdiction, namely which country's courts would have jurisdiction to hear these cases. The issue will, first of all, be assessed under EU law and US law, which have specific regulations in this respect. The US law is especially important in terms of place of jurisdiction because of the unique position of Alien Tort Statute, which will be analysed herein below. Following the comparative legal analysis, Turkish law will then be analysed within the scope of jurisdiction in transnational tort claims and some suggestions *de lege ferenda* will be given under Turkish law, resulting from the comparative analysis made under EU law and US law.

5.1.1 Jurisdiction in FDL Claims Under EU Acquis and US Law

Before analysing Turkish law provisions on jurisdiction rules that might apply in FDL claims, it would be useful to assess the jurisdiction rules under the EU acquis and US law, as these laws are mostly relevant as home country laws. In terms of the EU, the focus here will be on UK case law, which is amongst the pioneers in FDL cases that shed some light on jurisdiction issues. Moreover, the ATS in US law, especially, provides a unique solution to the jurisdiction questions concerning FDL claims, which will be analysed in this section.

P. Kara, *Tort Liability in Multinational Corporate Groups*, Ius Gentium: Comparative Perspectives on Law and Justice 107,
https://doi.org/10.1007/978-3-031-29336-8_5

5.1.1.1 The EU Acquis: Brussels I Recast

In order to initiate legal action before the courts of an EU member state, it would first of all be necessary to determine that the relevant courts have international jurisdiction, which would be assessed under a specific regime, provided that this is applicable to the relevant case.[1] In the event that the defendant's residence is within the borders of an EU member state, a special regulation would apply in determining the jurisdiction of courts in civil and commercial disputes. The 1968 Brussels Convention on Jurisdiction and the Enforcement of Judgments in Civil and Commercial Matters[2] and the Council Regulation (EC) No 44/2001 of 22 December 2000 on jurisdiction and the recognition and enforcement of judgments in civil and commercial matters[3] ('Brussels I'), the latter being based upon the Brussels Convention and abrogating it by entering in force on 1 March 2002, regulated the international jurisdiction of courts in commercial and civil law disputes, as well as the recognition and enforcement of judgments amongst EU member states. Due to the incapacity of the Brussels I regulations in certain aspects, the Regulation (EU) No 1215/2012 of the European Parliament and of the Council of 12 December 2012 on jurisdiction and the recognition and enforcement of judgments in civil and commercial matters[4] ('Brussels I Recast') was enacted, regulating the same issues, and the majority of these provisions entered into force as of 10 January 2015 by abrogating Brussels I.

The provisions of the Brussels I Recast shall apply in cases where the defendant's place of residence is in one of the EU member states; otherwise, the incident will remain outside its scope of application.[5] In fact, the Brussels I Recast explicitly stipulates that in cases where the defendant's place of residence is not in an EU member state, the jurisdiction shall be determined in accordance with the domestic law of the relevant state, without consideration of the Brussels I Recast provisions (Article 6/1). Accordingly, an FDL claim where the defendant parent company is residing in an EU member state would be subject to Brussels I Recast; where the parent company is a Turkish company with subsidiaries abroad, on the other hand,

[1] Van Den Eeckhout (2017), p. 41.

[2] Convention of 27 September 1968 on jurisdiction and the enforcement of judgments in civil and commercial matters: OJ L 304 (30.10.1978). The non-member states may also join the Brussels Convention. Within scope of the negotiations held with EFTA states, Lugano Convention (Convention on jurisdiction and the enforcement of judgments in civil and commercial matters done at Lugano on 16.09.1988: OJ L 319 (25.11.1988)), which basically bears the same regulations as the Brussels Convention is signed.

[3] For detailed information on the reasons and results of the incorporation of Brussels Convention provisions onto the EU regulation please see Sakmar and Ekşi (2002), pp. 728–735.

[4] Regulation (EU) No 1215/2012 of the European Parliament and of the Council of 12 December 2012 on jurisdiction and the recognition and enforcement of judgments in civil and commercial matters: OJ L 351/21 (20.12.2012). As per Article 66 of the Brussels I Recast, its provisions will apply only to "*legal proceedings instituted, to authentic instruments formally drawn up or registered and to court settlements approved or concluded on or after 10 January 2015*". Thus Brussels I provisions will continue to apply to all legal proceedings instituted before this date.

[5] Roorda and Ryngaert (2016), p. 787.

Brussels I Recast would no longer be applicable. Therefore, the analysis concerning Brussels I Recast is restricted to the scenario where the parent company (P) is located in an EU member state, with a subsidiary (S) located in Turkey, where the damages occur.

It is worth noting that in order to decide on the application of the Brussels I provisions, the courts will need to examine the merits of the case to be able to determine the *prima facie* existence of a claim by establishing a link between the forum and the claim.[6] Therefore, it will be required to conduct a substantive legal analysis to be able to then conduct a private international law analysis. This is expressed in case law, such as the decision of Fraser J in *Okpabi & Ors v RDS,*[7] where it was held that it is not unreasonable to assume jurisdiction in cases where there is a real issue to be tried. The District Court of the Hague in Dutch Shell proceedings, *Akpan v RDS*[8] also rejected the arguments of the defendants that the claimants abused the law by initiating the lawsuit before Dutch courts, as the defendant company was registered in the UK. The court considered that it had jurisdiction under Article 7 of the Dutch Code of Civil Procedure,[9] which stipulated that a foreign subsidiary can be sued before Dutch courts in the case of a joint hearing with the parent company, provided that the claims are connected sufficiently to be able to conduct an efficient joint hearing.[10] The court further considered that the parent company might assume liability based on tort for a subsidiary's actions under Nigerian law, which was found to be the law applicable to the dispute.[11] This decision shows that foreign subsidiaries can be sued before Dutch courts in cases where the relevant claim justifies a joint hearing with the parent company, which is subject to Dutch jurisdiction, and a substantive legal analysis should be made for this purpose before deciding on the question of jurisdiction.

5.1.1.1.1 Scope of Application of Brussels I Recast

According to the general rule of jurisdiction under Brussels I Recast, the courts of the defendant's place of residence shall have jurisdiction, regardless of the defendant's nationality (Article 4/1). Hence the defendant's place of residence is set as a general ground of jurisdiction and constitutes a precondition for connecting the case to the

[6] Weller and Pato (2018), p. 401; van Dam (2011), p. 230.

[7] Okpabi & Ors v Royal Dutch Shell Plc & Anor [2018] EWCA Civ 191.

[8] Friday Alfred Akpan v Royal Dutch Shell Plc and Shell Petroleum Development Co Nigeria Ltd. (District Court of The Hague, 337050/HA ZA 09-1580, 2013).

[9] Article 7 "Jurisdiction over counter actions, joinders and interventions" of Dutch Code of Civil Procedure. The English text of the code is available at http://www.dutchcivillaw.com/civilprocedureleg.htm.

[10] Cambou (2015), p. 353.

[11] Weller and Pato (2018), p. 407.

EU, which triggers the application of the Brussels I Recast system.[12] This rule is said to promote legal certainty and provide an advantage to the defendant in being sued before the courts of the place country of its own residence.[13]

If the defendant is a company, the place where it has its (a) statutory seat, (b) central administration or (c) principal place of business will be deemed as its place of residence (Article 63/1). Brussels I Recast provides a specific rule for the UK regarding the definition of a statutory seat, which is stated as, "*the registered office or, where there is no such office anywhere, the place of incorporation or, where there is no such place anywhere, the place under the law of which the formation took place*" (Article 63/2). Hence, the place of incorporation of the company is given priority and it is deemed sufficient to have the defendant company incorporated in an EU member state to fall within the scope of Brussels I Recast. Consequently, EU member state courts have jurisdiction over those cases concerning parent companies located within their territory and can adjudicate extraterritorial cases concerning FDL claims filed against parent companies within their territory.[14]

The provisions of Brussels I Recast shall also apply in cases where the defendant company is not incorporated in an EU member state, but is effectively run from an EU member state.[15] In fact, in such a case, it might be considered that the central administration is in the EU and therefore the company would be deemed to have its domicile within EU borders. At this point, the term 'effectively run' should be interpreted correctly, as not all administrative operations would lead to the conclusion that the company is run by another. *Baughen* refers to the UK Court of Appeal decision in *Young v Anglo-American,*[16] where it was held that the central administration is "*the place where a company carries out functions and not where others carry out functions that affect it*". It was, therefore, not sufficient that the UK parent company of a South African subsidiary was making the major decisions concerning the corporate group to deem that the central administration was located in the UK.[17] In light of these explanations, if the defendant parent company in an FDL action is incorporated in an EU member state, then there is no question that Brussels I Recast provisions would apply. Furthermore, in cases where the defendant parent company is incorporated elsewhere but 'effectively run' from a company located within the EU (such as where its business operations are carried out by the relevant company), then the case would again fall within the scope of Brussels I Recast.

[12] Isidro (2016), p. 78.
[13] Aristova (2018), p. 10.
[14] Palombo (2019), p. 278.
[15] Baughen (2015), p. 173.
[16] Young v Anglo-American South Africa Limited [2014] EWCA Civ. 1130.
[17] Baughen (2015), p. 173.

5.1.1.1.2 The Case of Multiple Tortfeasors

In cases of multiple defendants domiciled in different member states, each one may be sued in its own domicile (Article 8/1). Therefore, in the case of an MNC with a parent company and several subsidiaries domiciled in different EU member states, the claimants may—if they wish—initiate legal action against each entity involved in the relevant tort before the courts of the member states where they are incorporated. Suing both the transnational subsidiary that is involved in the alleged human rights violation and the parent company might be beneficial to the plaintiffs in terms of establishing a shared liability and facilitating the reach and gathering of evidence.[18]

An example in practice for the above-mentioned jurisdiction rule on multiple tortfeasors is the *Motto & Ors v Trafigura* case.[19] The case concerned claims for deaths and injuries caused by the allegedly toxic waste carried by the charterer Trafigura Ltd., a UK company, and the parent company Trafigura Beheer BV, a Dutch company, that was ultimately discharged in Abidjan, Cote D'Ivoire. The claimants, who were individuals that suffered damages in Cote D'Ivoire due to the disposal of the toxic waste, successfully sued both Trafigura Ltd. and Trafigura Beheer BV in the countries of their own domicile.

The assessment of jurisdiction in cases of multiple tortfeasors may be different when the parent is domiciled in an EU member state but the subsidiary is not. In the *Lungowe v Vedanta* case, which was brought against both the English parent company, Vedanta Resources Plc, and its Zambian subsidiary, Konkola Copper Mines Plc (KCM), the trial judge found English courts to be the proper place for jurisdiction, stating that "*The alternative – two trials on opposite sides of the world on precisely the same facts and events – is unthinkable*." The Court of Appeal supported the trial judge's view that England was the most appropriate place to hear claims against both Vedanta and KCM, as it would not have been efficient to have parallel proceedings on identical facts taking place in two different jurisdictions, considering that England would already have jurisdiction for the case against Vedanta (para. 117). However, the UK Supreme Court, upon reviewing the case, rejected the lower courts' approach and based its judgment on *forum non conveniens*. This part of the judgment will be discussed further in the relevant section.

In its judgment the UK Supreme Court admitted that the question of jurisdiction was the most difficult issue in the appeal (para. 66).[20] The UK Supreme Court held that, although the proper place to hear this case would be the Zambian courts—considering many factors including the connection with the claim, the place of the alleged damages, the place where most of the evidence was located, the high number of witnesses and victims who were unable to travel due to poverty etc.—there was

[18] Isidro (2016), p. 81.

[19] Motto & Ors v Trafigura [2011] EWCA Civ 1150.

[20] Lungowe v Vedanta [2019] UKSC 20 (10.04.2019).

sufficient evidence, based on previous cases, that Zambia did not constitute a jurisdiction where substantial justice could be achieved for the claimants. Accordingly, the UK Supreme Court rejected the companies' appeal based on the substantial justice issue. In the verbal summary judgment declared online by Lord Briggs from the UK Supreme Court,[21] the issue of jurisdiction was addressed in detail. The court declared that Zambia would be the natural choice and most appropriate place to hear this case, given that the claims were all subject to Zambian law, that all claimants lived there, that the alleged pollution and damages occurred there, that most of the evidence was located there, and that the dialects of the people could also be understood by the Zambian courts.

The claimants argued, however, that Vedanta's place of domicile under Article 4 of Brussels I Recast was England and that they wanted to sue both defendants before the same courts in order to avoid the risk of conflicting judgments. The claimants further pointed to the lack of substantial justice in Zambia, not because of a lack of fair trial, but due to a lack of funding, legal aid and conditional fee agreements, which were basically preventing them from suing these companies before the Zambian courts. The defendants, on the other hand, contended that the claimants abused EU law by bringing claims against both KCM and Vedanta before the English courts, thereby using Vedanta as an anchor defendant. The judge of the lower courts agreed with the claimants, stating that it was not an abuse of EU law to use Vedanta as an anchor defendant in this case, as Vedanta had incurred liability of negligence, and England was the proper place of jurisdiction as claimants could not obtain proper funding in Zambia.

The UK Supreme Court disagreed with the analysis of the lower courts on the point that the risk of conflicting judgments could be used as a 'trump card' by the claimants, as it was accepted by the lower courts. Instead the court declared that the claimants in this case had the right to choose between English and Zambian jurisdiction, to which Vedanta had agreed to submit, and that the connection of all factors to Zambia could outweigh this 'trump card'.

Accordingly, the UK Supreme Court stated that it would have rejected the claimants' jurisdiction request, had it not been for the substantial justice issue; however, the lack of access to justice in Zambia meant that the case could proceed against both defendants in England. In his conclusion, Lord Briggs offered a gentle reminder of the need for proportionality and economy in the litigation of issues about jurisdiction. This decision shows that English courts may tend to assume jurisdiction over parent companies domiciled in England, regardless of where the tort is committed and without any *forum non conveniens* control, which is seen as justifiable and predictable for both parties.[22]

---

[21] UK Supreme Court, Vedanta Resources PLC and another (Appellants) v Lungowe and others (Respondents) (10.04.2019), https://youtu.be/_s7YvSnX63w.

[22] Aristova (2018), p. 14.

As unique examples up until now, in *Vava v Anglo American South Africa Ltd*[23] and in *Young v Anglo American South Africa Ltd*,[24] the claimants sued only the foreign subsidiaries, without including the parent companies as defendants, before the English courts. In these cases, the claimants were not able to bring any claims against the English parent company, Anglo American Plc, as this company only became a shareholder after the occurrence of the incidents in dispute. Therefore, they contended that England was the domicile of the subsidiaries, within the meaning under Brussels I Recast, as it was where the 'central administration' was located.

The Court of Appeal concluded that Anglo American Plc was not the direct shareholder of the South African subsidiary, that it had no significant influence on the board meetings and auditing of the subsidiary, while it exercised a certain degree of control over its subsidiary's important decisions.[25] The Court of Appeal also made an interpretation of Article 63 (then Article 60) of Brussels I Recast, stating that the provision was meant to be interpreted to provide the option of three places of domicile for companies (i.e. statutory seat, central administration, principal place of business) to the claimants' advantage (para. 37). The Court of Appeal then accepted the definition of 'central administration' as "*the place where the company concerned, through its relevant organs according to its own constitutional provisions, takes the decisions that are essential for that company's operations*" (paras. 40–45). Accordingly, the Court of Appeal dismissed the appeal by upholding the judge's decision that there was no 'good arguable case' for the central administration of the company being in England.

The *Young v Anglo American* decision shows that it is challenging to claim jurisdiction over a foreign subsidiary under Brussels I Recast. The decision has been criticised for disregarding the complex structure of the multinational groups of our time by leaning on the 'central administration' definition made by *Everling* (which is also Article 48 of the Treaty on the Functioning of the EU) back in 1964.[26]

Furthermore, although the decision was successful in drawing a clear framework for the application of Article 63 of Brussels I Recast, the decision referred to day-to-day operations as a company's 'essential operations', which seems to leave out important decisions surrounding budgeting, financing and other important projects.[27] Hence the decision fails to address the question: if a subsidiary's important decisions—such as those concerning acquiring or disposing of businesses, budgets, business plans, appointment of senior management—are made by the parent company, with the day-to-day business decisions being made by the subsidiary itself, then which of these places would be deemed the 'central administration' of the

[23] Vava v Anglo American South Africa Ltd. [2013] EWHC 2131 (QB).

[24] Young v Anglo American South Africa Ltd. [2014] EWCA Civ 1130.

[25] "*(...) the judge did note that Mr Guy Philipps QC, counsel for AASA, "did not dispute" that AASA would not make an important decision such as, for example, to dispose of shares in a subsidiary company such as AOL, "otherwise than in accordance with [AA's] wishes"."* (para. 20).

[26] Aristova (2018), p. 18.

[27] Aristova (2018), p. 19.

subsidiary? In such a case, it seems quite illogical to accept that the place where the day-to-day operations are carried out would be deemed the place of central administration.

5.1.1.1.3 General Principle of Jurisdiction in Tort Claims Under Brussels I Recast

As per the special rules on jurisdiction in tort claims under Brussels I Recast, courts of the place where the harmful event occurred or may occur shall be deemed to have jurisdiction (Art. 7/2). This rule provides an optional choice of jurisdiction to the claimant, in addition to the courts of its own domicile within an EU member state under the general rule of Article 4/1.[28]

The special rule on jurisdiction in tort claims is interpreted as a two-fold one by the ECJ, in the sense that it is set to cover both the place where the tortious act is committed and the place where the damage has occurred.[29] The ECJ, in its *Handelskwekerij v Mines de Potasse d'Alsace* judgment,[30] did a thorough analysis of the interpretation of the concept of 'the place where the harmful event occurred' by evaluating the expected outcomes of various types of interpretation. Within this analysis, the ECJ stipulated that the failure to act is an essential element of the tortious act, while damage is a mere consequence thereof, which favoured—in the ECJ's opinion—the interpretation of the place where the tortious act is committed (p. 1741). The ECJ has also stated that favouring this rule would provide legal certainty to the tortfeasor, as the tortfeasor would know the laws of the place where it has acted (p. 1741). On the other hand, as to interpreting the rule as the place of damage, the ECJ has stated that damage is required to form a tortious act, as the mere existence of an act is not sufficient, and therefore the place of damage is significant (p. 1742). The ECJ also stipulated that the rule of the place of damage would be advantageous in environmental damage claims, where it would mostly result in the

[28] See the Opinion of Advocat General Léger in Roche Nederland and others (C-539/03 - 08.12.2005) for the optional status of the special jurisdiction rule in tort claims under Brussels Convention (paras. 10-11).

[29] Magnus and Mankowski (2016), p. 276. See also ECJ judgment dated 29.07.2019, numbered Case C-451/18 in Tibor-Trans v DAF Trucks NV cartel case, where the ECJ stated that "*the place where the harmful event occurred is intended to cover both the place where the damage occurred and the place of the event giving rise to it, so that the defendant may be sued, at the option of the applicant, in the courts for either of two places*" (para. 25).

[30] Handelskwekerij G. J. Bier B.V. v Mines de Potasse d'Alsace S.A. (preliminary ruling requested by the Gerechtshof of The Hague) Case 21/76 (30.11.1976). The case was handled under the provisions of the then in force 1968 Brussels Convention on jurisdiction and the enforcement of judgments in civil and commercial matters (OJ L 299, 31.12.1972). Having said that, Article 5/3 of the 1968 Brussels Convention bears the same provision on jurisdiction in tort claims with Article 7/2 of Brussels I Recast, as it refers to 'the place where the harmful event occurred', with the difference that it does not bear any reference to the 'the place where the harmful event may occur' as the Brussels I Recast.

victim's domicile (p. 1742). Finally, the ECJ makes the following conclusions on the interpretation of the 'place where the harmful event occurred' (p. 1743):

> Accordingly, Article 5 (3) of the Convention can be interpreted as meaning that 'the place where the harmful event occurred' may be understood as meaning, as well as the place where the act occurred, either the place of the damage or the place in which the essential aspect of the legal sphere of the tortious or delictual act is located, so that where a tortious or delictual act has occurred there is a choice between these three places. The arguments in favour of interpreting Article 5 (3) as meaning the place most favourable to the injured party would not appear to be sufficiently conclusive.

As the ECJ has expressed in the quoted judgment, the concept of 'the place where the harmful event occurred' can be interpreted as the place of committed act or the place of damage. Hence the courts of either one of these places (on condition that they are in an EU member state) shall have jurisdiction.[31] The choice of jurisdiction between these two options is left to the discretion of the plaintiff. This is referred to as the principle of ubiquity and it is intended to favour the plaintiff, who is a tort victim.[32]

In the event that the place where the harmful event has occurred is interpreted merely as the place where the damage has occurred, this special rule of jurisdiction for tort claims might result to the detriment of victims in FDL claims. The place of damage is described as the place where the harmful event has produced effects on the values or assets of the victim.[33] In FDL claims, the damaged values and assets of victims are located in the host country, where the victims are residing. Consequently, the place of damage will be considered the host country, where the victims have suffered physical damages such as health issues and injuries due to the operations of the transnational subsidiary.

On the other hand, in light of the ECJ's interpretation, the place where the harmful event occurred might also be interpreted as the place where the tortious act that gave rise to the damage was committed. If the claimants in an FDL claim are able to prove that the damage arose due to a decision by the parent company, which is domiciled in an EU member state, then the parent company's home country might be accepted as the place where the harmful event (in this case, the relevant decision or omission) occurred.[34] The ECJ's judgment in *Fiona Shevill v Presse Alliance*[35] might be useful

---

[31] Van Den Eeckhout (2017), p. 42.

[32] Magnus and Mankowski (2016), p. 277.

[33] Magnus and Mankowski (2016), p. 303.

[34] Weller and Pato (2018), p. 400, fn. 11. In the opinion of Van Den Eeckhout, the jurisdiction regulated under Article 7/2 of Brussels I Recast constitutes an additional ground of jurisdiction to the general rule under Article 4/1 of Brussels I recast (in conjunction with Article 63/2), which addresses the courts of the place of the defendant's domicile, thus the courts of the parent company's headquarters (i.e. the home country courts) (Van Den Eeckhout 2017, pp. 42–43).

[35] ECJ judgment dated 07.03.1995, numbered C-68/93 in Fiona Shevill et al. v Presse Alliance SA concerned claim for damages due to the publication of a defamatory newspaper article, where the ECJ held that the place where the tortious act was committed was the place of the company's headquarters.

here in order to successfully prove that the place of the tortious act is the headquarters of the relevant company (in this case, the parent company) that took a certain decision concerning the activities of its subsidiary or failed to do so. Hence the tables might be turned to the benefit of the plaintiffs in FDL claims, who seek to have their claims heard before the courts of the parent company's home country. The harmful event is accepted as the event causing the damage suffered by the victim, thus it should be the precondition of the relevant damage.[36] If it is accepted that the 'harmful event' that took place is in fact the parent company's decision or omission with regard to the operations of its transnational subsidiary, which gave rise to the relevant damages, then the courts of the home country would have jurisdiction. Of course, this depends on the substantive legal analysis of the matter, especially concerning the liability of the parent company.

It is also important to consider if the assessment would be any different in cases of a potential omission by the parent company, as this is a frequent type of alleged tort in FDL claims. There are two conditions that should be considered for this purpose: (1) the place where the parent company is under the obligation to act and (2) the place of inactivity.[37] In my opinion, it would be reasonable to deem that the place of the harmful event in cases of an omission is the place where the relevant party had the obligation to act in a certain manner, thus in cases of FDL claims, indicating the home country where the parent company is located. The place of inactivity should also be considered as the home country in this example, as the parent company failed to take an action or a decision to act at its headquarters.

The general principle of jurisdiction under Article 7/2 also makes reference to the courts of the place where the harmful event may occur. Accordingly, in addition to the courts of the place where the harmful event has already occurred, the courts of the place where there is a possibility for a harmful event to occur shall also have jurisdiction. This rule is important in the sense that it takes into account potential damages that have not yet materialised, but which may do in the near future. The principle of ubiquity will also apply here, thus the place where the future activity giving rise to the damage will happen and the place where the future damage will occur shall be deemed to have jurisdiction.[38]

[36]Magnus and Mankowski (2016), p. 282. See also ECJ judgment dated 29.07.2019, numbered Case C-451/18 in Tibor-Trans v DAF Trucks NV cartel case, where the ECJ referred to its settled precedents stating that "*the term 'place where the harmful event occurred' cannot be construed so extensively as to encompass any place where the adverse consequences of an event, which has already caused damage actually occurring elsewhere, can be felt. Consequently, it stated that this notion cannot be construed as including the place where the victim claims to have suffered financial damage following initial damage arising and suffered by him in another State*" (para. 28).

[37]Magnus and Mankowski (2016), p. 287.

[38]Magnus and Mankowski (2016), p. 339.

5.1.1.1.4 Choice of Jurisdiction Amongst Parties to a Tort Claim Under Brussels I Recast

According to Brussels I Recast, the parties to a tort claim are free to determine the place of jurisdiction (Art. 25). This right is granted to the parties in relation to the already existing disputes, as well as any potential disputes that may arise in a legal relationship. The choice of jurisdiction should be made in writing, which includes any form that is agreed between the parties including an electronic form. The validity of the choice of jurisdiction agreement shall be subject to the law of the member state designated in the agreement. The jurisdiction agreed upon by the parties shall be exclusive, unless the parties have agreed otherwise. Therefore, this alternative shall be assessed prior to other rules of jurisdiction.

In FDL claims, as the defendant parent company and the tort victims in the host country do not usually have any legal relationship prior to the relevant tort, it is unlikely that the option of a prior choice of jurisdiction would be relevant. However, it might be possible to agree on a jurisdiction after the occurrence of the tortious act, even though this option is also quite unlikely, considering that the parties interests conflict with each other on the point of jurisdiction. Furthermore, such an *ex post* agreement on the choice of jurisdiction bears risks of injustice, as the parties' leverage and power are disproportionate and thus the choice may result in favour of the defendant corporation. I, therefore, believe that the choice of jurisdiction does not sit well with the nature and main purpose of FDL claims.

5.1.1.1.5 Forum Non Conveniens

The proposal for a regulation of the European Parliament and of the Council on jurisdiction and the recognition and enforcement of judgments in civil and commercial matters[39] contained certain provisions that referred to *forum necessitatis* and *forum non conveniens*; however, these provisions of the proposal were then not retained in Brussels I Recast. Nevertheless, the doctrine of *forum non conveniens* has a significant role in jurisdiction analysis under the EU acquis.

As per Brussels I Recast, the courts of a state have jurisdiction in respect of the persons residing within its borders. Accordingly, it is not possible for EU member state courts to decide on the lack of jurisdiction based on *forum non conveniens* doctrine for companies that are located within the EU borders.[40]

---

[39] The proposal for a regulation of the European Parliament and of the Council on jurisdiction and the recognition and enforcement of judgments in civil and commercial matters, COM/2010/0748 final - COD 2010/0383, http://eur-lex.europa.eu/legal-content/EN/TXT/?uri=CELEX%3A52010PC0748.

[40] Having *forum non conveniens* regulated under Brussels I Recast would deprive the FDL plaintiffs of a significant advantage against the ATS, under which *forum non conveniens* can be invoked (Van Den Eeckhout 2017, p. 48).

The above-mentioned rule is emphasised in *Owusu v Jackson*,[41] where the ECJ decided that if the defendant is residing in an EU member state, the EU courts cannot reject jurisdiction by reason of closer connection with another country. The UK Court of Appeal has also recently acknowledged the effect of the *Owusu v Jackson* decision on the *Lungowe v Vedanta* judgment, stating that Article 4 of the Brussels I Recast does not allow English courts to decline a mandatory jurisdiction where the defendant is a company established in England and Wales (para. 34).[42] It therefore appears that this judgment has put an end to the practice of *forum non conveniens* in those EU member states that are subject to Brussels I Recast, regardless of the jurisdiction of the defendant or whether the alternative jurisdiction is an EU member state or not.[43] It is also accepted after observing the ECJ's approach to *forum non conveniens* that this doctrine will no longer apply within the scope of Brussels I Recast either.[44]

Having said that, some potential ways to exercise *forum non conveniens* are discussed in legal doctrine. For instance, as per Articles 33 and 34 of the Brussels I Recast, in the event that the courts of a member state are seised while the same action is pending before the courts of a third country, the courts of the member state are entitled to decide to stay the proceedings, if this seems necessary for the proper administration of justice.[45] Furthermore, in some cases, where the defendant is not domiciled in an EU member state, the domestic rules on *forum non conveniens* of the member states may apply as per the exception made under Article 6/1. Accordingly, in the event that a claimant would like to sue a foreign subsidiary with an English parent, the jurisdiction shall be decided based on the domestic rules of English law,[46] which has recently abandoned the *forum non conveniens*. However, if a member state domestic law were to continue following this doctrine, it could be possible to apply it under the exception of Article 6/1.

At this point, it would also be necessary to consider the English case law on *forum non conveniens*. In English law, a two-fold test is envisaged in the *Spiliada Maritime Corp. v Cansulex Ltd.*[47] judgment for the application of the *forum non conveniens* doctrine: (i) that there is a "clearly and distinctly" more appropriate forum to hear the case, and (ii) that there can be a fair trial for the parties in the alternative

[41] Owusu v Jackson C-281/02 [2005] EUECJ.

[42] It would be worth to consider that the English courts' approach to *forum non conveniens* doctrine under Brussels Convention may change due to Brexit, resulting in the UK's exit from the scope of Brussels Convention along with other EU legislation. In such a case, English courts may reject jurisdiction over a parent company where there is a more appropriate forum for seeing the dispute; except when the claimant lacks financial and litigation strength in the natural forum, where English courts might apply a kind of *forum necessitatis* and accept jurisdiction. For further details, see Ahmed (2022), pp. 27–28.

[43] Zerk (2006), p. 126; Cambou (2015), p. 352.

[44] Magnus and Mankowski (2016), p. 109.

[45] Weber and Baisch (2016), pp. 682–683.

[46] Baughen (2015), p. 175.

[47] Spiliada Maritime Corp. v Cansulex Ltd [1987] 1 AC 460.

jurisdiction.[48] Accordingly, the defendant, who tries to base its defence on *forum non conveniens,* will firstly need to prove that there is clearly a more appropriate jurisdiction than the venue where the lawsuit was initiated. Then if the court agrees with the defendant's argument, it will discontinue the case. In this case, the plaintiff will have to prove that there cannot be a fair trial in the alternative jurisdiction.[49] For instance, the plaintiff might show that there are time bars in other jurisdictions or that there is no legal aid.[50]

To give some examples, in *Connelly v RTZ,*[51] the House of Lords acknowledged that the lack of legal aid in the appropriate alternative jurisdiction might qualify as a reason for commencing the trial before the English courts, provided that the plaintiff is able to prove that substantial justice will not be done in the appropriate jurisdiction (para. 29–30). The *Connelly v RTZ* decision was reinforced in *Lubbe v Cape,*[52] where it was decided that the class action initiated by the claimants required efficiency, cost-effectiveness, lawyer supervision, expert advice and evidence, and that for these reasons England was in fact the appropriate jurisdiction, rather than South Africa.[53] In the opinion of *Isidro*, the courts in both *Connelly v RTZ* and *Lubbe v Cape* acknowledged that any other way would deny the claimant substantial justice, which is an argument of *forum necessitatis* that is not regulated under Brussels I Recast system.[54]

The long-awaited judgment of the Court of Appeal on *Lungowe v Vedanta*[55] cleared the way for foreign nationals to seek remedies before English courts against UK-based MNCs for their activities in other countries, as it clarified that the practice of *forum non conveniens* would be discontinued.[56] This was also confirmed by the UK Supreme Court judgment in *Lungowe v Vedanta* case,[57] where the court also noted that the discontinuance of the *forum non conveniens* doctrine would not prevent the defendant from seeking the elimination of a claim based on the abuse of process or the lack of a reasonable cause of action or from seeking reverse summary judgment based on the lack of a triable issue against that defendant (para. 17).

---

48 De Jonge (2011), pp. 109–110; Meeran (1999), p. 162; Eroğlu (2008a), pp. 105–106; Zerk (2006), p. 124.

49 Eroğlu (2008a), p. 106.

50 Bantekas (2004), p. 342.

51 Connelly v RTZ [1997] UKHL 30 (24th July, 1997).

52 Lubbe and Others v Cape Plc., [2000] UKHL 41.

53 Choudhury (2005), p. 55.

54 Isidro (2016), p. 80.

55 Lungowe v Vedanta [2017] EWCA Civ 1528.

56 For further information on this decision see Aristova (2017), http://conflictoflaws.net/2017/court-of-appeal-allows-in-england-claims-against-english-based-multinational-for-overseas-human-rights-violations/.

57 Lungowe v Vedanta [2019] UKSC 20 (10.04.2019).

The UK Supreme Court decision in *Lungowe v Vedanta* addressed another significant issue concerning jurisdiction: the non-availability of substantial justice in the naturally proper jurisdiction. The court declared the lack of both adequate funding and legal aid, as well as the lack of conditional fee agreements for lawyers (whereby they would be appointed by the claimants on a 'no win, no fee' basis) as factors leading to the non-availability of substantial justice, although there was no issue concerning fair trial.

The stay of proceedings on the grounds of *forum non conveniens* was made subject to allegations of breach of Article 6 of the European Convention of Human Rights[58] (ECHR) in the *Lubbe v Cape*[59] case before the English courts. In this case, the plaintiffs argued that the court's decision of stay of proceedings on the basis that South African courts were a more adequate venue would violate their rights to a fair trial under Article 6 of the ECHR due to the lack of funding and legal representation in South Africa. Even though this aspect of the plaintiffs' claim was not specifically addressed by the court, this claim shows that Article 6 of the ECHR can extend to legal procedures in which access to a court in Europe is sought.[60] The UK Supreme Court in its *Lungowe v Vedanta* judgment referred to the need to make an adjustment to the practice of avoiding *forum non conveniens* by English courts, in a manner that might make it reasonable for an anchor defendant to submit to the jurisdiction of the foreign defendant in cases where the relevant foreign jurisdiction is the proper place, leaving aside the risk of irreconcilable judgments (para. 40). The UK Supreme Court also declared that there was no need to refer to the ECJ, as no abuse of EU law was found (para. 41).

5.1.1.1.6 Forum Necessitatis

Another doctrine that is relevant to jurisdictional analysis is *forum necessitatis*. This doctrine is explicitly regulated under Swiss law. As per Article 3 of Switzerland's Federal Code on Private International Law,[61] if the relevant code "*does not provide for jurisdiction in Switzerland and if proceedings abroad are impossible or cannot reasonably be required to be brought, the Swiss judicial or administrative authorities at the place with which the facts of the case are sufficiently connected shall have jurisdiction*". This doctrine is also recognised in Dutch law. As per Article 9/b of the Dutch Code of Civil Procedure (entitled "Tacit choice of forum ('*forum necessitatis*')"), in the event that "*a civil case outside the Netherlands appears to*

[58] European Convention on Human Rights, as amended by Protocols Nos. 11 and 14, supplemented by Protocols Nos. 1, 4, 6, 7, 12, 13 and 16; Rome, 4.XI.1950.

[59] Lubbe v. Cape Plc. [2000] UKHL 41.

[60] Enneking (2009), p. 919.

[61] For the official Italian version see: Legge Federale Sul Diritto Internazionale Privato del 18 dicembre 1987 (Stato 1 Aprile 2017), https://www.admin.ch/opc/it/classified-compilation/19870312/index.html.

be impossible", the Dutch courts will assume jurisdiction, even though they did not have it in the first place. The European Court of Human Rights, in its judgment in *Naït-Liman v Switzerland* case,[62] decided that in cases of violations of international law (such as torture in the relevant case) it was under the plaintiff's right to not to initiate legal action before the courts of the country where its rights were violated (the country of torture in the relevant case), and hence Swiss courts' declination of jurisdiction would constitute violation of the plaintiff's right to a fair trial protected under Article 6 of the ECHR. This judgment is surely a reflection of the doctrine of *forum necessitatis*.

Forum necessitatis was also suggested by the European Commission to be included in Brussels I Recast.[63] However, it was then not kept in the final text that was agreed upon between the member states. It is stated in legal doctrine that the deletion of *forum necessitatis* does not stem from the incompatibility of the concept in international law, but rather from the concerns on the part of member states on the mandatory nature of this doctrine, although they had not yet included it in their national laws.[64] The explanation given by the Netherlands regarding their negative response to the Commission's suggestion refers mainly to the very nature of the Brussels I regime, as this is not aimed at creating new grounds for jurisdiction, but to form a division of jurisdictional powers between member states.[65] Accordingly, full harmonisation of these rules would go against the closed system of the Brussels I regime. Having said that, the non-inclusion of *forum necessitatis* in Brussels I Recast does not mean that this doctrine would be completely abandoned in legal disputes concerning member states.

In legal doctrine, some scholars criticise the practice of *forum necessitatis* as being risky, as it may create a possibility of 'forum shopping' for the victims and this could create legal uncertainty for defendant companies.[66]

However, *forum necessitatis* can be quite useful to plaintiffs in FDL claims, considering that these victims often encounter jurisdictional obstacles when they initiate legal action against parent companies before the courts of the home country. In fact, the doctrine of *forum necessitatis* might be used as a last resort in cases where it is impossible or unreasonable to initiate legal action in another forum, provided that there is always a connection between the claim and the relevant forum.[67] The required connection might be open to different interpretations, however, in general the plaintiff's residence, nationality, and the presence of the defendant's assets are

---

[62] European Court of Human Rights, Naït-Liman v Switzerland [GC], no. 51357/07, 15 March 2018.

[63] COM (2013) 554: Proposal for a Regulation of the European Parliament and of the Council amending Regulation (EU) No 1215/2012 on jurisdiction and the recognition and enforcement of judgments in civil and commercial matters.

[64] Nwapi (2014), p. 33.

[65] Roorda and Ryngaert (2016), pp. 807–808.

[66] Roorda and Ryngaert (2016), p. 785.

[67] Roorda and Ryngaert (2016), p. 808.

deemed as a sufficient or close enough connection in this respect.[68] Depending on the specifics of the case, the required connection might be deemed to exist in respect of the defendant parent company's administrative centre, where the decisions concerning the transnational subsidiaries are also made (especially decisions such as the subsidiaries' health and safety policies, environmental policies, including monitoring and supervision of the same). Accordingly, this interpretation might allow the plaintiffs of FDL claims to prove that the home country courts are the *forum necessitatis* to hear their claims.

5.1.1.2 US Law: Alien Tort Statute

The US law has specific legislation in force, and while this was not enacted to address FDL claims, it has become perhaps the most commonly used legislation for this purpose: the Alien Tort Statute (ATS), also known as Alien Tort Claims Act (ATCA).[69]

5.1.1.2.1 The Purpose and Scope of Application of Alien Tort Statute

One of the most important sources for procedural law in respect of FDL cases is the ATS, which stipulates that "*The district courts shall have original jurisdiction of any civil action by an alien for a tort only, committed in violation of the law of nations or a treaty of the United States*".[70] Accordingly, US district courts shall have jurisdiction in civil law cases concerning a tort which breaches international law or US conventions that was initiated by a foreigner (a non-US citizen). The ATS, therefore, grants the power to exercise extraterritorial jurisdiction to the US courts in protection of human rights[71] and has a unique position in comparative law in this respect.

It is stated that the reason district courts were given direct jurisdictional authority under the ATS is because state courts were seen to be biased against foreigners.[72] Accordingly, the ATS paved the way for actions concerning torts to be initiated and heard before the US courts, regardless of the place where the tort was committed or the nationality of the person who committed it.

Although ATS was enacted in 1789, it was only in the 1980s that it began to be used in respect of human rights violations and there have been different interpretations referring to its practice throughout the years. Considering the differences in political atmosphere and global issues, it is no surprise that there are ongoing debates on what the scope of the ATS should be and how it should be interpreted. At the time

[68] Nwapi (2014), p. 34; Roorda and Ryngaert (2016), p. 797.

[69] 28 U.S.C. § 1350; it was embedded in a statute that was enacted in 1789.

[70] 28 U.S.C. § 1350; Alien's Action for Tort.

[71] De Schutter (2010), p. 170.

[72] Haider (2012), p 1365.

when ATS first came into effect, the most common and important violations of international law were violations of safe conduct, infringement of the rights of ambassadors and piracy. Even now, while conservatives contend that the scope of ATS should be interpreted in line with the main purpose for which this act was first enacted, human rights defenders claim that this should be interpreted widely so as to fit the spirit of the time.[73]

It is worth noting that ATS claims are based on violations of the law of nations (interpreted as customary principles of international law) or on violations of US laws. Therefore, the material scope of ATS is different to and seems more restrictive than common tort law, considering that generally tort rules are sufficiently broad to cover human rights violations (e.g. torture, slavery, unlawful execution), while the opposite is not always the case.[74] In fact, as it will be discussed further below, the recent judgments on ATS claims do not offer any positive prospects to human rights victims. If the US Supreme Court continues its restrictive approach in the application of ATS for tort claims initiated by foreigners, this might result in an increase in claims based on general tort law, as a reasonable alternative to ATS claims.

5.1.1.2.2 Relevant Case Law Under Alien Tort Statute

There has been a series of court decisions related to claims concerning transnational human rights violations from the 1980s to the current day. It would be beneficial to go through some specific cases in order to understand the rise of ATS-based claims and the approach of the US courts in this respect.

Filártiga v Peña-Irala

Filártiga v Peña-Irala[75] was the first case to set a precedent in relation to the US courts' jurisdiction in a tort claim that concerned the violation of international law, which was committed by foreigners outside the US.

In this judgment, the court ruled that US jurisdiction could extend to tortious acts causing the violation of international law that are committed within the borders of the US and abroad.[76] This case did not concern any violation by a corporate actor. It was filed by the parents of a Paraguayan teenager, who had been allegedly tortured to death by another Paraguayan citizen, after trials before the Paraguayan courts that did not reach any conclusion. The US courts assumed jurisdiction in this lawsuit, where both the plaintiff and the defendant were Paraguayan citizens and where the alleged tort did not occur in the US. Following this landmark judgment, the scope of ATS was extended in practice.

[73] Fielding (2008), pp. 516–517.

[74] Webb (2013), p. 155.

[75] Filártiga v Peña-Irala 630 F.2D 876 (2D Cir. 1980).

[76] De Jonge (2011), p. 100; Zerk (2006), p. 207.

The *Filártiga v. Peña-Irala* decision is important in the sense that it identified the three-pronged test to check if a wrong constitutes any violation of international law: (1) the wrong should be a violation that commands the general assent of civilised nations, (2) the wrong should be clearly and unambiguously prohibited, and (3) the states should clearly express that the wrong is of mutual concern.[77]

Union Carbide Corporation/Dow Chemicals (Bhopal)

This incident occurred on 2-3 December 1984 in Bhopal, India, and concerned a leak of methyl isocyanate (MIC) gas from the pesticide factory owned, managed and operated by Union Carbide India Limited (UCIL). This led to a tremendous death toll (unofficial estimates were 7000–8000 initial deaths, and 15,000–20,000 subsequent deaths), as well as serious and permanent injuries (around 50,000 permanently disabled amongst around 500,000 injured people).[78]

According to the information provided on the disaster by Union Carbide Corporation on its website, the plant had been in operation since the 1960s on a site that was owned and leased from Madhya Pradesh State Government, which had selected the location of the plant.[79] At the time of the incident, the shareholding structure of UCIL (the owner and operator of the Bhopal plant) consisted of 50.9% of shares held by Union Carbide Corporation (UCC),[80] a company located in the US, 22% of shares held by the Indian government, and the remaining shares held by 23,500 private Indian investors through the Bombay Stock Exchange.

Initially, the plaintiffs who suffered injuries filed several lawsuits before the US courts claiming the responsibility of both UCIL and UCC for the incident. These lawsuits were merged through a multi-district litigation process. Throughout the proceedings, UCC's main line of defence was that the construction, engineering, operation and management of the plant was conducted by Indian companies and workers, and there was no connection with UCC despite the shareholding in UCIL. In turn, the plaintiffs argued that the plant's operations were largely supervised and monitored by UCC, who was also responsible for the decision to store the toxic material which led to the disaster,[81] and therefore it should be held legally liable.

In May 1986, US District Court Judge Keenan dismissed the lawsuit based on *forum non conveniens*, finding that India was the more suitable forum for the case,

---

[77]Fielding (2008), p. 517.

[78]Union Carbide/Dow lawsuit (re Bhopal), Business & Human Rights Resource Centre, https://www.business-humanrights.org/en/latest-news/union-carbidedow-lawsuit-re-bhopal/.

[79]Bhopal Plant History and Ownership, Union Carbide Corporation, https://www.bhopal.com/bhopal-plant-history-ownership.html. It is worth noting that United Carbide Corporation has distinguishably tried to show that the construction phase of the plant was almost fully undertaken by Indian firms and workers, under the supervision of UCIL, and that UCC was not involved in the design, construction and operation of the plant.

[80]Union Carbide Corporation became a wholly owned subsidiary of Dow Chemical Company in 2001.

[81]Enneking (2012), p. 94.

on the condition that UCC would waive any rights to statute of limitations and accept Indian courts' jurisdiction to hear the case, which UCC accepted. Amongst the reasons for this judgment, Judge Keenan cited the convenience of obtaining evidence and lowering costs, but he mainly based his judgment on Indian law being the most adequate applicable law in this case, as the incident occurred in India and the related parties (i.e. victims) were located there, and consequently the Indian courts would be in the best position to apply Indian law.[82] It is, in fact, ironic that the judge expressed his concerns that had the case been allowed to continue in the US courts, this would imply a kind of imperialism: "*it would be sadly paternalistic, if not misguided*".[83]

In the meantime, the Bhopal Gas Leak Disaster Act was enacted in India, which allowed the Indian government to act as trustee and representative for the Bhopal victims, and for this reason, the Indian government appeared as a plaintiff in class actions before the US courts.[84] In 1989, the Supreme Court of India approved the settlement reached by agreement for UCC's liability for the amount of USD 470 million, while the actual amount of claimed damages was more than USD 3 billion. In 1991, the Supreme Court of India, which was asked to review the case, refused to reconsider compensation claims but issued an order that UCC and its affiliates should establish a hospital for the Bhopal victims. In 2010, an Indian court issued a judgment imposing sanctions of imprisonment and monetary fines on eight Indian former plant employees and an arrest order on the former CEO of UCC.[85] Unsurprisingly, the decision of extradition for the former CEO was never applied.

Judge Keenan's consistent approach of refusing plaintiffs' cases on several grounds, including the main ground of *forum non conveniens*, continued through several multi-district litigation processes, starting with the 1986 judgment, then continuing in 1989, 1992 and 1993. *Krishnan* strongly criticises the appointment of Judge Keenan to subsequent cases concerning Bhopal but falling outside the previous multi-district litigation framework, with claims of environmental damages to the area and its water sources and damages to private property, which also resulted in the dismissal of plaintiffs' claims.[86] Judge Keenan was also appointed by the Court of Appeals in 2001 to decide on the case alleging liability for environmental damages against UCC and the then CEO of UCC, which was—in line with the rest of the judgments—finally dismissed in favour of the defendants.

[82] Krishnan (2020), p. 13.

[83] Baxi (2016), p. 29; Krishnan (2020), p. 13.

[84] Krishnan (2020), pp. 4–5.

[85] Enneking (2012), p. 95.

[86] Krishnan (2020), p. 6. The mentioned cases include Sajida Bano v Union Carbide Corporation and Warren Anderson, No. 99 Civ. 11329 (JFK), Janki Bai Sahu v Union Carbide Corporation and Warren Anderson, No. 04 Civ. 8825 (JFK) (Sahu I), Jagarnath Sahu v Union Carbide Corporation and Madhya Pradesh State, No. 07 Civ. 2156 (JFK) (Sahu II) – for detailed information on the cases see EarthRights International, Sahu v Union Carbide, https://earthrights.org/case/sahu-v-union-carbide/.

In the end, the Bhopal disaster, which is often recognised as the worst industrial disaster in the world's history, resulted in a settlement (the fairness of which is still debated) without any acknowledgement by any corporate entity allegedly involved in the occurrence of the incident. In other words, the settlement reached between the Union of India and UCC effectively closed the door on the faces of the victims.

Doe v Unocal

Another important decision in ATS-based case law is *Doe v Unocal.*[87] This case has specific importance given that the California District Court decided for the first time that it was possible to initiate legal action based on ATS not only against real persons, but also against private companies.

The case concerned the development of a facility in Andaman Sea, 40 miles offshore from Burma, to retract natural gas and oil and transport it to Thailand. Unocal Corporation, a US corporation, was one of four parties involved in the joint venture. According to the claimants' allegations, Unocal's joint venture party, a Burmese state authority, used violence against local people in order to relocate villages, including murder, rape, torture, as well as forced labour, which were all known to and perhaps even assisted by the other joint venture parties.[88]

The judge accepted that the plaintiffs had effectively proved that Unocal was aware and had benefited from the forced labour and slavery, and thus it had acted in joint action with the perpetrators, and therefore the US courts could assume jurisdiction as these acts constituted a violation of *jus cogens.*[89] Although the case was finally settled out of court,[90] it still points to the expansion of corporate complicity in aiding and abetting international law violations.[91] The case also showed how wide a scope ATS can achieve even in cases filed against corporate actors.

Sosa v Alvarez-Machain

In *Sosa v Alvarez-Machain*,[92] where both the plaintiff and the defendant were Mexican citizens and the alleged tortious action had also occurred outside the US territory, the US Supreme Court held that, although limited, certain specific violations of international law could be made subject to legal action under ATS. The relevant violations were declared as the ones pertaining to the eighteenth century

[87] Doe v Unocal 395 F.3d 932 (9 Cir. 2002).

[88] Christmann (2000), pp. 207–208.

[89] Christmann (2000), pp. 213, 217.

[90] Several interpretations were made on the out-of-court settlement of this case: (i) Unocal had accepted responsibility and its obligation to compensate the victims, and (ii) Unocal had only wanted to dismiss the case without any formal admission of liability and avoiding any damage to its reputation (see Smith and Pangsapa 2011, p. 225). My opinion favours the second interpretation.

[91] Fielding (2008), p. 518.

[92] Sosa v Alvarez-Machain 542 U.S. 692, 738 (2004).

when ATS was first enacted, namely: (i) violations of safe conducts, (ii) offences against ambassadors and (iii) individual actions arising out of prize captures and piracy. Hence according to this judgment, in order for a currently applicable rule of customary international law to be recognised within the scope of ATS, it should be "*specific, universal and obligatory*".[93]

As per this judgment, in the event that the defendant has a 'minimal contact' with the US, the US courts shall have jurisdiction, regardless of whether the violations occurred within or outside its borders.[94] This approach is declared to be fairly liberal as it poses a wide application scope, whereby it might be sufficient to deem that a corporation doing business and having regular and systematic activity in the US would fall within the scope of the US courts' jurisdiction.[95] On the other hand, this decision shows that claims under ATS are actionable based on the principles of customary international law, rather than the common law tort system.[96]

The *Sosa v Alvarez-Machain* case is also significant for the reason that it is the case where the European Commission expressed an opinion on ATS for the first time by submitting an *amicus curiae* brief to the proceedings before the US Supreme Court.[97] In this brief, the European Commission stated that as the ATS has extra-territorial reach and in certain cases also applies to the nationals of and legal entities domiciled in EU member states, the US Supreme Court was asked to interpret the ATS from both the substantive and jurisdictional perspectives in accordance with the principles of international law (p. 6). The European Commission expressed its own stance on this issue by stating that the substantive principles of the ATS should be determined according to the customary international law, which is evolutionary in nature, and therefore the US courts must act diligently in referring to the international law that existed at the time of the conduct in dispute (p. 7). The European Commission also referred to the jurisdictional reach of the ATS by making the following comments:

> Hence, the Alien Tort Statute should be interpreted to reach conduct with no nexus to the United States only where that exercise accords with principles governing universal jurisdiction. (...) To the extent recognized, it should apply only to a narrow category of conduct and should be exercised only when the claimant would otherwise be subject to a denial of justice (p. 16).

The quoted interpretation of the European Commission, undoubtedly, restricts the scope of the ATS jurisdiction, which is not in line with the liberal approach of the US Supreme Court in its judgment.

---

[93] Webb (2013), p. 135.

[94] Enneking (2009), p. 914.

[95] Enneking (2009), p. 914.

[96] Enneking (2009), pp. 914–915.

[97] Brief of Amicus Curiae the European Commission in Support of Neither Party, Sosa v Alvarez-Machain, No. 03-0339, January 23, 2004, 542 US 692(2004); Enneking (2009), p. 910.

Khulumani v Barclay National Bank

In *Khulumani* et al. *v Barclay National Bank* et al.,[98] the US Court of Appeals permitted class actions under the ATS by South Africans who were harmed by the apartheid regime that lasted from 1948 to 1994, claiming that around fifty MNCs aided and abetted the apartheid regime, and actively and willingly collaborated with them to maintain the apartheid regime.[99] The plaintiffs contended that the MNCs had supported the regime by providing funds, supplying the required computer systems and equipment, and by continuing to do business in South Africa, even though it was then recognised that the apartheid regime committed consistent violations of international law. In their claims, the plaintiffs argued that the defendant corporations "*knew of the racist policies of apartheid; that they nevertheless so engaged in the transactions in and with the Union of South Africa; and that, had they not done so, the apartheid regime would have collapsed, apartheid would have ended sooner, and plaintiffs would not have suffered some or all of their injuries*".[100]

The claims were first brought before the US District Court for the Southern District of New York,[101] which dismissed the claims on the grounds that aiding and abetting was not actionable under the ATS.[102] The legal proceedings lasted for years and resulted in the dismissal of the plaintiffs' claims against the majority of the defendants, keeping only the claims against Ford Motor Company and International Business Machines Corporation (IBM), which concerned aiding and abetting the apartheid regime by selling and providing military vehicles and computers to security forces. In rejecting the claims against the other non-US-based defendants, in the judgment of 28 August 2014, the US District Court judge specifically required the plaintiffs to show that the remaining defendants' actions touch and concern US territory with sufficient force to be allowed under the ATS.

---

[98] Khulumani et al. v Barclay National Bank et al. US Court of Appeals Second Circuit 05-2141, 05-2326 (12 October 2007). Within framework of Apartheid cases, Three groups of plaintiffs (Ntsebeza, Digwamaje and Khulumani) initiated lawsuits before US courts against various corporate defendants (Lungisile Ntsbeza et al. v. Daimler AG et al., and Khulumani et al. v. Barclays National Bank et al., the cases are collectively referred to as South African Apartheid Litigation).

[99] It is worth noting that the allegation of aiding and abetting the Apartheid regime in South Africa does not exactly fall within scope of this study, as the study focuses on violations of bodily integrity due to the activities of transnational subsidiaries in a corporate group. Nevertheless, the outcome of the alleged aiding and abetting is the violation of bodily integrity of the people. Therefore, the case was studied hereunder.

[100] Khulumani et al. v Barclay National Bank et al. US Court of Appeals Second Circuit 05-2141, 05-2326 (12 October 2007), p. 70.

[101] There were three groups of plaintiffs that filed several actions before federal district courts; namely, the Khulumani plaintiffs, the Ntsebeza plaintiffs and the Digwamaje Plaintiffs.

See In re S. African Apartheid Litig., 346 F. Supp. 2d 538, 542 (S.D.N.Y. 2004) and In re S. African Apartheid Litig., 238 F. Supp. 2d 1379, 1380–81 (J.P.M.L. 2002).

[102] In re South African Apartheid Litigation, 238 F. Supp. 2d 1379 (J.P.M.L. 2002).

However, then the judge referred to the Kiobel II judgment,[103] where the US Supreme Court held that the ATS would apply to violations of the law of nations occurring outside the US territory only to the extent that such violations touch and concern the US territory with sufficient force, and the concurring opinions submitted thereto. In assessing the US Court of Appeals Second Circuit's opinion in the Apartheid case, the judge came to the conclusion that the Second Circuit adopted the narrower approach of the two views expressed in the concurring opinions in Kiobel II, which is to delimit the application of ATS to those cases where the relevant conduct occurred on US territory and where it caused a violation of international law. In this case, therefore, the judge decided that the conduct subject to allegations did not occur on US territory, thus they did not touch or concern US territory, hence the claims should not be allowed to proceed under ATS.

The plaintiffs brought the case before the US Court of Appeals. In its *per curiam* opinion, the Second Circuit of the US Court of Appeals decided that aiding and abetting was, in principle, actionable under the ATS. However, there was a disagreement between the judges as to whether the decision should be based on customary international law or on federal common law.[104]

Finally, the Supreme Court was consulted with a writ of a *certiorari* by some of the corporate defendants, but the Supreme Court refused to grant a *certiorari.*[105] The Supreme Court held that while actions such as providing information on anti-apartheid activists to the South African security forces, selling armaments and related equipment with the knowledge that they would be used for killings, selling computer hardware to the government with knowledge that this would be used to register individuals and arbitrarily denationalise them would constitute an act of aiding and abetting, extending loans or selling automobiles to the government should not be deemed a violation of international law.[106] The Supreme Court also rejected the appeal of the plaintiffs challenging the decision that they failed to show that the defendant's conduct in the US had a sufficiently close link with the human rights violations committed by the South African apartheid regime.[107]

This case is important for ATS practice as it demonstrates a significant advantage of the ATS system, which is to allow a claim to be filed on behalf of an unidentified

---

[103] Kiobel v. Royal Dutch Petroleum Co., 133 S. Ct. 1659 (2013).

[104] Judge Katzmann referred to the US Supreme Court's *Sosa v Alvarez-Machain* judgment, where it was stated that the scope of ATS liability was defined by the law of nations and that aiding and abetting was made subject to international treaties concerning organized crime and terrorism. Judge Hall, on the other hand, argued that the ATS did not provide any guidance on the grounds of secondary liability, and therefore, the federal courts were to look into the federal common law to fill the loophole.

[105] SCOTUS Opinion no. 07-919 (27.03.2008). The Supreme Court stated that while the defendants argued that the mere act of doing business in South Africa did not amount to aiding and abetting under the ATS, they had not raised this defense during the proceedings (p. 1).

[106] De Jonge (2011), p. 104.

[107] Apartheid reparations lawsuits (re So. Africa), Business & Human Rights Resource Centre, https://www.business-humanrights.org/en/latest-news/apartheid-reparations-lawsuits-re-so-africa/.

group of people—i.e. in this case, "*all persons who lived in South Africa between 1948 and the present and who suffered damages as a result of apartheid*".[108]

Morrison v National Australia Bank

The presumption against extraterritoriality in ATS claims was firstly addressed in detail in *Morrison v National Australia Bank,*[109] which concerned claims based on foreign application of the US securities legislation. The plaintiffs, who were ordinary share purchasers from the National Australia Bank, alleged that the share prices were artificially inflated due to the deceptive statements made by the bank, which were based on a misleading accounting of the bank's subsidiaries located in the US.

In this case, the US Supreme Court ruled that a court would presume that a statute is *"primarily concerned with domestic conditions"* unless *"there is the affirmative intention of the Congress clearly expressed"*, in which case it would apply extraterritorially.[110] The new test determined with this judgment suggests that in cases where the fraud concerns securities traded on foreign exchanges or foreign platforms, this would not be subject to the protections provided under the US securities legislation.

Kiobel v Royal Dutch Petroleum

Referring to the recent ATS practice, it can be observed that the US courts have adopted a more conservative approach over time. The case *Kiobel v Royal Dutch Petroleum* was initiated by the wife of an Ogoni activist, Esther Kiobel, whose husband was a member of the Movement for the Survival of the Ogoni People, a group that protested against the environmental damage caused by the oil companies' activities in Ogoniland. Her husband was executed by the military government along with other members of the group. The claimants alleged that Shell provided support to the Nigerian military—in the form of transport, food and other needs—and hence was complicit in the Nigerian military's torture and other violations under the ATS.[111] The lawsuit concerned a different aspect of the Dutch Shell[112] and English

[108] van Dam (2015), p. 488.

[109] Morrison v National Australia Bank 130 S Ct 2869 (2010).

[110] Webb (2013), p. 136.

[111] Kiobel lawsuit was predated by Wiwa lawsuit, which was initiated by the heirs of the Ogoni activist Ken Saro-Wiwa, who was executed together with Barinem Kiobel by the military government. In Wiwa lawsuit, it was also alleged that Shell supported and aided the Nigerian military government and facilitated the commission of various human rights violations. The parties reached an out-of-court settlement in 2009, without any admission of liability by Shell. See Shell lawsuit (re Nigeria - Kiobel & Wiwa), Business & Human Rights Resource Centre, https://www.business-humanrights.org/en/latest-news/shell-lawsuit-re-nigeria-kiobel-wiwa/.

[112] Oguru, Efanga, Milieudefensie v Royal Dutch Shell Plc and Shell Petroleum Development Co Nigeria Ltd. (District Court of The Hague, C/09/330891/HA ZA 09-0579, 2013); Friday Alfred Akpan v Royal Dutch Shell Plc and Shell Petroleum Development Co Nigeria Ltd. (District Court

Shell[113] lawsuits, which mainly concerned the environmental damage aspects of Shell's activities in Nigeria through its Nigerian subsidiary SPDC.

In *Kiobel v Royal Dutch Petroleum,* the Second Circuit of the Court of Appeals[114] held that there were no international courts which ruled for the liability of a corporation under international law and this showed that there was, in fact, no corporate liability under international law. The Second Circuit's majority also stated that although there were some international treaties which would impose certain liabilities on corporations, this was limited to their specific subjects, and thus would not lead to any assumption that corporations were liable under international law.

In response to the majority in the Second Circuit's decision, Judge Leval expressed his dissenting opinion that there was no stipulation in international law that would lead to the interpretation that whilst private individuals would be liable for their violations, corporations would not be liable for the consequences of their violations. *Haider* connects this opinion to the Lotus principle, which concerns an incident between a French and Turkish steamer in the high seas resulting in death, where the Permanent Court of International Justice held that the Turkish courts could assume jurisdiction over the case although the incident took place outside Turkish waters, as there was nothing in international law that would prohibit them from doing so. In *Haider*'s opinion, "*the Lotus principle stands for the proposition that whatever is not explicitly forbidden is permitted*", which supports the dissenting opinion of Judge Leval in the *Kiobel* judgement, that the lack of corporate liability in international law actually renders it permissible.[115]

Following the Second Circuit's judgment, the US Supreme Court has granted a *certiorari.*[116] This was not unexpected considering that there were splits on the question of corporate liability under the ATS within the Second Circuit and also amongst different circuits.[117] The US Supreme Court held that the US laws should only be applied extraterritorially in cases where the lawsuit "*touches and concerns*" the US "*with sufficient force*". The US Supreme Court stated that the presumption against extraterritoriality applies to the ATS, which is interpreted as a general presumption against the extraterritorial application of the US law, with the exception of an intent from the Congress to the contrary.[118]

of The Hague, 337050/HA ZA 09-1580, 2013); Barizaa Manson TeteDooh v Royal Dutch Shell Plc and Shell Petroleum Development Co Nigeria Ltd. (District Court of The Hague, C/09/337058/HA ZA 09-1581, 2013).

[113] Okpabi & Ors v Royal Dutch Shell Plc & Anor [2018] EWCA Civ 191.

[114] Kiobel et al. v Royal Dutch Petroleum Co. et al. [2010] USCA 621 F.3d 111.

[115] Haider (2012), p. 1373.

[116] SCOTUS Certiorari To The United States Court of Appeals for the Second Circuit No. 10–1491 (17.04.2013).

[117] Stewart and Wuerth (2013), p. 605.

[118] Dittmers (2017), p. 14.

It might be argued that the aforementioned indications could be deemed as leaving some room for manoeuvre.[119] Still, with this decision, the US Supreme Court declared that as the case was initiated by non-US citizens against non-US citizens due to an alleged tort that was committed outside US borders, there were no grounds to base it on ATS.[120] The US Supreme Court further held that ATS is subject to a *"presumption against extraterritoriality"* and that the mere existence of a foreign company in the US was not *per se* sufficient to sue it before the US courts with allegations that it helped or motivated a violation which was committed outside US borders.[121] According to the majority opinion of the judgement, liability under ATS claims is determined by customary international law, thus companies cannot be sued under the ATS because they have no liabilities under international law.[122] The US Supreme Court therefore dismissed the plaintiffs' claims based on a lack of subject matter jurisdiction.

The European Commission also expressed its views on this case through its brief as *amicus curiae,*[123] where it stated that the extraterritorial application of the ATS is in line with customary international law to the extent that this is limited to the *"most grave violations of the law of nations"*, such as torture, genocide or other conduct committed outside any state's territory, such as piracy (p. 4–5). This opinion of the EU stands apart from any presumption against extraterritoriality.[124]

With the *Kiobel* decision, there was a change in the approach recognised under *Doe v Unocal*[125] that companies may also be subject to lawsuits under the ATS for any violations of international law. In fact, the *Kiobel* judgment significantly limited the possibility of initiating lawsuits before US courts for issues that are not clearly connected with the US.[126] Thus, this judgment can be interpreted as prohibiting the extraterritorial reach of US laws and protecting jurisdictional prerogatives of *lex loci delicti.*[127] Despite this negative improvement on the side of ATS-based FDL claims, there have been developments in claims based on tort law and more specifically tort of negligence.[128]

Along with other issues, the *Kiobel* judgment is also criticised based on the argument that the court failed to address (or, as a matter of fact, chose to purposefully leave open) certain key points that are important to ATS claims: (i) whether

---

[119] Enneking (2014), p. 50.

[120] Weber and Baisch (2016), p. 680.

[121] Weber and Baisch (2016), p. 680.

[122] De Jonge (2011), p. 106.

[123] Brief of the European Commission on behalf of the European Union as Amicus Curiae in Support of Neither Party, June 13, 2012, Kiobel v. Royal Dutch Petroleum Co., 133 S.Ct. 1659 (2013) (No. 10-1491).

[124] Kaeb and Scheffer (2013), p. 853.

[125] Doe v Unocal 395 F.3d 932 (9 Cir. 2002).

[126] Van Dam (2015), p. 487.

[127] Kaeb and Scheffer (2013), p. 852.

[128] Enneking (2013), p. 136.

corporate liability falls within the scope of the ATS, (ii) what the standard would be for touching and concerning the US territory with sufficient force to displace the presumption against extraterritoriality, (iii) whether the acts of aiding and abetting fall within the scope of ATS, (iv) whether domestic remedies should be exhausted before being able to file an ATS claim, and (v) whether principles of prescriptive comity should be applicable to ATS claims.[129]

Nevertheless, it might be suggested that tort victims might still be allowed to initiate legal action before US courts based on ATS. First of all, the *Kiobel* judgment requires a sufficiently close nexus with the US in order to accept jurisdiction in transnational tort claims, even where these are initiated by a non-US citizen. The required nexus (i.e. *"touch and concern the US territory with sufficient force"*) should be deemed to exist where the defendant parent company is headquartered in the US. Therefore, this decision might be deemed to favour foreign corporations over American corporations,[130] as foreign corporations would not be eligible to be sued under the ATS. It may even be argued that the *"touch and concern with a sufficient force"* requirement might be deemed to exist where a foreign corporation has continuous and systematic presence in the US, as it was declared by the US Supreme Court in *Daimler AG v Bauman.*[131]

Furthermore, although it may seem to some scholars that initiating legal action against companies may no longer be possible, there appears to be no obstacle to initiating legal action against individuals—such as directors, managers or other employees.[132] This might also lead to an increase in cases of piercing the corporate veil, based on issues such as corporate governance, compliance and record-keeping.[133] It is worth noting, however, that the burden of proof in such a case would not be easy to fulfil, as it would be necessary to prove not only that the relevant directors or managers knew about the harm but also that they intended to cause it.[134] In any case, I believe that due to the very nature of FDL claims, suing individuals would not create any viable solution. In fact, the desired outcome of these claims would be to render the parent companies of MNCs liable, instead of directing these claims against the parent company's or its transnational subsidiary's directors or managers. It is, therefore, obvious that the *Kiobel* judgment has dramatically changed the ATS landscape.

ATS was nonetheless criticised on several grounds, regardless of the situation after *Kiobel*. According to *Choudhury*, there are three shortcomings of the ATS system for corporate liability: (1) the need for a state actor or state aid, which leaves the corporate abuses without a state component outside the scope of ATS; (2) the requirement for establishing personal jurisdiction by the US courts, thus where a

[129] Webb (2013), pp. 132, 139.

[130] Chander (2013) p. 829.

[131] Daimler AG v Bauman, 571 U.S. (2014).

[132] Enneking (2012), p. 269.

[133] Erb and Pell (2012), p. 1075.

[134] Haider (2012), p. 1384.

sufficient connection exists between the court and the defendant, and; (3) *forum non conveniens*.[135] The ATS was also found to be unclear as to whether the plaintiffs needed to first exhaust domestic legal remedies or the degree of knowledge or intent to be sought for the establishment of secondary liability (e.g. aiding and abetting).[136] The most recent case law shows that all these concerns are still valid for the effectiveness of the ATS in terms of the liability of corporations.

To continue these criticisms of ATS, in *Dine*'s opinion, ATS provides a court procedure that leaves a "*final escape hatch*" for the defendants and it also concerns civil suits that can be settled without any admission of liability by the defendants.[137] The possibility for settlement seems to dominate the future of ATS claims, as defendant companies opt for the settlement option as soon as they understand that they are risking in facing a viable claim. Undoubtedly, this makes no contribution to FDL claims, as the defendant parent companies of MNCs are well-equipped and ready to pay the settlement as long as they can avoid liability. This situation also prevents the formation of settled case law on ATS claims, which constitutes a step back from achieving legal certainty.

Another important problem with the ATS is that it is based on human rights, which are linked to the principle of states being subject to liability, not private actors such as corporations.[138] This issue was the key point of the *Kiobel* judgment, which is expected to continue to affect the ATS practice. There are also shortcomings concerning the types of violations that might fall within the scope of the ATS. Research indicates that the case law based on ATS so far shows that eight torts are recognised as violations of international law: war crimes, torture, summary execution, genocide, disappearance, prolonged arbitrary detention, slavery and cruel, inhuman or degrading punishment.[139] This leaves out a considerable amount of torts, including labour rights violations, environmental damages, seizure or expropriation of property, and supporting armed forces, which the courts have explicitly refused to recognise as violations of international law.[140]

The question of the presumption against extraterritoriality has so far been the subject of several decisions in ATS litigation, yet the courts have refrained from taking a clear stance with concerns on diplomatic and political impacts. The US Supreme Court decided both in the *Sosa* and *Kiobel* judgments that the scope of the ATS was purely jurisdictional and in *Kiobel* the majority decided that the presumption against extraterritoriality was to be decided on the merits of the case. The majority opinion in *Kiobel* further stated that if the extraterritorial application of the statute might give rise to diplomatic strife, in that US citizens might also be drawn to the courts of a foreign state in cases of conducts taking place within the US,

---

[135] Choudhury (2005), pp. 48–49.

[136] Erb and Pell (2012), p. 1073.

[137] Dine (2012), p. 53.

[138] Dine (2012), p. 53.

[139] Fielding (2008), p. 520.

[140] Fielding (2008), p. 521.

and therefore this issue should be decided by the political branches, instead of the courts.[141] However, it is still not clear if the majority was referring to the Congress in its legislative capacity or if it was also referring to the executive branch's *amicus curiae* briefs and statements of interest.[142] To end the obscure situation caused by the *Kiobel* judgment, it was suggested that the Congress should clarify the extraterritorial effects of the ATS without confining its application to the closeness of the actions with the US.[143]

It is worth noting that there is, in fact, significant diplomatic concern regarding the ATS practice. The seemingly wide extraterritorial reach of the ATS has so far allowed the US courts to assume jurisdiction in cases where neither the plaintiffs nor the defendants were US nationals and the incident took place outside the US territory. However, this approach has caused certain concerns on the part of the foreign states, where the defendant corporations are domiciled, and often even led them to submit *amicus curiae* briefs to the US courts.[144] In the *Kiobel* judgment, the majority opinion noted that the presumption against extraterritoriality prevented an international relations crisis between the US and other countries, and that the Congress should express its opinion on the subject.[145]

Jesner v Arab Bank

The concerns surrounding the diplomatic aspects of the ATS practice were clearly expressed in the *Jesner v Arab Bank*[146] decision.

The case concerned claims of injury and death caused by terrorist attacks in the Middle East that were allegedly facilitated or caused by Arab Bank, PLC, by allowing a transfer of the funds that were allegedly used in the terrorist attacks. The defendant was a Jordanian bank with branches around the world, including the US. The claimants contended that the relevant transfers were also realised through the bank's New York offices. The claimants submitted an important argument for subjecting the corporations to international law rules, contending that in cases where a corporation's human agents (e.g. directors) have violated international law by using that corporation, then the relevant corporation should be deemed to assume liabilities and responsibilities under international law.

In this case, the US Supreme Court finally dealt with the question of corporate liability under international law and reached the conclusion that it should be upon the Congress, and not the US Supreme Court, to decide whether to extend the scope of ATS to cover foreign corporations or not. However, it then held that foreign

[141] Stewart and Wuerth (2013), p. 607.
[142] Stewart and Wuerth (2013), p. 612.
[143] Chander (2013), p. 834.
[144] Chander (2013), p. 831.
[145] Carey (2016), p. 460.
[146] Jesner et al. v Arab Bank, PLC, 584 U.S. No. 16-499, (24.04.2018).

corporations may not be defendants in lawsuits brought under the ATS.[147] The US Supreme Court discussed the relevant question in detail by making references to previous judgments and to the importance of diplomatic relationships between states, and finally concluded that the issue actually falls within the scope of politics, rather than being juridical:

> These and other considerations that must shape and instruct the formulation of principles of international and domestic law are matters that the political branches are in the better position to define and articulate. For these reasons, judicial deference requires that any imposition of corporate liability on foreign corporations for violations of international law must be determined in the first instance by the political branches of the Government.[148]

The decision in *Jesner v Arab Bank* generated significant disappointment amongst human rights defenders, as it seems to have put a full stop on ATS practice in claims against foreign corporations, which significantly hinders the extraterritorial scope of the ATS. Thus with this decision, it has become clear that claims concerning foreign corporations are not considered within the scope of the ATS and thus foreign corporations cannot be sued for alleged violations of customary international law.

Despite the US Supreme Court's clear approach on the question of foreign corporations, there are still a couple of issues left unanswered with this judgment. First of all, it seems that the US-based corporations are still considered to fall within the scope of ATS, as long as the relevant violation of international law touches and concerns the US territory with sufficient force, as required under the *Sosa* judgment. The majority opinion in the *Jesner* case led by Justice Kennedy referred to the criteria set out in the *Sosa* judgment to question whether the alleged violation by corporations of customary international law can be deemed "*a norm that is specific, universal and obligatory*". Justice Kennedy stated that corporate liability is not recognised by international law or by international tribunals, yet he refrained from drawing a clear conclusion on this issue, after hearing the dissenting opinions of other judges.[149] Accordingly, it is to be seen whether US-based corporations will also be deemed to fall outside the ATS's scope, in the event that it is recognised that corporate liability is not a norm that is specific, universal and obligatory.[150] However, for now, it seems that it is still technically possible to sue US corporations under the ATS.

The *Jesner* decision is harshly criticised in legal doctrine for favouring market fundamentalism over the administration of justice and for giving corporations the rights of personhood, without the responsibilities.[151] In fact, Justice Kennedy stated that agreeing to impose liability on corporations would discourage US companies

---

[147] Jesner et al. v Arab Bank, p. 27.

[148] Jesner et al. v Arab Bank, p. 29.

[149] Dodge (2019), p. 133.

[150] Hughes-Jennett et al. (2018), https://www.hlregulation.com/2018/04/27/foreign-corporations-cannot-be-sued-under-the-alien-tort-statute-jesner-v-arab-bank-the-verdict/.

[151] Ryerson (2018), https://corpaccountabilitylab.org/calblog/2018/4/24/supreme-court-rejects-liability-for-foreign-corporations-in-international-human-rights-cases.

from making investments in foreign countries, where they can actually contribute to their economic development and which in the end leads to improvements in human rights. This view is lacking at the very core of the dispute on corporate liability for human rights violations, as it fails to acknowledge the clash between business on the one hand and human rights on the other. In other words, if the contributions of the developed home countries to the economies of developing host countries were to result in an ultimate improvement in the human rights conditions of those host countries, there would be no FDL cases in the first place. In fact, the implications of foreign investment—if left without the adequate safeguards for employees, environment and local people—have proven to be significantly damaging to human rights.[152] Under any circumstances, imposing "*a blanket ban on corporate liability*", as stated in Justice Sotomayor's dissenting opinion, is not the adequate solution to foreign policy concerns. Justice Sotomayor stated that the law is in a better position to address certain issues: "*There can be, and sometimes is, a profit motive for these types of abuses. Although the market does not price all externalities, the law does*". Accordingly, it would not be reasonable to leave human rights issues out of the law's reach, as this would lead to corporations enjoying personal rights while not assuming responsibilities arising therefrom.

Nevertheless, and rather unfortunately, the current trend of ATS cases seems to be insufficient in many aspects in addressing and remedying claims by human rights victims. In fact, as per the recent case law, the criteria for a successful ATS claim appears to be the following: (1) the defendant should not be a foreign corporation, i.e. it should be a US-based corporation; (2) the plaintiff should be foreign; (3) the claim should be based on one of the universally-recognised international norms (torture, crimes against humanity, genocide, etc.); (4) the facts of the case should touch and concern US territory with sufficient force and; (5) the case should not create any foreign policy concerns.[153] Against this background, for now it seems that holding corporations accountable for their violations of international human rights norms has become significantly challenging,[154] while claiming liability for issues other than universally-recognised international norms has become nearly impossible.

John Doe I v Nestle

Following the US Supreme Court's *Jesner* judgment, the Ninth Circuit of the Court of Appeals has held an opinion that could revive the ATS claims, at least to some extent. In *John Doe I v Nestle,*[155] which was appealed by the plaintiffs after the

[152]Ryerson (2018), https://corpaccountabilitylab.org/calblog/2018/4/24/supreme-court-rejects-liability-for-foreign-corporations-in-international-human-rights-cases.

[153]Ryerson (2018), https://corpaccountabilitylab.org/calblog/2018/4/24/supreme-court-rejects-liability-for-foreign-corporations-in-international-human-rights-cases.

[154]Dodge (2019), p. 137.

[155]John Doe I v Nestle 9th Cir. No. 17-55435 (23.10.2018).

District Court's decision that the claim should be dismissed due to an impermissible extraterritorial application of the ATS, the Ninth Circuit questioned the grounds of the District Court's decision and then decided to reverse and remand it. However, the US Supreme Court reversed the decision of the Court of Appeals and remanded the case on 17.06.2021.[156]

The facts of this case concern child slave labour[157] in cocoa farms in the Ivory Coast, which Nestle and Cargill allegedly both aided and abetted by providing financial support, equipment and training to these farms, by entering into exclusive supply agreements with them, and by continuing their relationship with them despite the fact that they regularly visited the farms several times a year and thus should have had known the situation. The defendant Nestle, USA is located in Virginia and the defendant Cargill, Inc. in Minneapolis. Both of these companies are carrying out operations within the US, with operational decisions taken at their US headquarters.

In the opinion of the Court of Appeals, it is referred to the principles in *Sarei v Rio Tinto, PLC* decision[158] for holding corporations liable for aiding and abetting slavery: (1) "*There is no categorical rule of corporate immunity or liability*"; (2) "*corporate liability under an ATS claim does not depend on the existence of international precedent enforcing legal norms against corporations*"; and (3) "*norms that are 'universal and absolute', or applicable to 'all actors', can provide the basis for an ATS claim against a corporation*". It is thereby stated that in the decision of *Nestle I*, it was held that the prohibition of slavery is universal and therefore should be applicable to all actors, including corporations.

The Ninth Circuit recognised the US Supreme Court's *Jesner* decision, stating that foreign corporations cannot be sued under the ATS, but moved on drawing the conclusion that this does not eliminate all corporate liability and that the ATS could apply to domestic corporations. It is also reiterated in this opinion that the application of the ATS is not limited only to principal offences but can also refer to a direct violation of the law of nations or conduct that constitutes aiding and abetting another's violation of the law of nations, thus concluding that aiding and abetting is considered within the scope of torts committed in violation of the law of nations.

The Ninth Circuit then continued to question whether the case involved a permissible domestic application, although other conduct was committed outside the US territory. By referring to several decisions whereby a transfer of funds and use of an escrow account in a US bank were considered domestic conduct, the Ninth Circuit held that the financial support agreements signed with cocoa farms were originated in the US headquarters of the defendant companies, which led to the conclusion that there was specific and domestic conduct that would put the claim within the focus of the ATS.

---

[156] Nestle USA, Inc. v Joe Doe et al. Nos. 19–416 and 19–453, 593 U.S. (17.06.2021).

[157] While the scope of this study does not comprise child labour, this decision is examined only for purposes of the analysis on the ATS practice.

[158] Sarei v Rio Tinto, PLC 671 F.3d 736, 746 (9th Cir. 2011) (en banc).

The US Supreme Court, in reversing the decision of the Court of Appeals, referred to *Jesner v Arab Bank* decision[159] to emphasize that courts cannot create new causes of action against foreign corporations under the ATS. The Supreme Court further declared that to be able to adopt an extraterritorial reach of the ATS, the plaintiffs should have proven that the conduct regulated by the ATS had occurred within the US. Unlike the Court of Appeals, the Supreme Court did not accept the plaintiffs' argument for extraterritoriality that the major decisions of the companies were taken in the US, stating that general corporate activity, such as decision making, cannot justify domestic application of the ATS and that a "*more domestic conduct than general corporate activity*" should be present.[160] This interpretation is definitely not in favour of FDL claimants, as the grounds of their applicable law and jurisdiction claims raise on the argument that the harming act (i.e. the decision or the omission to take the decision concerning the relevant activity of the transnational subsidiary) took place in the home country. This approach of the US Supreme Court, which is supported by majority, appears to be closing the door on FDL claims as it delimits the scope of application of the ATS to the three types of international tort described in the eighteenth century.[161]

Jam v IFC

The *Jam v. International Finance Corporation (IFC)*[162] case concerned allegations of IFC's contribution to environmental damages and human rights abuses through their funding of a power plant project in Gujarat, India: Tata Mundra Coastal by Gujarat Power Ltd. The plant caused considerable pollution, damaging the waterways and farmland in the area where it operated. The lawsuit was initiated before the US District Court for the District of Columbia in 2015, which ruled in IFC's favour for the immunity reasons that will be discussed below. The US Court of Appeals also upheld the lower court's judgment, which was appealed and granted a writ of a *certiorari* by the US Supreme Court.

The claimants based their corporate accountability claims on an internal audit report of the IFC, whereby it was found that the company constructing and operating the power plant did not comply with the environmental and social action plan, and also that the IFC failed to supervise the process adequately. The IFC's defence was

[159] Jesner et al. v Arab Bank, PLC, 584 U.S. No. 16-499, 24.04.2018.

[160] Nestle USA, Inc. v Joe Doe et al. Nos. 19–416 and 19–453, 593 U.S. (17.06.2021), p. 5.

[161] Justice Sotomayor, although concurring with the majority opinion, notes that the delimitation of the scope of the ATS with the three international torts recognised in 1789 would contravene with the history of the ATS and previous case law. In doing so, she emphasizes the change in international and national legal landscape after the eighteenth century and states that today's torturers, slave traders, and perpetrators of genocide are *hostis humani generis*, such as the pirates of the eighteenth century. See Opinion of Sotomayor, J., in Nestle USA, Inc. v Joe Doe et al. Nos. 19–416 and 19–453, 593 U.S. (17.06.2021).

[162] Budha Ismail Jam et al. v. International Finance Corporation, Supreme Court of the United States, No. 17–1011, 27.02.2019.

based on its allegedly absolute immunity from lawsuits and judicial proceedings, which was found to be inflated by the court.

The opinion of the Supreme Court is ground-breaking in the sense that it declared that the World Bank Group, including the IFC, did not have absolute immunity from all lawsuits, as was claimed by the defendants. In fact, the aforementioned institutions were granted the same immunity from lawsuits with foreign governments under the International Organisations Immunities Act (1945). However, this immunity was further restricted under the opinion of the State Department in 1952. The judicial immunity granted to foreign states was then restricted in the Foreign Sovereign Immunities Act (1976), whereby immunity from lawsuits was avoided for actions based on commercial activity with sufficient connection to the US. The Supreme Court, in this decision, held that the interpretation of the immunity granted to the World Bank Group was linked to the immunity granted to foreign states, which should be understood as a wilful choice by the lawmaker; the immunity of the World Bank Group, therefore, should also be understood to exclude any lawsuit or judicial proceedings initiated based on commercial activity with sufficient connection to the US. Accordingly, in this case, the Supreme Court allowed the claimants' action and sent the case to the lower courts for litigation.

On 14 February 2020, the US District Court of Columbia held in favour of the defendants, rejecting the plaintiffs' case.[163] The court assessed the Foreign Sovereign Immunities Act,[164] which governs the immunities of international organisations as well as foreign states, and which was relied upon by IFC to argue that it had absolute immunity from suit. The court considered these exceptions to immunity identified in the Foreign Sovereign Immunities Act: (i) when an action is based upon a commercial activity carried out in the US by an international organisation; or (ii) an act performed in the US in connection with a commercial activity of the international organisation elsewhere. An activity carried out in the US is described as an activity that has substantial contact with the US. At this point, the court delved into an assessment of which activity was the one that allegedly violated plaintiffs' rights and whether this activity had any substantial connection with the US. The court then distinguished between the activities of taking the decision to fund the plant and that of failing to supervise or monitor construction and operation of the funded project or ensure its compliance with the environmental and social sustainability requirements in the loan agreement. While the decision to fund the plant and sign the loan agreement was made in Washington DC, the court declared that the plaintiffs had failed to provide evidence that IFC's failure to monitor and supervise the project – which was considered as the gravamen of the plaintiffs' claims—was also effectively decided upon in the US.

This decision by the District Court is surely against the interests of plaintiffs in FDL claims, as it shows the court's approach that when the defendant's action is an

[163] Budha Ismail Jam et al. v. International Finance Corporation, United States District Court for the District of Columbia, Civil Action No. 15-612 (JDB), 14.02.2020.

[164] Foreign Sovereign Immunities Act, Public Law 94-583, 21 October 1976.

omission or a failure to take measures, the place where these measures are addressed is taken as the place of tort, rather than the place where the decisions are taken. This approach, if adopted and supported by other courts too, might create a significant barrier for FDL claims. The court rejected the argument that IFC's decision to sign the loan agreement and fund the project caused the damages incurred by the plaintiffs. Instead, it concluded that the relevant activity should be regarded as IFC's "*subsequent failure to take sufficient steps or exercise due care to prevent and mitigate harms to the property, health, [and] livelihoods of those who live near the plant*". The court decided that the aforementioned activity took place in India and therefore that it did not have a substantial connection with the US.

Although the decision will probably be appealed by the plaintiffs, for the time being the fate of the corporate accountability of financial institutions in respect of the projects they are funding has been decided.

5.1.2 International Jurisdiction of Turkish Courts in FDL Claims

Similar to applicable law, Turkish law does not bear any specific provisions concerning the jurisdiction of Turkish courts in FDL claims. Therefore, provisions concerning the jurisdiction in tort claims might be applicable, which are assessed in further detail below.

5.1.2.1 General Principles Regarding International Jurisdiction Under Turkish Law

As per Article 40 of PIPC, the international jurisdiction of Turkish courts is determined by the rules of domestic law which stipulate courts' territorial jurisdiction.[165] In other words, the existence of domestic jurisdiction is deemed sufficient and also necessary for the existence of international jurisdiction.[166] In this respect,

[165] Şanlı et al. (2018), p. 373. The mentioned rule of Article 40 of PIPC that makes the international jurisdiction subject to the rules of domestic jurisdiction has also procedural consequences. Accordingly, the same rules on jurisdiction and proceedings regarding objecting against jurisdiction shall apply in international disputes as the domestic ones. Therefore, in a case that was initiated before Turkish court that had no jurisdiction, if the defendant does not raise any objection, then it will be deemed that the parties have reached an implied agreement on jurisdiction. If the defendant raises an objection, the Turkish court shall reject jurisdiction, but it shall not be able to determine the foreign court that has jurisdiction in that specific case. See Doğan (2020), p. 52.

[166] Doğan (2020), pp. 60–61; Nomer (2015), p. 455; Sarıöz (2012), p. 156; Şanlı et al. (2018), p. 373. These rules of jurisdiction that govern both domestic and international disputes are defined as "rules having double function" (Doğan 2020, p. 61; Sarıöz 2012, p. 156). Concurring with this opinion, see also decision of Turkish Court of Appeal, 21th Civil Chamber, numbered 2016/17700 E., 2016/14575 K., dated 24.11.2016. Çelikel/Erdem state that PIPC adopts a mix approach in

the nationality of the parties to the dispute is not important; thus as long as the Turkish courts have jurisdiction in light of Turkish law provisions, even disputes amongst two foreign parties might be heard before the Turkish courts.[167] The rules concerning jurisdiction in Turkish law are regulated under several codes, including but not limited to the CC, the Turkish Civil Procedure Code No. 6100 (CPC) and the TCC. In cases that fall within the scope of the relevant provisions, Turkish courts will have international jurisdiction. Yet, in order to accept the jurisdiction of Turkish courts, it is required that the relevant dispute have a connection with Turkey.[168]

According to the general rule of jurisdiction[169] under Article 6 of CPC, the courts of the place of residence of the defendant (real person or legal entity) at the time of the filing of the case shall have jurisdiction to hear the case. In cases where the defendant has no place of residence in Turkey the courts of the place where the defendant has its habitual residence in Turkey will be deemed to have jurisdiction (Art. 9 CPC). The definitions of the terms 'of residence' and 'habitual residence' shall be made under *lex fori*.[170] The general rule on jurisdiction is a non-exclusive jurisdiction clause, hence it renders it possible to initiate proceedings in other alternative jurisdictions stipulated by special rules of jurisdiction in specific cases.[171]

As per the relevant provisions of Turkish law, the residence of real persons is the place where they reside with an aim of settlement (Art. 19 CC). The residence of legal entities, on the other hand, is the place of residence stipulated in its statute or articles of association and, if no place is stipulated, then the place where the administrative work is managed (Art. 51 CC).[172] If a claim also concerns the activities of a company's branch, then the courts of the place of residence of the relevant branch shall also have jurisdiction (Art. 14 CPC).

In the event that the defendant is a foreign company with a branch located in Turkey, then the courts of the place where the branch is located shall also have jurisdiction (Art. 14/1 CPC). This special jurisdiction clause shall apply only to disputes concerning the operations of the relevant branch in Turkey.[173] It is, however, not quite possible to conclude that this provision would also provide

---

determining international jurisdiction of Turkish courts, whereby jurisdiction in disputes with a foreign element are determined in accordance with domestic rules of jurisdiction, but with support of rules on international jurisdiction where needed (Çelikel and Erdem 2020, p. 561).

[167] Doğan (2020), p. 61.

[168] Süral (2012), p. 168.

[169] Albayrak and Mavzer (2019), p. 282; Şanlı et al. (2018), p. 376. General rule of jurisdiction, in principle, applies to all types of lawsuits. There are also special rules of jurisdiction, which apply to certain types of lawsuits and in exceptional cases. See Çelikel and Erdem (2020), pp. 563–564.

[170] Çelikel and Erdem (2020), p. 564; Şanlı et al. (2018), p. 376.

[171] Exclusive jurisdiction is accepted only in exceptional cases where this is clearly stipulated by law (Albayrak and Mavzer 2019, p. 283). By the same token, special jurisdiction rules do not abrogate the jurisdiction of the court authorized by general jurisdiction rule (Çelikel and Erdem 2020, p. 570).

[172] Doğan (2020), p. 64; Şanlı et al. (2018), p. 377.

[173] Süral (2012), p. 182.

grounds for FDL cases. First of all, the relevant cases concern a parent company's tort of negligence in relation to the operations of its transnational subsidiaries, which led to the damages. Therefore, the tortious act is not the subsidiary's but the parent company's. Furthermore, the legal status of a branch is different to that of a subsidiary; while a branch has no separate legal personality to the main company's, a subsidiary has a separate legal personality and is a company independent of its shareholders. Hence, engaging in such a wide interpretation of this provision would be misleading.

In cases where there is more than one defendant, it is possible to file the lawsuit at the courts of residence of one of these defendants (Art. 7 CPC). According to this provision, if one of the defendants is resident in Turkey, this would be sufficient to establish the international jurisdiction for Turkish courts.[174] The conditions for jurisdiction of a common court are set as: (i) the presence of more than one defendant; (ii) having the same subject of claim; and (iii) legal grounds for jurisdiction of a common court.[175] However, as per Art. 7/2 of CPC, if it is determined that the lawsuit has been initiated with the sole purpose of suing one of the defendants in a court which is not its place of residence, then the court may decide to reject jurisdiction upon the relevant defendant's objection. This rule might also be useful when an FDL claim is brought against the transnational subsidiary as the defendant. Especially in those cases where the parent company resides in Turkey, while the subsidiary is located in a less-developed host country, the plaintiffs might base their claims on this clause and file the lawsuit against both the parent company and subsidiary before the Turkish courts.

5.1.2.2 Jurisdiction in Tort Claims Under Turkish Law

The specific rule on jurisdiction in tort cases is regulated under Article 16 of CPC. Accordingly, the courts of the place where (i) the tortious act is committed or (ii) the damage has occurred or might possibly occur or (iii) the victim is residing shall also have jurisdiction.[176] Thus, the legislator has granted the plaintiff the right to initiate a tort claim in either one of these jurisdictions.

There are various interpretations of the concept 'the place where the tortious act is committed' in Turkish law. This concept was also regulated under Article 21 regarding jurisdiction in tort claims of the abrogated Civil Procedural Code No. 1086.[177]

---

[174] Şanlı et al. (2018), p. 378.

[175] Albayrak and Mavzer (2019), p. 285.

[176] The abrogated Turkish Civil Procedure Code no. 1086 (OJ dated 02.07.1927 numbered 622, abrogated as of 20.07.2016), the courts of the place where the tort took place would have jurisdcition in disputes arising out of torts. Hence, the new provision under Article 16 of CPC has a much wider scope, as it refers to both the place where the tortious act is committed and the place where the damage occurred or might potentially ocur, as well as an alternative jurisdiction of the plaintiff's place of residence.

[177] Civil Procedural Code No. 1086, OJ 02.07.1927/622.

Unlike the provision currently in force, this article referred only to the place where the tortious act took place. Therefore, it was then debated whether this concept should be understood as the place where the tortious act is committed or as the place where the damage has occurred. The Turkish Court of Appeal interpreted the place of tortious act as the place where the damage occurred and thus where the tortious act was completed.[178] According to the dominant opinion in Turkish legal doctrine at the time of the abrogated Civil Procedural Code, this description of the place where the tortious act took place should be understood as the place where the essential elements of tort have occurred and the tortious act was completed.[179] It was also stated that the concept of place of tortious act should be interpreted widely, so as to cover both the place where the act is committed and the place where the damage has occurred.[180] As the place of tortious act is kept in the wording of Article 16 of CPC, the opinions in legal doctrine on the former Civil Procedural Code should also be taken into account in interpreting this concept. According to *Nomer*'s opinion, the place of tortious act is considered the place where the tortious act is completed, thus where the final action constituting the tort is committed.[181] *Nomer* also opines that for torts that result in damages in several different countries, the place of jurisdiction should be the place where the tortious act is committed, rather than the place of damage, in order to link the relevant tort to one jurisdiction and dismiss the plaintiff's potentially arbitrary choice of forum.[182] As a matter of fact, considering the place of tortious act as the place where the unlawful act was committed[183] seems more in line with the wording of the provision. As for omissions that result in tort, it is stated that the place where the tortious act is committed shall be the place where the omitted action has been regulated to take place.[184]

Amongst the three options provided to the claimant under Article 16, the first option of the place where the tortious act is committed provides a viable solution to FDL claimants. In fact, as also discussed in relation to applicable law, it might be argued that the parent company's tort took place in the home country where it has its headquarters and where its decisions are taken, including the ones concerning its transnational subsidiaries' operations. In torts committed via media, the ECJ had considered that the place where the tortious act was committed was the headquarters of the publisher.[185] Considering especially that most FDL claims are based upon the

[178]Turkish Court of Appeal 3rd Civil Chamber decision dated 24.12.1956 and numbered 8766/6523.

[179]Albayrak and Mavzer (2019), p. 291; Kılıçoğlu (2012), p. 180; Kuru (2001), p. 483.

[180]Demir and Sıdıka (2008), p. 66.

[181]Nomer (2015), p. 462.

[182]Nomer (2015), p. 356.

[183]Albayrak and Mavzer (2019), p. 292.

[184]Sarıöz (2012), p. 161.

[185]Sarıöz (2012), p. 168. The ECJ decision referred dated 07.03.1995, numbered C-68/93 in Fiona Shevill et al. v Presse Alliance SA concerned claim for damages due to the publication of a defamatory newspaper article, whereby the ECJ held that "*the expression 'place where the harmful event occurred' (...) must be understood as being intended to cover both the place where the*

omission of the parent company to take adequate measures and decisions concerning the operations of its transnational subsidiaries, the place where the tortious act is committed might indeed be deemed as the place where these actions ought to have been taken, but were then omitted. Accordingly, the claimant might successfully argue that the courts of the home country have jurisdiction in the relevant legal action.

The second alternative jurisdiction in tort claims is granted to the courts of the place where the damage has occurred or might potentially occur. The place of damage is described as the place where the victim's material or moral interests were effectively violated.[186] This refers to the place where the damage produced concrete results, which is said to cover only the place where the direct victim's loss occurred, namely the place of direct damage.[187] Indirect and ricochet damages are not taken into account in the determination of the place of damage. In respect of FDL claims, as discussed further hereunder in this section on the tort analysis of these claims, a typical example of direct damage suffered by the victims could be the deaths and illnesses they suffered due to the deterioration of environmental conditions within their surroundings. Accordingly, the place of damage in these claims results in being the host country, where the victims are residing. This outcome offers no viable grounds for FDL claims, which aim to be heard before the courts of the home country.

The possibility of initiating the lawsuit in the jurisdiction where the damage 'might occur' creates a favourable situation for cases where the damage has not yet occurred, but is expected to occur in the near future. This provision is in line with the provision under Brussels I recast (Art. 7) which also refers to the place where the harmful event occurred or may occur. A typical example of how this provision might be useful could be the case of environmental damages, where only the risk of occurrence of a damage can be deemed sufficient to establish liability.[188] In light of this rule, in cases where an incident has occurred in a foreign country which is expected to cause damages in Turkish territory, then the plaintiff would be entitled to initiate a tort claim before the Turkish courts. However, similarly to the jurisdiction of the place of damage, the place where the damage might occur does not seem to

damage occurred and the place of the event giving rise to it, so that the defendant may be sued, at the option of the plaintiff, either in the courts for the place where the damage occurred or in the courts for the place of the event which gives rise to and is at the origin of that damage" (para. 20). The ECJ also stated in this judgment that the place of the harmful event should be understood as important as the place of damage in terms of evidence and conduct of proceedings (para. 21).

[186] Sarıöz (2012), p. 166.

[187] *Sarıöz* makes this interpretation in light of the provisions of 1968 Brussels Convention on jurisdiction and the enforcement of judgments in civil and commercial matters (OJ L 299, 31/12/1972 P. 0032 - 0042), which refers to the place where the harmful event has occurred for jurisdiction in disputes arising out of tort; see Sarıöz (2012), p. 167. With the enactment of Brussels I Recast, however, the interpretation of the place of harmful event has been widened so as to cover both the place of the tortious act and the place of damage. This issue is further analysed herein on the question of jurisdiction in tort claims under Brussels I Recast provisions.

[188] Sarıöz (2012), p. 171.

offer viable grounds for FDL claims, as this rule would address the courts of the host country, rather than those of the home country.

In Turkish legal doctrine it is accepted that in cases of transboundary torts, where the place of tort is different from the place of damage, courts in both of these places would be deemed to have international jurisdiction and the plaintiff would have the discretion to choose one of these.[189] In fact, in those cases where a tortious act is committed in a foreign country, while the damage has occurred in Turkey, the Turkish courts would be able to assume jurisdiction in this case.[190]

The third alternative jurisdiction for tort claims is set as the plaintiff's place of residence. However, despite its clear advantage to the plaintiff under normal circumstances,[191] this rule is criticised as positioning the plaintiff as the weaker party against the defendant, and does not justify departing from the general rule of jurisdiction under Article 6 of the Law No. 6100, which addresses the defendant's place of residence.[192] Moreover, according to one opinion, this rule might be deemed *ex orbitant* in the recognition and enforcement stage before a foreign court and thus might lead to the rejection of recognition and enforcement claim.[193] Under any circumstances, it is worth noting that the alternative to filing the lawsuit at the courts of the victim's place of residence would not abrogate the general rule of jurisdiction of the defendant's place of residence; hence the plaintiff will also be able to initiate legal action at the defendant's residence.[194] The reason for this is that the rule on jurisdiction in tort claims is not an exclusive rule and does not concern public policy.[195] Therefore, it would remain the choice of the plaintiff to file the lawsuit at his/her own place of residence, at the place of tort or at the defendant's place of residence. Finally, the alternative of the victim's residence courts is not very useful in FDL claims, as it goes against the main purpose of these actions, which is to hear the case before the more developed home country's courts.

It is also important to emphasise that the general rule of jurisdiction, the place of the defendant's residence, is also available as the rule for tort claims does not concern public policy, nor does it confer an exclusive jurisdiction and in principle the special rule of jurisdiction does not abrogate the general rule.[196] Therefore, the

[189] Nomer (2015), p. 94.

[190] Sarıöz (2012), p. 167.

[191] The possibility to initiate the lawsuit before the courts of the plaintiff's place of residence is considered to be less burdensome for the plaintiff compared to the defendant's place of residence (see Özel 2012, p. 31).

[192] Çelikel and Erdem (2020), pp. 577–578.

[193] Şanlı et al. (2018), p. 388, fn. 114; Demirkan (2013), p. 224; Özel (2012), p. 34.

[194] Doğan (2020), p. 66.

[195] Albayrak and Mavzer (2019), p. 292; Kuru (2001), p. 486.

[196] Çelikel and Erdem (2020), p. 570; Kuru (2001), p. 486. See also Turkish Court of Appeal 4th Civil Chamber decision dated 24.04.1967 and numbered 4033/3760, whereby it was held that the jurisdiction rule in tort claims (under Art. 21 of the former Civil Procedural Code) does not confer an exclusive jurisdiction, but rather it constitutes a secondary rule, and therefore, it does not lift the jurisdiction of the courts of the place of the defendant's residence. Turkish Court of Appeal 20th

special rules of jurisdiction offer alternatives to the plaintiff in addition to the jurisdiction addressed under the general rule. Accordingly, plaintiffs in FDL claims should be able to claim the jurisdiction of the home country's courts, as this is where the defendant parent company resides.

5.1.2.3 Jurisdiction in Specific Claims Concerning Corporate Groups Under Turkish Law

Turkish law carries a specific provision concerning lawsuits initiated against a parent company for its alleged misuse of the subsidiary's resources, which introduces a new competent court for the international jurisdiction of Turkish courts with the reference of Article 40/1 of PIPC.[197] Article 202/1(e) of TCC stipulates that the claims made under this article by the shareholders and/or creditors of the Turkish subsidiary against the parent company for its failure to rectify the damages suffered by the subsidiary can be initiated before the courts of the place where the subsidiary is established in Turkey, in cases where the parent is located outside of Turkey. This is seen as an innovative regulation, considering that it allows MNCs to be sued in a single jurisdiction, provided that a subsidiary is domiciled there.[198] In this way, claims concerning the liability of the foreign parent company can be successfully brought before Turkish courts, provided that the subsidiary is located in Turkey. This is interpreted as a provision similar to the ATS, which also addresses the international jurisdiction of US courts in tort claims concerning violations of US laws or international law initiated by non-US citizens under certain circumstances.[199]

Turkish Court of Appeal has made it clear that this provision does not constitute a special jurisdiction rule, and hence it does not precede the general rule on jurisdiction under Article 6 of Turkish Civil Procedure Law No. 6100 (i.e. the defendant's place of residence).[200] The same judgment also stipulates that as Article 202/1(e) strictly regulates alternative jurisdiction in lawsuits based on Article 202/1 of TCC, there is no room for adapting this rule to other cases concerning corporate groups. Having

---

Civil Chamber has settled precedents where it held that the special jurisdiction rule in tort claims does not abrogate the general rule of jurisdiction, as it does not constitute an exclusive rule of jurisdiction, and that the plaintiffs are entitled to choose in between the alternative jurisdictions; see decision numbered 2016/3672E. 2016/5923K. and dated 30.05.2016, the decision numbered 2016/3857E. 2016/6766K. and dated 13.06.2016, the decision numbered 2015/9603E. 2015/9990K. and dated 22.10.2015, the decision numbered 2015/3153E. 2015/10737K. and dated 05.11.2015. It should be noted that the mentioned decisions concern domestic disputes, rather than international ones with a foreign element, but these rules are also applicable in international disputes with the reference of Article 40 of PIPC (Çelikel and Erdem 2020, p. 570).

[197] Tekinalp (2013), p. 557.

[198] Eroğlu (2008b), p. 262.

[199] Anker-Sorensen (2014), p. 22.

[200] Turkish Court of Appeal, 11th Civil Chamber decision numbered 2016/551 K. 2016/1281 and dated 10.2.2016.

said that, the provision concerning groups of companies with full dominance[201] (Art. 206) clearly states that the compensation claims under Article 206/1 in full dominance cases would be subject to Article 202/1(e), which creates a dilemma in view of the mentioned judgment of the Turkish Court of Appeal.

Under any circumstances, Article 202/1 of TCC refers to cases where the board of the parent company breaches its duty of care towards the subsidiary; in other words, it shifts the board liability from the subsidiary level to the parent company level.[202] Therefore, it might be beyond the bounds of possibility to include claims from involuntary creditors (including FDL claimants) within the scope of this article. In fact, the provision exemplifies situations for the parent company's liability to compensate the subsidiary in respect of creditor claims, which all seem to cover voluntary creditors, i.e. the commercial counterparties.

Moreover, the parent company liability regulated in this article is not against the creditors, but against the subsidiary, although the creditors are permitted to make a claim in this respect. Hence, in the unlikely case that the involuntary creditors do initiate legal action against the parent for the restitution of the losses suffered by the subsidiary (so that eventually they would be receiving the alleged compensation from the subsidiary), the claims against the parent would still not cover the claims for compensation for the breach of duty of care; it would concern the parent's liability under Article 202/1 of the TCC, which refers to an exercise of control by the parent over its subsidiary to the detriment of the subsidiary. Therefore, it seems that this provision does not grant suitable legal grounds for the claims of involuntary creditors in multinational tort claims.

5.1.2.4 Choice of Jurisdiction Amongst the Parties to a Tort Claim

Turkish law allows the choice of a foreign court jurisdiction amongst the parties to a claim that bears a foreign element, unless it falls within the scope of exclusive jurisdiction[203] (Art. 47/1 PIPC). The choice of jurisdiction needs to concern a dispute with a foreign element (e.g. nationality or residence of a party, place

[201] Under Turkish law, full dominance is defined as direct or indirect ownership of %100 of the shares or the voting rights of a company (Art. 203 of TCC).

[202] Okutan Nilsson (2011), p. 96.

[203] Exclusive jurisdiction concerns whether Turkish courts are vested with exclusive jurisdiction in terms of private international law, which may be understood from a teleological interpretation of the relevant provision concerning jurisdiction (Doğan 2020, p. 79). Turkish Court of Appeal too has expressed in its judgments that exclusive jurisdiction may be understood from the purpose and wording of the relevant provision and the characteristics of disputes with a foreign element (20th Civil Chamber, 2018/5596E. 2018/7557K. and dated 26.11.2018, 18th Civil Chamber, 2013/19774E. 2014/6261K. and dated 07.04.2014).

where the tortious act is committed), which arose from a relationship of obligation such as a tort liability or contract,[204] and it should be made in writing.[205]

The parties may decide on the choice of jurisdiction by entering into an agreement or by inserting a clause into an agreement. The relevant provision does not provide any limitations as to the method of choice of jurisdiction, as long as this is made in writing. It is worth noting that the condition of having the choice of jurisdiction in writing is not a condition of validity, but rather a condition of proof.[206] Therefore, the choice of jurisdiction shall be taken into consideration only when it is proven in writing. This is also evident from the clear wording of Article 47 of PIPC.

It is important to assess whether any choice of foreign court jurisdiction amongst the parties, made in line with the requirements, would abrogate the jurisdiction of Turkish courts. In light of the clear wording of the relevant provision, the jurisdiction agreed upon by the parties is considered exclusive, thus abrogating any jurisdiction of the Turkish courts, unless the foreign court rejects jurisdiction.[207] In the event that a choice of jurisdiction is made between the parties in a form satisfactory to the requirements under Article 47 of PIPC, whereby a foreign court has been authorised, then the Turkish court that has international jurisdiction to hear the case shall decide that it has no jurisdiction in the relevant case.[208] However, it is required that the defendant raises an objection concerning the choice of jurisdiction, otherwise, the Turkish court will be seen to have jurisdiction.

Under Turkish law, it is accepted that the agreement on the choice of jurisdiction should not contravene Turkish public policy. According to the Turkish Court of Appeal's landmark judgment on this matter, "*The agreement on the choice of jurisdiction should not fall against public policy and should not hinder the country's public policy. Events that severely hinder and fall against rules of morals and good faith, fundamental principles and values of the society and law, as well as the*

---

[204] Accordingly, it is not possible to agree on a choice of jurisdiction for disputes that fall outside the scope of obligation relations, such as, for instance, family law related issues, inheritance law, rights in rem. Under Turkish law, obligation relations arise in contract, tort, unjust enrichment and negotiorum gestio. See Çelikel and Erdem (2020), p. 639; Doğan (2020), p. 78.

[205] Süral (2012), p. 192; Demir İskenderoğlu (2008), p. 98.

[206] Çelikel and Erdem (2020), p. 643; Doğan (2020), p. 83.

[207] Çelikel and Erdem (2020), p. 652; Doğan (2020), pp. 85–86. Turkish Court of Appeal also held that a court that acquires jurisdiction by way of a valid agreement, it becomes vested with an exclusive jurisdiction (General Assembly of Civil Chambers, numbered 1998/12-287E. 1998/325K. and dated 06.05.1998). Having said that, as per the exception regulated under Article 47/2 of PIPC, it is not possible to abrogate the jurisdiction of the courts authorized under Articles 44, 45 and 46 of PIPC in disputes concerning employment contracts and relationship, consumer contracts and insurance contracts, which are referred to as contracts with social elements (see Doğan 2020, p. 80).

[208] In this manner, a duly made agreement on the choice of jurisdiction, which authorizes a foreign law in the relevant dispute, shall abrogate the international jurisdiction of Turkish courts (Demir Gökyayla 2011, p. 52). See also Çelikel and Erdem (2020), p. 652.

fundamental rights stipulated in the Constitution violate public policy".[209] In light of this judgment, it is evident that in order to abrogate the international jurisdiction of Turkish courts by way of an agreement on choice of a foreign jurisdiction, the relevant agreement should be valid under Turkish law; otherwise, if the agreement contravenes Turkish public policy, then the jurisdiction of the Turkish courts shall not therefore be abrogated.[210]

In principle, the choice of a foreign jurisdiction might be possible in FDL claims. The relevant article concerning the choice of foreign court jurisdiction does not clearly regulate whether the choice of jurisdiction can be made after the occurrence of the tortious act. In the absence of such a clear stipulation, considering that the choice of foreign court jurisdiction is recognised for tort claims,[211] it might be concluded that this agreement can be reached after the occurrence of the tortious act, where there is no prior relationship existing between the parties. However, the wording "*a dispute arising from an obligation relation*" in Article 47/1 of PIPC is interpreted as a certain dispute arising amongst the parties and, therefore, disputes that might arise in future from relationships of obligation that have not yet been established cannot be made subject to choice of jurisdiction agreements.[212] This interpretation closes the door to agreements on choice of jurisdiction in FDL claims, as it implies that there should be a materialised dispute in order to agree on such a choice.

Even if one were to argue that it might be possible to engage in choice of jurisdiction agreements in FDL claims, considering the nature of these claims – where parent companies of MNCs usually have the power and leverage to impose their choice of jurisdiction on others—it is also worth evaluating what would happen in those cases where the jurisdiction chosen by the parties is not fit for a fair trial. *Demir Gökyayla*, who has assessed this matter in depth, states that Turkish courts should be able to assume jurisdiction in the event that the jurisdiction chosen by the parties is not able to provide a fair trial; this should be evident in terms of several factors such as the lack of separation of powers between the executive and judiciary, potential or factual discrimination against foreign parties, or lack of independence of the judiciary.[213] This issue can be quite crucial in FDL claims. In fact, in these claims, the defendant parent companies usually try to rebut the claims of tort victims by putting forth that the case should have been addressed against the transnational subsidiary before the host country courts. If, at any point, it might have been possible for the parties to agree on a choice of jurisdiction, the parent company would have pushed to agree upon the jurisdiction of the host country. Although this is unlikely to happen in practice, it is nevertheless important to assess the potential impact of such

[209]Turkish Court of Appeal General Assembly of Civil Chambers decision numbered 1998/12-287E. 1998/325K. dated 06.05.1998.

[210]Demir Gökyayla (2011), p. 64.

[211]Nomer (2015), p. 484.

[212]Doğan (2020), p. 81.

[213]Demir Gökyayla (2011), pp. 53–54.

a choice of jurisdiction on FDL claims. It seems from the opinion of *Demir Gökyayla* that if the host country is not able to ensure a fair trial for transnational tort victims for any reason (in this case, it might be the host country's need for foreign investment and the state's alliance with MNCs for this purpose), then the choice of jurisdiction may be disregarded and the court with international jurisdiction may assume jurisdiction.[214]

PIPC regulates the above-named conditions on the choice of jurisdiction of foreign courts, but does not regulate the choice of jurisdiction of Turkish courts. Therefore, based on the general rule under Article 40 of PIPC that Turkish courts' international jurisdiction shall be determined in accordance with the provisions of domestic law, the provisions of Law No. 6100 shall also apply in relation to the choice of jurisdiction of Turkish courts. Having said that, as per Article 17 of Law No. 6100, which regulates choice of jurisdiction, the possibility of agreeing upon the jurisdiction of Turkish courts is granted only to merchants and public legal entities, as the provision allows agreement on choice of jurisdiction only in disputes that have arisen or may potentially arise between public legal entities and/or merchants.[215] Therefore, the aforementioned provision regulating choice of Turkish courts' jurisdiction is not analysed hereunder, given that the victims in an FDL claim are not merchants or acting in the capacity of merchants in these claims.

5.1.2.5 Jurisdiction in Claims Concerning Violation of Personal Rights

Turkish law includes an exceptional rule of jurisdiction concerning claims arising from the violation of personal rights. According to the relevant clause (Art. 25/5 CC), the plaintiff alleging violation of his/her personal rights is entitled to bring the lawsuit before the courts of his/her own residence or the courts of the defendant's residence. This rule does not constitute an exclusive jurisdiction, thus the plaintiff would be free to bring the lawsuit before the courts of the defendant's residence (under general rule of Art. 6 of CPC), or before the courts of the place where the tortious act is committed or where the damage occurred (Art. 16 of CPC), or before the courts of his/her own residence.[216] Therefore, this is a right concerning alternative jurisdiction brought in favour of the victim of personal rights violation.

---

[214] Demir Gökyayla (2011), p. 56. *Demir Gökyayla* also refers to the implications of the availability of a fair trial under Article 6 of the UNDHR, which protects the right to a fair trial, and states that any objective and reasonable suspicion that the courts of the chosen jurisdiction might not provide an independent and impartial trial should justify the right to initiate the relevant case before Turkish courts (Demir Gökyayla 2011, p. 58). It is, in fact, challenging to prove with concrete evidence that a country's courts will not be able to provide fair trial. Therefore, it should be sufficient to put forward objective and reasonable suspicion on this issue, in a way that would create an opinion on the judge (Demir Gökyayla 2011, pp. 67–68).

[215] The main aim of this provision is to protect the weak party in relationships between real persons and merchants or legal entities (the weak party being the real persons); see Kılıçoğlu (2012), p. 190.

[216] Aşit (2017), pp. 480–481.

In the event that the victims of a transnational tort allege violation of their personal rights, this clause under Turkish law could be of important assistance. In cases where the parent company is located outside of Turkey and the claims concern the operations of its Turkish subsidiary, victims can successfully rely on this clause to sue the parent company before the courts of the parent company's place of residence. However, it must be noted that the claim should concern the violation of personal rights, which constitutes a special type of tort, as further explained in the chapter on substantive legal analysis of this study.

5.1.2.6 Forum Non Conveniens

At this point, it would also be relevant to refer to the *forum non conveniens* doctrine, which stipulates that a court may decide to stay proceedings due to lack of jurisdiction if there is a more appropriate jurisdiction for that lawsuit. Thus, in such a case, the court where the lawsuit was first initiated may hold that a court of another jurisdiction would be competent to hear the case, if it were more closely related to the subject matter. In the event that the court deems another forum more appropriate, the burden to prove why justice cannot be achieved in that forum shifts onto the claimant.[217]

In order to apply *forum non conveniens*, it is necessary for more than one country's courts to have international jurisdiction to hear the relevant claim.[218] Otherwise, in cases where there is only one country's courts with international jurisdiction, *forum non conveniens* would not be relevant. This doctrine is described by *Ekşi* as a kind of abandonment of their chauvinist attitudes, more in line with international comity.[219]

Several factors are considered in determining whether there is a more appropriate jurisdiction to hear the case. It may be suggested that the proximity to the relevant incident and to evidence is especially important.[220] Other factors that may be considered in this respect are the enforceability of the court decision, the reasonable duration of the legal procedures, as well as legal costs and legal aid.[221]

---

[217] Meeran (1999), p. 162.

[218] Ekşi (1994), p. 71.

[219] Ekşi (1994), p. 74.

[220] Nomer (2015), p. 489.

[221] It might be worth noting the situation of legal aid and conditional fee agreements for lawyers under Turkish law. In fact, as per Article 163 of the Lawyers Act in Turkey, lawyers' agreements should refer to a monetary amount or value in return for the legal service provided by the lawyer. Turkish Court of Appeal in its General Assembly of Joint Chambers' decision (numbered 2017/6E. 2018/9K. and dated 05.10.2018) defines the lawyers' agreement as "*a synallagmatic agreement executed by and between the lawyer and the client, whereby the lawyer undertakes to provide legal service and the client, in principle, undertakes to make the payment of the fee in return for the legal service*". The decision also states, in light of the relevant provisions of the Lawyers Act, that a lawyers' agreement should include a certain monetary value as lawyer's fee, as this is a mandatory

It may be suggested that the majority of *forum non conveniens* claims and courts' decisions on lack of jurisdiction appear in litigation concerning the involuntary creditors, i.e. tort victims, rather than voluntary creditors in commercial disputes. This stems from the fact that there is generally an agreement between commercial parties that would determine the authorised jurisdiction, whereas this is not the case for tort victims and, therefore, it may occur more often that the defendants claim *forum non conveniens* and/or the courts reject jurisdiction on this basis.[222]

This doctrine might be seen as an incentive for MNCs to engage in a complex corporate organisational structure with their transnational subsidiaries. However, what should also be carefully considered is how it would be possible to apply the *forum non conveniens* doctrine in an FDL case with complex decision-making structures involved. For instance, although the damages arising from the mining activities of a transnational subsidiary occurred in the host country, the decision to operate the mine and the financing of the project were probably taken in the home country, at the headquarters of the parent company. Thus it might be difficult for the defendant parent company to claim that the host country's courts are the right courts to hear the case. Therefore, the complex structures of MNCs, especially their decision-making mechanisms, might be deemed to render the *forum non conveniens* doctrine ineffective and not practically applicable.[223]

In terms of Turkish law, as the international jurisdiction is determined by exercising standard reference rules under the relevant legislation, *forum non conveniens* is often considered to be incompatible with it.[224] The application of this doctrine is also seen to violate Article 36 of the Turkish Constitution, which

---

element thereof. Furthermore, as per Article 164 of the Lawyers Act, it is not possible to determine a legal fee below the minimum fees set every year by the Turkish Bar Association. In the event that a legal service is given without legal fee, the issue will be notified to the bar association board and a legal fee will be determined between the amount of 10–20% of the value of the claim on the date of the finalization of the relevant court order or, in case the claim's value cannot be put in monetary terms, the legal fee will be determined according to the minimum fee tariff set by the Turkish Bar Association. Therefore, Turkish law does not allow for conditional fee agreements for lawyers. On the other hand, legal aid is regulated under Turkish law. As per Article 176 of the Lawyers Act, legal aid concerns the provision of legal services to those who cannot afford lawyers' fees, as well as other legal costs and expenses. As per Article 334 of CPC, individuals who cannot wholly or partially afford the legal costs and expenses, without significantly risking theirs and their family's living, are entitled to request legal aid on the condition that their claims are not clearly groundless. Foreigners are also entitled to benefit from legal aid, subject to the condition of reciprocity. Although legal aid is regulated and as a benefit for those who satisfy the sought conditions, there are also criticisms on its well-functioning in practice. In the opinion of *Elveriş/Kutucu/Yaşar*, the appointment of lawyers in legal aid cases is not subject to transparent and objective terms, and the bar association's monitoring on the lawyers' services remain unsatisfactory as the bar association has no authority to effectively monitor performance or to apply disciplinary sanctions on lawyers. The insufficient budget allocated for legal aid is also considered as a problem in legal aid system in Turkey. See Elveriş et al. (2005), pp. 48–49, 51.

[222] Eroğlu (2008a), p. 104.

[223] Eroğlu (2008a), p. 119.

[224] Nomer (2015), p. 119.

stipulates that the Turkish courts cannot refrain from hearing lawsuits that fall within their authority and jurisdiction.[225] Furthermore, according to one opinion in Turkish legal doctrine, the main purpose of *forum non conveniens* is to delimit the vast jurisdictional authorities of the courts in the Anglo-American judicial system, such as the assumption of jurisdiction in the case of service of the claim petition to the defendant even in cases where the defendant was only temporarily present within their jurisdiction.[226]

According to a Turkish Court of Appeal decision, the parties to the lawsuit who had ceased all connections with Germany at the time of World War II could not possibly initiate legal action in Germany, and therefore Turkish courts should assume jurisdiction.[227] However, it is suggested that *forum non conveniens* should be strictly applied, so as to refer to cases with a *force majeure* or public policy only, and in the event that Turkish courts assumed jurisdiction, where there was no sufficient connection with Turkey, this should be deemed an exercise of exorbitant jurisdiction.[228]

5.1.2.7 Forum Necessitatis

Another relevant doctrine relating to the jurisdictional analysis of FDL claims is *forum necessitatis*, which is mostly used in civil law jurisdictions and which says that even in cases where none of the conditions required for an authorised jurisdiction are present, if there is no other adequate jurisdiction because of an impossible or unreasonable situation, the relevant case can be heard before the court where it was initiated. Accordingly, the courts shall accept jurisdiction and hear the relevant case, provided that the case is connected to the forum where the plaintiff is seeking to initiate legal action and that there are unsurmountable obstacles preventing the lawsuit from being initiated in another country.[229]

The above-mentioned impossibility can be practical, such as the legal infrastructure being inaccessible, or legal, such as the claim being non-justiciable in the forum that would otherwise have jurisdiction.[230] Unreasonableness, on the other hand, refers to non-legal or practical difficulties hindering the possibility of initiating legal action in a foreign forum, such as a state of war or other types of ongoing violence affecting the legal system or making it unsafe to travel there in order to initiate legal action.[231] As there are no clear definitions of 'impossibility' or 'unreasonableness'

[225] Şanlı et al. (2018), p. 369.

[226] Nomer (2015), p. 490.

[227] Turkish Court of Appeal 2nd Civil Chamber, E. 37, K. 1922, 06.04.1945.

[228] Şanlı et al. (2018), p. 373.

[229] Weber and Baisch (2016), p. 683.

[230] Roorda and Ryngaert (2016), p. 794; Nwapi (2014), p. 35.

[231] Nwapi (2014), p. 36.

within the scope of the *forum necessitatis* doctrine, the examples are not exhaustive and different interpretations are always possible from case to case.

The doctrine of *forum necessitatis* has a crucial role to play in FDL cases. In fact, the plaintiffs in these cases may from time to time face difficulties, oppression or even physical violence because of their intention to initiate legal action against MNCs operating in their countries. Also, in the majority of cases, the plaintiffs cannot even access a judicial system that would provide an effective remedy. Many developing or least developed countries that are in the position of a host country tend to want to protect foreign investments and thus might even act against FDL claims. The doctrine of *forum necessitatis* is, therefore, seen as a 'safety valve' that ensures access to justice, which would otherwise not have been possible in many cases.[232]

As for Turkish law, there are no specific provisions that would require Turkish courts to assume jurisdiction in cases where it is impossible to hear the case before any other country's courts. The need for a Turkish court to assume jurisdiction as *forum necessitatis* usually arises in cases where a foreign court was authorised by a choice of jurisdiction agreement between the parties, but where initiating proceedings before such a foreign court then become impossible.[233] It is accepted in Turkish legal doctrine that in cases where there is no other competent jurisdiction, Turkish courts can assume jurisdiction due to the presence of a *force majeure* (a legal or practical impossibility) or for reasons of public policy.[234] However, it is also stated that the Turkish courts' assumption of jurisdiction in this way would be limited to those cases where foreign plaintiffs cannot initiate legal action before foreign courts due to any cause connected to the Turkish authorities and should be assessed on a case-by-case basis.[235]

5.1.3 Interim Conclusion on Place of Jurisdiction in FDL Claims

In light of the foregoing analysis on Turkish private international law, EU acquis, ATS and the relevant case law, it is possible to determine the advantages and disadvantages of these regulations for FDL claims.

First of all, it seems crucial to engage in the substantive legal analysis in order to assess the private international legal aspects of the case. In fact, in order to be able to comment on what would be deemed the place of tort or the place of damage, it should firstly be assessed what the tortious act and the damage would be in the relevant case. This point is one of the most challenging ones in FDL cases. While the plaintiffs contend that the tortious act is the parent company's decision or omission

---

[232] Nwapi (2014), p. 29.

[233] Çelikel and Erdem (2020), p. 563.

[234] Çelikel and Erdem (2020), p. 562; Ekşi (1994), p. 177.

[235] Çelikel and Erdem (2020), p. 562; Ekşi (1994), p. 177.

to act in relation its transnational subsidiary, the defendants usually state that the tortious act should be the transnational subsidiary's operation or action, rather than the parent company's action. Based on this reasoning, this study has sought to assess the concept of tort and damage in FDL claims, before moving forward into the analysis of applicable law and jurisdiction.

Once a hopeful resource for human rights defenders, the ATS now seems to have lost its spark. The recent case law shows that the courts do not tend to adopt a liberal interpretation of ATS by keeping the scope wide enough to include claims against foreign corporations. Despite the calls for the Congress to step in and clarify the extraterritoriality issue, the Congress has so far remained silent. According to some, the Congress would find more incentive to step in and provide guidance if the criticised restrictions on the practice of ATS continue to exist, which might ultimately lead the way to the adoption of new legislation that would ensure corporate accountability in MNCs in a clearer context.[236] However, it seems illogical to expect the Congress to decide that foreign victims may commence legal action against US corporations for claims of human rights violations.

In general, following the recent restrictive approach by the US Supreme Court on ATS cases, it seems that the victims of corporate violations may choose to look elsewhere to remedy the damages they suffer, such as general tort law provisions, which may prove to provide better remedy. In fact, tort law provides a wider ground of claim for plaintiffs when compared to the restrictive approach under the ATS, which requires claims to be based on the violation of customary international law.[237]

Another positive side of tort law compared to the ATS is the restrictive application of the doctrine of *forum non conveniens*, which constitutes a significant barrier for plaintiffs. The doctrine of *forum non conveniens* is interpreted differently in various jurisdictions. In the US, it is accepted that only a court which is qualified as a severely inappropriate jurisdiction can reject jurisdiction.[238] Within this context, the court will first check if the alternative jurisdiction is appropriate for the relevant dispute, which is fulfilled by investigating and examining evidence, witness statements and relevant expenses.[239] As evaluated in the relevant section above, recent case law on *forum non conveniens* in the UK shows that the courts are not allowed to decline jurisdiction on the basis that there is a more appropriate jurisdiction in cases where the defendant is residing in an EU member state. This situation constitutes a strong advantage for tort victims against ATS, under which the application of *forum non conveniens* is still adopted. The abandonment of *forum non conveniens* constitutes an advantage for the Brussels I Recast regime over the ATS regime in FDL cases as it might be seen as a way to recovery for the narrower jurisdiction under Brussels I Recast.[240]

[236] Carey (2016), p. 466.

[237] Webb (2013), p. 155.

[238] De Jonge (2011), p. 110.

[239] Zerk (2006), pp. 120–121.

[240] Enneking (2009), pp. 917–918.

There are certain views expressed that Brussels I Recast constitutes the equivalent of the ATS in Europe, as it provides a means for tort claims to be brought against companies domiciled in the EU for their actions outside the EU.[241] However, it can be stated that the scope of application for the Brussels I Recast regime is narrower than the US regime under the ATS. In fact, while Brussels I Recast provides jurisdiction over corporations that are incorporated in an EU member state, the ATS finds it sufficient to have *"continuous and systematic activities"* in the US to accept jurisdiction.[242] Furthermore, the Brussels I Recast regime provides a rather closed system, in the sense that if a claim falls within its scope, the courts can only assume jurisdiction based on this regulation, without applying any domestic laws.[243] Despite all the aforementioned advantages of ATS over Brussels I Recast, the recent case law under ATS seems to have narrowed its scope of application significantly. Therefore, for the time being, it proves to be challenging to draw a conclusion from the comparison of ATS and Brussels I Recast in terms of FDL claims.

On a further note, the wider approach adopted by Brussels I Recast—by regulating that the place of jurisdiction is the place of harmful event, which might include the place of the tortious action or the place of damage—is not compliant with the approach adopted by Rome II, as the general rule on applicable law in tort claims is the law of the place where the damage occurred. Accordingly, the court of the place of tortious action will have jurisdiction, while it might not be allowed to apply its own country's rules, if the damage has occurred in another country, which might create difficulties in legal practice.[244]

Turkish law's position on place of jurisdiction for FDL claims is also quite favourable towards tort victims. The general rule of defendant's residence, which is in line with Brussels I Recast, provides a viable solution for plaintiffs in these cases, as long as the defendant is the parent company. The general rule of jurisdiction in tort claims also provides the alternatives of place of tortious act, place of damage and victim's residence. Amongst these options, the place of tortious act would seem the most beneficial one for tort victims in FDL claims, as long as the tortious act is proven as the parent company's action or omission.

As an interim conclusion, it might be stated that the way forward in FDL claims seems to lie in general tort claims, departing from ATS-based claims, especially in consideration of the most recent case law under the ATS.

[241] Kaeb and Scheffer (2013), pp. 854–855.

[242] Enneking (2009), p. 916.

[243] Roorda and Ryngaert (2016), p. 803.

[244] Huber and Bach (2011), p. 71.

5.2 Applicable Law in FDL Claims: A Comparative Analysis Through Turkish Law and EU Acquis

In FDL claims, it is necessary to determine which law would apply to the dispute. To this end, the relevant EU regulation will be examined, and then followed by the relevant Turkish legislation. As discussed in the previous chapter on substantive legal analysis, and as further assessed under the section on the question of jurisdiction, the legal qualification of FDL claims are to be made under *lex fori*, which would most likely result as tort claims with a foreign element—thus requiring assessment under the tort law provisions of the applicable law determined by private international law provisions. The analysis in this section will focus on the EU regulation that has global application and the relevant Turkish law.

5.2.1 Applicable Law in FDL Claims Under Rome II

Regulation (EC) No 864/2007 on the law applicable to non-contractual obligations[245] (Rome II) is a crucial source for determining the applicable law in FDL claims, especially considering that it has universal application (Art. 3). In other words, Rome II applies not only to non-contractual relations between EU member states, but also to the ones between non-member states, regardless of whether the relevant dispute is linked to any EU member state.[246] Needless to say, Rome II is also important in determining the applicable law in FDL claims where the parent company is located in an EU member state. Hence, to recall a previous scenario, reference is made to the case where the parent company is located in the UK, with a Turkish subsidiary operating a gold mine in Turkey, where the alleged damages occurred.

[245] Regulation (EC) No 864/2007 of the European Parliament and of the Council of 11 July 2007 on the law applicable to non-contractual obligations (Rome II): OJ L 199/40 (31.07.2007). Rome II is applicable to the disputes concerning damages that were occurred as of January 11, 2009, when its substantive provisions have become applicable in EU member states' courts. The aim of Rome II was to harmonize the conflicts of law provisions in different member states concerning non-contractual obligations in civil and commercial matters, which is declared as an autonomous concept considering that there may be different legal interpretations by the member states (para. 11 of the Preamble). Having said that, the meaning of 'non-contractual obligations' for the purposes of Rome II is set out as "*(...) tort/delict, unjust enrichment, negotiorum gestio or culpa in contrahendo*". To this end, consensual obligations (i.e. voluntary undertakings) are considered as contractual, while non-consensual obligations are deemed to form non-contractual obligations within the meaning under Rome II (See Scott 2009, p. 66). From this aspect, it is clear that FDL claims that are claims addressed by involuntary creditors (tort victims) against parent companies of MNCs would be within the scope of Rome II.

[246] Tarman (2008), p. 198.

5.2.1.1 General Principle of Applicable Law in Tort Claims Under Rome II

The law applicable to disputes concerning torts is regulated under Chapter II of Rome II. Article 4/1 sets the general principle as the law of the country where the damage has occurred (*lex loci damni*). Hence Rome II does not adopt the general rule of the law of the place where the tort is committed (*lex loci delicti commissi*). In the preamble of Rome II (paras. 15–18), it is stated that the rule of *lex loci delicti commissi*, which is adopted by many EU member states, fails to provide a unified practice, thus giving rise to legal uncertainty.[247] For this purpose, *lex loci damni* is found to provide a clearer and more stable basis for applicable law, as the place where the damage has occurred is usually clear, i.e. where the injury was suffered, the property was damaged etc. In fact, the place of damage refers to the place where the direct damage resulting from the tortious act has occurred.[248] It is also stated in the preamble of Rome II (para. 16) that this principle strikes a balance between the interests of the tortfeasor and the victim, in that adopting the place where the tort is committed would be in the tortfeasor's favour, while the domicile of the victim would clearly be in the victim's favour.

The general rule of *lex loci damni* under Rome II is applicable also to transboundary torts,[249] where the damage occurs in a different country to the place where the event giving rise to the damage took place. As the rule of *lex loci damni* accepted under Rome II adopts a strict approach, in determining the place of damage, no consideration will be given to the place of the tortious act or the place where indirect or potential damages arise.[250] Accordingly, the law of the place of damage shall be applicable to tort claims, including transboundary ones, that fall within the scope of Rome II. However, the acceptance of *lex loci damni* in tort claims would abrogate the benefits expected by FDL claims. It is difficult to argue that *lex loci damni* would be the home country, instead of the host country, as the damages incurred by the victims of FDL claims take place in the host country. For instance, in the scenario previously used, people living in the vicinities of the gold mine operated by S suffered health damages. In this case, the place of the damage would be the host country and accordingly, at first glance, the applicable law would also be the host country's law. Based on this scenario, it is possible to state that the general rule of applicable law under Rome II is not favourable to the plaintiffs of FDL claims. Arguing that in cases where a damage has occurred in the host country due to an act or omission of the parent company in the home country (e.g. a breach of duty of care), then the event giving rise to the damage will have occurred in the home

---

[247] The rule of *lex loci delicti commissi* is also considered to be rather incidental and difficult to determine in most cases, which supports the shift towards the rule of *lex loci damni* (Öztekin Gelgel 2006, p. 96).

[248] Çelikel and Erdem (2020), p. 467.

[249] Enneking (2012), p. 214.

[250] Öztekin Gelgel (2006), p. 100.

country and that home country law would be applicable as *lex loci damni* would blur the difference between *lex loci damni* and *lex loci delicti commissi*, and goes against the clear purpose of Rome II in preferring *lex loci damni* as the general rule in tort claims. Moreover, it is difficult to successfully argue that the mere existence of a negligence or omission by the parent company in monitoring or supervising its transnational subsidiary would justify applying the *lex loci delicti commissi*, as the clear preference of Article 4/1 of Rome II is *lex loci damni.*[251] Based on this analysis, in my opinion, this rule does not provide sufficient grounds to accommodate FDL claims.

For this reason, revising Rome II would be a significant option in terms of providing efficient legal grounds for FDL claims. Although *lex loci damni* may be proven to be advantageous to the victims of traditional tort cases, as the place of damage is usually the place of the victim's residence and they are familiar with the law, the situation is quite the opposite with FDL claims. Therefore, an additional provision on the general rule of applicable law might be regulated, stating that the home country's laws (as *lex loci delicti commissi*) may be chosen as the applicable law by the plaintiff, provided that a link is proven between the harmful event and the parent company.[252] It is, in fact, quite reasonable to subject the parent company to the laws of the country where it is seated, as the parent company in such a case would not be able to claim that it has no knowledge of the relevant law, which already regulates its activities.[253]

Having said that, the general rule on applicable law under Article 4/1 is only applicable if (i) the parties have not agreed upon the choice of applicable law, (ii) the special rules under Articles 5–9 are not applicable, (iii) the places of residence of the parties are not in the same country, and/or (iv) a more closely connected law cannot be found.[254]

5.2.1.2 Choice of Applicable Law Amongst the Parties to a Tort Claim

Rome II regulates the choice of law as the general rule and the first degree *renvoi* for applicable law in tort claims.[255] Therefore, this law would be applied primarily and the other rules of reference would no longer be exercised, except the overriding mandatory provisions of the law of forum (addressed in Art. 16).[256] The parties may freely negotiate and choose the applicable law by way of either (i) reaching an

---

[251] Van Den Eeckhout (2017), p. 51.

[252] Kessedjian (2017), p. 149.

[253] Kessedjian (2017), p. 150.

[254] Huber and Bach (2011), p. 70.

[255] Çelikel and Erdem (2020), p. 467; Öztekin Gelgel (2006), pp. 115, 233. In fact, the law chosen as applicable by the parties is considered as the most closely conntected law (Öztekin Gelgel 2006, p. 117).

[256] Huber and Bach (2011), p. 3133; Öztekin Gelgel (2006), p. 116.

agreement after the occurrence of the harmful event (*ex post*), or (ii) if they are business parties pursuing commercial activity, by reaching an agreement even before the occurrence of the harmful event (*ex ante*) (Art. 14). The parties are free to make the choice of law either expressed or implied, to the extent that it is clearly understood without any doubt (*"demonstrated with reasonable certainty by the circumstances"*). There are no restrictions concerning which law to choose, thus the parties may as well agree upon a neutral third country's law.[257] This rule is described as a modern approach that favours party autonomy in non-contractual obligations, which would support legal certainty and foreseeability in terms of applicable law.[258]

Clearly, in FDL claims, the second option where the parties are involved in commercial activity would not be applicable, as the victims are mostly real persons who might not be involved in commercial activity. Therefore, the only option remains the first one, which is to reach an agreement after the occurrence of the harmful event. For the purposes of FDL claims, it seems unlikely that such an agreement will be reached in the first place, as the parties' preference of laws would be different.[259] Even if an agreement is reached, this would result in favouring MNCs in practice, considering the difference of power and leverage the parties possess. Having said that, it is worth noting that this option is legally available.

5.2.1.3 The Exception of Common Residence

Article 4/2 of Rome II brings an exception to the general rule of *lex loci damni* in torts. Accordingly, the law of the country where both parties have their habitual residence at the time of the damage shall be applied in tort disputes (principle of common residence). In such a case, the law of the place where the damage has occurred will no longer be relevant in determining the applicable law.

The term of 'habitual residence' for companies and other legal entites within the meaning of this provision is defined as the 'place of central administration' (Art. 23/1 (1) of Rome II).[260] However, if the damaging incident is related to the operation of a branch, agency or other establishment, then the place where the relevant branch, agency or establishment is located would be treated as the habitual residence (Art. 23/1(2) of Rome II).

---

[257] Graziano (2009), p. 118.

[258] Graziano (2009), p. 114, 131.

[259] See also *Enneking*, who states that in FDL cases it is unlikely for the parties to reach an agreement on applicable law especially when causes such as the level of protection of the victims and the level of damages vary under the law applicable to the case; Enneking (2012), p. 215.

[260] Under Turkish law it is generally not recognised that legal entities might have a 'habitual residence', as this concept is deemed to refer to real persons only. It is, however, pointed out that should the concept be accepted also for legal entities, then the place of de facto management, where the administrative operations are carried out, should be considered as the 'habitual residence' of a legal entity. See Arslan (2012), p. 143.

First of all, considering that FDL claims are filed against parent companies residing in home countries and the victims reside in the host countries where the subsidiaries operate, this exception does not seem particularly relevant. However, it might still pose a danger to the plaintiffs. In fact, the defendant parent company might argue that the damages relate to the operations of its subsidiary, which is located in the host country, and that the exception of common residence should be applied in light of Art. 23/1(2) of Rome II. Therefore, this exceptional rule would also not be suitable for the claims brought by FDL plaintiffs.

5.2.1.4 The Exception of the More Closely Connected Law

Article 4/3 of Rome II brings another exception to applicable law in tort claims. In cases where the incident is more closely connected to another country, the relevant country's law shall apply. It is stated in the Preamble (para. 18) that this provision should be understood as an 'escape clause' from Articles 4/1 and 4/2, *"where it is clear from all the circumstances of the case that the tort/delict is manifestly more closely connected with another country"*.

According to the Explanatory Memorandum on Rome II,[261] this exception refers to cases where there is a pre-existing relationship between the parties, which might justify not following the general rule. As it is stipulated under the Explanatory Memorandum, the discretion to adopt this exception or to follow the general rule rests with the court, depending on the court's impression of whether the pre-existing relationship between the parties constitutes a manifestly closer connection. Hence, in the event that the court deems a third country's law more closely connected to the relevant tort, it might completely disregard the law applicable under the general rule of *lex loci damni* (and also the law of common residence, if relevant) and apply the more closely connected law.[262] Considering that this is an exception to the general rule and an escape clause, regarding also the general aim of Rome II of providing certainty and predictability on applicable law, it is important that it is applied restrictively.[263]

The concept of 'close connection' is not clearly defined under Rome II. There may be several factors to take into account in this respect: (1) a connection between the parties, such as common residence or being parties to a contract; (2) a connection with the relevant tort, such as the harmful event and the damage occurred; and (3) other connections such as the country where the parties are insured.[264] It is also

[261] Proposal for a Regulation of the European Parliament and the Council on the Law Applicable to Non-Contractual Obligations, Explanatory Memorandum, Brussels, 22.7.2003 COM(2003) 427 final 2003/0168 (COD), https://eur-lex.europa.eu/LexUriServ/LexUriServ.do?uri=COM:2003:0427:FIN:EN:PDF.

[262] Öztekin Gelgel (2006), p. 105.

[263] Huber and Bach (2011), p. 99; Enneking (2012), pp. 215–216; Van Den Eeckhout (2017), p. 52.

[264] Fentiman (2009), pp. 98–99.

important to note that this rule in no way suggests that the primarily applicable law should be weakly connected to the relevant tort.[265] In other words, although the primary law has a certain connection with the relevant tort, if there is another law with a more manifest connection, then the latter shall apply.

At first glance, it seems difficult to link this exception to FDL claims, considering that these claims do not usually present a pre-existing relationship between the parties.[266] Therefore, it might be difficult to retract a manifestly closer connection with another country based on a pre-existing relationship. The connection based on the parties' common residence would also not work in FDL claims, as the victims and the parent company reside in different countries.

On the other hand, it might be possible to argue that a closer connection exists with the home country, as the relevant country has a connection with the harmful event that gave rise to the damage. For instance, in the event that the violation and damage have arisen due to a lack of supervision, an omission or an action by the parent company, then it might be argued that the law of the country where the parent is domiciled could be deemed as the manifestly connected one.[267] In fact, this approach leads to the law of the country where the tortious act is committed, i.e. in this case, where the parent company has taken an action or decision, or it has failed to do so while it was legally obliged. This is suggested by way of a teleological interpretation of the exception under Article 4/3 of Rome II for the purpose of providing some protection to the victim, by giving the victim the alternative to choose between the law of the place of damage and the law of the tortious act.[268] The opposite opinion, on the other hand, suggests that such a teleological interpretation of this clause would be against the conscious legislative preference that opted for the choice of applicable law under Article 14 and for the victim's unilateral right to choose the applicable law under Article 7.[269] It is, in fact, challenging to draw a straightforward conclusion on the interpretation of Article 4/3 of Rome II. It would be required to interpret the relevant obligation of monitoring or surveillance imposed on the parent company by the relevant domestic laws in order to decide whether the relevant domestic law could be deemed the manifestly more closely connected law in that specific case. *Palombo* refers to the duty of vigilance under French law and stipulates that it would be difficult to argue that French law would be considered more closely connected to an extraterritorial tort rather than the host country solely based on the parent company's obligation of due diligence.[270] In light of all these opinions, I still believe that, although argumentative, this exception might be used by the plaintiffs of an FDL claim as grounds to base their claims on

[265] Fentiman (2009), p. 109.

[266] Enneking (2012), p. 215.

[267] van Dam (2015), p. 489; van Dam (2011), p. 231; Enneking (2008), p. 300; Weller and Thomale (2017), p. 524.

[268] Thomale and Hübner (2017), p. 391.

[269] Mansel (2018), p. 457.

[270] Palombo (2019), p. 480.

under the home country's laws, given that there is no clear stipulation under Rome II in this respect and thus a case-by-case analysis will in any case be adopted.

5.2.1.5 The Exceptions of Public Policy and Overriding Mandatory Rules

Rome II regulates a rule of exception in cases where the applicable law is not in line with the public policy of the forum. Accordingly, if the applicable law determined as per the Rome II provisions contravenes the public policy of the relevant forum, then the application of this law may be refused (Art. 26).

Rome II also recognises 'Overriding Mandatory Provisions' (Art. 16). As per this article, the rules that are of a mandatory nature in the law of the forum, which are applicable to the non-contractual obligation, cannot be restricted by the application of Rome II provisions. These mandatory provisions are deemed the provisions of domestic law which provide mandatory compliance for the protection of political, social or economic order of the member state.[271] For this reason, it is not possible to exclude or modify these provisions by contract. In cases of tort claims too, it will not be possible to exclude the overriding mandatory provisions of the most closely connected law by way of choice of law amongst the parties.[272] Overriding mandatory provisions are directly applicable without having regard to the provisions of applicable law resulting from the conflict of laws provisions.[273] This particular feature differentiates overriding mandatory provisions from public policy in legal practice. The concept of public order or public policy may be interpreted differently in different jurisdictions. In fact, the European Court of Justice (ECJ) declared in a past decision that it cannot rule on what is meant by public policy, as this is a national concept, but it can review how this exception is applied by the member state courts.[274] Although no explicit definition of public policy is made under EU law, this concept should be interpreted so as to cover fundamental rights acknowledged by the EU and by the ECHR.[275]

As per Article 17 of Rome II, in cases where the law of the country where the harmful act was committed is not applicable to the relevant dispute, it may still be possible to take into account the rules of safety and conduct of that country, if this is found appropriate for the case at hand. The rules of safety and conduct cover all

[271] van Dam (2015), p. 489; Öztekin Gelgel (2006), p. 248. As per this definition, some examples for overriding mandatory provisions are regulations that concern foreign trade, import-export, foreign exchange, competition, as well as those that concern workers' health and safety, social security, union freedom and protection of cultural assets (Öztekin Gelgel 2006, p. 249).

[272] Yılmaz (2016), p. 3133.

[273] Öztekin Gelgel (2006), p. 248.

[274] Renault v. Maxicar, Case C-38/98 (11 May 2000), [2000] ECR I-02973; Enneking (2008), p. 306.

[275] Tarman (2008), p. 217.

regulations concerning safety and conduct, for instance road safety rules.[276] It is important to note that 'taking into account' should not be deemed the same as 'applying' these rules. Nevertheless, this article allows the higher standards of the home country to be taken into account, even in cases where the law of the host country is applicable, which might be significant in transnational tort claims.[277] In fact, this article paves the way for applying the law of the country where the tortfeasor was under the obligation to act in a certain way, at least in determining whether or not it acted in fault.[278] Depending on the substantive legal assessment of the place where the tort is deemed to have been committed in FDL claims, this article may significantly assist plaintiffs in having the home country's laws applied to the actions of the parent company.

5.2.1.6 Environmental Claims

Rome II regulates a specific rule for the applicable law in respect of environmental damages (Art. 7). This rule, along with others concerning product liability, unfair competition, intellectual property and industrial action, is brought in for cases "*where the general rule does not allow a reasonable balance to be struck between the interests at stake*".[279] Accordingly, a victim of environmental damage may choose to base his/her claim on the law where the damage has occurred (as per Art. 4) or on the law of the place where the event giving rise to the damage has occurred.[280] Considering the nature of environmental damage, which is mostly difficult to determine and with its effects often materialising slowly over time, Rome II has been criticised for not providing any option to choose the law of the place where the damage may eventually occur. Having said that, the law of the place of occurrence of the event giving rise to the damage is considered the most closely connected law in these cases, and therefore, it is deemed sufficiently adequate in terms of environmental claims.[281]

This rule is different from the manifestly more closely connected country exception under Article 4/3, in the sense that it gives the plaintiff the discretion to choose between the two laws, rather than leave it to the court to decide. Therefore, the

---

[276] Preamble para. 34 of Rome II.

[277] Enneking (2008), p. 305.

[278] Huber and Bach (2011), p. 68.

[279] Preamble para. 19 of Rome II.

[280] Moreover, the parties' right to choose the applicable law as per Article 14 of Rome II is reserved, thus the parties will be able to choose the applicable law by way of an agreement entered into after the occurrence of the event giving rise to damage (Art. 14/1(a)). The option to enter into an agreement on choice of applicable law after the occurrence of the event giving rise to damage is granted only for commercial parties and therefore, it will not apply in FDL cases. The exception of the more closely connected law shall also apply in cases where the relevant connection is clear from the circumstances (Öztekin Gelgel 2006, p. 167).

[281] Öztekin Gelgel (2006), p. 170.

provision benefits the claimants who are well-informed of the substantive laws in question, as they are free to choose between two different legal systems.[282] If the parent company's failure to act to prevent the harms caused by its transnational subsidiary's operations is considered as the event giving rise to the damage, then the place where it should have acted might be deemed as the home country.[283] In fact, it might be stated that on the basis of the alternative provided under Article 7, the victims in FDL cases might opt for the law of the home country, where the parent company has its headquarters or where the parent company is obliged to make policy decisions concerning its transnational subsidiaries.[284] For instance, in the case of environmental damage occurring in Turkey due to the activity of a subsidiary pertaining to a corporate group with a parent in the UK, then the victims of this environmental damage may also request that English law be applied to their claims. This alternative provided for victims of environmental damages is seen as increasing the level of environmental protection, as it significantly discourages companies domiciled in a country where the statutory provisions on environmental liability are high from causing pollution in a country where the statutory provisions on environmental liability are low.[285]

This provision of Rome II is considered more favourable than ATS in the US, based upon the reasoning that it takes into account the different legal standards in different countries and gives the victim an opportunity to choose the most favourable one.[286] The main purpose of this rule is said to rely on the 'polluter pays' principle, which is adopted in European environmental law.[287] The environmental damage rule constitutes a significant exception to the general rule of applicable law under Rome II, which is most relevant in FDL claims, as it paves the way for the claimants to seek remedy under the applicable law of the developed home country, even though the damage has occurred in the developing host country.

As per the explicit wording of Article 7, and as also mentioned in the Explanatory Memorandum on Rome II, "*the rule covers both damage to property and persons and damage to the ecology itself, provided it is the result of human activity*".[288] It is also mentioned in the Preamble of Rome II that the term 'environmental damage' should be interpreted as "*adverse change in a natural resource, such as water, land or air, impairment of a function performed by that resource for the benefit of another*

[282] Bogdan (2009), p. 222.

[283] Palombo (2020) p. 65.

[284] Van Den Eeckhout (2017), p. 53. Van Dam states that the parent company should have actively participated in causing the damage occurred due to the activity of its transnational subsidiary (van Dam 2011, pp. 231–232).

[285] Weller and Pato (2018), p. 402, fn. 24; Enneking (2012), p. 216.

[286] Enneking (2009), p. 930.

[287] Enneking (2012), p. 216. *Enneking* also stipulates that the environmental damage rule is based on the fact that the tortfeasor in these cases (e.g. the parent company in home country) obtains an economic benefit from the activities of the subsidiary that lead to environmental damage; Enneking (2012), p. 216.

[288] Explanatory Memorandum on Rome II, p. 19.

natural resource or the public, or impairment of the variability among living organisms".[289] It is also important that the environmental damage affected not individuals but the public in general, as per the definition of environmental damage made in the Recital.[290] In fact, environmental damage in a narrower sense, which refers to those who cause certain damages to property or to person – damages that can be determined – are within the protective scope of Article 7, while damages that result from the deterioration of an ecological system, which affects a whole society rather than individuals and which is difficult, if not impossible, to be calculated in terms of compensation are normally not within the scope of Article 7.[291] However, in the event that this type of ecological damage causes a certain determinable harm to certain individuals living in the region which is under impact, then the damage suffered by the relevant individuals due to the deterioration of ecological system might be claimed under Rome II.[292]

Nuclear damage is kept outside the scope of Rome II by the ruling under Article 1/2(f). The reasoning for such an exception might be linked to the difficulty in determining the extent and amount of damage in most nuclear incidents, as these affect the whole society rather than just a certain number of individuals and hence concern a public law issue rather than a civil law claim. Accordingly, in cases where a nuclear incident caused certain harm to an individual (e.g. bodily injury caused by nuclear waste), the relevant damage—although it might be considered as an environmental damage in the narrow sense which should normally be covered within Rome II—shall not be within the scope as per the clear exception.[293] Therefore, it appears that the aforementioned exception differentiates between the claims for damages by an individual harmed due to a nuclear incident and the claims for damages by an individual who suffered a certain harm due to the deterioration of an ecological system. This outcome seems quite unjust, considering that both the deterioration of an ecological system and nuclear damage generally concern people en masse, rather than individuals, and thus are seen as environmental damage in a broader sense; however, while one of them leaves a door open to claims by individuals, the other one shuts the door on all claims, regardless of whether or not they can be determined or calculated. Nevertheless, in view of the clear rule of exception, it is not possible to adopt a liberal approach regarding nuclear damages, which are set to fall outside the scope of Rome II.

The rule of exception on environmental claims might constitute an effective legal basis for addressing FDL claims under a home country's laws. However, this point would again depend on the interpretation of the concept of the place where the damaging act has occurred. Considering that in FDL claims the damaging act is the parent company's act or omission, the place where this occurs might be

[289] Preamble para. 24 of Rome II.

[290] Bogdan (2009), p. 224.

[291] Öztekin Gelgel (2006), pp. 162–163.

[292] Öztekin Gelgel (2006), p. 163.

[293] Öztekin Gelgel (2006), p. 163.

deemed the administrative centre of the parent company, where the decisions are made. In fact, although the result of the relevant act or omission takes place in the host country, this means that the place of damage is the host country, while the place of the damaging act is the home country. In cases where environmental damage has caused a certain harm but without any direct impact on the victim's being or assets, the place of residence or place of headquarters of the person or entity who has committed the relevant act might be recognised as having the law that is most closely connected to the dispute.[294] In FDL claims, the victims are usually indirectly affected by the parent company's decisions or omissions, which makes it possible to adopt this approach and deem the place of the damaging act to be the home country, and the applicable law to be the home country's laws.

There are also the opposite opinions in legal doctrine, suggesting that the event giving rise to the damage cannot be interpreted merely as the decisions of the parent company, and that this should be understood as the immediate cause of the physical damage that occurs.[295] It is difficult to agree with this opinion, which significantly restricts the scope of FDL in a way that would almost eliminate it entirely. In fact, based on this opinion, the victims in multinational tort claims would not stand a chance of successfully addressing their claims under the laws of the home country where the parent company is located. Against the background of FDL claims concerning serious torts with mass effects, it seems the simplest option to stick with the traditional approach of recognising the event giving rise to the damage as the immediate cause of the relevant physical damage. Another point in support of this opposing opinion would be to consider the environmental damage rule as applicable only to the more classic transboundary damage, such as damage that occurs in a neighbouring country due to river pollution or the explosion of a plant dealing with dangerous substances.[296] This approach would leave out FDL claims, which mostly concern damage occurring in the host country due to an act or omission of environmental policy by a parent company. In fact, these are more sophisticated transboundary tort claims compared to the classic ones. However, even this approach remains groundless, as there is no stipulation in Rome II that would delimit its application to classic transboundary environmental damage, and also as the Rome II adopts a universal application and favours legal certainty.[297] As a matter of fact, determining the place of damage might be challenging in most environmental damage cases, considering that the types of damages are usually quite extensive and ongoing.[298] This feature of environmental damage also justifies the option of leaving the choice of alternative applicable laws to the party suffering the relevant damage. Therefore, in my opinion, the environmental damage rule provides the essential

[294] Öztekin Gelgel (2006), p. 168.

[295] Mansel (2018), p. 461.

[296] Enneking (2012), p. 217.

[297] Enneking (2012), p. 217.

[298] Öztekin Gelgel (2006), p. 158.

grounds for FDL claims, most of which concern environmental damage within the meaning of the relevant article.

On a further note, if the liability of the parent company were to be deemed a secondary liability arising due to the operations of the transnational subsidiary, then Article 15(g) of Rome II might be applicable.[299] According to this provision, the law governing the relevant non-contractual obligation shall also govern liability for the acts of another person. Furthermore, if the liability of the parent company were deemed a form of shareholder liability only, then this would be excluded from the scope of Rome II by the explicit rule under Article 1/2(d).[300] However, I believe that these two options are not available for FDL claims, as these claims concern the primary liability of the parent company, rather than a secondary one, and they are based on tort liability rather than shareholder liability. Therefore, in my opinion, the rule on environmental damages might be used as effective grounds in FDL claims and determine the future of these claims.

5.2.2 Applicable Law in FDL Claims Under Turkish Law

As assessed in the previous chapter on substantive legal analysis, and as also stated in the qualification analysis made under this chapter on the question of jurisdiction, FDL claims concern tort liability. Therefore, the assessments in this section on applicable law for FDL claims are made in light of the applicable law provisions for tort claims under Turkish law.

5.2.2.1 General Principle of Applicable Law in Tort Claims Under Turkish Law

The Turkish Code on Private International and Procedural Law No. 5718[301] (PIPC) regulates the general rule (Art. 34) and special rules (Art. 35-38) applicable to torts bearing a foreign element. Hence the general rule under Article 34 shall apply, unless the tort claims fall within the scope of the special rules under Articles 35-38.[302] These special rules concern the violation of personal rights via press, radio, TV or internet, product liability, unfair competition and prevention of competition, which are not relevant in terms of FDL claims. Therefore, the analysis hereunder is made within the framework of the general rule under Article 34.

[299] Bogdan (2009), p. 229.

[300] Bogdan (2009), p. 230.

[301] Milletlerarası Özel Hukuk ve Usul Hukuku Hakkında Kanun, No. 5718, OJ dated 12.12.2007 and numbered 26728.

[302] The general rule on applicable law shall apply to torts that do not fall within scope of the cases mentioned under Articles 35-38; see Tiryakioğlu (2010), p. 213.

As per the general rule under Article 34/1 of PIPC, to the extent that no choice of law is made under Article 34/5, tort liability will be subject to the laws of the country where the tortious act is committed (*lex loci delicti commissi*).[303] This is, in fact, regarded as the law that is most closely connected to the relevant tortious act.[304] It is considered that the committed tortious act has violated the public order of the country where it has been committed and, therefore, should be subject to sanctions decided under the laws of that same country.[305] Having the law of the country where the tortious act is committed as the applicable law is said to be in line with the interests of the parties and the security of the transaction, and provides legal certainty in terms of the question of applicable law.[306] The tortfeasor would most likely know the laws of the place where it has committed the relevant tortious act and might as well be held liable thereunder.[307]

In those cases where the damage occurs in the same place as the tortious act, it is clear that the laws of the relevant country shall be applicable to the dispute. On the other hand, in the event that the tortious act is committed in a different country to the country where the damage has occurred, then the law of the place of damage (*lex loci damni*) would apply instead of the law of the place where the tortious act was committed (Art. 34/2).[308] Adopting the rule of the place of damage is based on the reasoning that this would be the place where the interests protected by law were harmed.[309]Accordingly, although at first glance the place of the tortious act appears as the general rule, the law of the country where the damage has occurred shall apply primarily.[310] In fact, as *Şanlı/Esen/Ataman-Figanmeşe* correctly point out, there would be no difference in legal terms if the wording of the article were to directly address the law of the country where the damage occurred.[311] Therefore, the

[303]By regulating *lex loci delicti commissi* as the general rule, PIPC departs from the provisions of Rome II, which adopts the general rule of *lex loci damni* in tort claims (Çelikel and Erdem 2020, p. 462).

[304]Çelikel (2010), p. 392; Çelikel and Erdem (2020), p. 461.

[305]Doğan (2020), p. 438; Tekinalp (2009), p. 430.

[306]Tekinalp (2009), p. 430.

[307]Tekinalp (2009), p. 432.

[308]Tiryakioğlu (2010), p. 214.

[309]Tekinalp (2009), p. 432.

[310]Tekinalp (2009), p. 436. It is worth noting that Turkish Court of Appeal has adopted a view conflicting with this approach. In a case concerning a car accident that took place in Turkey, where the plaintiff resided in Germany who was on vacation in Turkey, the Court of Appeal decided that despite the rule under Article 34/1 of PIPC, the damage should have been detected in Germany. The Court of Appeal, in this decision, acknowledged the rule under Article 34/1 of PIPC, which points out to the assessment of damage under Turkish law and before Turkish courts, but has then ruled that the appreciated damage should reflect the real damage incurred which would have been possible to be determined under the circumstances in Germany. See Turkish Court of Appeal, General Assembly of Civil Chambers decision numbered 2014/703 E., 2016/497 K. and dated 06.04.2016.

[311]Şanlı et al. (2018), pp. 310–311.

question of how to determine the place where the damage has occurred becomes important.

In *Nomer*'s opinion, the place where the damage has occurred is the place where the asset that is subject to a right is present at the time of the occurrence of the damage, provided that the damage is a *de facto*, tangible, direct and present damage.[312] *Sarıöz* describes the place of damage as the place where the victim's material or moral interests were effectively violated.[313] This refers to the place where the damage produced material results, namely the place where the direct victim's loss occurred, referring again to the place of direct damage.[314] Hence the place where an indirect, a richocet or a moral damage has occurred as a result of a tortious act would not be deemed the place of damage.[315] This description is also in line with the interpretations of the place of damage made under Rome II, which similarly refers to the place of direct damage, without considering the place of commitment of the tortious act or the place of indirect potential damages.[316] The law of the place of damage is considered more beneficial to both parties since it constitutes an unbiased and objective rule, even if in certain cases it might be completely incidental to them.[317]

The discussions vary in cases of transboundary torts. If, for instance, the toxic waste created by the activities of a transnational subsidiary is carried away by a river or sea to eventually reach other places, then the country where the damage has occurred shall be considered the place where the toxic waste reached, thus where the pollution has occurred. In fact, in such a case, although the act causing the damage is the subsidiary's activity—or in the case of FDL claims, the parent company's breach of duty of care—the place of damage might be considered the place where the pollution has occurred by sea,[318] which results in the host country.

The prevalence of the law of the place of damage over the place of commitment of the tortious act, which is accepted under Turkish law, might seem problematic in terms of FDL claims. To recall, the main purpose of these claims is to have them heard under the law that has sufficiently addressed liability issues and that is able to accommodate FDL claims, which is generally the law of the home country. In typical cases of FDL, it is possible to argue that the tortious act committed by the parent company is the failure to monitor and supervise its transnational subsidiary's health and safety policies, environmental risks or other relevant matters (i.e. the breach of duty of care). This might lead to a consequence where the place the tortious act is

---

312 Nomer (2015), p. 356.

313 Sarıöz (2012), p. 166.

314 Sarıöz (2012), p. 167.

315 Yılmaz (2016), p. 3126.

316 Çelikel and Erdem (2020), p. 467; Öztekin Gelgel (2006), p. 117; Tekinalp (2009), p. 433.

317 Nomer (2015), p. 356.

318 There is an opinion in Turkish legal doctrine that in respect of environmental pollution incidents caused by sea vessels or air vessels, the law of the place where the tortious act is committed shall apply—unless there is a multinational convention on this matter. Nomer (2015), p. 358.

committed happens to be the home country, where the parent company has failed to make adequate decisions at its management body or where it has generally acted negligently in this respect. It would be a success for FDL claimants if the questions on applicable law would be settled at this point. However, the problem arises on considering that the place of damage is different to the place of the tortious act, i.e. while the place of damage is the host country, where the claimants have suffered alleged damages, the place of the tortious act might prove to be the home country. As per the clear preference of the legislator, the place of the damage (i.e. the host country jurisdiction) prevails, which results in potential disappointment for the claimants, who are eventually stuck with their own country's insufficient laws.

On a further note, in torts that concern an act of omission, it is discussed whether the applicable law should be considered the law of the tortfeasor's place of residence or the law that addresses the obligation to act, the generally accepted rule being the latter.[319] In FDL claims, this interpretation might result in having the home country's laws as the applicable law in the relevant dispute. Having said that, in order to be able to reach such a conclusion, the home country's laws should have a specific rule that obliges the parent company to act in a certain manner in relation to the activities of its transnational subsidiary (i.e. a duty of care imposed on the parent company). In the event that this is regulated, it might be possible to argue that the parent company's omission, which is subject to the FDL claim, is regulated under the home country's laws and consequently the law applicable to the dispute should also be the home country's laws. Needless to say, this interpretation requires a thorough substantive legal analysis on the matter.

5.2.2.2 Choice of Applicable Law Amongst the Parties to a Tort Claim

Turkish law allows the parties to a tort claim to choose the applicable law, to the extent that the choice is made explicitly and after the occurrence of the tortious act (Art. 34/5 PIPC). Hence there are two conditions set for the validity of choice of applicable law between the parties to a tort claim: (1) the choice shall be made in explicit form; and (2) the choice shall be made after the occurrence of the tortious act. This is considered as the first degree *renvoi,*[320] taking priority over the law of the place where the tortious act has occurred or the place of damage.[321] In other words, the parties' choice of applicable law shall abrogate all other rules of reference,

[319]Tekinalp (2009), p. 433; Kayık (2011), p. 65; Demirkan (2013), p. 227.

[320]The Turkish corresponding term to 'renvoi' is discussed in legal doctrine, which is divided in between the terms 'atıf' or 'yollama'. Despite these discussions, renvoi is recognized as the application of the conflict of laws principles of foreign law, which is applicable as per the conflict of laws principles of lex fori (Mesci, Barış, Milletlerarası Özel Hukukta Atıf (Renvoi) (Renvoi in Private International Law, Master's Thesis, January 2014, pp. 3–4).

[321]Şanlı et al. (2018), p. 309.

including but not limited to the law with a closer connection, and shall apply to the case together with all its mandatory and complementary provisions.[322]

In legal doctrine, this article is criticised as granting only a limited right, and that in principle the choice of law should also be made before the occurrence of any tortious act.[323] I do not agree with this opinion, on the grounds that it would, first of all, be unpractical, if not impossible, to have an agreement between the parties before the occurrence of the tortious act, in cases where there is no prior relationship between the parties. An *ex post* choice of applicable law is practical and sufficient for tort claims, considering that the legal relationship between the parties to a tort is formed only after the occurrence of damage.[324] If there is a prior relationship, such as a contract, the law of the place of contract might still be applicable, it being the more closely connected law. We therefore believe that any option to allow the choice of law before the occurrence of the tortious act could result to the benefit of the stronger party, who would be in a position to unilaterally dictate its own choice.

As mentioned, for a valid choice of applicable law in tort claims, Turkish law requires the existence of an explicit agreement between the parties (Art. 34/5 PIPC).[325] According to one opinion in Turkish legal doctrine, the term 'explicit' should not be interpreted restrictively here, but the parties' implied choice of law should also be deemed valid in cases where this is clear from the circumstances.[326] Moreover, it has been observed that the parties' implicit choice of law usually results in *lex fori* and that such choice should be accepted as valid.[327] Therefore, in addition to an explicit choice of law made between the parties, if the parties' choice of law can be clearly understood by their actions, such as where the plaintiff has filed his/her claim under a certain law and the defendant has responded to the same under the conditions of the same law, the implicit choice of law might also be accepted.

Besides the two conditions stipulated above, there are no restrictions concerning which law to choose as the applicable law between the parties to a tort claim. Hence the parties are free to decide on any applicable law, regardless of whether this law might have any connection to the tort or not, and the judge is bound to the parties' choice of law.[328] This aspect surely shows that the relevant provision of Turkish law prioritises freedom of contract amongst the parties.

---

[322] Tarman (2010), p. 7, 9.

[323] Nomer (2015), p. 361. *Çelikel/Erdem* compares Article 34/5 of PIPC with Article 14/1 of Rome II, emphasizing that PIPC does not recognize implicit choice of law in tort claims; see Çelikel and Erdem (2020), p. 465. *Tiryakioğlu* also emphasizes that the provision regulating the choice of applicable law in tort claims has a narrower scope than the one concerning contractual relations (Art. 24/1 PIPC); Tiryakioğlu (2010), p. 214.

[324] Tarman (2010), p. 11.

[325] This aspect of Turkish law is different from the implied agreement recognised under Rome II (i.e. "*demonstrated with reasonable certainty by the circumstances of the case*"), which will be assessed further in this chapter.

[326] Doğan (2020), p. 440.

[327] Doğan (2020), p. 440.

[328] Tarman (2010), pp. 13–14.

It is worth noting that in FDL cases, there is normally no pre-existing relationship between the parties (i.e. the parent company and the claimants). Although it might be a relief to know that the parties are entitled to agree upon the applicable law after the occurrence of the tortious act, this option seems rather difficult to achieve in practice. The parties to the FDL claim would most likely reach no agreement on the question of applicable law, considering that this issue is one of the pillars of the claim and the parties would most probably have opposing interests (e.g. with the parent company trying to have the host country's law as the applicable law, and the plaintiffs trying to have the home country's law as the applicable law).

5.2.2.3 The Exception of the More Closely Connected Law

As per Article 34/3 of PIPC, if there is a country that is more closely connected to the relevant tort, then that country's law will apply. Hence, regardless of whether it is the law of the place of the tortious act or the law of the place of damage, if the relevant tort has a closer connection with a third country, then the law of the relevant third country shall be the law applicable to the dispute.[329] The relevant provision does not stipulate any criteria to determine this 'close connection'. Therefore, the courts shall apply the exception of the law of more closely connected country as regulated under Article 34/3 in cases where the objective test provided thereunder is met, by taking into account the interests guarded in private international law, as well as normal life experience.[330] As per the wording of the article (i.e. "shall apply" instead of "might apply"), the judge has no discretionary power in applying the more closely connected country's law; instead this exception has a mandatory application which creates an obligation for the judge.[331] Therefore, in the event that there is a law determined to have a closer connection to the relevant tort act, the aforementioned law shall apply. Having said that, this exception is considered a complementary rule that would be used in support of the main one and thus it shall not be used primarily.[332]

Common nationality or common place of residence of the parties to the tort claim or the country of *lex fori* are considered as laws that might be most closely connected.[333] For work accidents, the law of the usual work place may also qualify as the more closely connected law.[334]

---

[329] Doğan (2020), p. 439. On the other hand, *Erdem/Çelikel* state that the exception of the more closely connected law does not result in a complete abandonment of the rule of the place of damage and the place of tortious act; see Çelikel and Erdem (2020), pp. 463–464.

[330] Doğan (2020), p. 439.

[331] Çelikel (2010), p. 393; Çelikel and Erdem (2020), p. 464; Tiryakioğlu (2010), p. 214. Compare with Tekinalp (2009), pp. 435–436; Kayık (2011), p. 72.

[332] Yılmaz (2016), p. 3120.

[333] Şanlı et al. (2018), p. 312.

[334] Nomer (2015), p. 360.

The rule of common nationality is mostly adopted in cases where the place of the tortious act has a weak connection with the case, while both the victim and the tortfeasor have the same nationality.[335] This rule is especially used when the two parties to a tort claim happen to be in the same foreign country, accidentally, where the tortious act occurs. Considering that in FDL claims the parent company and the victims would very unlikely have the same nationality, this exception is not relevant or exercisable in practice. The common habitual residence exception also does not sit right with FDL claims, where the alleged tortfeasor is a legal entity. In fact, the term 'habitual residence', as opposed to 'place of residence' or 'domicile' under Turkish law, is deemed to refer to real persons only, as the place of *de facto* residence in the will and discretion of the relevant person.[336] As for the law of the place where a work accident took place, even if the relevant tort were to be deemed a work accident, the relevant claim would be addressed towards the employer, thus the transnational subsidiary and not towards the parent company. Therefore, this exception too becomes irrelevant to FDL claims.

Amongst the other alternatives to trigger the rule of the most closely connected law, I believe that the only potentially viable one in an FDL claim would be *lex fori* of the court of jurisdiction. Having said that, in order to apply the rule of the most closely connected law in such a case, it would be required for the place where the tortious act is committed (which forms the general rule) to have a temporary and weak connection with the relevant tort. To consider an FDL claim, in cases where the applicable law is determined as the host country's law, it would be necessary to successfully prove that the relevant tort has a temporary and weak connection with the host country. This might not be an easy task in practice. It might, nevertheless, be argued that: (1) the tortious act is the parent company's omission to take certain measures or to effectively monitor its transnational subsidiary, which took place in the home country; (ii) the host country is the place where the damage has occurred, but the tortious act (i.e. parent company's omission) is regulated under the laws of the home country; and (iii) as the laws of the home country were violated, then the most closely connected law should be the home country's laws. However, all of this analysis is based on successfully proving that the tortious act is the parent company's omission in the relevant case and that the parent company has acted in violation of the home country's laws, which depends on the substantive legal analysis of the matter.

5.2.2.4 The Exceptions of Public Policy and Overriding Mandatory Rules

In cases where the conflict of law provisions point to a foreign law in dispute with a foreign element, the application of the relevant foreign law will not be exclusive, as it

[335] Tekinalp (2009), p. 438; Yılmaz (2016), p. 3122.

[336] Arslan (2012), p. 141; Yılmaz (2016), p. 3123.

is a generally accepted rule that the foreign law shall be applicable only to the extent that it does not contravene the public policy of the country of *lex fori.*[337] This general rule is also regulated under Turkish private international law. Accordingly, if the law determined as applicable by way of the rules in the relevant legislation is found by the judge to go against public policy, this law would no longer be applicable and Turkish law would apply instead (Art. 5 PIPC).

The concept of public policy is not defined in law, yet there are various definitions put forward in legal doctrine. *Çelikel/Erdem* defines public policy as a conglomeration of institutions and rules that ensure good provision of public services and security and order, as well as compliance with those rules concerning peace and morality amongst the public.[338] As the moral and social rules of different countries might vary, it is difficult to adopt a unified general definition of the concept of public policy in international law; hence the concept might vary in time and place.[339] The Turkish Court of Appeal has also taken a joint chambers' decision on 'public policy' in order to unify the different interpretations of several civil chambers, whereby the definition was made as "*a whole set of rules that protect the fundamental structure and interests of the public*".[340] The decision referred to the challenges of defining the concept of public policy, as it tends to vary in time and place from one case to another, and in those states where a violation of a mandatory norm would in most cases go against public policy, there may be mandatory norms that when violated do not result in non-compliance with public policy.[341] Hence, the mere fact that a foreign law provision goes against the mandatory provisions of *lex fori* cannot be deemed a violation of public policy of the country of *lex fori*, considering that

[337] Çelikel and Erdem (2020), p. 140; Tekinalp (2009), p. 49; Yöney (2018), p. 185.

[338] Çelikel and Erdem (2020), p. 141.

[339] Doğan (2020), p. 256.

[340] Turkish Court of Appeal General Assembly Joint Chambers' Decision, numbered 2010/1E. 2012/1K, dated 10.02.2012, published on the OJ dated 20.09.2012 and numbered 28417.

[341] The relevant Joint Chambers' decision determined the scope of public policy in Turkish domestic law as the following: "Incompliance with fundamental values of Turkish law, general Turkish manners and morals, fundamental understanding of justice on which Turkish laws are based, general politics on which Turkish laws are based, fundamental rights and freedoms stipulated in the Constitution, rules that are based upon the common principle valid in international arena and on the principle of good faith in civil law, moral principles that are jointly adopted by civilized societies and legal principles that express the understanding of justice, level of civilization of the public, political and economic regime and human rights and liberties" (Turkish Court of Appeal General Assembly Joint Chambers' Decision, numbered 2010/1E. 2012/1K, dated 10.02.2012, published on the OJ dated 20.09.2012 and numbered 28417). It is important to note that the mere difference in the regulations of a foreign law and Turkish law does not, per se, constitute a violation of Turkish public policy; in order to have such a violation, the application of foreign law provisions should fall against Turkish law's fundamental values (Doğan 2020, p. 260). These fundamental values cover the provisions of the Turkish Constitution, as well as certain fundamental principles such as the principle of good faith (Çelikel and Erdem 2020, p. 154; Doğan 2020, p. 262).

different countries may have different social, political and economic values, which may be reflected differently in their legal systems.[342]

In light of the interpretations made in legal and judicial doctrine on public policy, the UNDHR, as an international treaty that regulates fundamental rights and freedoms, should also be deemed to concern matters of public policy, and consequently violation of its provisions should be deemed to contravene public policy.[343]

The application of public policy rules under Turkish law is not unlimited. In light of the wording of Article 5 of PIPC, it is accepted in Turkish legal doctrine that the intervention of public policy is exceptional and therefore the application of this provision should also be restricted to certain cases.[344] Moreover, the provision refers to a 'clear' incompliance with public policy, which also delimits the scope of application of this exception. This 'clear' incompliance with public policy is interpreted as being capable of causing unbearable consequences in terms of public policy and public conscience.[345] The judge shall consider the matters of public policy *ex officio* in each case.[346]

There are also overriding mandatory rules in domestic laws, which shall apply even though the applicable law is a foreign law, without taking into consideration the conflict of law provisions.[347] In terms of cases subject to a foreign applicable law, the impact of overriding mandatory rules of Turkish law is determined by Article 6 of PIPC. Although there is no clear definition of overriding mandatory rules under Turkish law, in legal doctrine these are defined as mandatory rules that serve to protect the state's social, economic and political order and that shall be applied directly and independently from the applicable law.[348] These are considered as legal provisions that cannot be excluded, delimited or changed by contract.[349] The most crucial characteristic of overriding mandatory norms is deemed to be their purpose of protection. The norms that were put in place with an aim to protect public interests

[342] Yöney (2018), p. 187.

[343] Sarıöz Büyükalp (2018), p. 75.

[344] Çelikel and Erdem (2020), p. 145; Kayık (2011), p. 86; Tarman (2010), p. 25; Tekinalp (2009), p. 49.

[345] Çelikel and Erdem (2020), p. 147. See also decision of Turkish Court of Appeal 2nd Civil Chamber numbered 2011/10335E. 2012/4239K. and dated 29.02.2012, and decision of Turkish Court of Appeal 2nd Civil Chamber numbered 2016/15771E. 2017/1737K. and dated 09.02.2017, where the public policy concept was discussed in detail.

[346] Tekinalp (2009), p. 49.

[347] Doğan (2020), p. 276; Nomer (2015), p. 183; Yılmaz (2016), p. 3130. On this point, it is also important to consider the position of UNDHR as an international treaty that is ratified and enforced in Turkey. *Sarıöz Büyükalp* discusses whether the provisions of UNDHR should be considered as part of domestic law or as mandatory overriding rules of foreign law in terms of conflict of laws. The scholar concludes that the UNDHR is neither and it shall be applicable not alongside the provisions of PIPC, but prior to those, as a legal system above the domestic law that regulates fundamental rights and freedoms. See Sarıöz Büyükalp (2018), pp. 73–74.

[348] Çelikel and Erdem (2020), p. 155; Nomer (2015), p. 183; Tarman (2010), p. 17; Yılmaz (2016), p. 3130; Yöney (2018), p. 190.

[349] Yılmaz (2016), p. 3130.

and the state's economic and socio-political interests, rather than to protect the interests of individuals, are considered as overriding mandatory norms.[350]

There may be three types of overriding mandatory rules: (i) those of *lex fori*, (ii) those of *lex causae* and (iii) those of a third country.[351] Article 6 of PIPC regulates only the overriding mandatory rules of *lex fori*, as Turkish law. This means that Turkish judge will directly apply the overriding mandatory rules to any dispute, including the ones of an international nature, without looking into the conflict of law provisions and the applicable law that they point to. In other words, in a case concerning an overriding mandatory rule, a Turkish judge shall directly apply the relevant provision of Turkish law and decide on the merits of the case accordingly.[352]

The concepts of public policy and overriding mandatory rules are often confused with each other. However, actually, the application and practice of these two concepts are different to each other. Rules of public policy are generally not in writing, as they represent general and abstract rules of a state, while overriding mandatory rules are mostly put in writing and refer to concrete and specific issues.[353] In cases of public policy, the judge firstly looks into the conflict of laws provisions to determine the applicable law, which results as a foreign law, and then if certain provisions of the relevant applicable foreign law go against Turkish public policy, the judge would refrain from applying them and instead apply Turkish law provisions (Art. 5 PIPC). On the other hand, in cases of overriding mandatory rules, the judge will not look into the conflict of laws provisions to determine applicable law, but will directly apply the overriding mandatory rules, even if the dispute has a foreign element (Art. 6 PIPC). Therefore, the main difference between these two concepts lies at the point of the power of overriding mandatory rules compared to public policy, in that they would be directly applicable even in foreign element disputes without checking conflict of laws provisions and applying the relevant foreign law.[354] Although this situation creates an understanding that overriding mandatory norms are more powerful than public policy, the scope of public policy is actually much wider than that of overriding mandatory norms. In fact, while overriding mandatory norms usually involve commercial matters and especially contracts, the scope of public policy also extends to matters concerning individuals and family law.[355]

[350] Doğan (2020), pp. 276–277; Nomer (2015), p. 184.

[351] Çelikel and Erdem (2020), p. 156; Doğan (2020), p. 277. Overriding mandatory rules of *lex causae* will not affect the application of the relevant foreign law, considering that it is *lex causae* that will apply to the relevant case with all its provisions, including the overriding mandatory rules. Overriding mandatory rules of *lex fori* and of a third country's law would, on the other hand, intervene in the application of *lex causae* (see Yöney 2018, p. 191).

[352] Doğan (2020), p. 279.

[353] Takavut (2018), p. 29.

[354] Çelikel and Erdem (2020), p. 161; Nomer (2015), pp. 185–186; Takavut (2018), p. 28; Yöney (2018), p. 188.

[355] Takavut (2018), p. 27.

5.2.2.5 Claims Against the Tortfeasor's Insurer

There is also another exception to the general rule on applicable law (Art. 34/4 PIPC),[356] which stipulates that the tort victim can claim for the damage vis-à-vis from the defendant's insurer, provided that the law applicable to the tort or to the insurance agreement permits it. This is regulated as an alternative that might be selected by the tort victim bringing the tort claim. Depending on the applicable law on which the claim is based, i.e. whether on tort or on insurance agreement, the claim will either be on tort or on insurance.[357] In any case, the amount for which the insurer is responsible cannot exceed the amount of insurance under the insurance agreement.[358]

As the provision addresses the law applicable to the tort or to the insurance agreement, it will be necessary to make a substantive legal analysis under these laws to check if any such claim towards the defendant's insurer is allowed thereunder.[359] Under Turkish law, in liability insurance, the damaged person is entitled to have direct recourse to the damaging person's insurer up to the amount insured within the statute of limitations applicable for the relevant insurance agreement (Art. 1478 TCC). Therefore, in the event that the law applicable to tort or the law applicable to the relevant insurance agreements happens to be Turkish law, it would be possible for the tort victim to take direct action against the damaging party's liability insurer as per Article 1478 of the TCC.

It is important to note that the right to have direct recourse to the insurer is regulated only for liability insurance under Turkish law, and not for other types of insurance. The purpose of the provisions concerning the right to direct action against the insurer is described as to provide certain security for tort victims by granting them the right to have direct recourse to the insurer, who is deemed to be in a better position financially than the tort victim, in a way that would facilitate the procedures and provide a faster and more effective remedy for the victim.[360]

Although this provision might seem to constitute a viable alternative for tort victims in transnational tort claims, its application and effect in practice might prove to be challenging. First of all, the provision explicitly requires that either the law applicable to the insurance agreement or the law applicable to the tort should

[356] The alternative of addressing direct claims against the tortfeasor's insurance has been introduced in Turkish law with the enactment of PIPC in 2007. The reasoning of the article states that this provision was introduced in line with the improvements under international conventions and newly enacted codes on private international law.

[357] Çelikel and Erdem (2020), p. 465.

[358] Ekşi (2015), p. 45.

[359] Tiryakioğlu (2010), p. 215. *Tiryakioğlu* also states that this provision would especially be effective in cases where the law applicable to tort does not provide any ground for direct application to the insurer, while the law applicable to insurance agreement does; in such a case, the law applicable to the insurance agreement shall apply taking priority over the law applicable to tort. See Tiryakioğlu (2010), p. 215.

[360] Ekşi (2015), p. 313, fn. 503.

regulate direct action against insurers. It is, therefore, required to make an assessment under both of these laws to draw a conclusion on whether the provision would apply to the relevant case. Furthermore, considering the high amount of damages suffered in transnational tort claims, the limit on the insurer's liability in terms of the amount of insurance might hinder any advantage expected from this provision. In light of these concerns, the aforementioned alternative does not pose an effective legal basis for FDL claims.

5.2.2.6 Special Rule on Applicable Law for Corporate Groups

TCC provisions on corporate groups also provide a specific rule on applicable law. According to Article 195/1 of TCC, Turkish law provisions concerning corporate groups would apply in cases where the parent company, or any subsidiary of a corporate group, has its headquarters in Turkey. Furthermore, as per Article 195/5 of TCC, Turkish law provisions concerning corporate groups would apply also in cases where the parent company is an undertaking with its headquarters or place of residence either in Turkey or abroad.[361] Accordingly, in the event that there is a corporate group within the meaning under the relevant provisions of TCC, where either the parent company or the parent undertaking or any of the subsidiaries is located in Turkey, then Turkish law provisions on corporate groups would be applicable.

The above-mentioned wording of Article 195/1 is quite wide with the purpose that the liability regime within corporate groups is widely adopted.[362] Therefore, in light of this provision, the Turkish law provisions concerning coprorate groups shall be seen as overriding mandatory rules that will apply regardless of the law applicable to the relevant dispute. The main purpose of this provision is to provide certain protection to the Turkish shareholders and Turkish creditors of the Turkish subsidiaries against foreign investors[363] by ensuring a level of transparency and liability within the corporate group.[364]

Although Article 195/1 might be considered as an overriding mandatory rule, in that the corporate group provisions of Turkish law would be applicable to a certain case, the substantive legal analysis presented here on the matter shows that the relevant provisions do not provide an effective legal basis for FDL claims. Therefore, the disputed applicability of the Turkish law provisions on corporate groups would not lead to any effective outcome in this respect.

[361] In *Çakır Çelebi*'s opinion, by the provisions of Article 195/1 and 195/5, the legislator has aimed to provide protection to the vulnerable subsidiaries located in Turkey, rather than their parents, which might as well be located abroad (Çakır Çelebi 2018, p. 30).

[362] Tekinalp (2013), p. 556.

[363] Okutan Nilsson (2011), p. 95.

[364] Tekinalp (2013), p. 556.

5.2.3 Interim Conclusion on Applicable Law in FDL Claims

Under both Turkish law and Rome II, in the case of a foreign element tort, it would first of all be necessary to establish whether there is a valid agreement on the choice of applicable law between the parties. If so, this law would be applicable in the first instance. However, as already mentioned, this option does not seem practical or fair in FDL claims.

In the absence of a choice of applicable law, Turkish law addresses the general rule of *lex loci delicti commissi* (or *lex loci damni* in cases where the damage occurred in a different place), while Rome II points to the special provisions. Amongst these special provisions, in FDL claims, Article 7 of Rome II on environmental damages might apply, which is not regulated under Turkish law. In the event that none of the special provisions or exceptions are relevant, then the general rule on the law of the place of damage would apply. However, if there is a more closely connected law, then this exception would abrogate all other rules.

The law of the place of damage, which is adopted by Rome II and (for cases where the places of the damaging act and of the damage are not the same) by Turkish law, is not suitable for FDL claims as it results in the law of the host country. The law of the place of the tortious act (or the damaging incident) might better accommodate FDL claims, based on the reasoning that the parent company's acts or omissions take place in the home country and therefore this should be deemed as the place where the tortious act is committed. The exception of the more closely connected law might also be useful at this point in proving that the place of the tortious act has the closest connection with the relevant claim.

In light of the analysis made under the relevant Turkish law and Rome II, in terms of FDL claims, it seems important to determine firstly the place where the tortious act or damaging act has occurred. If it can be proven that this place is the home country, where the parent company's headquarters are located and where it is supposed to have taken the decisions that led to the relevant damages by the operations of subsidiaries, then the plaintiffs would attain the desired outcome. All of this would depend on the substantive legal analysis of the case, which complicates the situation.

The exception of environmental damages under Rome II, which gives the claimant the opportunity to sue the parent company in the place of the damaging incident, might also prove to be successful in FDL claims, depending on the interpretation of the place of the damaging incident. In any case, this rule of exception is useful and beneficial to plaintiffs as it provides them, and not the courts, with an alternative to initiate legal action before the courts of the place of damage or the place of the damaging incident. This rule could be adopted by Turkish law for the purposes of environmental claims.

References

Online Sources

Apartheid reparations lawsuits (re So. Africa), Business & Human Rights Resource Centre. https://www.business-humanrights.org/en/apartheid-reparations-lawsuits-re-so-africa

Bhopal Plant History and Ownership, Union Carbide Corporation. http://www.bhopal.com/Bhopal-Plant-History-and-Ownership

EarthRights International, Sahu v Union Carbide. https://earthrights.org/case/sahu-v-union-carbide/

Legge Federale Sul Diritto Internazionale Privato del 18 dicembre 1987 (Stato 1° Aprile 2017). https://www.admin.ch/opc/it/classified-compilation/19870312/index.html

Union Carbide/Dow lawsuit (re Bhopal), Business & Human Rights Resource Centre. https://www.business-humanrights.org/en/latest-news/union-carbidedow-lawsuit-re-bhopal/

Legislation, Reports, Resolutions and Opinions

Brief of Amicus Curiae the European Commission in Support of Neither Party (January 23, 2004) Sosa v Alvarez-Machain. No. 03-0339, 542 US 692

Brief of the European Commission on behalf of the European Union as Amicus Curiae in Support of Neither Party (June 13 2012) Kiobel v. Royal Dutch Petroleum. Co., 133 S.Ct. 1659 (2013) (No. 10-1491), available at: https://www.americanbar.org/content/dam/aba/publications/supreme_court_preview/briefs/10-1491_neither_amcu_eu.authcheckdam.pdf

Proposal for a Regulation of the European Parliament and the Council on the law applicable to non-contractual obligations (ROME II). http://eur-lex.europa.eu/legal-content/EN/TXT/?uri=celex:52003PC0427

Proposal for a Regulation of the European Parliament and the Council on the Law Applicable to Non-Contractual Obligations (22.7.2003) Explanatory Memorandum, Brussels, COM(2003) 427 final 2003/0168 (COD). https://eur-lex.europa.eu/LexUriServ/LexUriServ.do?uri=COM:2003:0427:FIN:EN:PDF

Proposal for a Regulation of the European Parliament and of the Council on jurisdiction and the recognition and enforcement of judgments in civil and commercial matters; COM/2010/0748 final - COD 2010/0383. http://eur-lex.europa.eu/legal-content/EN/TXT/?uri=CELEX%3A52010PC0748

UK Supreme Court (10.04.2019) Vedanta Resources PLC and another (Appellants) v Lungowe and others (Respondents). https://youtu.be/_s7YvSnX63

Literature

Ahmed M (2022) Private international law and substantive liability issues in tort litigation against multinational companies in the English courts: recent UK supreme court decisions and post-Brexit implications. J Priv Int Law 18:56–82

Albayrak H, Mavzer T (2019) Haksız Fiilden Doğan Davalarda Ortak Yetkili Mahkeme Sorunu (The problem of the common competent court in jurisdiction of tort cases). SÜHFD 27(2): 279–306

Anker-Sorensen L (2014) Parental liability for externalities of subsidiaries: domestic and extraterritorial approaches. University of Oslo Faculty of Law Legal Studies, Research Paper Series 2014/36

Aristova E (2017) Court of Appeal allows in England claims against English-based multinational for overseas human rights violations. http://conflictoflaws.net/2017/court-of-appeal-allows-in-england-claims-against-english-based-multinational-for-overseas-human-rights-violations/

Aristova E (2018) Tort litigation against transnational corporations in the English courts: the challenge of jurisdiction. Utrecht Law Rev 14(2):6–21

Arslan İ (2012) Milletlerarası Özel Hukukta Mutad Mesken Kavramı (The concept of habitual residence in private international law). Master's Thesis, Istanbul

Aşit R (2017) Kişilik Hakkı İhlallerinde Yetkili Mahkemeler (place of jurisdiction in case of violation of personal rights). MÜHF – HAD 23(2):467–492

Bantekas I (2004) Corporate social responsibility in international law. Boston Univ Int Law J 22: 309–347

Baughen S (2015) Human rights and corporate wrongs. Edward Elgar Publishing

Baxi U (2016) Human rights responsibility of multinational corporations, political ecology of injustice: learning from Bhopal thirty plus. BHRJ 1:21–40

Bogdan M (2009) The treatment of environmental damage in regulation Rome II. In: Ahern J, Binchy W (eds) The Rome II regulation on the law applicable to non-contractual obligations: a new international litigation regime. Brill | Nijhoff, Leiden – Boston, pp 219–230

Çakır Çelebi FB (2018) Şirketler Topluluğunda Hakim Teşebbüs (Dominant Undertaking in Group Companies). TFM 4(1):19–32

Cambou D (2015) The Dutch Shell case: foreign direct liability claims as an avenue for holding multinational corporations accountable for human rights violations. In: Cernic JL, Van Ho T (eds) Human rights and business: direct corporate accountability for human rights. Wolf Legal Publishers, pp 347–365

Carey MJ (2016) How concerned should we be: the conundrum of Kiobel's touch and concern test and corporate liability under the Alien Tort Statute. Suffolk Univ Law Rev 49:451–468

Çelikel A (2010) Milletlerarası Özel Hukuk (Private International Law). Revised 10th edn. Istanbul

Çelikel A, Erdem BB (2020) Milletlerarası Özel Hukuk (Private International Law). 16th edn. Istanbul

Chander A (2013) Unshackling foreign corporations: Kiobel's unexpected legacy. Am J Int Law 107(4):829–834

Choudhury B (2005) Beyond the alien tort claims act: alternative approaches to attributing liability to corporations for extraterritorial abuses. Northwest J Int Law Bus 26:43–75

Christmann T (2000) The Unocal case: potential liability of multinational companies for investment activities in foreign countries. Southern Cross Univ Law Rev 4:206–224

De Jonge A (2011) Transnational corporations and international law, accountability in the global business environment. Edward Elgar Publishing

de Schutter O (2010) International human rights law. Cambridge University Press
Demir Gökyayla C (2011) Seçilen Mahkemede Adil Yargılama Yapıl(a)mayacağı Şüphesi Yetki Anlaşmasının Geçerliliğini Etkiler mi? (Does the suspicion on the fair trial before the chosen jurisdiction affect the validity of the jurisdiction clause). Dokuz Eylül Üniversitesi Hukuk Fakültesi Dergisi 13(2):51–70
Demir İskenderoğlu SA (2008) Türk Mahkemelerinin Milletlerarası Yetkisi (International Jurisdiction of Turkish Courts). Master's Thesis, Ankara
Demirkan U (2013) Hukuk Muhakemeleri Kanunu'nun 8 İla 16'ncı Maddeleri Arasında Düzenlenmiş Olan Özel Yetki Kuralları (Special Jurisdiction Rules Regulated in Articles 8 to 16 of Civil Procedure Code). Master's Thesis, Istanbul
Dine J (2012) Jurisdictional arbitrage by multinational companies: a National law Solution. J Human Rights Environ 3:44–69
Dittmers H (2017) The applicability of the alien tort statute to human rights violations by private corporations. J Sci Human Art 4(2) http://www.josha-archive.org/system/articles/merged_pdfs/000/000/296/original/tmp_pdf_the-applicability-of-the-alien-tort-statute-to-human-rights-violations-by-private-corporations.pdf?1497009414
Dodge WS (2019) Corporate liability under the US Alien tort statute: a comment on Jesner v Arab Bank. BHRJ 4:131–137
Doğan V (2020) Milletlerarası Özel Hukuk (Private international law). Revised 6th edn. Ankara
Ekşi N (1994) Türk Milletlerarası Yetki Sisteminde Objektif İlişki İlkesi (Principle of Objective Connection in the System of Turkish International Jurisdiction). PhD Thesis, Istanbul
Ekşi N (2015) Milletlerarası Özel Hukuk Açısından Sigortacıya Doğrudan Başvuru Hakkını Kısıtlayan veya Ortadan Kaldıran Yabancı Yasaların Türk Mahkemelerince Dikkate Alınıp Alınmayacağı Sorunu (The Issue Whether Turkish Courts Can Apply Foreign Laws which Prohibit or Limit Direct Action Against Insurers under Turkish PILA). Uluslararası Ticaret ve Tahkim Hukuku Dergisi (J Int Trade Arbitr Law) 4 (2):31–61
Elveriş İ, Kutucu S, Yaşar İ (2005) Türkiye'de Adli Yardım Sisteminin Değerlendirilmesi (Analysis of legal aid system in Turkey). In: Elveriş İ (eds) Türkiye'de Adli Yardım, Karşılaştırmalı İnceleme ve Politikalar (Legal Aid in Turkey, Policy Issues and a Comparative Perspective, Round Table Discussion 16 April 2004, Istanbul Bilgi University
Enneking L (2008) The common denominatory of the Trafigura case, foreign direct liability cases and the Rome II regulation, an essay on the consequences of private international law for the feasibility of regulating multinational corporations through tort law. Eur Rev Priv Law 2:283–311
Enneking L (2009) Crossing the Atlantic? The political and legal feasibility of European foreign direct liability cases. George Wash Int Law Rev 40:903–938
Enneking L (2012) Foreign direct liability and beyond. Eleven International Publishing
Enneking L (2013) Multinationals and transparency in foreign direct liability cases. Dovenschmidt Quarterly 3:134–147
Enneking L (2014) The future of foreign direct liability? Exploring the international relevance of the Dutch Shell Nigeria case. Utrecht Law Rev 10(1):44–54
Erb N, Pell O (2012) Kiobel's new focus on extraterritoriality under the Alien Tort Statute could put resolution of the corporate liability issue indefinitely out of reach. Geo J Int Law 43:1073–1076
Eroğlu M (2008a) Multinational enterprises and Tort liabilities, an interdisciplinary and comparative examination. Edward Elgar Publishing
Eroğlu M (2008b) Limited liability in Turkish law. Eur Bus Org Law Rev 9:237–265
Fentiman R (2009) The significance of close connection. Ahern J, Binchy W (eds) The Rome II regulation on the law applicable to non-contractual obligations: a new international litigation regime. Brill | Nijhoff, Leiden – Boston, pp 85–112
Fielding A (2008) Yahoo? Reining in the wild west with the alien tort claims act. Human Rights Rev 9:513–523
Graziano TK (2009) Freedom to choose the applicable law in tort – articles 14 and 4(3) of the Rome II regulation. Ahern J, Binchy W (eds) The Rome II regulation on the law applicable to

non-contractual obligations: a new international litigation regime. Brill | Nijhoff, Leiden – Boston, pp 113–132

Haider Z (2012) Corporate liability for human rights abuses: analyzing Kiobel & alternatives to the Alien Tort Statute. Geo J Int Law 43:1361–1390

Huber P Bach I (eds) (2011) Rome II Regulation: Pocket Commentary. Munich

Hughes-Jennett J, Berthet A, Prior S (2018) Foreign corporations cannot be sued under the Alien Tort Statute – Jesner v Arab Bank: the verdict. Hogan Lovells Focus on Regulation. https://www.hlregulation.com/2018/04/27/foreign-corporations-cannot-be-sued-under-the-alien-tort-statute-jesner-v-arab-bank-the-verdict/

Isidro MR (2016) Business and human rights abuses: claiming compensation under the Brussels I recast. Human Rights Int Legal Discour 10(1):72–93

Kaeb C, Scheffer D (2013) The paradox of Kiobel in Europe. Am J Int Law 107:852–857

Kayık A (2011) Milletlerarası Özel Hukukta Haksız Fiiller ve Uygulanacak Hukuk (Torts and Applicable Law in Private International Law). Master's Thesis, Kayseri

Kessedjian C (2017) Implementing the UN principles on business and human rights in private international law: European perspectives. In: Zamora Cabot FJ, Urscheler LH, De Dycker S (eds) Implementing the U.N. Guiding Principles on Business and Human Rights – Private International Law Perspectives, pp 141–152

Kılıçoğlu M (2012) 6100 Sayılı Hukuk Muhakemeleri Kanunu El Şerhi (Civil Procedural Code No. 6100 Manual)

Krishnan JK (2020) Bhopal in the federal courts: how Indian victims failed to get justice in the United States, (Forthcoming). Rutgers University Law Review

Kuru B (2001) Hukuk Muhakemeleri Usulü, vol 1, 6th edn, Istanbul

Magnus U, Mankowski P (2016) European Commentaries on Private International Law ECPIL. Vol. I, Brussels Ibis Regulation – Commentary, Dr. Otto Schmidt, Munich

Mansel HP (2018) Internationales Privatrecht de lege lata wie de lege ferenda und Menschenrechtsverantwortlichkeit deutscher Unternehmen (international private law *de lege lata* as well as *de lege ferenda* and human rights responsibility for German companies). ZGR 2–3:439–478

Meeran R (1999) The unveiling of transnational corporations: a direct approach. In: Addo MK (ed) Human rights standards and the responsibility of transnational corporations. Kluwer Law International

Mesci Barış (2014) Milletlerarası Özel Hukukta Atıf (Renvoi) (Renvoi in Private International Law). Master's Thesis

Nomer E (2015) Devletler Hususi Hukuku (private international law), 21st edn, Istanbul

Nwapi C (2014) Jurisdiction by necessity and the regulation of the transnational corporate actor. Utrecht J Int Eur Law 30(24):24–43

Okutan Nilsson G (2011) Şirketler Topluluğu (groups of companies). Bankacılar Dergisi (Bankers' J) 79:90–103

Özel S (2012) Haksız Fiillere İlişkin Davalarda Türk Mahkemelerinin Yetkisini Belirleyen HMK m. 16 Kuralının Karşılaştırmalı Hukuk Açısından Değerlendirilmesi (Comparative Legal Analysis on Article 16 of Turkish Code on Private International and Procedural Law on Jurisdiction of Turkish Courts in Tort Claims). Bahçeşehir Üniversitesi Hukuk Fakültesi Kazancı Hukuk Dergisi 8(91–92):7–37

Öztekin Gelgel G (2006) Akit Dışı Borç İlişkilerine Uygulanacak Hukuk Hakkındaki Avrupa Birliği Düzenlemesi (EU Regulation on Applicable Law in Non-Contractual Obligations). Istanbul

Palombo D (2019) The duty of Care of the Parent Company: a comparison between French law, UK precedents and the Swiss proposals. BHRJ 4:265–286

Palombo D (2020) The case for legal reform - business and human rights: the obligations of the European home states. Hart Publishing, Oxford

Roorda L, Ryngaert C (2016) Business and human rights litigation in Europe and Canada: the promises of forum of necessity jurisdiction. RabelsZ 80:783–816

Ryerson C (2018) Supreme Court Rejects Liability for Foreign Corporations in International Human Rights Cases. Corporate Accountability Lab, https://legaldesign.org/calblog/2018/4/24/supreme-court-rejects-liability-for-foreign-corporations-in-international-human-rights-cases

Sakmar A, Ekşi N (2002) Hukuki ve Ticari Konularda Mahkemelerin Milletlerarası Yetkisi ve Mahkeme Kararlarının Tanınması Tenfizi Hakkında AB Konsey Tüzüğü (EC Council regulation on the international jurisdiction of courts in civil and commercial matters and the recognition and enforcement of court decisions). İstanbul Hukuk Fakültesi MHB 22:721–743. http://www.journals.istanbul.edu.tr/iumhmohb/article/viewFile/1019002958/1019002556

Şanlı C, Esen E, Ataman-Figanmeşe İ (2018) Milletlerarası Özel Hukuk (Private International Law), 6th edn Istanbul

Sarıöz Aİ (2012) HMK'nın 16. Maddesi Uyarınca Haksız Fiillerden Doğan Uyuşmazlıklarda Yetkili Mahkemenin Tespiti ve Hükmün Türk Milletlerarası Usul Hukuku Açısından Değerlendirilmesi (Determination of the Court's Jurisdiction in Disputes Arising from Torts According to Article 16 of Turkish Civil Procedure Code and the Evaluation of this Article under Turkish Private International Law). T.C. Maltepe Üniversitesi Hukuk Fakültesi Dergisi 1: 155–181

Sarıöz Büyükalp Aİ (2018) AİHS ve AİHM Kararlarının da İncelenmesi Suretiyle Adil Yargılanma Hakkının Türk Milletlerarası Usul Hukuku Üzerindeki Etkileri (Impacts of Right to a Fair Trial on Turkish Private International Law upon Analysing UNDHR and ECHR Judgments). On İki Levha Yayıncılık

Scott A (2009) The scope of 'non-contractual obligations'. In: Ahern J, Binchy W (eds) The Rome II regulation on the law applicable to non-contractual obligations: a new international litigation regime. Martinus Nijhoff Publishers, Leiden – Boston, pp 57–83

Smith MJ, Pangsapa P (2011) Clusters of injustice: human rights, labour standards and environmental sustainability. In: Voiculescu A, Yanacopulos H (eds) The business of human rights – an evolving agenda for corporate responsibility. Zed Publications, pp 214–234

Stewart DP, Wuerth I (2013) Kiobel v. Royal Dutch Petroleum Co.: the supreme court and the alien tort statute. Am J Int Law 107(3):601–621

Süral C (2012) Hukuk Mahkemeleri Kanunu'nun Türk Mahkemelerinin Milletlerarası Yetkisine Etkisi (The effect of new civil procedure law on the international jurisdiction of Turkish courts). TBB Dergisi 100:167–216

Takavut İD (2018) Milletlerarası Ticari Tahkimde Doğrudan Uygulanan Kurallar (Overriding Mandatory Rules in International Commercial Arbitration). On İki Levha Yayıncılık

Tarman ZD (2008) Akit Dışı Borç İlişkilerine Uygulanacak Hukuk Hakkındaki Avrupa Topluluğu Tüzüğü (Roma II) (EC Regulation on the Law Applicable to Non-Contractual Liabilities – Rome II). AÜHFD 57(2):193–222. http://dergiler.ankara.edu.tr/dergiler/38/262/2351.pdf

Tarman ZD (2010) 5718 Sayılı Milletlerarası Özel Hukuk ve Usul Hukuku Hakkında Kanun (MÖHUK) Uyarınca Yabancılık Unsuru Taşıyan Akit Dışı Borç İlişkilerinde Hukuk Seçimi (Choice of law in non-contractual relations with a foreign element according to law no. 5718 concerning private international law and international civil procedure). BATİDER 26(2):5–34

Tekinalp G (2009) Milletlerarası Özel Hukuk Bağlama Kuralları (Rules of Renvoi in Private International Law), 10th edn, Istanbul

Tekinalp Ü (2013) Sermaye Ortaklıklarının Yeni Hukuku (New law of capital partnerships). 3rd edn. Revised with Changes and Secondary Legislation, Istanbul

Thomale C, Hübner L (2017) Zivilgerichtliche Durchsetzung völkerrechtlicher Unternehmensverantwortung (Civil judicial enforcement of international corporate responsibility). Juristenzeitung 8:385–397

Tiryakioğlu B (2010) Haksız Fiiller, Genel Olarak Haksız Fillere, Haksız Rekabete ve Rekabetin Engellenmesine Uygulanacak Hukuk (Applicable Law to Torts, Unfair Competition and Obstruction of Competition), Avrupa'da Devletler Özel Hukuku ve Yeni Türk Milletlerarası Özel Hukuk ve Usul Hukuku Hakkında Kanun'un Akitler ve Ticaret Hukukuna İlişkin

Hükümleri (European Private International Law and the Provisions of the New Turkish Code on Private International and Procedural Law). Legal Yayınları, pp 212–219
van Dam C (2011) Tort law and human rights: brothers in arms on the role of tort law in the area of business and human rights. J Eur Tort Law 2(3):221–254
van Dam C (2015) Human rights obligations of transnational corporations in domestic tort law. In: Cernic JL, Van Ho T (eds) Human rights and business: direct corporate accountability for human rights. Wolf Legal Publishers, pp 475–497
Van Den Eeckhout V (2017) The private international law dimension of the principles in Europe. In: Zamora Cabot FJ, Urscheler LH, De Dycker S (eds) Implementing the U.N. Guiding Principles on Business and Human Rights – Private International Law Perspectives, pp 35–62
Webb O (2013) Kiobel, the Alien Tort Dtatute and the common law: human rights litigation in this present, imperfect world. Aust Int Law J 20:131–160
Weber RH, Baisch R (2016) Liability of parent companies for human rights violations of subsidiaries. EBLR:669–695
Weller M, Pato A (2018) Local parents as 'anchor defendants' in European courts for claims against their foreign subsidiaries in human rights and environmental damages litigation: recent case law and legislative trends. Unif Law Rev 23(2):397–417
Weller MP, Thomale C (2017) Menschenrechtsklagen gegen deutsche Unternehmen (Human rights lawsuits against German companies). ZGR 4:509–526
Yılmaz G (2016) Türk Milletlerarası Özel Hukuku ve Roma II Tüzüğü Kapsamında Haksız Fiilden Doğan Akit Dışı Borç İlişkilerine Uygulanacak Hukukun Mukayeseli Olarak İncelenmesi (Comparative analysis of the applicable law to tort liabilities within the scope of international private law and Rome II regulation). MÜHFD-HAD 22(3):3111–3142
Yöney C (2018) Yabancı Hukukun Uygulanması (Application of Foreign Law). On İki Levha Yayıncılık
Zerk JA (2006) Multinationals and corporate social responsibility, limitations and opportunities in international law. Cambridge University Press

Chapter 6
Conclusion

Due to their economic powers and their dispersion around the world, MNCs have a global influence and that they should therefore be subject to effective regulation in order to balance their power in the international arena. Concerns on MNCs reach a peak when it comes to involuntary creditors who are not able to negotiate or shift their losses elsewhere, such as tort victims affected by the transnational operations of MNCs in host countries. Globalisation, which triggered both the formation and expansion of MNCs while creating its own victims on the other side of the spectrum, has also led to the necessity of regulating these structures, as the sensitivity and diligence of consumers, investors and other stakeholders on respecting human rights also keep growing. Soft law instruments, including CSR tools, often remain insufficient in ensuring compliance, especially in host countries which are usually developing or least-developed countries, and it has therefore become a pressing need to regulate this issue in statutory law.

Although there are still theoretical obstacles to effectively regulating MNCs, these can be overcome by establishing a legal framework which would sufficiently and reasonably cover these corporate structures. There have been recent attempts to regulate MNCs in domestic laws, through imposing mHRDD obligations on companies. This method does not only serve as an *ex ante* identification and prevention of risks of human rights abuses that may arise from corporate activities, but it also provides a viable legal ground for a parent company's tort liability for its subsidiary's actions. The UN's efforts in drafting an international legal instrument to regulate State responsibility for putting in place legal mechanisms for business and human rights are also noteworthy, as such a legal instrument might serve to have unified and internationally recognised mechanisms in domestic statutory laws on mHRDD.

In light of the substantive legal analysis made hereunder, it is possible to conclude that Turkish law has no sufficient legal grounds to accommodate FDL, but it does have great potential to do so. The currently available provisions on corporate groups in TCC pave the way for a wide interpretation of the concept, which might extend to

P. Kara, *Tort Liability in Multinational Corporate Groups*, Ius Gentium: Comparative Perspectives on Law and Justice 107,
https://doi.org/10.1007/978-3-031-29336-8_6

cover companies within a control relationship. Having said that, the corporate group provisions in TCC do not regulate any outward liability, such as parent company liability towards involuntary creditors, including tort victims.

The analysis of Turkish tort law addresses the need to regulate a parent company's duty of care in statutory law, as otherwise it would be challenging to establish tort liability for a parent company's negligent act in terms of omitting to supervise and monitor its transnational subsidiary's operations. On the other hand, some of the strict liability grounds, such as liability for dangerous activities (Art. 71 TCO) or liability of the polluter (Art. 28 Environmental Law) might arguably serve to accommodate FDL claims, depending on whether it is possible to prove that the parent company has been economically and organisationally in control of the subsidiary's operations.

Accordingly, this study proposes the introduction of a new type of liability for parent companies in terms of duty of care, regulated under the civil liability, by taking into account the relevant case law before the English courts, as well as the UN's working draft of a legally binding instrument in business and human rights. It is also suggested that a new regulation be adopted on mHRDD, in light of the evolving legislation in several EU member states. These two suggestions aim to construct the required legal basis for effectively regulating MNCs under Turkish law.

In terms of issues of jurisdiction and applicable law, which stand in the core of FDL, the current Turkish law and the EU acquis examined hereunder do not seem to pose clear beneficial grounds for addressing these claims before the home country's courts and under the home country's laws, as desired by FDL plaintiffs. Having said that, there are alternatives that can be used and these points are definitely considered in upcoming legislations, such as the UN's working draft of a legally binding instrument in business and human rights and the domestic legislations on mHRDD. Without losing hope from litigation, private arbitration also appears as a powerful alternative in FDL claims with the finalization of the Hague Rules on BHR, which will surely create a considerable impact in the future of FDL.

To conclude, it is possible to say that FDL is a growing and dynamic area of law, and Turkish law will most certainly have to play its part in this process. The complexity and multidisciplinary nature of the issue makes it difficult to regulate in law. In effect, FDL touches upon many different fields of law—including tort, corporate law, environmental law, but also criminal law, tax law, human rights and even corruption. Therefore, it might take some time to efficiently cover all aspects of the issue, which requires an understanding that sustainability and the protection of the environment should be prioritised in our lives and in our laws, as a pressing need of our times.